MERRILL

Solving Problems in

Chemistry

A MODERN COURSE

Richard G. Smith
Bexley High School
Bexley, Ohio

Gary K. Himes
International Minerals and Chemicals
Glendale, Arizona

Consultant

Robert C. Smoot
McDonogh School
McDonogh, Maryland

MERRILL

PUBLISHING COMPANY

A MERRILL SCIENCE PROGRAM

Chemistry: A Modern Course
Chemistry: A Modern Course, Teacher Edition
Chemistry: A Modern Course, Teacher Resource Package
Chemistry: A Modern Course, Transparency Package
Chemistry: A Modern Course, Test Bank
Laboratory Chemistry
Laboratory Chemistry, Teacher Annotated Edition
Laboratory Chemistry, Computer-Assisted Data-Checking Software
Solving Problems in Chemistry

Series Editor: Mary Beth Gallant
Project Editor: Teresa Anne McCowen
Project Designer: Brent Good
Cover Illustration: computer graphic, Slidemasters, Inc.

ISBN 0-675-06432-5
Published by
MERRILL PUBLISHING COMPANY

Columbus, Ohio

PREFACE

Solving Problems in Chemistry helps to develop problem-solving skills essential to the study of chemistry, through the use of Example and practice problems. The chapters contain brief explanations of basic chemistry principles. A variety of Example problems are provided to illustrate these principles. The factor-label method of problem-solving is used as part of the step-by-step process in solving the Example problems. Answers to all practice problems are provided at the end of the book, enabling students to check their own progress.

The authors offer a wide range of expertise in the field of chemistry. The seventh edition of *Solving Problems in Chemistry* reflects a blend of their experiences in the high school and college classroom as well as in industry. Emphasis has been placed on practical applications. Environmental concerns, career information, and everyday uses of chemicals have been integrated into the problems where appropriate. In using this book, it is hoped that today's chemistry students will become familiar with ways in which the principles and concepts of chemistry affect their daily lives.

Solving Problems in Chemistry is designed for use with the text **Chemistry: A Modern Course.** This problems book can also be used as a supplement to other standard first-year textbooks, as a guide to independent study, or as a reference in reviewing basic chemistry principles. Students will find *Solving Problems in Chemistry* a valuable aid in achieving a better understanding of chemistry. Teachers will find it a time-saving resource for planning an introductory chemistry course for today's students.

CONTENTS

CHEMISTRY SKILLS

1

The factual style of writing in science textbooks is different from the narrative style of most other books you read. Thus, reading science requires special skills. In order to be successful in chemistry, you must adjust to the amount of factual information presented. You must read critically and sense relationships among ideas, as well as build on previous knowledge. You must master a new, technical vocabulary. Skills are needed to use supplementary materials, like this problems book, to enhance understanding. You must learn to interpret information presented in tables, graphs, and diagrams. Laboratory experimentation also requires special skills to interpret and apply scientific knowledge. In this chapter you will learn some techniques that can help you master these skills.

1:1 READING SCIENTIFIC MATERIALS

Reading for meaning, or comprehension, is one of the most important skills to master. Once the foundation is laid for strong comprehension the other skill areas will be facilitated. For example, if you have a basic understanding of the concepts presented in a particular chapter, new vocabulary words will be grasped more quickly from context clues. Problems and laboratory activities will also gain perspective.

When previewing or reading you should identify the main ideas in the material. The **main idea** is the most important concept described in a passage. The main idea can be located at any point in a paragraph and may not be a single sentence. The main ideas in a sequence of paragraphs can serve as a summary of the material.

You should always try to understand what you read and avoid rote memorization. One way to broaden your understanding is to look for statements that support the main idea. Some of these statements may be real world examples of the main idea; others may be conclusive research data. Supporting statements often explain the "how" or "why" questions you may have about the main idea. You should associate these supporting statements with the main idea. These associations will help you increase your knowledge from factual repetition of main ideas to broader understanding of the concept described.

One additional type of statement you should look for as you read is linking sentences. Linking sentences provide perspective on the material. The linking sentences tie the main idea to previously learned material or to material to be presented later. Use linking sentences to determine where to store new information in your mind. As you add new information to various compartments of information your knowledge base will expand. You will also avoid trying to remember lots of unrelated concepts.

Let's practice some of these suggestions with a paragraph from your textbook.

> Carbon atoms may bond to each other by the overlap of an orbital of one carbon atom with an orbital of another carbon atom. *The carbon-carbon single bond is a sigma type bond.* Many carbon atoms may bond in this manner to form a chain or ring. Recall from Chapter 11 that carbon exhibits catenation. Plastics, synthetic fibers, and synthetic rubber all contain molecules with hundreds or thousands of carbon atoms joined in chains and rings.

The main idea is italicized. This information alone is not very helpful to our general understanding of carbon bonding. However, if you remember that carbon atoms may bond by orbital overlap and they bond in chains or rings, two "how" questions are answered. The fourth sentence serves as a link with previous information. The last sentence provides real world application of the main idea.

1:2   DRAWING CONCLUSIONS

You may be asked to draw conclusions concerning a passage you have read. The answer to the question may not be stated directly in the passage. However, by understanding the main idea and some supporting details you can make an educated guess. For example, you know that pressure is caused by the collisions of particles with the walls of their container. You also know that temperature increases the speed of particles. You conclude that pressure increases with an increase in temperature because the particles would have more collisions.

When you make conclusions you may use inductive reasoning. **Inductive reasoning** involves applying specific concepts to general situations to form a conclusion. For example, consider the following.

> Hans Geiger and Ernest Marsden subjected a very thin sheet of gold foil to a stream of subatomic particles. They found that most of the particles passed right through the sheet. From this observation Rutherford concluded that the atom is mostly empty space. They also found that a few particles (about 1 in 8000) bounced back in almost the opposite direction from which they started. Rutherford explained this observation as meaning that there was a very small "core" to the atom. The core contained all the positive charge and almost all the mass of the atom. This core is now called the nucleus.

Rutherford used inductive reasoning to develop this theory of atomic structure. He used specific data from the Geiger-Marsden experiment to develop a general description of atomic structure.

Deductive reasoning involves applying general concepts to answer specific problems. Following is an example of how deductive reasoning is used

> Every system has some internal energy which is designated by U. The internal energy is a state function. Since we will be interested only in ΔU, changes in the internal energy of a system, we do not have to know absolute values of U for systems.

General information about the change in internal energy is used to find specific answers to the problems in Chapter 20.

PROBLEMS

Read the following paragraph and answer the questions that follow.
> The density of gases and vapors is most often expressed in grams per cubic decimeter. We express it in these units because the usual density units, g/cm^3, lead to very small numbers for gases. It is possible to calculate the density of a gas at any temperature and pressure from data collected at any other temperature and pressure. Assuming that the number of particles remains the same, a decrease in temperature would decrease the volume and increase the density. An increase of pressure would decrease the volume and increase the density. The following problem illustrates this calculation. (Remember 1000 cm^3 equals 1 dm^3.)

1. The purpose of this passage is to describe
   a. how many cm^3 are in 1 dm^3
   b. the units used for gas density
   c. typical density units
   d. the effects of temperature and pressure on gas density

2. In what units is gas density measured?
   a. g/cm^3 c. g/dm^3
   b. 1000 cm^3 d. 1 dm^3

3. What value must remain constant in order to determine gas density?
   a. number of particles   c. pressure
   b. temperature   d. volume

4. Which of the following is not mentioned in the paragraph?
   a. effects of temperature   c. usual density units
      decrease   d. gas density units
   b. effects of pressure decrease

5. What can you expect to learn in the text that would follow this paragraph?
   a. effects of temperature on volume
   b. effects of pressure on volume
   c. how to calculate gas density
   d. conversion units for density

6. Compare gas density units with usual density units. You would conclude that
   a. gases are less dense than other forms of matter
   b. gases are more dense than other forms of matter
   c. gases have the same density as other forms of matter

7. In order to answer question 6 you must use
   a. deductive reasoning   b. inductive reasoning

8. If the temperature of a sample of gas changed from 52°C to 23°C, the
   volume of the gas would
   a. increase   b. decrease   c. remain the same

9. In order to answer question 8 you must use
   a. deductive reasoning   b. inductive reasoning

1:3 GRAPHING

Throughout your study of chemistry you will be required to prepare
graphs or interpret graphs of experimental data. Thus you should be familiar with the composition of a graph.

The data that you will be using involves two variables, dependent and
independent. The quantity that is deliberately varied is the **independent
variable.** The quantity that changes due to variation in the independent
variable is the **dependent variable.** The independent variable is plotted on
the horizontal axis. This axis is referred to as the **abscissa** or x axis. The
dependent variable is plotted on the vertical axis. The vertical axis is referred to as the **ordinate** or y axis.

Graph titles should clearly state the purpose of the graph and include
the dependent and independent variables. For example, Figure 1-1 is titled

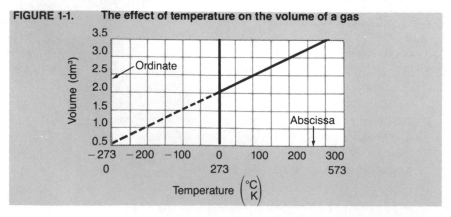

FIGURE 1-1.   The effect of temperature on the volume of a gas

volume vs. temperature of a gas. Each axis should be labeled with the appropriate variable and units of measurement. For Figure 1-1 the abscissa is labeled Temperature (K, C°), indicating that the scale is marked in both kelvins and Celsius degrees. The ordinate is labeled Volume (dm³), with the scale marked in cubic decimeters. Each axis has equal intervals. The intervals are 0.5 dm³ for the ordinate and 100°C or K for the abscissa.

1:4   INTERPRETING GRAPHS

Sometimes it is necessary to find a value for a variable at a point along the graph that is not one of the original data points. For example, on Figure 1-1 assume that we want to know the volume of a gas when the temperature is 75°C. The original data was not recorded at 75°C. In order to determine the volume of the gas at 75°C you must **interpolate,** or read from the graph between data points. By interpolating we can see that the volume of the gas is 2.3 dm³ at 75°C.

If a value is needed that is beyond the limits of the graph you must extrapolate. Reading a graph beyond the limits of the experimentally determined data points is **extrapolation.** To determine the theoretical volume of a gas at −273°C we must extrapolate to find the answer, 0 dm³. You should be cautious when extrapolating data. The relationship between the variables may not remain the same beyond the limits of your investigation.

CHAPTER REVIEW PROBLEMS

Read the following paragraph and answer the questions that follow.

An immediate application of electrochemistry is its use in quantitative analysis. For example, suppose that it is necessary for you to determine the percentage of copper in a given water soluble copper compound. A sample of the compound of known mass could be dissolved in water and inert electrodes inserted. The mass of the cathode should be measured before the current is applied. As the current is passed through the cell, metallic copper plates onto the electrode of known mass. When the action is complete and current no longer flows, all the copper is plated. The mass of the electrode is again measured. The difference in mass (due to the copper) is compared to the mass of the sample to find the percentage of copper in the sample. Electroanalysis is a useful tool of the chemist.

1. The best title for this passage is
   - **a.** Electroanalysis
   - **b.** Electrochemistry
   - **c.** Copper Analysis
   - **d.** Chemistry Tools
2. All the copper has been plated when
   - **a.** the copper compound dissolves in water
   - **b.** the percentage of copper in the sample is determined
   - **c.** current no longer flows
   - **d.** the mass of the electrode is measured

3. Which of the following is not mentioned as a step in plating copper?
    a. a sample of copper compound is dissolved in water
    b. the electrodes are attached to a power source
    c. the mass of the cathode is measured
    d. electrodes are inserted into the copper solution

4. With what topic is this passage most closely associated?
    a. finding mass of substances   **c.** electrochemistry
    b. electricity   **d.** chemistry of copper

5. Electroanalysis is
    a. an application of electrochemistry
    b. a useful tool of the chemist
    c. a form of quantitative analysis
    d. all of the above

6. You should conclude that the mass of the cathode
    a. increases with plating   **c.** remains the same with plating
    b. decreases with plating

7. In order to answer question 6 you must use
    a. deductive reasoning   **b.** inductive reasoning

The effects of temperature and pressure on the percent yield of NH_3

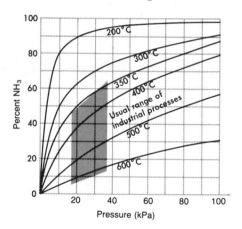

FIGURE 1-2.

8. What is the title of the graph?
9. What variable is plotted along the abscissa?
10. What variable is plotted along the ordinate?
11. In what units is pressure measured?
12. What is the interval for each block along the y axis?
13. At 70 kPa and 600°C, what is the percent yield of NH_3?
14. Predict the percent yield of NH_3 at 120 kPa and 200°C.
15. Considering the usual range of industrial processes, what is the maximum yield that can be expected?
16. In order to obtain at least a 90% yield, in what temperature range would NH_3 be produced (pressure not to exceed 100 kPa)?

MEASURING AND CALCULATING

2

Chemistry is a physical science based on measurements. A chemist uses these measurements to form conclusions about the behavior of matter. The units of the measurement designate the quantity being measured. If scientists are to understand one another, units that are familiar to all scientists must be used. Standard units have been adopted so that scientists everywhere can communicate their findings.

2:1 THE INTERNATIONAL SYSTEM (SI)

During the past two centuries, many versions of the metric system have been used. One system, called the **International System of Units (SI),** was established by international agreement. SI is used commonly by scientists in all countries. The most common SI units used in chemistry are listed in Table A-1 of the Appendix.

In the SI system there is one base unit for each category of measurement—mass, length, time, and so on. These base units are multiplied by factors of ten to form larger and smaller units. The factors are indicated by prefixes attached to the base units. Table A-2 of the Appendix lists the SI prefixes. A kilometer, for example, is 1000 meters; a microgram is one millionth of a gram; a nanomole is one billionth of a mole.

Two situations that often confuse students are the measurements for mass and weight and temperature and heat. Mass and weight are different quantities and are not interchangeable in usage. **Mass** is a measure of the quantity of matter in an object and is measured in grams. **Weight** is a measure of gravitational attraction on an object and is measured in Newtons. Only mass will be used in this book. **Temperature** is a measure of the kinetic energy of particles. While the standard unit of temperature is the kelvin (K), the size of the Celsius degree (C°) is equal to the kelvin.

$$K = °C + 273$$

Heat is a means of energy transfer and is measured in joules.

2:2 SIGNIFICANT DIGITS

The accuracy of the answer to a problem depends upon the accuracy of the numbers used to express each measurement. The **accuracy** of any measurement depends upon the instrument that is used and upon the observer. The digits in an answer that imply more accuracy than the measurements justify are not significant and should be dropped. The digits that remain truly indicate the accuracy of the original measurements. These remaining numerals are called significant digits. **Significant digits** consist of the definitely known digits plus one estimated digit.

Imagine that you have measured the length of a page in this book with a small ruler that is calibrated in tenths of a centimeter. You find that the edge of the page is between 22.6 and 22.7 cm. You estimate that the last digit is closer to 0.7. You record the measurement as 22.7 cm. You did not record the length as 22.6895 cm because you would be exceeding the accuracy of the ruler and your ability to estimate that number of decimal places. Since the last digit is estimated, it is said to be uncertain. Unless otherwise stated, the uncertainty in a measurement is assumed to be within ±1 in the last indicated digit. Therefore, the uncertainty of your measurement can be expressed as 22.7 ±0.1 cm. The last digit is uncertain but it is part of the measurement and is a significant digit. The significant digits of a measurement consist of all known digits plus one estimated digit.

If five people measured the same page in this book using the same ruler and recorded the length as 22.7 cm, we would say that the measurement is precise. Precision refers to the reproducibility of identical measurements of a quantity on the same instrument. The accuracy is determined by comparison of the measured value to an accepted or true value. The ruler, if poorly made, may give precise measurements that are not accurate. Measurements are written using the correct number of significant digits in order to indicate precision.

The following rules are used to determine the number of significant digits in a recorded measurement.

1. Digits other than zero are always significant.

        56.1   3 significant digits

2. Zeros between nonzero digits are always significant.

        3.108   4 significant digits

3. Any final zero used after a decimal point is significant.

        4.320   4 significant digits

4. Zeros used solely for spacing the decimal point (place holders) are not significant.

        400   1 significant digit

        0.0026   2 significant digits

Not all numbers used in a calculation are measurements. Exact numbers, such as counted numbers or defined numbers, may be part of the calculation. How many students are present in your chemistry class? The answer is an exact number. It contains no uncertainty. Exact numbers are sometimes said to have an infinite number of significant digits. Definitions, such as 1 minute = 60 seconds, contain exact numbers and do not limit the number of significant digits used in a calculation.

Example 1

Determine the number of significant digits and the uncertainty in the measurement 20.17 grams.

Solving Process:

Rules 1 and 2 indicate that there are 4 significant digits. The last digit is estimated and is uncertain. It occurs in the hundredth's place. The uncertainty is ±0.01 gram.

PROBLEM

1. Determine the number of significant digits and the uncertainty in each of the following.

a. 6.751 g	**f.** 30.07 g	**k.** 54.52 cm^3
b. 0.157 kg	**g.** 0.106 cm	**l.** 0.1209 m
c. 28.0 mL	**h.** 0.0067 g	**m.** 2.690 g
d. 2500 m	**i.** 0.0230 cm^3	**n.** 43.07 cm
e. 0.070 g	**j.** 26.509 cm	**o.** 6 352 001 g

2:3 HANDLING NUMBERS IN SCIENCE

The least accurate measurement determines the accuracy of an answer in an addition or subtraction problem. The answer must be rounded off to the highest decimal place containing uncertainty. Use the following guidelines when rounding measurements.

1. If the eliminated digit is less than 5, do not change the preceding digit.

Rounded to 3 digits	*Rounded to 2 digits*
2.473 becomes 2.47	3.64 becomes 3.6

2. If the eliminated digit is 5 or more, add 1 to the preceding digit.

Rounded to 3 digits	*Rounded to 2 digits*
8.276 becomes 8.28	0.478 becomes 0.48

In the addition and subtraction examples below the answers must be rounded to the tenth's place. In each case the least accurate measurement is expressed to tenths.

Add		**Subtract**
50.23 g		28.75 cm
23.7 g		17.5 cm
14.678 g		11.25 cm
88.608 g		
88.6 g	**Answer**	11.3 cm

In multiplication and division, the answer should have the same number of significant digits as the factor having the least number of significant digits (the least precise measurement) in the problem.

If you are using a calculator to obtain your numerical answer, you must be very careful to observe significant digits. The calculator may give you an answer of eight or more digits. All of these digits may not be justified by your data. For example, in the problem 4.8070/1.23 the number of significant digits is five and three, respectively. The calculator answer may appear as 3.908 130 081, but rounding the calculator answer to the smaller number of significant digits (three) gives a final answer of 3.91.

PROBLEMS

Express each answer in the correct significant digits.

2. Add.
   a. 16.5 cm + 8 cm + 4.37 cm
   b. 13.25 g + 10.00 g + 9.6 g
   c. 2.36 m + 3.38 m + 0.355 m + 1.06 m
   d. 0.0853 g + 0.0547 g + 0.037 g + 0.00387 g
3. Subtract.
   a. 23.27 km − 12.058 km   c. 350.0 m − 200 m
   b. 13.57 g − 6.3 g   d. 27.68 cm − 14.369 cm
4. Multiply.
   a. 2.6 cm × 3.78 cm   d. 3.08 km × 5.2 km
   b. 6.54 m × 0.37 m   e. 3.15 dm × 2.5 dm × 4.00 dm
   c. 0.036 m × 0.02 m   f. 35.7 cm × 0.78 cm × 2.3 cm
5. Divide.
   a. 35 cm^2 ÷ 0.62 cm   d. 40.8 m^2 ÷ 5.050 m
   b. 39 g ÷ 24.2 g   e. 3.76 km ÷ 1.62 km
   c. 0.58 dm^3 ÷ 2.15 dm   f. 0.075 g ÷ 0.003 cm^3

2:4   DERIVED UNITS

By combining basic SI units, we obtain measurement units used to express other quantities. Distance divided by time equals speed, m/s. If we multiply length by length, we get area, cm^2. Length cubed equals volume, dm^3.

Other derived units are given special names. The force that will cause a 1.00-kg mass to accelerate at 1.00 m/s^2 is defined as one newton, N. One pascal, Pa, is a pressure of one newton per square meter, N/m^2. Gas pressure is measured in pascals. Derived units are also used as labels in the factor label method of problem solving, Section 2:6.

2:5   CONVERSION FACTORS

In Table A-2 the values of the SI prefixes are described. Using these definitions and SI base units we can form conversion ratios to convert a given unit to any other related unit.

Example 2

How many meters are in 175 cm?

Solving Process:

Table A-2 defines centi- as 1/100. Therefore there are 100 cm in 1 m. Since 100 cm = 1 m, two ratios equal to 1 are possible.

$$\frac{100\ cm}{1\ m} \quad or \quad \frac{1\ m}{100\ cm} = 1$$

Since we wish to convert cm to m, we use the second ratio.

$$number\ of\ meters = \frac{175\ cm}{} \left| \frac{1\ m}{100\ cm} \right. = 1.75\ m$$

The centimeters divide out and the answer is given in meters. Since the multiplying ratio equals one, the quantity has not changed, merely the units in which it is expressed.

PROBLEM

6. Convert.

a. 0.75 kg to mg
b. 1500 mm to km
c. 1.00 day to seconds

d. 0.52 kilometer to meters
e. 65 grams to kilograms
f. 750 micrograms to grams

2:6   PROBLEM SOLVING—FACTOR LABEL METHOD

The study of chemistry requires skill in handling units and solving problems. You can develop this skill in problem solving by practice. Essentially, successful problem solving requires that you look for a pattern.

Problems consist of three parts: a known beginning, a desired end, and a connecting path or conversion method. For any word problem, first select the information that is given or known. Then decide what information you must find. The connecting path comes from your general knowledge and the chemistry knowledge you acquire on a regular basis through study. This connecting path involves the use of conversion factors.

Consider the following problem. Ask yourself what is known, what is desired, and what is the connecting path.

Example 3

An object is traveling at a speed of 7500 centimeters per second. Convert the value to kilometers per day.

Solving Process:

From the problem, the known value and the desired value can be written as ratios.

$$\frac{7500 \text{ centimeters}}{\text{second}} \quad \text{and} \quad \frac{? \text{ kilometers}}{\text{day}}$$

What relationships are known between centimeters and kilometers? Between second and day? Write them down.

$$100 \text{ cm} = 1 \text{ m} \quad 1000 \text{ m} = 1 \text{ km} \quad 60 \text{ s} = 1 \text{ min}$$
$$60 \text{ min} = 1 \text{ h} \quad\quad 24 \text{ h} = 1 \text{ day}$$

Use these relationships as ratios in such a way that seconds, minutes, hours, centimeters, and meters divide out. If the units don't divide out, your answer will have unusual units such as second squared.

$$\frac{\text{km}}{\text{day}} = \frac{7500 \text{ cm}}{\text{s}} \left| \frac{60 \text{ s}}{1 \text{ min}} \right| \frac{60 \text{ min}}{\text{h}} \left| \frac{24 \text{ h}}{\text{day}} \right| \frac{1 \text{ m}}{100 \text{ cm}} \right|$$

$$\left| \frac{1 \text{ km}}{1000 \text{ m}} = 6480 \frac{\text{km}}{\text{day}} = 6500 \frac{\text{km}}{\text{day}} \right.$$

Note that this example is for one chain of operations. Lengthy operations that require the use of more than one line will use the above format.

Example 4

One edge of a copper cube is carefully measured and found to be 2.162 cm. An atom of copper is 0.2560 nm in diameter. How many atoms of copper are contained in the cube?

Solving Process:

To develop your skill in solving problems, it is good practice to write down the given values, the desired quantity, and the relationships used to construct conversion factors.

Given: edge of cube = 2.162 centimeters (cm)
　　　　　diameter of copper atom = 0.2560 nanometer (nm)

Desired quantity: number of copper atoms in cube

Relationships: 10^9 nm = 1 m
　　　　　　　　10^2 cm = 1 m
　　　　　　　　Volume of cube = $edge^3$
　　　　　　　　Volume of atom = $\frac{4}{3} \pi r^3 = \frac{\pi d^3}{6}$

To relate the volume of a copper atom to the volume of the cube, length values must be in the same units.

$$\text{edge of cube} = \frac{2.162 \text{ cm}}{} \left| \frac{1 \text{ m}}{1 \times 10^7 \text{ } \mu\text{m}} \right| \frac{1 \times 10^9 \text{ nm}}{1 \text{ m}}$$

$$= 2.162 \times 10^7 \text{ nm}$$

$$\text{volume of cube} = edge^3 = (2.162 \times 10^7 \text{ nm})^3 = 1.011 \times 10^{22} \text{ nm}^3$$

$$\text{volume of copper atom} = \frac{\pi \, d^3}{6}$$

$$= \frac{\pi \, (0.2560 \text{ nm})^3}{6} = 8.785 \times 10^{-3} \text{ nm}^3$$

$$\text{number of atoms in cube} = \frac{1.011 \times 10^{22} \text{ nm}^3}{\text{cube}} \left| \frac{1 \text{ atom}}{8.785 \times 10^{-3} \text{ nm}^3} \right.$$

$$= 1.151 \times 10^{24} \text{ atoms/cube}$$

PROBLEMS

7. The following information is given in a science supply catalog:

   60 rubber stoppers = 500.0 grams = $4.89

   Each student in a class will need 4 stoppers. There are 24 students in the class. What mass of stoppers must be ordered and what will be the cost?

8. The speed of a skyrocket is measured and found to be 145.3 m/s. What is the rocket's speed in km/h?

9. The dimensions of an aquarium are found to be 76.7 cm, 114.5 cm, and 104.2 cm. What is its volume in m^3?

10. An aquarium filter will clean 275 cm^3 of water per minute. How long will it take to filter 125 dm^3 of dirty water?

11. A light-year is the distance light can travel in one year. If the sun is 150 000 000 kilometers away, how many light years is the sun from the earth? Assume that light travels at a speed of 3.00×10^{10} cm/s.

2:7   SCIENTIFIC NOTATION

The average distance between the earth and the sun is 150 000 000 kilometers. This large number can be written as 1.5×10^8 kilometers. The diameter of atoms is about 0.000 000 02 centimeter. This small number can be written as 2×10^{-8} centimeter.

Both large and small numbers can be manipulated with ease in multiplication and division problems by putting them in scientific notation. In **scientific notation** the number is expressed in the form $M \times 10^n$, where $1 \leq M < 10$ and n is an integer.

Numbers written as powers of 10 can be used to indicate the number of significant digits. The total number of digits in the first portion of a value (M above) in scientific notation indicates the number of significant digits.

Number of Significant Digits Required in Answer		Power of Ten
2		1.5×10^5
3	(Answer)	1.50×10^5
4	150 000	1.500×10^5
5		1.5000×10^5

Let us review the addition, subtraction, multiplication, and division of values expressed in scientific notation.

To add or subtract numbers with exponents ($M \times 10^n$), all exponents must be the same.

Example 5

Find the sum of $(6.5 \times 10^2 \text{ g}) + (2.0 \times 10^3 \text{ g}) + (30.0 \times 10^3 \text{ g})$.

Solving Process:

Method 1: Using longhand calculations

Change 6.5×10^2 to $M \times 10^3$

$$6.5 \times 10^2 = 0.65 \times 10^3$$
$$(0.65 \times 10^3) + (2.0 \times 10^3) + (30.0 \times 10^3) = (0.65 + 2.0 + 30.0) \times 10^3$$
$$= 32.7 \times 10^3$$
$$= 3.27 \times 10^4 \text{ g}$$

Method 2: Using a calculator

Enter the M part of the numer (6.5) into the calculator. Then instead of multiplying by 10^2, press the $\boxed{\text{EE}}$ or $\boxed{\text{EXP}}$ key followed by the value of the exponent. If the exponent is negative, change its sign by using the $\boxed{+/-}$ key.

The key stroke sequence for the above problem is

6.5 $\boxed{\text{EE}}$ 2 + 2.0 $\boxed{\text{EE}}$ 3 + 30.0 $\boxed{\text{EE}}$ 3 = 3.27×10^4 g

For multiplication problems involving numbers with exponents ($M \times 10^n$), multiply the values of M and add the exponents. The exponents do not need to be alike as they do in addition and subtraction in order to do longhand calculations.

Example 6

Find the product of $(4.0 \times 10^{-2} \text{ cm})(3.0 \times 10^{-4} \text{ cm})(2.0 \times 10^1 \text{ cm})$.

Solving Process:
Add the exponents: $-2 + (-4) + 1 = -5$
Multiply the values of M: $4.0 \times 3.0 \times 2.0 = 24$

$$(4.0 \times 10^{-2})(3.0 \times 10^{-4})(2.0 \times 10^{1}) = (4.0 \times 3.0 \times 2.0) \times 10^{-2-4+1}$$
$$= 24 \times 10^{-5} = 2.4 \times 10^{-4} \text{ cm}^3$$

Division is similar to multiplication except the exponents are subtracted instead of added. The exponents do not need to be the same. To divide exponential numbers ($M \times 10^n$), divide the values of M and subtract the exponent of the denominator from the exponent of the numerator.

Example 7

Divide (12.73×10^{-6} g) by (4.6×10^2 cm^3)
Solving Process:
Subtract the exponents: $-6 -(2) - 8$
Divide the values of M: $\dfrac{12.73}{4.6} = 2.8$

$$\frac{12.73 \times 10^{-6} \text{ g}}{4.6 \times 10^2 \text{ cm}^3} = \frac{12.73}{4.6} \times 10^{-6-2} = 2.8 \times 10^{-8} \text{ g/cm}^3$$

Example 8

$$\frac{(8.0 \times 10^6 \text{ cm}^3)(4.0 \times 10^3 \text{ kPa})(3.0 \times 10^2 \text{ K})}{(3.0 \times 10^4 \text{ kPa})(2.0 \times 10^2 \text{ K})}$$

Solving Process:

$$= \frac{(8.0 \times 4.0 \times 3.0) \times 10^{6+3+2} \text{ cm}^3}{(3.0 \times 2.0) \times 10^{4+2}}$$

$$= \frac{96}{6.0} \times \frac{10^{11}}{10^6} = 16 \times 10^{11-6} \text{ cm}^3$$

$$= 16 \times 10^5 = 1.6 \times 10^6 \text{ cm}^3$$

PROBLEMS

12. Express the following in scientific notation.

a. 0.000 03 cm   c. 55 000 000 m   e. 0.000 007 m
b. 8 000 000 g   d. 0.002 g   f. 65 000 km

13. Do the following calculations using scientific notation.

a. $(5.1 \times 10^{-4}$ cm$)(2.8 \times 10^{-3}$ cm$)$
b. $(6.5 \times 10^4$ m$)(3.27 \times 10^{-5}$ m$)$

c. $(4.00 \times 10^2 \text{ g}) \div (2.000 \times 10^2 \text{ cm}^3)$

d. $\dfrac{(6.33 \times 10^{-7} \text{ km})(2.189 \times 10^{-3} \text{ km})}{(3.007 \times 10^{-8} \text{ km})}$

e. $(7.072 \times 10^5 \text{ cm})(5.77 \times 10^{-3} \text{ cm})(2.0 \times 10^2 \text{ cm})$

f. $(7.5 \times 10^5 \text{ g}) \div (2.5 \times 10^2 \text{ g})$

g. $(9.000\ 00 \times 10^7 \text{ m}) \div (3.0000 \times 10^3 \text{ s})$

h. $\dfrac{(4 \times 10^5 \text{ m}^3)(345 \text{ K})(2.008 \times 10^2 \text{ kPa})}{(273 \text{ K})(1.013\ 25 \times 10^2 \text{ kPa})}$

2:8 DENSITY

One quantity used to characterize substances is density. **Density*** is the mass of a substance that occupies a given volume. Though the SI standard unit of volume is the cubic meter (m^3), it is more practical to express the density of solids and liquids in g/cm³. Gases are much less dense than solids or liquids. Their densities are usually given in g/dm³. The densities of gases will be discussed in detail in Chapter 18.

Table 2-1

Densities of Some Materials at 25°C (g/cm³)			
aluminum	2.699	mercury	13.534
carbon (diamond)	3.614	platinum	21.41
gold	19.32	potassium	0.862
iron	7.874	sodium	0.968
lead	11.342	water	1.00
magnesium	1.738		

Example 9

What is the density of a hydrochloric acid solution that has a mass of 17.84 g and occupies 15.00 cm³?

Solving Process:

$$density = \frac{mass}{volume}$$

$$= \frac{17.84 \text{ g}}{15.00 \text{ cm}^3}$$

$$= 1.189 \text{ g/cm}^3$$

The equation for density may be solved for volume or mass as well.

*Density varies with temperature. For convenience, we will assume that the density of solids and liquids does not vary significantly.

PROBLEMS

Calculate the density of the following materials.

14. 35.0 g of a substance that occupies 25.0 cm^3

15. 2.75 kg of a substance that occupies 250 cm^3

16. 2.80 g of a substance that occupies 2.00 dm^3

17. Determine the volume that 35.2 g of carbon tetrachloride will occupy if it has a density of 1.60 g/cm^3.

18. The density of ethanol is 0.789 g/cm^3 at 20°C. What is the mass of 150 cm^3 of this alcohol?

19. A block of lead measures 20.00 mm × 30.00 mm × 45.00 mm. Calculate the mass of this block, if the density of lead is 11.34 g/cm^3.

CHAPTER REVIEW PROBLEMS

1. A sign in a town gives the speed limit at 50 km/h. What is this speed in centimeters per second?

2. Convert.

   a. 3.50 m to cm   **c.** 0.52 km to mm

   b. 65 g to kg   **d.** 8.14 dm^3 to cm^3

3. Write the correct units to the answer for the following problem

lab	lump	bang	bam	bog^2	mess
	bog	lump	bog	bang	bam

4. Determine the number of significant digits in each of the following.

   a. 35 g   **f.** 0.004 m^3

   b. 3.57 m   **g.** 24.068 kPa

   c. 3.507 km   **h.** 268 K

   d. 0.035 kg   **i.** 20.040 80 g

   e. 0.246 cm   **j.** 730 000 kg

Perform the following calculations and express your answer to the proper number of significant digits.

5. (5.14 cm) (6.742 × 10^2 cm)

6. 2.8 × 10^3 g ÷ 6.86 × 10^2 cm^3

7. $\dfrac{(6.88 \times 10^2 \ m^3)(2.14 \times 10^2 \ K)}{(3.8 \times 10^2 \ K)}$

8. (7.500 00 cm) (2.040 × 10^3 cm) (3.0 × 10^2 cm)

9. 6.0 × 10^{-3} m ÷ 3 × 10^{-4} s

10. $\dfrac{(5 \times 10^3 \ cm^3)(8 \times 10^2 \ kPa)}{(4.5 \times 10^2 \ kPa)}$

11. 30.0 g of each of the following acids are needed. What volume of each should be measured out?

Acid	Density (g/cm³)
a. hydrochloric acid, HCl	1.1639
b. sulfuric acid, H_2SO_4	1.834
c. nitric acid, HNO_3	1.251

12. Use the densities given in Table 2-1 to determine which would be heavier—a ball of lead with a diameter of 2.00 cm or a cylinder of iron with a diameter of 3.00 cm and a height of 8.00 cm.

    (Volume of a sphere $= \dfrac{1}{6}\pi d^3$. Volume of a cylinder $= \pi r^2 h$.)

MATTER

Matter is anything that has the property of inertia. It can also be defined as anything that has mass and volume. Matter can be classified in a variety of ways. When matter is classified according to physical state, it can be solid, liquid, or gas. We may also classify matter according to composition as homogeneous or heterogeneous, substance or mixture, element or compound.

3:1 HETEROGENEOUS AND HOMOGENEOUS MATERIALS

Most of the things around us contain two or more different materials. Concrete, for example, contains sand, gravel, lime, and clay. Air is a mixture of oxygen, nitrogen, carbon dioxide, and other gases. If we look closely at a piece of concrete, we see it is not uniform throughout. Such nonuniform materials are called **heterogeneous mixtures.** The physically separate parts, such as sand, gravel, lime, and clay, are called phases. A **phase** is any region of a material with a uniform set of properties. The phase boundaries in heterogeneous materials are called **interfaces.**

Materials such as air, which consist of only one phase, are **homogeneous.** Within these materials there is a uniform distribution of particles. Homogeneous mixtures are called **solutions.** They contain a dissolved material called a **solute,** and a dissolving material called a **solvent.** As in all mixtures, the components of a solution may be present in varying amounts or concentrations.

3:2 ELEMENTS AND COMPOUNDS

Homogeneous materials that contain one kind of matter are called substances. A **substance** is a material with definite composition and properties. Substances composed of only one kind of atom are **elements.** Substances composed of atoms of two or more elements are **compounds.**

PROBLEM

1. Indicate which of the following is an element, compound, heterogeneous mixture, or solution.

a. ocean water	**e.** copper	**i.** aluminum foil
b. calcium	**f.** grain alcohol	**j.** milk
c. vitamin C	**g.** after-shave lotion	**k.** table salt
d. dry ice (solid CO_2)	**h.** hamburger	**l.** iron nail

3:3   PHYSICAL PROPERTIES AND CHANGES

A **physical property** is a characteristic that can be specified without reference to another substance. Physical properties are divided into two types, extensive and intensive. **Extensive properties** depend upon the amount of matter present. Mass, length, and volume are examples. **Intensive properties** do not depend upon the amount, but upon the nature of the substance. Density, solubility, boiling point, and conductivity are examples.

When a material changes form, but not chemical composition, a **physical change** has occurred. Grinding into powder, melting, boiling, and dissolving are examples. Physical changes are often used to separate mixtures. Salt may be separated from a saltwater solution by boiling off the water. Distillation, fractional crystallization, filtration, and precipitation are laboratory techniques that are used to separate the components of mixtures.

3:4   CHEMICAL PROPERTIES AND CHANGES

A familiar chemical reaction is burning. The color, density, and other characteristics of the ashes are different from the material before it was burned. A **chemical change** occurs when a substance burns because new substances with different properties are formed. **Chemical properties** relate to the ability of a substance to change to a different substance. For example, does it burn? Does it react with acids? Such questions help to determine the chemical properties of a substance.

PROBLEMS

2. Classify each of the following as a chemical or physical property.
   - **a.** reacts with H_2O
   - **b.** is red
   - **c.** conducts electricity
   - **d.** resists corrosion
   - **e.** boils at 88°C
   - **f.** dissolves in gasoline
   - **g.** is ductile
   - **h.** is flammable
   - **i.** is 1.5 m long
   - **j.** is malleable
   - **k.** is corrosive
   - **l.** freezes at −17°C

3. Classify each of the following as a chemical or physical change.
   - **a.** alcohol evaporating
   - **b.** a firefly lighting up
   - **c.** a battery charging
   - **d.** ice melting
   - **e.** an explosion
   - **f.** salt dissolving in H_2O
   - **g.** digesting food
   - **h.** hammering hot iron into a sheet

3:5   MEASURING ENERGY CHANGES

The heat required to change the temperature of a substance depends upon the amount and nature of the substance as well as the extent of the temperature change. For example, one gram of water requires 4.18 joules of energy to cause a temperature change of one Celsius degree. It takes only 0.987 J to raise the temperature of 1 g of AlF_3 one Celsius degree.

Energy can be transferred between a system and its surroundings. The amount of energy transferred can be calculated from the relationship

$$\begin{pmatrix} heat\ gained \\ or\ lost \end{pmatrix} = \begin{pmatrix} mass \\ in\ grams \end{pmatrix} \begin{pmatrix} change\ in \\ temperature \end{pmatrix} \begin{pmatrix} specific \\ heat \end{pmatrix}$$

$$q = (m)(\Delta T)(C_p)$$

where q is the heat added (or removed), m is the mass of the substance, T is the change in temperature, and C_p is a property of the substance called its **specific heat.** The specific heat of a substance varies with the temperature. Specific heat values are given in Table A-8.

Example 1

How much heat is required to raise the temperature of 68.0 g of AlF_3 from 25.0°C to 80.0°C?

Solving Process:

In addition to the temperature change and mass given in the statement of the problem we must consult Table A-8 in the Appendix to obtain the specific heat of AlF_3, 0.8948 J/g·C°.

$$q = m(\Delta T)C_p$$
$$= \frac{68.0\ g}{} \left| \frac{(80.0 - 25.0)\ °C}{} \right| \frac{0.8948\ J}{g \cdot C°} = 3350\ J$$

A calorimeter containing water is often used to measure the heat absorbed or released in a chemical reaction. The temperature change of the water is used to measure the amount of heat absorbed or released by the reaction. According to the law of conservation of energy, in an insulated system, any heat lost by one quantity of matter must be gained by another. Energy flows from the warmer material to the cooler material until the two reach the same temperature.

$$heat\ lost = heat\ gained$$
$$m(\Delta T)C_p = m(\Delta T)C_p$$

Example 2

Suppose a piece of lead with a mass of 14.9 g at a temperature of 92.5°C is dropped into an insulated container of water. The mass of water is 165 g and its temperature before adding the lead is 20.0°C. What is the final temperature of the system? C_p lead = 0.1276 J/g·C°

Solving Process:

We know the heat lost equals the heat gained. Since the lead is at a higher temperature than the water, the lead will lose energy. The water will gain an equivalent amount of energy.

(a) The heat lost by the lead is

$$q = (m)(\Delta T)(C_p) = \frac{14.9\,\cancel{g}}{} \left| \frac{(92.5°\cancel{C} - T_f)}{} \right| \frac{0.1276\,J}{\cancel{g} \cdot \cancel{C°}}$$

(b) The heat gained by the water is

$$q = (m)(\Delta T)(C_p) = \frac{165\,\cancel{g}}{} \left| \frac{(T_f - 20.0°\cancel{C})}{} \right| \frac{4.18\,J}{\cancel{g} \cdot \cancel{C°}}$$

(c) The heat gained must equal the heat lost

$$\frac{165\,\cancel{g}}{} \left| \frac{(T_f - 20.0°C)}{} \right| \frac{4.18\,\cancel{J}}{\cancel{g} \cdot \cancel{C°}} = \frac{14.9\,\cancel{g}}{} \left| \frac{(92.5°C - T_f)}{} \right| \frac{0.1276\,J}{\cancel{g} \cdot \cancel{C°}}$$

$$T_f = 20.2°C$$

PROBLEMS

4. How much heat is required to raise the temperature of 789 g of acetic acid, CH_3COOH, from 25.0°C to 82.7°C?

5. How much heat is released when 432 g of water cools from 71.0°C to 18.0°C?

6. Compute the heat released when 42.8 g of calcium carbide, CaC_2, cools from 74.2°C to 11.5°C.

7. If a piece of gold ($C_p = 0.129\ J/g \cdot C°$) with mass 45.5 g and a temperature of 80.5°C is dropped into 192 g of water at 15.0°C, what is the final temperature of the system?

8. A piece of unknown metal with mass 14.9 is heated to 100.0°C and dropped into 75.0 g of water at 20.0°C. The final temperature of the system is 28.5°C. What is the specific heat of the metal?

CHAPTER REVIEW PROBLEMS

Compute the energy changes associated with the following transitions using Table A-8.

1. 49.2 g acetic acid, CH_3COOH, is heated from 24.1°C to 67.3°C

2. 9.61 g ethanol, CH_3CH_2OH, is heated from 19.6°C to 75.0°C

3. 2.47 g sand, SiO_2, is heated from 17.1°C to 46.7°C

4. 31.9 g calcium sulfate, $CaSO_4$, is cooled from 83.2°C to 55.5°C

5. 63.6 g zinc sulfide, ZnS, is cooled from 95.5°C to 42.3°C

6. If a piece of silver ($C_p = 0.2165\ J/g \cdot C°$) with mass 14.16 g and a temperature of 133.5°C is dropped into 250.0 g of water at 17.20°C, what will be the final temperature of the system?

7. A piece of unknown metal with mass 17.19 g is heated to 100.00°C and dropped into 25.00 g of water at 24.50°C. The final temperature of the system is 30.05°C. What is the specific heat of the metal?

8. In order to make 4 cups of tea, 1.00 kg of water is heated from 22.0°C to 99.0°C. How much energy is required?

CHEMICAL FORMULAS

4

4:1 SYMBOLS

The chemical name for an element can be abbreviated to form a **chemical symbol.** Usually the chemical symbol contains the first letter of the element's name. If the names of two elements begin with the same letter, another letter from one name is added. For instance, B is boron, Br is bromine. The first letter is always uppercase, the second letter is always lowercase: Na is sodium, O is oxygen, and He is helium.

The use of upper and lowercase letters is important. For instance, the following elements and compounds are represented by the same letters.

Elements	Compounds
Co, cobalt	CO, carbon monoxide
No, nobelium	NO, nitrogen(II) oxide

For elements with atomic numbers greater than 103, the chemical symbols contain three letters. This system of naming will not be discussed here. See the Table of International Atomic Masses and the Periodic Table on the inside back cover of this book for names and symbols for these elements.

4:2 CHEMICAL FORMULAS

A **chemical formula** provides the clearest and simplest method of designating compounds. The chemical formula for a compound indicates the number and kind of elements in a compound. The chemical formula for vitamin A is $C_{20}H_{30}O$. Thus, in one molecule of vitamin A there are twenty carbon atoms, thirty hydrogen atoms, and one oxygen atom.

Compounds that consist of two elements are called binary compounds (HCl, H_2O, C_2H_6). The formula of a compound composed of a metal and a nonmetal is written with the symbol of the metal first, as in $NaCl$ and Al_2S_3. Generally, you can determine whether an element is a metal or a nonmetal by its position in the periodic table. Metals are listed at the left and center in the standard periodic table. Nonmetals are listed at the extreme right. Notice the diagonal line that divides the table into metallic and nonmetallic elements.

PROBLEMS

1. Which symbol would be written first in the formula for the compound formed from each of the following pairs of elements? Use the periodic table.

   a. S and Cu
   b. Bi and S
   c. N and Nb

   d. C and Mg
   e. Ta and Cl
   f. Al and As

2. Which element would be placed first in the formula for the compound formed from each of the following pairs of elements?

   a. oxygen, copper
   b. sulfur, potassium
   c. lithium, fluorine

   d. calcium, nitrogen
   e. sodium, chlorine
   f. magnesium, bromine

4:3 OXIDATION NUMBER

An atom or group of atoms that is positively or negatively charged is known as an **ion.** The charge that the atom or group of atoms has is called its **oxidation number.** For example, Mg represents the metallic element magnesium, while Mg^{2+} represents the magnesium ion. The oxidation number of the magnesium ion is $2+$. The nonmetallic element fluorine is represented by the symbol F, while F^- represents the fluoride ion. The oxidation number of the fluoride is $1-$.

Some metals have the same positive charge in all compounds. The elements in Group IA (1), such as lithium, sodium, and potassium, always have an oxidation number of $1+$. Group IIA (2) metals, such as magnesium, calcium, strontium, and barium, always have an oxidation number of $2+$. Aluminum always has a charge of $3+$.

In ionic compounds, the total positive charge is equal to the total negative charge. One Mg^{2+} ion with a charge of $2+$ will combine with two Cl^- ions to form $MgCl_2$. For $MgCl_2$ the total positive charge is $2+$ and the total negative charge is $2(1-)$ or $2-$. In a correctly written formula, the sum of the total positive charge and total negative charge is zero.

4:4 POLYATOMIC IONS

The term **polyatomic ion** is used to designate a group of atoms that act as a unit in a wide variety of chemical reactions. A common positive polyatomic ion is NH_4^+, the ammonium ion. A common negative polyatomic ion is hydroxide, OH^-.

Two common negative polyatomic ions are SO_4^{2-} and SO_3^{2-}. Prefixes and suffixes are used in the names of these ions to indicate the oxygen content of the polyatomic ion in relation to other ions in a series of similar ions.

	Prefix	Suffix	Example
	per	-ate	ClO_4^- perchlorate
Increasing		-ate	ClO_3^- chlorate
oxygen content		-ite	ClO_2^- chlorite
	hypo	-ite	ClO^- hypochlorite

Table 4-1

Some Common Oxyanions			
	IO_6^5 periodate		
BrO_3 bromate	IO_3 iodate	SO_4^{2-} sulfate	NO_3^- nitrate
		SO_3^{2-} sulfite	NO_2^- nitrite
BrO^- hypobromite	IO^- hypoiodite		

When more than one polyatomic ion is included in a chemical formula, the ion must be enclosed in parentheses to avoid confusion. For example, $Ca(OH)_2$ is not the same thing as $CaOH_2$. The subscript located to the right of the parenthesis indicates the number of polyatomic ions present The formula for magnesium hydroxide, $Mg(OH)_2$, contains two hydroxide ions There are three ammonium ions in $(NH_4)_3N$.

In more complex compounds the metallic ions are still written first. Hydrogen is indicated by adding the word "hydrogen" immediately in front of the name of the negative ion. For example, $NaHCO_3$ is sodium hydrogen carbonate. (Table A-7 lists additional polyatomic ions.)

Example 1

Write the formula for the compound made from calcium and the phosphate ion.

Solving Process:

Using Tables A-6 and A-7, we see the oxidation states of calcium and the phosphate ion are as follows

$$Ca^{2+} \qquad PO_4^{3-}$$

It is necessary to have three Ca^{2+} and two PO_4^{3-} in the compound to maintain neutrality. Writing calcium ions in the formula is simple, Ca_3.
For the phosphate ion, the entire polyatomic ion must be placed in parentheses to indicate that two phosphate ions are required.

$$Ca_3(PO_4)_2$$

PROBLEMS

3. Write formulas for the following compounds.
   a. lithium fluoride
   b. lithium chloride
   c. lithium bromide
   d. lithium iodide
   e. lithium oxide
   f. lithium sulfide
   g. calcium fluoride
   h. calcium chloride
   i. calcium bromide
   j. calcium hydroxide
   k. calcium oxide
   l. calcium sulfide

4. Write formulas for the following compounds.
   a. sodium cyanide
   b. sodium hydroxide
   c. sodium bromate
   d. sodium acetate
   e. barium cyanide
   f. barium hydroxide
   g. barium oxide
   h. barium sulfate

5. Write formulas for the following compounds.
   a. barium azide
   b. zinc molybdate
   c. cesium perchlorate
   d. aluminum silicate
   e. boron phosphide
   f. silver nitride
   g. cadmium oxalate
   h. potassium thiocyanate
   i. calcium hypophosphite
   j. aluminum hexafluorosilicate

6. Write formulas for the following compounds.
   a. calcium sulfate
   b. sodium nitrate
   c. potassium perchlorate
   d. aluminum sulfate
   e. potassium chlorate
   f. magnesium sulfite
   g. lithium nitrite
   h. sodium chlorite
   i. ammonium dichromate
   j. sodium nitrite

4:5   NAMING COMPOUNDS

There is a systematic method of naming practically all compounds. The names of only a few compounds, particularly acids, will not be included in our discussion of this system.

Compounds containing only two elements are called binary compounds. To name a binary compound, first write the name of the element having a positive charge. Then add the name of the negative element. The name of the negative element must be modified to end in -ide.

Example 2

Name the compound with the formula ZnO.

Solving Process:

The compound is formed by Zn^{2+} (zinc) and O^{2-} (oxide). It is named zinc oxide.

The binary compounds containing hydrogen and a nonmetal, called hydrides, often have common names, such as ammonia, NH_3; methane, CH_4; and water. These compounds will be discussed later.

Table 4-2

Names for Nonmetals in Binary Compounds				
B^{5-}	C^{4-}	N^{3-}	O^{2-}	F^-
boride	carbide	nitride	oxide	fluoride
	Si^{4-}	P^{3-}	S^{2-}	Cl^-
	silicide	phosphide	sulfide	chloride
		As^{3-}	Se^{2-}	Br^-
		arsenide	selenide	bromide
		Sb^{3-}	Te^{2-}	I^-
		antimonide	telluride	iodide
				At^-
				astatide

Compounds containing the ammonium ion are named by using the name "ammonium" followed by the appropriate name for the negative ion.

ammonium bromide	ammonium sulfide	ammonium nitride
NH_4Br	$(NH_4)_2S$	$(NH_4)_3N$

To name a compound containing a negative polyatomic ion, the appropriate positive ion name is followed by the name of the polyatomic ion.

sodium sulfate	magnesium carbonate	aluminum nitrate
Na_2SO_4	$MgCO_3$	$Al(NO_3)_3$

A number of metallic elements can form compounds in which the metal ions have different charges. For example, iron forms one series of compounds in which the iron is Fe^{2+}, and another series in which iron is Fe^{3+}. In naming these compounds, the charge (or oxidation number) of the metal is written in Roman numerals enclosed in parentheses following the metal. The Roman numeral system is thus used to differentiate between ions that have two or more possible charges. For example, $FeBr_2$ is iron(II) bromide, and $FeBr_3$ is iron(III) bromide. To name these compounds we must know the oxidation number of iron.

The following rules will enable you to determine the oxidation numbers of metal ions from the formulas of their compounds.

1. *In metallic halides and other binary metallic compounds, the halogen* (F, Cl, Br, and I) *always has an oxidation number of 1−*. $AuCl_3$ is gold(III) chloride (read as "gold three chloride"). The three Cl atoms have a combined oxidation number of 3−. Since the compound has no charge, the oxidation number of the gold atom must be 3+.

2. *In binary compounds that contain oxygen combined with a metal, the oxygen can usually be assumed to have an oxidation number of 2−.* FeO is iron(II) oxide.

3. *The sum of the charges of the atoms composing a polyatomic ion is the charge on the ion.* This charge is indicated as a superscript. The perchlorate ion, ClO_4^-, has a charge of $1-$ (the sum of the charges of one Cl atom and four O atoms). Since the sum of all the oxidation numbers in a compound is zero, in $Fe(ClO_4)_2$ the Fe must have an oxidation number of $2+$. This compound is named iron(II) perchlorate.

Example 3

Write the names of the compounds Cu_2O and CuO.

Solving Process:

From Rule 2 we know that O in these compounds has a $2-$ charge. Since the sum of all the oxidation numbers in a compound is zero, in Cu_2O the Cu must have a charge of $1+$. In CuO, the charge on Cu must be $2+$. The compounds are named

Cu_2O	CuO
copper(I) oxide	Copper(II) oxide

Some binary compounds composed of nonmetals form a series of two or more compounds such as CO and CO_2. The number of atoms of a given kind is indicated by the use of a Greek prefix preceding the name of the element to which it refers. The prefixes are *mono-*(1), *di-*(2), *tri-*(3), *tetra-*(4), *penta-*(5), *hexa-*(6), *hepta-*(7), and *octa-*(8). The prefix mono- is usually omitted except when it is used for emphasis, as in carbon monoxide. Common usage omits the double vowel. That is, CO is named carbon monoxide, not mono-oxide. CO_2 is carbon dioxide.

The names of the common acids do not follow the rules for naming other compounds. The rules for naming acids will be presented in Chapter 24. Table 4-3 lists names and formulas of acids commonly used in the laboratory. They should be memorized.

Table 4-3

Common Acids			
Formula	**Name**	**Formula**	**Name**
CH_3COOH	acetic	HNO_3	nitric
H_2CO_3	carbonic	H_3PO_4	phosphoric
HCl	hydrochloric	H_2SO_4	sulfuric

PROBLEMS

7. Name the following compounds.
   a. Na_2S
   b. Li_2O
   c. $MgBr_2$
   d. AlN
   e. CaF_2
   f. KI
   g. $MgSO_4$
   h. $Ca(ClO)_2$
   i. $Ba(NO_2)_2$

8. Name the following compounds.

a. $Mg(OH)_2$

b. CaO

c. $LiCH_3COO$

d. $ZnCl_2$

e. Na_3P

f. K_2Se

g. NH_4MgPO_4

h. KNO_2

i. $KNaCO_3$

9. Name the following compounds.

a. Na_2SO_4

b. $AgNO_3$

c. $ZnCr_2O_7$

d. NH_4CH_3COO

e. $KClO_4$

f. NH_4ClO_3

g. CaC_2O_4

h. $BaCO_3$

i. NaH_2PO_4

10. Write formulas for the following compounds.

a. manganese(III) chloride

b. iron(III) bromide

c. chromium(III) bromide

d. tin(IV) chloride

e. manganese(II) bromide

f. tin(IV) oxide

g. chromium(III) oxide

h. lead(II) oxide

i. manganese(VII) oxide

j. mercury(I) oxide

11. Name the following compounds. (Roman numeral system)

a. $TiCl_2$

b. $TiBr_4$

c. $CuCl$

d. PbI_2

e. $SnCl_4$

f. Sb_2O_5

g. CrO_3

h. Mn_3O_4

i. TiO_2

j. PbO

k. BiF_5

l. $NiBr_2$

m. $CuBr_2$

n. $PbCl_2$

o. CrF_3

12. Name the following compounds. (Roman numeral system)

a. $Fe_2(SO_4)_3$

b. $Cr(OH)_2$

c. $Hg_2(ClO_3)_2$*

d. $Fe(ClO_4)_2$

e. $MnSO_4$

f. $Hg(IO_3)_2$

g. $Pb(ClO_2)_2$

h. $Cu(CH_3COO)_2$

i. Cu_2SO_4

j. $CoSO_4$

13. Write formulas for the following compounds.

a. copper(II) chlorate

b. bismuth(III) telluride

c. manganese(III) sulfate

d. iron(III) nitrate

e. tin(IV) nitrate

f. chromium(III) sulfate

g. iron(II) hydroxide

h. copper(II) phosphate

i. mercury(I) nitrite

j. lead(II) nitrate

14. Write formulas for the following compounds.

a. dichlorine oxide

b. chlorine dioxide

c. carbon disulfide

d. chlorine trifluoride

e. dichlorine heptoxide

f. sulfur hexafluoride

15. Name the following compounds. (Greek prefixes)

a. CO_2

b. NO_2

c. SO_3

d. PCl_3

e. NO

f. P_2O_5

---

*Mercury exists as Hg_2^{2+}, mercury (I), in which two mercury atoms are bound together. It also exists as Hg^{2+}, mercury(II).

4:6 MOLECULAR AND EMPIRICAL FORMULAS

The **empirical formula** of a compound is the smallest whole number ratio of the number of atoms of each element in the substance. The **molecular formula** gives the actual number of atoms in the molecule. For instance, CH_2 is the empirical formula for the series of molecular compounds C_2H_4, C_3H_6, C_4H_8, and so on.

There is a definite relationship between the empirical and the molecular formula. Note that the molecular formula is always a whole number multiple of the empirical formula. As can be seen in Table 4-4 the empirical formula and the molecular formula are not always the same.

Table 4-4

Empirical and Molecular Formulas		
Compound	**Empirical Formula**	**Molecular Formula**
water	H_2O	H_2O
hydrogen peroxide	HO	H_2O_2
mercury(I) bromide	$HgBr$	Hg_2Br_2
methane	CH_4	CH_4
butane	C_2H_5	C_4H_{10}
ethene	CH_2	C_2H_4
butene	CH_2	C_4H_8

PROBLEM

16. Write the empirical formula for each of the following.

a. C_6H_6 (benzene)   f. SO_3

b. C_2H_2 (ethyne)   g. N_2O_4

c. $C_6H_{12}O_6$ (glucose)   h. NO_2

d. C_4H_{10} (butane)   i. $Ag_2C_4H_4O_6$

e. P_4O_{10} j. K_2S_4

4:7 COEFFICIENTS

The formula of a compound represents a definite amount of that compound. This amount is called a formula unit. It may be one molecule or the smallest number of particles giving the true proportions of the elements in the compound.

When we wish to represent two molecules of water we write $2H_2O$. The number prefixed as a multiplier is called the **coefficient.** For example, when the coefficient 3 is written before the formula unit Fe_2O_3, it means three times everything in the formula. In $3Fe_2O_3$ there are 6 iron atoms and 9 oxygen atoms.

PROBLEMS

17. Write the number of formula units represented by the following.

    a. 5NaCl   **d.** $ZnSO_4$

    b. H_2O **e.** $2CuSO_4$

    c. $6MgCl_2$ **f.** $12Pb(NO_3)_2$

18. Determine the number of atoms of each element in the following.

    a. $7H_2O$ **c.** $4Al_2O_3$

    b. $2(NH_4)_3PO_4$ **d.** $3CuSO_4$

CHAPTER REVIEW PROBLEMS

Write the formula for each of the following compounds.

1. a. sodium nitrite   **h.** cadmium oxalate

    b. sodium carbonate   **i.** cadmium carbonate

    c. sodium sulfate   **j.** cadmium sulfate

    d. potassium hydroxide   **k.** cadmium phosphate

    e. potassium nitrate   **l.** aluminum bromide

    f. potassium sulfite   **m.** aluminum nitrate

    g. potassium phosphate   **n.** aluminum sulfide

2. a. magnesium nitrate   **g.** iron(II) oxide

    b. magnesium sulfate   **h.** iron(II) hydroxide

    c. magnesium carbonate   **l.** iron(II) carbonate

    d. barium bromide   **j.** iron(II) sulfate

    e. barium nitrate   **k.** iron(III) phosphate

    f. barium sulfate   **l.** iron(III) bromide

3. a. strontium chloride   **f.** iron(III) sulfate

    b. strontium hydroxide   **g.** iron(III) phosphate

    c. strontium nitrate   **h.** mercury(II) bromide

    d. strontium sulfite   **i.** mercury(II) carbonate

    e. strontium sulfide   **j.** mercury(II) sulfide

Write the name for each of the following compounds.

4. a. $NaNO_3$ **e.** K_2CO_3 **i.** $CdSO_3$

    b. Na_2SO_3 **f.** K_2SO_4 **j.** CdS

    c. Na_3PO_4 **g.** $CdBr_2$ **k.** $AlCl_3$

    d. KNO_2 **h.** $Cd(NO_3)_2$ **l.** $Al(OH)_3$

5. a. $Mg(NO_2)_2$ **e.** $BaSO_3$ **i.** $FeBr_2$

    b. $MgSO_3$ **f.** $BaCO_3$ **j.** $Fe(NO_3)_2$

    c. $Mg_3(PO_4)_2$ **g.** $Al_2(SO_4)_3$ **k.** $FeSO_3$

    d. $Ba(NO_2)_2$ **h.** $AlPO_4$ **l.** FeS

6. a. $Ba_3(PO_4)_2$ **e.** $SrSO_4$ **i.** Fe_2S_3

    b. $SrBr_2$ **f.** $Sr_3(PO_4)_2$ **j.** $HgCl_2$

    c. $Sr(NO_3)_2$ **g.** $FeCl_3$ **k.** $Hg(NO_3)_2$

    d. $SrCO_3$ **h.** $Fe(NO_3)_3$ **l.** $HgSO_4$

7. Write the formula for each of the following compounds.
   a. sodium hydroxide
   b. mercury(II) sulfate
   c. calcium hypochlorite
   d. lead(II) phosphate
   e. aluminum chlorate
   f. ammonium sulfide
   g. copper(I) carbonate
   h. mercury(I) sulfide
   i. lead(II) acetate
   j. manganese(IV) oxide
   k. manganese(II) sulfate
   l. silver oxide
   m. zinc nitrate
   n. chromium(III) sulfite
   o. ammonium dichromate
   p. iron(III) oxide

8. Write the names for each of the following compounds.
   a. $NaCH_3COO$
   b. $Ni(NO_3)_2$
   c. Hg_2Cl_2
   d. $Sn_3(PO_4)_2$
   e. $Cr(OH)_2$
   f. $Zn(ClO_3)_2$
   g. $MgBr_2$
   h. CuN_3
   i. CaH_2
   j. $Ba(NO_2)_2$
   k. MnS
   l. $Sn(NO_3)_4$
   m. $(NH_4)_2SO_4$
   n. PbO
   o. KCN

9. Write the formula for each of the following compounds.
   a. magnesium nitrate
   b. silver acetate
   c. barium perchlorate
   d. potassium nitrite
   e. ammonium sulfate
   f. ammonium dichromate
   g. barium molybdate
   h. zinc thiocyanate

10. Write the name for each of the following compounds.
   a. $FeSO_4$
   b. NH_4ClO_3
   c. $Fe(CH_3COO)_2$
   d. $CuCrO_4$
   e. $Mg(NO_3)_2$
   f. $AlPO_4$
   g. Na_2SO_3
   h. $Ca(ClO_2)_2$
   i. $(NH_4)_2CO_3$
   j. Ag_2CrO_4
   k. $Ba_3(PO_4)_2$
   l. $KClO_4$

11. Write the formula for each of the following compounds.
   a. zinc hexafluorosilicate
   b. antimony(V) sulfide
   c. bismuth(III) telluride
   d. titanium(IV) iodide
   e. nickel(II) fluoride
   f. manganese(IV) oxide
   g. lead(IV) oxide
   h. calcium tartrate
   i. mercury(II) oxide
   j. cobalt(III) oxide

12. Write the name for each of the following compounds
   a. $Zn(SCN)_2$
   b. Sb_2O_5
   c. TiO
   d. InP
   e. Mn_2O_3
   f. $Cr(CH_3COO)_3$

13. Write the empirical formula for each of the following.
   a. C_6H_{14}
   b. CO_2
   c. N_2F_4
   d. $C_3H_6Cl_2$
   e. $C_5H_{10}O_2$
   f. $P_3N_3Cl_6$

14. Write the number of formula units expressed by each of the following.
   a. $5H_2O$
   b. $9O_2$
   c. $3(NH_4)_2SO_4$
   d. $6NF_3$
   e. $C_{12}H_{22}O_{11}$
   f. $4Fe_2O_3$

THE MOLE

5

5:1 ATOMIC MASS

The actual mass of an atom is extremely small. One type of hydrogen atom has a mass of 1.67×10^{-24} g and one type of oxygen atom has a mass of 2.66×10^{-23} g. Because these masses are impractical to use, chemists have defined an average **atomic mass scale** based on the mass of a carbon-12 atom. **Atomic mass** is the relative mass of an average atom of an element with carbon-12 atoms used as reference. For convenience, the carbon-12 atom has been arbitrarily assigned the atomic mass of 12 atomic mass units (u). An atomic mass unit is defined as 1/12 the mass of a carbon-12 atom. The mass of an average hydrogen atom is approximately 1/12 the mass of a carbon-12 atom. See the table of International Atomic Masses on the inside back cover.

This relationship between the masses of different elements is important because it enables the chemist to predict the amount of one element that will react with a given amount of a second element to yield a certain amount of product.

5:2 MOLECULAR MASS

Molecular mass is the sum of the atomic masses of the atoms in a molecule. Generally atomic masses will be rounded to tenths. For those elements with masses less than ten, masses will be rounded to hundredths unless more significant digits are suggested by the data of the problem.

Example 1

Find the molecular mass of vitamin A, one of the fat-soluble vitamins. Its molecular formula is $C_{20}H_{30}O$.

Solving Process:

carbon	20×12.0 u $= 240$ u
hydrogen	30×1.01 u $= 30.3$ u
oxygen	1×16.0 u $= \underline{16.0}$ u
	Molecular Mass $= 286$ u

33

5:3   FORMULA MASS

Ionic compounds do not exist in the form of molecules. The **formula mass** is the sum of the atomic masses of the ions present in the simplest or formula unit of an ionic compound. Both the molecular and formula masses are calculated in the same manner. It is possible to calculate masses without first determining whether the substance is ionic or molecular.

Formula mass is a more general term than molecular mass. Formula mass may be used in referrring to all compounds. Molecular mass should be used only to refer to molecular compounds.

Example 2

Determine the formula mass of calcium phosphate, $Ca_3(PO_4)_2$.
Solving Process:

calcium	3×40.1 u $= 120.3$ u
phosphorus	2×31.0 u $=\ \ 62.0$ u
oxygen	8×16.0 u $= \underline{128.0\ u}$
	Formula Mass $= 310.3$ u

PROBLEMS

1. Calculate the formula or molecular mass of each of the following compounds.

   a. H_2SO_4
   b. $NaOH$
   c. NH_4NO_3
   d. $Fe(CH_3COO)_3$

   e. $C_3H_5N_3O_3$, nitroglycerin
   f. $Al(NO_3)_3$
   g. $C_{63}H_{84}N_{14}O_{14}PCo$, vitamin B_{12}
   h. SO_2

2. Aspirin is used universally to decrease pain and fever. Calculate the molecular mass of 2-acetyloxybenzoic acid (aspirin) that has the following structural formula.

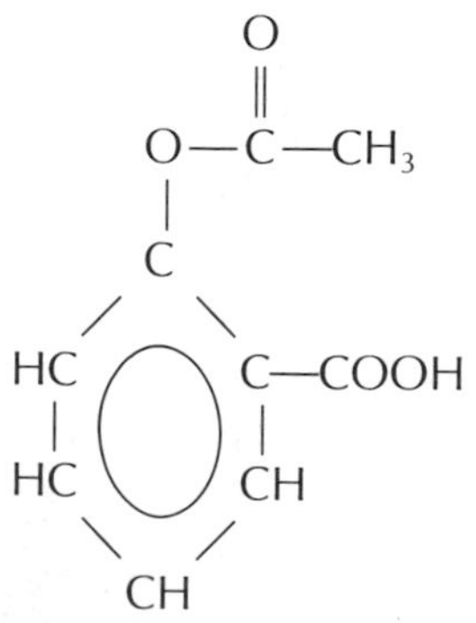

5:4   THE AVOGADRO CONSTANT

As stated earlier, the mass of a single atom or molecule is so small it cannot be measured easily. Laboratory quantities require many millions of atoms. If we express the international atomic masses of elements in grams, the masses can be readily measured in the laboratory.

Since atomic masses are relative quantities, the atomic mass in grams of one element contains the same number of atoms as the atomic mass in grams of any other element. It has been found that the atomic mass in grams of any element contains $6.022\ 045 \times 10^{23}$ atoms. This number is called the **Avogadro constant**, and is abbreviated, N_A. Another name for this quantity is the mole.

5:5 THE MOLE

The **mole** is the SI unit for amount of substance, and its symbol is mol. It represents both a formula mass and a number of formula units. Just as one million equals 1×10^6 things, one dozen equals 12 things, and one gross equals 144 things, one mole is 6.02×10^{23} things. Depending on the substance, the mass of the mole will be different. The mole is an important quantitative unit used in most chemical calculations. It is always understood to refer to one formula mass in grams, one atomic mass in grams, or one molecular mass in grams.

An element that is diatomic (such as nitrogen) can be measured as one mole of molecules or as one mole of atoms. Note the difference in Table 5-1.

Table 5-1

Mole Relationships			
Substance	**Mass**	**Number of particles**	**Moles**
C	12.0 g	6.02×10^{23} atoms	1 mol C
K^+	39.1 g	6.02×10^{23} ions	1 mol K^+
CO_2	44.0 g	6.02×10^{23} molecules	1 mol CO_2
NaCl	58.5 g	6.02×10^{23} ion pairs	1 mol NaCl
N_2	28.0 g	6.02×10^{23} molecules	1 mol N_2
N	14.0 g	6.02×10^{23} atoms	1 mol N

These relationships are important in a number of different chemical calculations. They will be used in this chapter and in subsequent chapters.

Conversion ratios are used to convert from one unit (such as grams) to a different unit (such as moles). Since the atomic mass in grams of an element = 1 mole of the element = 6.02×10^{23} atoms of an element, four conversion factors can be written.

$$\frac{1 \text{ mol } K^+}{39.1 \text{ g } K^+} \quad \text{or} \quad \frac{39.1 \text{ g } K^+}{1 \text{ mol } K^+}$$

$$\frac{1 \text{ mol } K^+}{6.02 \times 10^{23} \text{ } K^+} \quad \text{or} \quad \frac{6.02 \times 10^{23} \text{ } K^+}{1 \text{ mol } K^+}$$

The actual form used depends upon the units desired in the answer.

Example 3

Calculate the mass in grams of 2.23 mol of nitrogen molecules.
Solving Process:
To convert from moles to grams, use the conversion ratio 28.0 g N_2/mol N_2. This ratio gives the answer in grams by dividing out the unit mol.

$$\text{mass } N_2 = \frac{2.23 \text{ mol } N_2}{} \left| \frac{28.0 \text{ g } N_2}{1 \text{ mol } N_2} \right.$$

$$= 62.4 \text{ g } N_2$$

Example 4

Determine the number of atoms in 2.23 mol nitrogen molecules, N_2.
Solving Process:
The number of molecules in a mole is given by the Avogadro constant. To obtain atoms, this number must be multiplied by two, since N_2 is diatomic.

$$\text{atoms } N = \frac{2.23 \text{ mol } N_2}{} \left| \frac{6.02 \times 10^{23} \text{ molecules } N_2}{1 \text{ mol } N_2} \right| \frac{2 \text{ atoms } N}{1 \text{ molecule } N_2}$$

$$= 2.68 \times 10^{24} \text{ atoms } N$$

Example 5

Find the number of atoms in 16.0 g sulfur.
Solving Process:
Convert from grams to moles of sulfur, then from moles of sulfur to atoms of sulfur. This conversion will involve two ratios.

$$\text{atoms } S = \frac{16.0 \text{ g } S}{} \left| \frac{1 \text{ mol } S}{32.1 \text{ g } S} \right| \frac{6.02 \times 10^{23} \text{ atoms } S}{1 \text{ mol } S}$$

$$= 3.00 \times 10^{23} \text{ atoms}$$

PROBLEMS

3. Calculate the mass in grams of 0.354 mol of each of the following.
   a. ammonia gas, NH_3
   b. platinum metal, Pt
   c. cholesterol, $C_{27}H_{46}O$
   d. iron(II) ferricyanide, $Fe_3(Fe(CN)_6)_2$
4. Calculate the number of moles in 50.0 g of each of the following.
   a. borazon, BN
   b. thallium(I) sulfate, Tl_2SO_4
   c. calcium propanoate, $Ca(C_3H_5O_2)_2$
   d. penicillin G, $C_{16}H_{18}N_2O_4S$
5. Calculate the number of atoms, molecules, or ions for each of the following.
   a. 2.00 mol Na atoms
   b. 46.0 g Na atoms
   c. 3.00 mol K^+
   d. 68.0 g H_2S molecules

6. Calculate the mass in grams of each of the following.
   a. 6.02×10^{23} atoms of Na
   b. 3.01×10^{23} formula units of $Sr(OH)_2$
   c. 1.20×10^{24} molecules of CO_2
   d. 1.50×10^{23} ions of Na^+

5:6   MOLARITY

The mole is also used to express the concentration of a solution. A 1 molar solution contains 1 mole of solute dissolved in enough solvent (usually water) to make 1 cubic decimeter of solution.

$$\text{molarity } (M) = \frac{\text{number of moles of solute}}{\text{cubic decimeter of solution}}$$

Chemists express concentration in terms of **molarity** because they measure most solutions by volume and because they are interested in obtaining a certain number of particles. One mole of sodium chloride, NaCl, is 58.5 grams. If 2 moles of NaCl (117.0 grams) are dissolved in enough water to make 1 cubic decimeter of solution, the solution is a 2M solution. Fifty cubic centimeters of a solution will have the same concentration, 2M. The total number of particles changes when the volume is changed but the concentration of particles (the number of particles per unit volume) does not change.

Example 6

Calculate the molarity of 1.50 dm^3 of solution that contains 200.0 g of $MgCl_2$.

Solving Process:

The problem requires the calculation of molarity. Molarity is moles of solute per (divided by) dm^3 of solution. Therefore, the data concerning solute is placed in the numerator, and the data concerning the solution in the denominator. The solute data in the numerator is then converted to moles, and the solution data in the denominator to dm^3.

$$\text{molarity} = \frac{200.0 \text{ g MgCl}_2}{1.50 \text{ dm}^3} \; \middle| \; \frac{1 \text{ mol MgCl}_2}{95.3 \text{ g MgCl}_2}$$

$$= 1.40 \text{ mol/dm}^3 = 1.40M$$

Example 7

Calculate the molarity of a solution that contains 10.0 g of sodium hydroxide in 5.00×10^2 cm^3 of solution.

Solving Process:

Convert 10.0 g of NaOH per 5.00×10^2 cm^3 to moles of NaOH per dm^3 of solution.

$$\text{molarity} = \frac{10.0 \text{ g NaOH}}{5.00 \times 10^2 \text{ cm}^3} \; \middle| \; \frac{1 \text{ mol NaOH}}{40.0 \text{ g NaOH}} \; \middle| \; \frac{1000 \text{ cm}^3}{1 \text{ dm}^3}$$

$$= 0.500 \text{ mol/dm}^3 = 0.500M$$

PROBLEMS

7. Calculate the molarity of each of the following solutions.
    a. 0.500 dm^3 containing 30.0 g of acetic acid, CH_3COOH
    b. 2.000 dm^3 containing 49.0 g of phosphoric acid, H_3PO_4
    c. 1.50 dm^3 containing 102 g of potassium hydroxide, KOH

8. Calculate the mass of solute in the following solutions:
    a. 750.0 cm^3 of $CaCl_2$ solution that is 0.500M
    b. 3000.0 cm^3 of a KOH solution that is 2.50M
    c. 250.0 cm^3 of a Na_2SO_4 solution that is 2.00M

9. How many cubic decimeters of each solution can be made according to the following specifications?
    a. a 2.00M solution using 80.0 g sodium hydroxide
    b. a 0.500M solution using 80.0 g sodium hydroxide
    c. a 1.50M solution using 188 g silver nitrate, $AgNO_3$

5:7   PERCENTAGE COMPOSITION

The **percentage composition** of a compound gives the relative amount of each element present. The percent of an element in a compound is

$$\% = \frac{\text{number of atoms of element}}{} \left| \frac{\text{atomic mass of element}}{\text{formula mass of compound}} \right| 100$$

To calculate percentage composition:
(a) calculate the total mass for each element,
(b) calculate the formula mass for the entire compound,
(c) divide the total mass of each element by the formula mass of the compound, and
(d) multiply by 100.

Example 8

Find the percentage of nitrogen in ammonium nitrate, NH_4NO_3, an important source of nitrogen in fertilizers.

Solving Process:

Calculate the formula mass; then find the percentage.

$$
\begin{array}{lll}
\text{nitrogen} & 2 \times 14.0 & = 28.0 \\
\text{hydrogen} & 4 \times 1.01 & = 4.04 \\
\text{oxygen} & 3 \times 16.0 & = \underline{48.0} \\
& \text{Formula mass} & = 80.0
\end{array}
$$

$$\% N = \frac{\text{total mass N}}{\text{formula mass } NH_4NO_3} \left| 100 \right.$$

$$= \frac{28.0 \cancel{g}}{80.0 \cancel{g}} \left| 100 \right. = 35.0\% \text{ N}$$

PROBLEMS

10. Calculate the percentage composition of the following compounds.
    a. Fe_2O_3 **b.** Ag_2O **c.** HgO **d.** Na_2S
11. Determine the percentage of sodium in sodium sulfate, Na_2SO_4.
12. Urea, $CO(NH_2)_2$, and ammonia, NH_3, are two compounds used as a source of nitrogen in fertilizers. Calculate the percentage of nitrogen in each.

5:8 HYDRATES

Some crystals form **hydrates.** These compounds have water molecules adhering to their crystal structure. There is a fixed ratio of water molecules per formula unit. Examples are copper(II) sulfate pentahydrate, $CuSO_4 \cdot 5H_2O$, and calcium sulfate dihydrate, $CaSO_4 \cdot 2H_2O$. The raised dot indicates that the water molecules are not held tightly and can be driven off by heating the hydrate.

Example 9

In an experiment, a student gently heated a hydrated copper compound to remove the water of hydration. The following data was recorded:
  1. mass of crucible, cover, and contents before heating   21.54 g
  2. mass of empty crucible and cover   19.82 g
  3. mass of crucible, cover, and contents after heating
     to constant mass   20.94 g

Calculate (a) the experimental percent of water in the compound and (b) the percent error assuming that the compound is copper(II) sulfate pentahydrate.

Solving Process:
The mass of the original compound is found by subtracting item 2 from item 1. Calculate the mass of water lost by subtracting item 3 from item 1. Then calculate the percent of water.

$$\% \ H_2O = \frac{g \ H_2O \ removed}{g \ original \ compound} \ \bigg| \ 100$$

$$= \frac{0.60 \ g}{1.72 \ g} \ \bigg| \ 100 = 34.9\%$$

To calculate the percent error, we compare the experimentally determined value for the percent water with the value calculated from the formula for copper(II) sulfate pentahydrate, $CuSO_4 \cdot 5H_2O$. The calculated percent of water in the compound is 36.0%. Therefore the absolute error is

$$36.0\% - 34.9\% = 1.1\%$$

The percent error is

$$\% \text{ error} = \frac{\text{absolute error}}{\text{actual percentage}} \bigg| 100 = \frac{1.1\%}{36.0\%} \bigg| 100 = 3.1\%$$

PROBLEMS

13. Calculate the percentage of each of the following in the compound sodium sulfate decahydrate, $Na_2SO_4 \cdot 10H_2O$.
    a. Na   **b.** S   **c.** O   **d.** H_2O

14. Calcium chloride can exist as the anhydrous compound $CaCl_2$ or in three different hydrated forms that are mono-, di-, and hexahydrates. Calculate the following.
    a. the percent calcium in each compound
    b. the percent water in each of the three hydrates

15. In a laboratory experiment, barium chloride dihydrate was heated to completely remove its water of hydration. Calculate (a) the experimental percent of water, (b) the percent of $BaCl_2$, and (c) the percent error. The data below was obtained in the experiment.
    1. empty crucible and cover   20.286 g
    2. crucible, cover, and contents before heating   21.673 g
    3. crucible, cover, and contents after heating   21.461 g

5:9   EMPIRICAL FORMULAS

Recall from Section 4:6 that the empirical formula of a compound is the smallest whole number ratio of the number of atoms of each element in the substance. The molecular formula of a compound indicates the number of each atom in a molecule.

There is a definite relationship between the empirical and the molecular formula. Note that the molecular formula is always a whole number multiple of the empirical formula. For example, the empirical formula for ethyne is CH_2 and the molecular formula is C_2H_4 ($2 \times CH_2$). As can be seen in Table 4-4 the empirical formula and the molecular formula are sometimes identical. In Section 5:7, we used the formula of a compound to determine its percentage composition. Now we reverse the procedure and determine the empirical formula from the percentage composition. The elements in compounds combine in simple whole number ratios of atoms. To determine an empirical formula, masses of elements are converted to moles and then a ratio of moles is determined.

Example 10

Determine the empirical formula for sodium sulfite. Sodium sulfite contains 36.5% sodium, 25.4% sulfur, and 38.1% oxygen.

Solving Process:

The percentage composition data indicates that there are 36.5 g Na, 25.4 g S, and 38.1 g O in 100 g of compound.

Step 1. Find the number of moles.

$$\text{Na} \quad \frac{36.5 \text{ g Na}}{} \left| \frac{1 \text{ mol Na}}{23.0 \text{ g Na}} \right. = 1.59 \text{ mol Na}$$

$$\text{S} \quad \frac{25.4 \text{ g S}}{} \left| \frac{1 \text{ mol S}}{32.1 \text{ g S}} \right. = 0.791 \text{ mol S}$$

$$\text{O} \quad \frac{38.1 \text{ g O}}{} \left| \frac{1 \text{ mol O}}{16.0 \text{ g O}} \right. = 2.38 \text{ mol O}$$

Step 2. Determine the ratio of moles.

$$\begin{array}{ccc} \text{Na} & \text{S} & \text{O} \\ \frac{1.59}{0.791} = 2.01 & \frac{0.791}{0.791} = 1.00 & \frac{2.38}{0.791} = 3.01 \end{array}$$

The ratio is 2.01:1.00:3.01, Na:S:O.
The empirical formula is Na_2SO_3.

Example 11

What is the empirical formula of a compound that contains 53.73% Fe and 46.27% S?

Solving Process:

There are 53.73 g Fe and 46.27 g S in 100 g of compound.

Step 1. Find the number of moles.

$$\text{mol Fe} = \frac{53.73 \text{ g Fe}}{} \left| \frac{1 \text{ mol Fe}}{55.85 \text{ g Fe}} \right. = 0.9620 \text{ mol Fe}$$

$$\text{mol S} = \frac{46.27 \text{ g S}}{} \left| \frac{1 \text{ mol S}}{32.07 \text{ g S}} \right. = 1.443 \text{ mol S}$$

Step 2. Determine the ratio of moles.

$$\begin{array}{cc} \text{Fe} & \text{S} \\ \frac{0.9620}{0.9620} = 1.0000 & \frac{1.443}{0.9620} = 1.500 \end{array}$$

The ratio is 1.000:1.500, giving $FeS_{1.500}$

In the previous example problem, the relative numbers of atoms were small whole numbers and we could write the formula directly from them. The ratio 1 to 1.5 must be expressed in terms of whole numbers, since a fractional part of an atom does not exist. By multiplying both numbers in the ratio by two, we obtain two atoms Fe and three atoms S. The empirical formula is Fe_2S_3.

PROBLEMS

16. Calculate the empirical formula for compounds with the following compositions.

    a. Fe 63.5%, S 36.5%

    b. Mn 63.1%, S 36.9%

    c. K 26.6%, Cr 35.4%, O 38.0%

17. Calculate empirical formulas for the following two compounds containing sodium, sulfur, and oxygen.

    a. Na 32.4%, S 22.6% O 45.0%

    b. Na 29.1%, S 40.5%, O 30.4%

18. Calculate the empirical formulas for the following three iron ores.

    a. Fe 77.7%, O 22.3%

    b. Fe 72.4%, O 27.6%

    c. Fe 70.0%, O 30.0%

5:10 MOLECULAR FORMULAS

The molecular formula indicates not only the ratio of the atoms of the elements in a compound but also the actual number of atoms of each element in one molecule of the compound.

The molecular formula calculation is the same as the empirical formula calculation, except that the molecular mass is used in an additional step. The molecular formula is always a whole number multiple of the empirical formula.

Example 12

An organic compound is found to contain 92.25% carbon and 7.75% hydrogen. If the molecular mass is 78, what is the molecular formula?

Solving Process:

Determine the empirical formula.

Step 1. Find the number of moles.

$$C \quad \frac{92.25 \; \cancel{g \, C}}{} \left| \frac{1 \; mol \; C}{12.01 \; \cancel{g \, C}} \right. = 7.681 \; mol \; C$$

$$H \quad \frac{7.75 \; \cancel{g \, H}}{} \left| \frac{1 \; mol \; H}{1.01 \; \cancel{g \, H}} \right. = 7.67 \; mol \; H$$

Step 2. Divide by the smaller number of moles to determine ratio of moles.

$$\begin{array}{cc} H & C \\ \dfrac{7.67}{7.67} = 1.00 & \dfrac{7.681}{7.67} = 1.00 \end{array}$$

Step 3. Use the empirical formula to find the molecular formula.

The empirical formula is CH. Since the CH unit has a formula mass of 13 u and a molecular mass of 78 u there will be six units in each molecule.

$$13x = 78$$
$$x = 78/13 = 6.0$$

Six times the molecular formula is C_6H_6.

PROBLEMS

19. There are two oxides of phosphorus. Both oxides can exist in different forms depending on the temperature and the pressure. Calculate the empirical and molecular formulas from the following data.
    a. P 56.4%, O 43.7%, molecular mass 220
    b. P 43.6%, O 56.4%, molecular mass 284

20. The formula mass of a compound is 92. Analysis of the compound shows that there are 0.608 g of nitrogen and 1.388 g of oxygen. What is the molecular formula of this compound?

5:11 EMPIRICAL FORMULAS OF HYDRATES

The method used to calculate the formulas of hydrates is basically the same as that used to calculate other empirical formulas except that it is necessary to determine the number of moles of water involved.

Example 13

A hydrated compound has an analysis of 18.29% Ca, 32.37% Cl, and 49.34% H_2O. What is its formula?

Solving Process:

Step 1. Find the number of moles.

$$\text{mol Ca} = \frac{18.29 \text{ g Ca}}{} \left| \frac{1 \text{ mol Ca}}{40.08 \text{ g Ca}} \right. = 0.4563 \text{ mol Ca}$$

$$\text{mol Cl} = \frac{32.37 \text{ g Cl}}{} \left| \frac{1 \text{ mol Cl}}{35.45 \text{ g Cl}} \right. = 0.9131 \text{ mol Cl}$$

$$\text{mol } H_2O = \frac{49.34 \text{ g } H_2O}{} \left| \frac{1 \text{ mol } H_2O}{18.02 \text{ g } H_2O} \right. = 2.738 \text{ mol } H_2O$$

Step 2. Determine ratio of moles.

Ca	Cl	H_2O
$\frac{0.4563}{0.4563} = 1.000$	$\frac{0.9131}{0.4563} = 2.001$	$\frac{2.738}{0.4563} = 6.000$

The empirical formula is $CaCl_2 \cdot 6H_2O$. The raised dot between the $CaCl_2$ and the $6H_2O$ means that this substance is a hydrated compound.

PROBLEMS

21. The masses of the hydrates listed below were measured, heated to drive off the water of hydration, and cooled. Then the masses of the residues were measured. Find the formulas of the following hydrates.
    a. 1.62 g of $CoCl_2 \cdot xH_2O$ gave a residue of 0.88 g
    b. 1.21 g of $Pb(CH_3COO)_2 \cdot xH_2O$ gave a residue of 1.03 g
    c. 1.04 g $NiSO_4 \cdot xH_2O$ gave a residue of 0.61 g
    d. 1.26 g of $CaSO_4 \cdot xH_2O$ gave a residue of 0.99 g

22. A hydrated magnesium compound has a formula mass of about 174 and contains 31.0% water of hydration. From the following analysis, calculate the molecular formula: Mg 13.90%, P 17.74%, H 4.01%, O 64.30%.

CHAPTER REVIEW PROBLEMS

1. Calculate the formula (or molecular) mass of the following compounds:
    a. K_3AsO_4
    b. $Na_2B_4O_7 \cdot 10H_2O$
    c. $MnCl_2 \cdot 4H_2O$
    d. $Al_2(SO_4)_3 \cdot 18H_2O$
    e. N_2O_5
    f. $(NH_4)_3PO_4$
    g. Na_2CO_3
    h. $CHCl_2COOH$
    i. $NaCl$

2. Hydrocarbons and various oxides of nitrogen react photochemically (a chemical process that requires light) to form a variety of pollutants. The formula of one of the pollutants, peroxyacetylnitrate, is

What is the molecular mass of this compound?

3. An amino acid that cannot be made (synthesized) by the body and must be obtained in the diet is lysine. Determine the molecular mass of lysine, which has the formula

$$H_2N-(CH_2)_3-CHCOOH$$
$$|$$
$$NH_2$$

4. Calculate the mass in grams of each of the following.
    a. 6.38 mol O_2
    b. 4.00 mol Al
    c. 2.25 mol H_2SO_4
    d. 5.49 mol KI
    e. 1.500 mol $Ba(IO_4)_2$
    f. 0.602 mol $Ca(NO_3)_2 \cdot 3H_2O$

5. Calculate the number of moles in each of the following.
   a. 188.0 g Zn
   b. 160.0 g Br_2
   c. 293.0 g Fe
   d. 32.0 g SO_2
   e. 10.0 g Na_2S
   f. 84.2 g K_2SO_4

6. Calculate the number of atoms, molecules, or ions in each of the following quantities.
   a. 20.0 g Ca atoms
   b. 3.34 mol CO_2 molecules
   c. 68.0 g H_2S molecules
   d. 0.125 mol Mg^{2+} ions

7. Calculate the mass in grams of each of the following.
   a. 3.01×10^{23} atoms of S
   b. 2.41×10^{24} molecules of H_2O

8. Calculate the molarity of each of the following solutions.
   a. 500.0 cm^3 that contains 82.0 g $Ca(NO_3)_2$
   b. 250.0 cm^3 that contains 50.0 g $NiSO_4 \cdot 6H_2O$

9. Calculate the mass of solute in each of the following solutions.
   a. 250.0 cm^3 of a $Na_2SO_4 \cdot 7H_2O$ solution that is 2.00M
   b. 1.500 dm^3 of KH_2PO_4 solution that is 0.240M

10. How many cubic decimeters of solution can be made from each of the following?
    a. a 0.100M solution using 117 g NaCl
    b. a 1.25M solution using 55.0 g $Na_2S_2O_3 \cdot 5H_2O$

11. The sugar substitute sodium benzosulfimide (sodium saccharin) has a sweetness of about 500 times that of sucrose. Calculate the percentage of sodium and carbon in the sweetener. Its formula is

12. Copper phthalocyanine is a complex organic molecule possessing a brilliant greenish blue color. Millions of pounds are produced yearly to color products such as plastics, automobile finishes, rubber goods, and printing inks. Determine the percent carbon in copper phthalocyanine that has the formula $Cu(C_8H_4N_2)_4$.

13. Determine the percent of water in $MgSO_4 \cdot 7H_2O$.

14. Two compounds are analyzed and found to contain:
    a. 0.89 g K, 1.18 g Cr, 1.27 g O
    b. 1.03 g K, 0.69 g Cr, 0.84 g O
    Determine the empirical formulas for these two compounds.

15. To find the experimental empirical formula of a compound, a student heats a uniform coil of magnesium ribbon 35.00 cm long in a crucible. The resulting mixed product is treated with water, and subsequent heating gives an oxide of magnesium. The data is recorded as follows:

1. mass of empty crucible and cover   20.74 g
2. mass of two meters of magnesium ribbon   1.44 g
3. mass of crucible, cover, and final product   21.17 g

Determine the empirical formula for the oxide of magnesium.

16. A fat is composed, in part, of long chains of carbon and hydrogen atoms. In a reaction with a strong base, a fat forms a soap and glycerol. What is the empirical formula of a fat containing 76.5% C, 11.3% O and 12.2% H, if it has a molecular mass of 847?

17. Citric acid, an organic acid found in lemons and other citrus fruits, contains 37.5% carbon, 58.3% oxygen, and 4.20% hydrogen. What is the empirical formula of citric acid if it has a molecular mass of 192?

CHEMICAL REACTIONS

6

6:1 REPRESENTING CHEMICAL CHANGES

Scientists rely on a variety of shorthand methods for expressing chemical information. You have already seen how chemical symbols are used for the names of elements and chemical formulas for the names of compounds. A **chemical equation** is a shorthand expression that represents a chemical reaction. A **chemical reaction** is the process by which one or more substances are changed into one or more new substances. A chemical equation shows the relative amount of each substance taking place in a chemical reaction.

The starting substances in a chemical reaction are called **reactants.** The substances that are formed are called **products.** The general format for a chemical equation is

$$CO_2(g) + H_2O(l) \qquad \rightarrow \qquad H_2CO_3(aq)$$
$$\text{reactants} \qquad\qquad \text{yield} \qquad \text{products}$$

Reactants are generally written on the left side of chemical equations; products are written on the right side.

The letters in parentheses indicate the physical state of each substance involved in the reaction. The following symbols should be used in your work.

(g) gas   (cr) crystalline solid
(l) liquid   (aq) water solution

6:2 BALANCING EQUATIONS

The first step in writing a chemical equation is writing a word equation. It is composed of the names of the substances that are involved in a chemical reaction.

copper(I) chloride + hydrogen sulfide →
copper(I) sulfide + hydrochloric acid

The second step is writing a skeleton equation. This equation includes the chemical symbols and formulas for all the reactants and products identified in the word equation.

$$CuCl(aq) + H_2S(g) \rightarrow Cu_2S(cr) + HCl(aq)$$

The third step in writing a chemical equation is balancing the equation. The balanced equation includes the coefficients, numbers placed directly in front of the chemical formulas and symbols. The coefficients indicate the relative proportions of each substance involved in the chemical reaction.

$$2CuCl(aq) + H_2S(g) \rightarrow Cu_2S(cr) + 2HCl(aq)$$

This equation states that two moles of CuCl(aq) react with one mole of $H_2S(g)$ producing one mole of $Cu_2S(cr)$ and two moles HCl(aq).

Example 1

Sodium reacts with water to produce a metallic hydroxide and hydrogen gas. Write a balanced equation for the reaction.

Solving Process:

Step 1. Write the word equation. Determine the products and reactants.

$$\text{sodium} + \text{water} \rightarrow \text{sodium hydroxide} + \text{hydrogen}$$

Step 2. Write a skeleton equation. Since hydrogen is a diatomic gas, its formula is H_2. The formula for water may be written as HOH; this may make it easier to balance the equation.

$$Na + HOH \rightarrow NaOH + H_2$$

Step 3. Balance the equation. The metallic element sodium is balanced. One atom of sodium is on each side of the equation. There is one hydrogen atom on the reactant side (the H in OH has been accounted for) and 2 hydrogen atoms on the product side. Place a 2 in front of the HOH to balance the hydrogen atoms

$$Na + 2HOH \rightarrow NaOH + H_2$$

There are now 2OH on the left and 1 on the right. Place a 2 in front of the NaOH to give the same number of OH on each side.

$$Na + 2HOH \rightarrow 2NaOH + H_2$$

Put a 2 in front of the sodium metal. The balanced equation reads

$$2Na(cr) + 2HOH(l) \rightarrow 2NaOH(aq) + H_2(g)$$

Check to see if the equation is balanced.

	Reactants	Products
Na	2	2
H	4	4
O	2	2

PROBLEMS

Balance each of the following chemical reactions.

1. $Mg(cr) + O_2(g) \rightarrow MgO(cr)$
2. $Fe(cr) + O_2(g) \rightarrow Fe_2O_3(cr)$
3. $H_2O(l) + N_2O_3(g) \rightarrow HNO_2(aq)$
4. $Na_2O(cr) + H_2O(l) \rightarrow NaOH(aq)$
5. $Fe(cr) + H_2O(l) \rightarrow Fe_3O_4(cr) + H_2(g)$

Write equations for the following chemical reactions.

6. magnesium bromide(aq) + chlorine(g) → magnesium chloride(aq) + bromine(g)
7. chlorine(g) + sodium iodide(cr) → sodium chloride(cr) + iodine(g)

8. potassium nitrate(cr) $\rightarrow$ potassium nitrite(cr) + oxygen(g)

9. zinc(cr) + hydrochloric acid(aq) $\rightarrow$ zinc chloride(aq) + hydrogen(g)

10. calcium oxide(cr) + hydrochloric acid(aq) $\rightarrow$ calcium chloride(aq) + water(l)

6:3   CLASSIFYING CHEMICAL CHANGES

The products of a chemical reaction may often be predicted by applying known facts about common reaction types. While there are hundreds of different "kinds" of chemical reactions, only four general types of reactions will be considered: single displacement, double displacement, decomposition, and synthesis.

Single Displacement. One element displaces another element in a compound. A single displacement has the general form

$$element + compound \rightarrow element + compound$$
$$A + BX \rightarrow AX + B$$

The following are some general types of single displacement reactions.

1. An active metal will displace the metallic ion in a compound of a less active metal.

$$Fe(cr) + Cu(NO_3)_2(aq) \rightarrow Fe(NO_3)_2(aq) + Cu(cr)$$

2. Some active metals such as sodium and calcium will react with water to give a metallic hydroxide and hydrogen gas.

$$Ca(cr) + 2H_2O(l) \rightarrow Ca(OH)_2(aq) + H_2(g)$$

3. Active metals such as zinc, iron, and aluminum will displace the hydrogen in acids to give a salt and hydrogen gas.

$$Zn(cr) + 2HCl(aq) \rightarrow ZnCl_2(aq) + H_2(g)$$

4. An active nonmetal will displace a less active nonmetal.

$$Cl_2(g) + 2NaBr(aq) \rightarrow 2NaCl(aq) + Br_2(aq)$$

PROBLEMS

Balance the following reactions.

11. $Al(cr) + Pb(NO_3)_2(aq) \rightarrow Al(NO_3)_3(aq) + Pb(cr)$

12. $Cu(cr) + AgNO_3(aq) \rightarrow Cu(NO_3)_2(aq) + Ag(cr)$

13. $K(cr) + H_2O(l) \rightarrow KOH(aq) + H_2(g)$

14. $Cl_2(g) + LiI(aq) \rightarrow LiCl(aq) + I_2(g)$

Balance each of the following reactions after predicting the products.

15. aluminum(cr) + hydrochloric acid(aq) $\rightarrow$

16. iron(cr) + copper(II) sulfate(aq) $\rightarrow$ (iron(II) compound is formed)

17. zinc(cr) + sulfuric acid(aq) $\rightarrow$

18. chlorine(g) + magnesium iodide(aq) $\rightarrow$

19. sodium(cr) + water(l) $\rightarrow$

20. magnesium(cr) + hydrochloric acid(aq) $\rightarrow$

Double Displacement. The positive and negative ions of two compounds are interchanged in a double displacement reaction. The form of these reactions is easy to recognize.

$$compound + compound \rightarrow compound + compound$$
$$AX + BY \rightarrow AY + BX$$

The following are some general types of double displacement reactions.

1. A reaction between an acid and a base yields a salt and water. Such a reaction is a neutralization reaction.

$$2KOH(aq) + H_2SO_4(aq) \rightarrow K_2SO_4(aq) + 2H_2O(l)$$

2. Reaction of a salt with an acid forms a salt of the acid and a second acid that is volatile.

$$2KNO_3(aq) + H_2SO_4(aq) \rightarrow K_2SO_4(aq) + 2HNO_3(g)$$

This same reaction of a salt with an acid or base may yield a compound that can be decomposed. H_2CO_3, H_2SO_3, and $NH_3(aq)$ decompose to give a gas and H_2O.

$$CaCO_3(aq) + 2HCl(aq) \rightarrow CaCl_2(aq) + H_2CO_3(aq)$$
$$H_2CO_3(aq) \rightarrow CO_2(g) + H_2O(l)$$

3. Reactions of some soluble salts produce an insoluble salt and a soluble salt.

$$AgNO_3(aq) + NaCl(aq) \rightarrow AgCl(cr) + NaNO_3(aq)$$

PROBLEMS

Balance the following equations.

21. $Ca(OH)_2(aq) + HCl(aq) \rightarrow CaCl_2(aq) + H_2O(l)$

22. $KOH(aq) + H_3PO_4(aq) \rightarrow K_3PO_4(aq) + H_2O(l)$

23. $Al(NO_3)_3(aq) + H_2SO_4(aq) \rightarrow Al_2(SO_4)_3(aq) + HNO_3(aq)$

24. $Na_2SO_3(aq) + HCl(aq) \rightarrow NaCl(aq) + H_2O(l) + SO_2(g)$

Balance each of the following reactions after predicting the products.

25. sodium hydroxide(aq) + phosphoric acid(aq) $\rightarrow$

26. ammonium sulfate(aq) + calcium hydroxide(aq) $\rightarrow$

27. silver nitrate(aq) + potassium chloride(aq) $\rightarrow$

28. magnesium hydroxide(aq) + phosphoric acid(aq) $\rightarrow$

29. iron(II) sulfide(cr) + hydrochloric acid(aq) $\rightarrow$

30. ammonium sulfide(aq) + iron(II) nitrate(aq) $\rightarrow$

Decomposition. When energy in the form of heat, electricity, light, or mechanical shock is supplied, a compound may decompose to form simpler substances. The general form for this type of reaction is

$$compound \rightarrow two\ or\ more\ substances$$
$$AX \rightarrow A + X$$

The following are some general types of decomposition reactions.
1. When some acids are heated, they decompose to form water and an acidic oxide.
$$H_2CO_3(aq) \rightarrow CO_2(g) + H_2O(l)$$
2. When some metallic hydroxides are heated, they decompose to form a metallic oxide and water.
$$Ca(OH)_2(cr) \rightarrow CaO(cr) + H_2O(g)$$
3. When some metallic carbonates are heated, they decompose to form a metallic oxide and carbon dioxide.
$$Li_2CO_3(cr) \rightarrow Li_2O(cr) + CO_2(g)$$
4. When metallic chlorates are heated, they decompose to form metallic chlorides and oxygen.
$$2KClO_3(cr) \rightarrow 2KCl(cr) + 3O_2(g)$$
5. Most metallic oxides are stable, but a few decompose when heated.
$$2HgO(cr) \rightarrow 2Hg(l) + O_2(g)$$
6. Some compounds cannot be decomposed by heat, but can be decomposed into their elements by electricity.
$$2NaCl(l) \rightarrow 2Na(cr) + Cl_2(g)$$

PROBLEMS

Balance the following equations.
31. $KNO_3(cr) \rightarrow KNO_2(cr) + O_2(g)$
32. $PbO_2(cr) \rightarrow PbO(cr) + O_2(g)$
33. $NaOH(cr) \rightarrow Na_2O(cr) + H_2O(l)$
34. $MgCO_3(cr) \rightarrow MgO(cr) + CO_2(g)$
Balance each of the following reactions after predicting the products.
35. When heated, sulfurous acid, $H_2SO_3 \rightarrow$
36. When heated, calcium carbonate $\rightarrow$
37. When heated, iron(III) hydroxide $\rightarrow$
38. When heated, sodium chlorate $\rightarrow$
39. When heated, silver oxide $\rightarrow$
40. By electricity, water $\rightarrow$

Synthesis. In a synthesis reaction two or more simple substances are combined to form one new and more complex substance. Here the general form is

element or compound + element or compound → compound
$$A + X \rightarrow AX$$

The following are some general types of synthesis reactions.
1. Two or more elements combine to form a compound.
$$Fe(cr) + S(l) \rightarrow FeS(cr)$$

2. An acid anhydride, nonmetallic oxide, combines with water to give an acid.

$$SO_2(g) + H_2O(l) \rightarrow H_2SO_3(aq)$$

3. A basic anhydride, metallic oxide, combines with water to form a base.

$$Na_2O(cr) + H_2O(l) \rightarrow 2NaOH(aq)$$

4. A basic oxide combines with a nonmetallic oxide to form a salt.

$$CO_2(g) + Na_2O(cr) \rightarrow Na_2CO_3(cr)$$

PROBLEMS

Balance the following equations.

41. $Na(cr) + Cl_2(g) \rightarrow NaCl(cr)$

42. $Br_2(g) + H_2O(l) + SO_2(g) \rightarrow HBr(aq) + H_2SO_4(aq)$

43. $CaO(cr) + H_2O(l) \rightarrow Ca(OH)_2(aq)$

44. $P_2O_5(cr) + BaO(cr) \rightarrow Ba_3(PO_4)_2(cr)$

Balance each of the following reactions after predicting the products.

45. barium oxide(cr) + water(l) $\rightarrow$

46. sulfur(IV) oxide(g) + magnesium oxide(cr) $\rightarrow$

47. carbon dioxide(g) + water(l) $\rightarrow$

48. magnesium(cr) + oxygen(g) $\rightarrow$

49. nitrogen(III) oxide(g) + water(l) $\rightarrow$

50. iron metal(cr) + oxygen(g) $\rightarrow$ (iron(III) compound is formed)

6:4 MASS-MASS RELATIONSHIPS

Stoichiometry is the study of quantitative relationships in chemical reactions. A basic idea used in solving stoichiometric problems is the mole concept (see Chapter 5). If you are given the mass of one substance and know the balanced equation, you can calculate the reactants needed or the products produced because the equation shows relative number of moles of reactants and products. A general procedure for mass-mass problems uses the following steps.

1. Write a balanced equation.
2. Convert from mass of given material to moles.
3. Determine the mole ratio from the coefficients of the balanced equation and convert from moles of given material to moles of required material.
4. Express the moles of required material in grams.

The setup for a mass-mass calculation follows the format given below.

$$\left(\begin{array}{c} start\ with \\ grams\ given \end{array} \right) \rightarrow \left(\begin{array}{c} grams \\ to\ moles \end{array} \right) \rightarrow \left(\begin{array}{c} use \\ mole\ ratio \end{array} \right) \rightarrow \left(\begin{array}{c} moles \\ to\ grams \end{array} \right) \rightarrow \left(\begin{array}{c} end\ with \\ grams\ required \end{array} \right)$$

Example 2

Calculate the mass of HCl needed to react with 10.0 g Zn.

Solving Process:

Step 1. Begin with the balanced equation.

$$Zn(cr) + 2HCl(aq) \rightarrow ZnCl_2(aq) + H_2(g)$$

Step 2. Convert grams of zinc to moles.

$$\frac{10.0 \text{ g Zn}}{} \, \Bigg| \, \frac{1 \text{ mol Zn}}{65.4 \text{ g Zn}}$$

Step 3. Determine the mole ratio that exists between Zn and HCl and convert from moles Zn to moles HCl.

1 mole Zn reacts with 2 moles HCl

$$\frac{10.0 \text{ g Zn}}{} \, \Bigg| \, \frac{1 \text{ mol Zn}}{65.4 \text{ g Zn}} \, \Bigg| \, \frac{2 \text{ mol HCl}}{1 \text{ mol Zn}}$$

Step 4. Convert moles of HCl to grams of HCl.

$$\text{grams HCl} = \frac{10.0 \text{ g Zn}}{} \, \Bigg| \, \frac{1 \text{ mol Zn}}{65.4 \text{ g Zn}} \, \Bigg| \, \frac{2 \text{ mol HCl}}{1 \text{ mol Zn}} \, \Bigg| \, \frac{36.5 \text{ g HCl}}{1 \text{ mol HCl}}$$

$$= 11.2 \text{ g HCl}$$

Note that the conversion ratios are chosen and arranged so all the units divide out except the desired unit, in this case, grams of HCl. Since all the ratios are equal to 1, multiplying by one of them, or by all of them, changes only the units of the answer.

Example 3

Calculate the mass of O_2 produced if 2.50 g $KClO_3$ are completely decomposed by heating.

Solving Process:

Step 1. Write the balanced equation.

$$2KClO_3(cr) \rightarrow 2KCl(cr) + 3O_2(g)$$

Step 2. Convert mass of $KClO_3$ to moles.

$$\frac{2.50 \text{ g KClO}_3}{} \, \Bigg| \, \frac{1 \text{ mol KClO}_3}{123 \text{ g KClO}_3}$$

Step 3. Determine the mole ratio that exists between $KClO_3$ and O_2.

2 moles $KClO_3$ yield 3 moles O_2

$$\frac{2.50 \text{ g KClO}_3}{} \, \Bigg| \, \frac{1 \text{ mol KClO}_3}{123 \text{ g KClO}_3} \, \Bigg| \, \frac{3 \text{ mol O}_2}{2 \text{ mol KClO}_3}$$

Step 4. Convert moles of O_2 to grams.

$$\text{grams O}_2 = \frac{2.50 \text{ g KClO}_3}{} \, \Bigg| \, \frac{1 \text{ mol KClO}_3}{123 \text{ g KClO}_3} \, \Bigg| \, \frac{3 \text{ mol O}_2}{2 \text{ mol KClO}_3} \, \Bigg| \, \frac{32.0 \text{ g O}_2}{1 \text{ mol O}_2}$$

$$= 0.976 \text{ g O}_2$$

PROBLEMS

Solve the following problems. The reactions may not be balanced.

51. If 20.0 g of magnesium react with excess hydrochloric acid, how many grams of magnesium chloride are produced?

$$Mg(cr) + HCl(aq) \rightarrow MgCl_2(aq) + H_2(g)$$

52. How many grams of chlorine gas must be reacted with excess sodium iodide if 10.0 g of sodium chloride are needed?

$$NaI(aq) + Cl_2(g) \rightarrow NaCl(aq) + I_2(cr)$$

53. How many grams of oxygen are produced in the decomposition of 5.00 g of potassium chlorate?

$$KClO_3(cr) \rightarrow KCl(cr) + O_2(g)$$

54. What mass of copper is required to replace silver from 4.00 g of silver nitrate dissolved in water?

$$Cu(cr) + AgNO_3(aq) \rightarrow Cu(NO_3)_2(aq) + Ag(cr)$$

55. If excess ammonium sulfate reacts with 20.0 g of calcium hydroxide, how many grams of ammonia are produced?

$$(NH_4)_2SO_4(aq) + Ca(OH)_2(cr) \rightarrow CaSO_4(cr) + NH_3(g) + H_2O(l)$$

56. If excess sulfuric acid reacts with 30.0 g of sodium chloride, how many grams of hydrogen chloride are produced?

$$NaCl(aq) + H_2SO_4(aq) \rightarrow HCl(g) + Na_2SO_4(aq)$$

57. How much silver phosphate is produced if 10.0 g of silver acetate react with excess sodium phosphate?

$$AgCH_3COO(aq) + Na_3PO_4(aq) \rightarrow Ag_3PO_4(cr) + NaCH_3COO(aq)$$

58. How many grams of sodium hydroxide are needed to completely neutralize 25.0 g of sulfuric acid?

$$NaOH(aq) + H_2SO_4(aq) \rightarrow Na_2SO_4(cr) + H_2O(g)$$

CHAPTER REVIEW PROBLEMS

Balance the following reactions.

1. $HgO(cr) \rightarrow Hg(l) + O_2(g)$

2. $H_2O(l) \rightarrow H_2(g) + O_2(g)$

3. $Al(cr) + Pb(NO_3)_2(aq) \rightarrow Al(NO_3)_3(aq) + Pb(cr)$

4. $Cu(cr) + AgNO_3(aq) \rightarrow Cu(NO_3)_2(aq) + Ag(cr)$

5. $K(cr) + H_2O(l) \rightarrow KOH(aq) + H_2(g)$

6. $MnO_2(cr) + HCl(aq) \rightarrow MnCl_2(aq) + Cl_2(g) + H_2O(l)$

7. $Cl_2(g) + LiI(aq) \rightarrow LiCl(aq) + I_2(g)$

8. $F_2(g) + H_2O(l) \rightarrow HF(aq) + O_3(g)$

9. $AgNO_3(aq) + K_2SO_4(aq) \rightarrow Ag_2SO_4(aq) + KNO_3(aq)$

10. $NH_3(g) + O_2(g) \rightarrow N_2O_4(g) + H_2O(g)$

Write a balanced equation and indicate the reaction type (single or double displacement, decomposition, or synthesis) for each of the following reactions.

11. aluminum nitrate(aq) + sodium hydroxide(aq) →
   aluminum hydroxide(cr) + sodium nitrate(aq)

12. sulfur trioxide(g) → sulfur dioxide(g) + oxygen(g)

13. phosphoric acid(aq) + magnesium hydroxide(aq) →
   magnesium phosphate(cr) + water(l)

14. ammonium nitrite(cr) → nitrogen(g) + water(l)

15. ammonia(g) + oxygen(g) → nitrogen(II) oxide(g) + water(g)

16. barium chloride(aq) + sodium sulfate(aq) → sodium chloride(aq) +
   barium sulfate(cr)

17. iron(III) oxide(cr) + carbon monoxide(g) →
   iron(cr) + carbon dioxide(g)

18. magnesium hydroxide(aq) + ammonium phosphate(aq) →
   magnesium phosphate(cr) + ammonia(g) + water(l)

19. aluminum(cr) + copper(II) chloride(aq) →
   aluminum chloride(aq) + copper(cr)

20. iron(cr) + silver acetate(aq) → iron(II) acetate(aq) + silver(cr)

Balance each of the following reactions after predicting the products.

21. magnesium hydroxide(aq) + phosphoric acid(aq) →

22. iron(II) sulfide(cr) + hydrochloric acid(aq) →

23. ammonium sulfide(aq) + iron(II) nitrate(aq) →

24. sulfuric acid(aq) + potassium hydroxide(aq) →

25. aluminum sulfate(aq) + calcium phosphate(cr) →

26. barium carbonate(cr) + hydrochloric acid(aq) →

27. silver acetate(aq) + potassium chromate(aq) →

28. ammonium phosphate(aq) + barium hydroxide(aq) →

29. chromium(III) sulfite(aq) + sulfuric acid(aq) →

30. calcium hydroxide(aq) + nitric acid(aq) →

31. In a series of steps in an experiment, copper metal is converted into various compounds and then back to copper metal by treating the original copper stepwise with nitric acid, sodium hydroxide, heat, sulfuric acid, and zinc metal. Write the five equations representing these chemical changes if the overall experiment can be represented as:

$$Cu \rightarrow Cu(NO_3)_2 \rightarrow Cu(OH)_2 \rightarrow CuO \rightarrow CuSO_4 \rightarrow Cu$$

32. One type of fire extinguisher contains concentrated sulfuric acid that reacts with a solution to produce carbon dioxide. What solution, sodium hydrogen carbonate or sodium carbonate, would give the greater amount of carbon dioxide in a reaction with the same amount of acid?

33. If iron pyrite, FeS_2, is not removed from coal, oxygen from the air will combine with both the iron and the sulfur as the coal burns. Write a balanced chemical equation illustrating the formation of iron(III) oxide and sulfur dioxide.

34. Sodium sulfite, Na_2SO_3, can be used for the removal of SO_2 produced as a by-product in manufacturing operations. The SO_2 reacts with a sodium sulfite solution to form sodium hydrogen sulfite. The $NaHSO_3$ solution is heated to regenerate the original sodium sulfite for reuse. Write the equation for this reaction.

35. Molten iron and carbon monoxide are produced in a blast furnace by the reaction of iron(III) oxide and coke (carbon). If 25.0 kg of pure Fe_2O_3 are used, how many moles of iron can be produced?

36. Ammonia gas produced as a by-product in an industrial reaction can be reacted with sulfuric acid in order that the gas does not escape into the atmosphere. The product, ammonium sulfate, can be used as a fertilizer. Determine how many kilograms of acid are required to produce 1000.0 kg of $(NH_4)_2SO_4$.

37. Coal gasification is a process that is carried out industrially in a series of steps. The net reaction involves coal (carbon) reacting with water to form methane, CH_4, and carbon dioxide. How many kilograms of methane can be produced from 1.00×10^3 kg of coal?

38. A source of acid rain is automobile exhaust. Nitric oxide, formed in an internal combustion engine, reacts with oxygen in the air to produce nitrogen dioxide. The NO_2 reacts with water to form nitric acid. It is determined that the average car produces 10.0 m^3 of exhaust gas per mile driven. Assume that the average concentration of NO_2 in auto exhaust is $100.0 \text{ } \mu g/m^3$ and that traffic surveys have shown an average of 2.00×10^6 vehicle miles driven per day. From this data, determine the kilograms of nitric acid that could be produced annually.

$$2NO_2 + H_2O \rightarrow HNO_2 + HNO_3$$

39. Photosynthesis is a complex process composed of many steps. The initial reactants are carbon dioxide and water and the final products are glucose and oxygen gas. If a plant needs to make 30.0 g of glucose, $C_6H_{12}O_6$, through the process of photosynthesis, how many grams of water are required?

ATOMIC STRUCTURE

7

7:1 EARLY ATOMIC THEORIES

Scientists use models to explain atomic structure, because atoms cannot be seen directly. Models help provide mental images for concepts such as atomic structure. The research and theories described in this section will help you develop a mental model for what scientists believe atoms would look like if individual atoms could be seen.

In the 1800's John Dalton proposed an atomic theory of matter. His theory had four main points: (1) all matter is composed of atoms which cannot be broken apart; (2) all atoms of the same element are identical in mass (and other properties); (3) atoms of different elements are different in mass (and other properties); (4) atoms unite in definite ratios to form compounds. Dalton's theory is that atoms have fixed masses. An atom of one element has the same mass no matter what other elements it combines with. In a given chemical compound, the elements are always combined in the same proportion by mass. This statement is the **law of definite proportions.** Dalton's theory was modified when subatomic particles and isotopes were discovered.

Since the late 1800's there has been a great deal of scientific research to determine the actual structure of atoms. In 1897, J. J. Thompson used cathode ray tubes in a magnetic field to determine the charge to mass ratio for an electron. A few years later, Robert Millikan designed his "oil drop" experiment to provide the data needed to calculate the mass of the electron. In 1913, Henry Moseley used X rays to find the relationship between wavelength and atomic number. Based on his work we know that the number of protons determines the identity of the element.

Niels Bohr and Ernest Rutherford used spectroscopy to expand their knowledge of atomic structure. They viewed the atom as a central nucleus of positive charge surrounded by electrons. Today we know that absorption and emission spectra are like fingerprints for the elements. Bohr pictured the hydrogen atom as an electron circling a nucleus. The electron moves from its ground state or normal state if it absorbs a photon, energy of a certain frequency. When an electron drops from a larger orbit to a smaller one, a definite amount of energy is radiated.

7:2 ISOTOPES AND ATOMIC NUMBER

The **atomic number** of an element is represented by the symbol Z. The atomic number is the number of protons in the nucleus. Since an atom is electrically neutral, the number of electrons must equal the number of protons. The atomic number can be found in the table of atomic masses inside the back cover of this book. The number of protons determines the identity of the element.

Isotopes are atoms of an element that are exactly alike chemically but slightly different in mass. Isotopes have the same number of protons but a different number of neutrons. The number of neutrons determines the particular isotope of the element.

The particles that make up an atomic nucleus are called **nucleons.** The total number of nucleons, protons plus neutrons, in an atom is called the **mass number,** A. Thus, the number of neutrons = $A - Z$. Isotopes are often symbolized by placing the atomic number and mass number to the left of the chemical symbol. The mass number is a superscript, the atomic number a subscript. The isotope of radon, an indoor air pollutant, is

$$\text{mass number (protons + neutrons)} \atop \text{atomic number (protons)} \quad {}^{222}_{86}\text{Rn}$$

The name of this isotope is radon-222.

Example 1

Compute the number of electrons, protons, and neutrons in the atom of carbon with $A = 14$, and write its nuclear symbol.

Solving Process:

The atomic number, Z, is read from the table of atomic masses. The atomic number (number of protons) of carbon is 6. Because the atom is electrically neutral, the number of electrons equals the atomic number. The mass number, A, is the total number of nucleons. This particular isotope of carbon has a mass number of 14.

$$\text{number of neutrons} = A - Z = 14 - 6 = 8$$

In carbon-14, there are 6 protons, 8 neutrons, and 6 electrons. Its nuclear symbol is ${}^{14}_{6}\text{C}$.

PROBLEMS

1. Use the table of atomic masses inside the back cover to compute the number of electrons, neutrons, and protons in the following nuclides. Write the symbol for each nuclide.

   a. Cr $A = 50$ **d.** Ir $A = 193$
   b. Cl $A = 37$ **e.** Si $A = 29$
   c. Mg $A = 26$ **f.** Ne $A = 22$

2. Moseley used X rays to determine the atomic numbers of the elements. Identify each of the following elements by name.

   a. 1 proton   **d.** 12 protons
   b. 4 protons   **e.** 20 protons
   c. 8 protons   **f.** 30 protons

7:3   AVERAGE ATOMIC MASS

The atomic mass unit, u, is used to measure atomic mass. The carbon-12 nuclide is the standard for the atomic mass scale. One carbon-12 atom has a mass of 12 atomic mass units. The subatomic particles that we have studied have the following atomic masses.

$$\text{electron} = 9.109\ 53 \times 10^{-28}\ \text{g} = 0.000\ 549\ \text{u}$$
$$\text{proton} = 1.672\ 65 \times 10^{-24}\ \text{g} = 1.0073\ \text{u}$$
$$\text{neutron} = 1.674\ 95 \times 10^{-24}\ \text{g} = 1.0087\ \text{u}$$

As you can see, the masses of the protons and neutrons in an atom make up nearly all of the atom's mass.

The **average atomic mass** of an element can be determined from relative amounts of each isotope. In a naturally occurring element, the fractional abundance is the fraction of a particular isotope in the total sample of atoms. The atomic masses in the atomic mass table and the periodic table are based on the weighted average of the masses of all isotopes of an element. The average atomic mass of the element is used in most chemical calculations.

Example 2

Chlorine has two isotopes. Chlorine-35 has an actual mass of 34.9689 u and chlorine-37 has a mass of 36.9659 u. In any sample of chlorine atoms, 75.771% will be chlorine-35 and 24.229% will be chlorine-37. Calculate the average atomic mass of chlorine.

Solving Process:

Each of the isotopic masses is multiplied by its fractional abundance. Then the products are added.

$$(34.9689)(0.75771) + (36.9659)(0.24229) = 35.453\ \text{u}$$

PROBLEMS

3. Calculate the average atomic mass of magnesium using the following data for three magnesium isotopes.

isotope	mass (u)	fractional abundance
Mg-24	23.985	0.7870
Mg-25	24.986	0.1013
Mg-26	25.983	0.1117

4. Calculate the average atomic mass of iridium using the following data for two iridium isotopes.

isotope	mass (u)	fractional abundance
Ir-191	191.0	0.3758
Ir-193	193.0	0.6242

CHAPTER REVIEW PROBLEMS

Indicate whether each of the following statements is true or false. Correct the false statements.

1. Dalton's atomic theory includes a statement that says atoms of the same element are identical.
2. Dalton's theory states that atoms have variable masses.
3. J. J. Thompson is credited with the "oil drop" experiment.
4. The mass of an electron is equal to the mass of a proton.
5. The mass of a proton is approximately equal to the mass of a neutron.
6. Millikan devised an experiment to determine the charge on an electron.
7. The atomic number represents the number of protons in a nucleus and is represented by the symbol Na.
8. The proton has a mass of approximately 1 u.
9. The difference in mass of isotopes of the same element is due to the different number of protons in the nucleus.
10. The isotope carbon-12 is used as the relative mass standard for the atomic mass scale.
11. Calculate the average atomic mass of chromium.

isotope	mass (u)	fractional abundance
Cr-50	49.946	0.043 500
Cr-52	51.941	0.838 00
Cr-53	52.941	0.095 000
Cr-54	53.939	0.023 500

12. How many protons are in the nucleus of each of the following elements?
    a. uranium   c. helium
    b. selenium   d. unnilseptium
13. Give the number of neutrons in each of the following isotopes.
    a. titanium-46   c. $^{34}_{16}S$
    b. nitrogen-15   d. $^{65}_{29}Cu$
14. Fill in the blanks in the table below for neutral atoms. Use only the information given in the table.

	Atomic Number	Mass Number	Number of protons	Number of neutrons	Number of electrons
calcium-43			20		
lead-211				129	
plutonium-242	94				
chromium-50					24

ELECTRON CLOUDS AND PROBABILITY 8

8:1 QUANTUM NUMBERS

Einstein demonstrated that light not only has wave properties but also particle properties. DeBroglie reasoned that if light, which is considered a wave, has particle properties then particles of matter might show wave characteristics. Schrödinger expanded these concepts to describe electrons and to develop a theory called quantum mechanics or wave mechanics. **Quantum mechanics** allows us to determine the probability of finding an electron at a certain place in the atom. We do not know an electron's exact position. In fact, *it is impossible to know both the position and speed of an electron with absolute certainty*. This statement is the **Heisenberg Uncertainty Principle.**

Quantum mechanics uses four different **quantum numbers** to describe each electron in an atom. Three of the quantum numbers, n, l, and m, describe the atomic orbital. An **atomic orbital** is a region in space where there is a high probability of finding the electrons. The fourth quantum number, s, is used to designate a magnetic property of electrons called spin.

The **principal quantum number,** n, is used to describe the energy of the electron. The energy of an electron is determined by its average distance from the nucleus. The energy level in an atom is related to the radius of the electron cloud. The n quantum number can have values of 1, 2, 3, ... n. Each energy level, or quantum number, has n different sublevels. Each sublevel is described by the second quantum number l. The numerical values for l are the integers from 0 to (n − 1). The l values are usually designated by letters, s for l = 0, p for l = 1, d for l = 2, and f for l = 3. All of the sublevels, except the s sublevel, have more than one orbital. Each orbital in a sublevel will have the same energy and usually the same shape as all the others in that sublevel.

The orbitals differ in their orientation in space around the nucleus. The third quantum number, m (magnetic quantum number), is used to describe each orbital within a sublevel. The values for m are integers from −l to +l. For example, when l = 1, the sublevel is p. Since m can have any value from +l to −l, its values are −1, 0, and +1. Thus there are three orbitals in the p sublevel, one located along each of the three perpendicular axes.

When an electron moves, it generates a magnetic field. The fourth quantum number, s, describes the direction of electron spin around its axis. There are two values permitted by the theory, $+1/2$ and $-1/2$. These values can be thought of as describing clockwise and counterclockwise electron rotation around its axis. According to the **Pauli Exclusion Principle** *no two electrons in an atom can have the same set of quantum numbers.* Thus, only two electrons, having opposite spins, can occupy an orbital. As a result, each sublevel can hold a maximum of twice as many electrons as the number of orbitals in the sublevel.

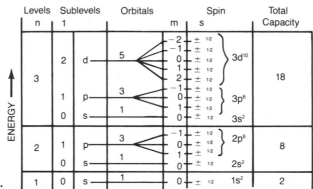

FIGURE 8-1.

PROBLEMS

1. Extend Figure 8-1 by showing the permitted values for each of the quantum numbers in the fourth energy level.

2. What is the maximum number of electrons that can occupy the fourth energy level?

3. Complete the following table.

sublevel	s	p	d	f
l value				

4. How many sublevels are there in the third energy level?

5. How many electrons can occupy any single orbital?

6. Complete the following table for the sublevels represented by the following quantum numbers.

n	2		4	4	5
l	0	2		3	
sublevel designation		$3d$	$4p$		$5s$

7. When $n = 5$, what are the possible values for l?

8. When $l = 2$, what are the possible values of m?

8:2   ORDER OF FILLING SUBLEVELS

The **electron configuration** of an atom is used to describe the electron distribution in the sublevels. Each sublevel symbol is written following a coefficient that represents the energy level containing the sublevel. Each sublevel symbol has a superscript on the right giving the number of electrons in the sublevel. For example, the electron configuration of the boron atom (atomic number 5) is written $1s^2 2s^2 2p^1$.

The order of filling corresponds to the increasing energy of the sublevels. By filling the sublevels of the lowest energy first, we have a model of an atom in the ground state. In many atoms with higher atomic numbers, the sublevels are not regularly filled. There is a rule of thumb that will give a correct configuration for most atoms in the ground state. We will explore the exceptions more fully in the next chapter. This rule of thumb is the **arrow diagram** and is shown in Figure 8-2. If you follow the arrows from tail to head, listing the orbitals passed as you move from left to right, you can find the electron configuration of most atoms.

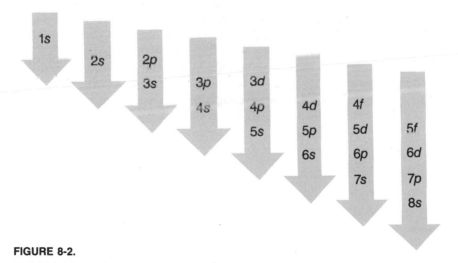

FIGURE 8-2.

Example 1

Write the electron configuration of arsenic ($Z = 33$).

Solving Process:

The arrow diagram above gives us the order $1s$, $2s$, $2p$, $3s$, $3p$, $4s$, $3d$, $4p$. The sublevels are then filled to capacity with the 33 electrons present in arsenic beginning with $1s$, then $2s$, and so on. The final 3 electrons are placed in the $4p$. The electron configuration is $1s^2 2s^2 2p^6 3s^2 3p^6 4s^2 3d^{10} 4p^3$.

The sum of the superscripts equals the atomic number, 33.

PROBLEMS

9. Which of the following show the correct order of filling?

   a. $1s2s2p$
   b. $1s2s2p3s3p$
   c. $1s2s3s$

   d. $1s2s2p3s3p4s$
   e. $1s2s2p3p3d4s$
   f. $1s2s2p3s3p4s4p$

10. Write the name of the element represented by each of the following configurations.

    a. $1s^22s^22p^5$
    b. $1s^22s^22p^63s^2$

    c. $1s^22s^22p^63s^23p^64s^23d^{10}4p^1$
    d. $1s^22s^22p^63s^23p^4$

11. Write the electron configuration for each of the following elements using the diagonal rule.

    a. aluminum $(Z = 13)$
    b. iron $(Z = 26)$
    c. cadmium $(Z = 48)$

    d. carbon $(Z = 6)$
    e. barium $(Z = 56)$
    f. hafnium $(Z = 72)$

8:3   ORBITAL FILLING DIAGRAMS

The electron configuration gives the number of electrons in each sublevel but does not show how the orbitals of a sublevel are occupied by the electrons. The result of Hund's Rule predicts that one electron enters each orbital of a sublevel before any orbital is doubly occupied. For example, the electron configuration for nitrogen is $1s^22s^22p^3$. Nitrogen has three electrons in the $2p$ sublevel, and each of these electrons occupies a separate orbital. In the orbital filling diagram each box stands for an orbital. Arrows are used to indicate the direction of electron spin.

Example 2

Construct an orbital filling diagram for fluorine $(Z = 9)$.
Solving Process:
Step 1. Write the electron configuration using the diagonal rule.

$$1s^22s^22p^5$$

Step 2. Construct an orbital filling diagram using a box for each orbital. Use arrows to represent the electrons in each orbital.

Recall that each electron occupies an empty orbital within a sublevel, rather than pair with another.

8:4 ELECTRON DOT DIAGRAMS

The Lewis electron dot diagram is useful when showing how atoms bond together. In these diagrams the outer energy level electrons, those with the largest value of n, are represented by dots placed around the letter symbol of the element.

Example 3

Write the Lewis electron dot diagram for selenium ($Z = 34$).

Solving Process:

Step 1. Write the orbital filling diagram for the outer energy level of selenium using the diagonal rule.

$1s^2 2s^2 2p^6 3s^2 3p^6 4s^2 3d^{10} 4p^4$

Step 2. The symbol of the element represents the nucleus and all the electrons except those in the outer energy level. Each "side" (above, below, left, right) of the symbol represents an orbital. Draw dots on the sides to represent only the outer electrons ($4s$ and $4p$). Show them as paired or unpaired based on the orbital diagram.

$:\overset{\cdot}{\underset{\cdot}{Se}}\cdot$

PROBLEMS

12. Predict electron configurations using the diagonal rule for atoms of the following elements.

    a. Li   c. Be   e. B   g. C
    b. N   d. O   f. F   h. Ne

13. Draw orbital filling diagrams for the elements listed in problem 12.
14. Draw Lewis electron dot diagrams for the elements in problem 12.

CHAPTER REVIEW PROBLEMS

1. Heisenberg stated that, at the same time, it was impossible to know what two things about an electron? exact position/velocity
2. How many quantum numbers are there? 4
3. What letter denotes the quantum number for the principal energy level? N
4. What four letters are used to represent the sublevels within a principal energy level? s p d f
5. What is the maximum number of electrons that may occupy one orbital? 2
6. Who stated that no two electrons in the same atom could have the same set of four quantum numbers? Pauli

7. The Lewis electron dot diagram is used to represent only which electrons in an atom? *outer energy level*

8. What is the arrow diagram used to predict? *~~electron~~ can order of filling Sublevels*

9. How many sublevels are possible in the third energy level? *3*

10. How many orbitals are there in an *f* sublevel? *7*

11. What is the maximum number of electrons that can occupy a *d* sublevel? *10*

12. Which sublevel may contain a maximum of three pairs of electrons? *P*

13. What must be true about the spins of two electrons occupying the same orbital? *they are opposite*

14. Write the electron configuration for each of the following elements.

   a. lithium ($Z = 3$)   **d.** mercury ($Z = 80$)
   b. radium ($Z = 88$)   **e.** tin ($Z = 50$)
   c. sodium ($Z = 11$)   **f.** krypton ($Z = 36$)

15. Draw the orbital filling diagrams for the following elements.

   a. titanium ($Z = 22$)   **c.** aluminum ($Z = 13$)
   b. sodium ($Z = 11$)   **d.** phosphorus ($Z = 15$)

16. Draw the Lewis electron dot diagram for the elements listed in problems 14 and 15.

PERIODIC TABLE

9

9:1 MODERN PERIODIC TABLE

In 1869 Dmitri Mendeleev, a Russian chemist, prepared a periodic table of the elements. The elements were arranged in order of their atomic masses in horizontal rows so that the elements in any vertical column had similar properties. In 1914, Moseley determined the atomic numbers of the elements from their X-ray spectra. He then reordered the elements in the periodic table according to increasing atomic number. This arrangement gave rise to our modern **periodic law.** It states that *the properties of the elements are a periodic function of their atomic numbers.*

In the modern periodic table we place elements with similar electron configurations in the same column or group. We also list the elements in the column in order of their increasing principal quantum numbers. The numbers along the left side of the periodic table on the inside back cover are the values for n, the energy levels. The first two columns (1 2) consist of elements that have electrons filling the s sublevel. The elements in the last six columns on the right (13-18) are elements that have electrons filling the p sublevels. The 10 columns in the center of the chart (3-12) contain the transition elements whose electrons are filling an inner d sublevel having a quantum number of $(n - 1)$. The two horizontal rows at the bottom of the periodic table represent the elements with a quantum number of $(n - 2)$ whose electrons are filling the inner f sublevel.

9:2 ELECTRON CONFIGURATION

The periodic table can be used to read the electron configuration of an element. The written configuration of any element in Group 1 (IA) will end in s^1. The coefficient of s^1 is easily found from the table because the number of the period indicates the energy level. Group 2 (IIA) elements end their electron configuration with s^2. The same procedure can be used for Groups 13 (IIIA) through 18 (VIIIA). There the endings are p^1 through p^6 preceded by a coefficient that is the same number as the period. For example, arsenic $(Z = 33)$ is in period 4 and Group 15 (VA). Its electron configuration will end in $4p^3$.

For Groups 3 (IIIB) through 12 (IIB) the endings are d^1 through d^{10} preceded by a coefficient that is one less than the period number. For the lanthanides, the endings are f^1 through f^{14} preceded by a coefficient that is two less than the period number.

To understand some of the exceptions to the diagonal rule, it is necessary to know that there is a special stability associated with certain electron configurations in an atom. An atom with eight electrons in the outer level has a special stability. *An atom having a filled or half filled sublevel is also more stable.* For example, chromium is predicted to have two electrons in its 4s sublevel and four electrons in its 3d sublevel. Actually it has only one electron in its 4s sublevel and five electrons in its 3d sublevel. Thus, the atom has two half-full sublevels instead of one full sublevel and one with no special arrangement. Copper is similar. It has one electron in its 4s sublevel and ten electrons in its 3d sublevel. Most of the exceptions from predicted configurations can be explained in this way.

PROBLEMS

1. Give the group number for the elements that have the following electron configurations.

   a. $1s^2 2s^2 2p^1$
   b. $1s^2 2s^2$
   c. $1s^2 2s^2 2p^6 3s^2 3p^5$
   d. $1s^2 2s^2 2p^6 3s^2 3p^4$
   e. $1s^2 2s^2 2p^6 3s^2 3p^6 4s^2 3d^3$
   f. $1s^2 2s^2 2p^6 3s^2 3p^6 4s^2 3d^{10}$

2. Give the names of each of the elements listed in problem 1.

3. Write the electron configurations for the following elements.

   a. potassium ($Z = 19$)
   b. mercury ($Z = 80$)
   c. lithium ($Z = 3$)
   d. phosphorus ($Z = 15$)
   e. calcium ($Z = 20$)
   f. indium ($Z = 49$)

4. In what period would the element with the configuration $1s^2 2s^2 2p^6 3s^2 3p^6 4s^2 3d^{10} 4p^6 5s^1$ be located?

5. Which two elements in the fourth period have configurations that are apparent contradictions to the diagonal rule?

9:3 METALS AND NONMETALS

Many of the columns in the table have family names. Group 1 (IA), except hydrogen, is called the **alkali metal family.** Group 2 (IIA) is called the **alkaline earth metal family.** Groups 1 (IA) and 2 (IIA) of the periodic table contain the most active metals.

On the other side of the table are the nonmetals. Group 16 (VIA) is called the **chalcogen** (KAL kuh juhn) **family.** Group 17 (VIIA) is known as the **halogen family.** The elements of Group 18 (VIIIA) are called the **noble gases.**

The majority of elements are **metals.** We are all familiar with typical metallic properties. Metals have a luster and are malleable. They conduct heat and electricity well. **Nonmetals** are generally gases or brittle solids at room temperature. They are usually poor conductors of heat and electricity. Exceptions are diamond, an excellent conductor of heat, and graphite, an electrical conductor. Elements with three or fewer electrons in the outer level are considered to be metals. Elements with five or more electrons in the outer level are considered to be nonmetals. There are some elements that have properties of both metals and nonmetals. These elements are called **metalloids.** These elements lie to the right and left of the stairstep line on the periodic table. Aluminum is usually considered to be a metal.

The elements in the B Groups are called **transition elements.** They all show metallic properties. The elements 57 through 70, the **lanthanides,** and 89 through 102, the **actinides,** have two electrons in the outer energy level and are metals.

PROBLEMS

6. Classify the following elements as metal, metalloid, or nonmetal.
   - **a.** cadmium
   - **b.** fluorine
   - **c.** californium
   - **d.** carbon
   - **e.** calcium
   - **f.** germanium

7. Are the transition elements metals or nonmetals?

Match each of the following terms with a letter from the periodic table.

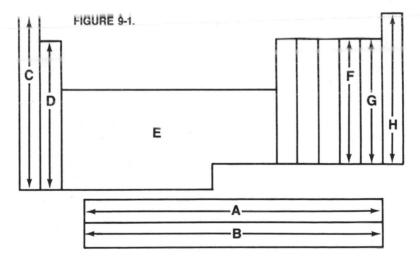

FIGURE 9-1.

8. alkali metals
9. alkaline earth metals
10. lanthanides
11. actinides

12. chalcogens
13. halogens
14. noble gases
15. transition metals

CHAPTER REVIEW PROBLEMS

1. How are substances that are gases or brittle solids at room temperature classified?

2. Would an element with two outer electrons be a metal or nonmetal?

3. What Russian scientist designed the first periodic table?

4. Which group of elements contains the most active metals?

5. Which group of elements has eight outer electrons?

6. To which quantum number is the period number of an element related?

7. For the transition elements, as the atomic number increases, to which sublevel are electrons being added?

8. According to the octet rule, how many pairs of outer electrons do the most stable atoms have?

9. In the lanthanide series, as the atomic number increases, to which sublevel are electrons being added?

10. Write the electron configurations of the following elements.
    a. silicon ($Z = 14$)   c. copper ($Z = 29$)
    b. krypton ($Z = 36$)   d. cesium ($Z = 55$)

11. Identify the elements whose electron configurations end with the following.
    a. $4s^2 3d^2$ d. $7s^2 5f^6$
    b. $2s^2 2p^6$ e. $4s^2 3d^{10} 4p^5$
    c. $4s^1 3d^5$ f. $3s^1$

12. Write the electron configurations of the following elements.
    a. iodine ($Z = 53$)   c. nickel ($Z = 28$)
    b. oxygen ($Z = 8$)   d. strontium ($Z = 38$)

13. Classify the following elements as metals, metalloids, or nonmetals.
    a. chlorine ($Z = 17$)   d. arsenic ($Z = 33$)
    b. tungsten ($Z = 74$)   e. promethium ($Z = 61$)
    c. radium ($Z = 88$)   f. uranium ($Z = 92$)

PERIODIC PROPERTIES 10

10:1 RADII OF ATOMS

The periodic table is a powerful tool of the chemist. Similar properties of the elements occur at predicted intervals. The properties are periodic because both the position and properties arise from the electron configurations of the atoms.

As you look at the periodic table from top to bottom, each period represents a new energy level. *As the principal quantum number increases, the size of the electron cloud increases.* Chemists discuss the size of atoms by referring to their radii. As you look across the periodic table, all the atoms in a period have the same principal quantum number. The positive charge on the nucleus increases by one proton for each element. This increase in charge results in the outer electron cloud being pulled closer to the nucleus. Thus, *atoms generally decrease slightly in size from left to right across a period.*

PROBLEM

1. From each of the following pairs, use the periodic table to select the atom that is larger in radius.
   a. Sn, Sr   **c.** Na, Rb   **e.** S, P   **g.** B, Al
   b. Cl, I   **d.** Mg, Be   **f.** Ac, U   **h.** Au, Ba

10:2 RADII OF IONS

Generally, when atoms unite to form compounds, their structures become more stable. Ionic compounds are formed from atoms that have lost or gained electrons in order to obtain a noble gas configuration. A **noble gas configuration** is particularly stable because the eight outer electrons fill the outer sublevels. Metals, on the left and in the center of the table, tend to lose electrons, forming positive ions by losing electrons. This loss of electrons results in the formation of a smaller metallic ion. Nonmetals are located on the right side of the table. Nonmetallic ions are formed by atoms gaining electrons. The negatively charged nonmetallic ions are larger than the atoms from which they are formed.

PROBLEM

2. From each of the following pairs of particles, select the particle that is larger in radius.
   a. Ca, Ca^{2+} **c.** As^{3-}, P^{3-} **e.** Mg^{2+}, Be^{2+} **g.** C, C^{4-}
   b. F^-, Cl^- **d.** Pb^{4+}, Pb **f.** Te^{2-}, Te **h.** Ag, Ag^+

10:3 PREDICTING OXIDATION NUMBERS

The outer, high energy electrons are involved in the reaction of atoms with each other. Recall that the noble gas configuration of eight outer electrons is stable. Filled s and p sublevels result in eight outer electrons. Oxidation numbers can be predicted from electron configurations.

Consider the metals in Group 1 (IA). Each atom has one electron in its outer level. The loss of this one electron will give these metals the same configuration as a noble gas. Group 1 (IA) metals have an oxidation number of 1+. In Group 2 (IIA) we would expect the loss of the two s electrons for the atom to achieve the same configuration as the prior noble gas. That loss leads to a prediction of 2+ oxidation number for the alkaline earth metals.

In the B groups there are atoms in which the highest energy electrons are not in the outer level. Scandium has the configuration $1s^2 2s^2 2p^6 3s^2 3p^6 4s^2 3d^1$. Its outer level is the fourth level containing two electrons. Scandium's highest energy electron, however, is the one in the $3d$ sublevel. The transition elements may lose not only the outer level electrons, but also some lower electrons. Therefore, the transition elements have oxidation numbers varying from 2+ (representing loss of the two outer s electrons) to 8+. We would expect scandium to show only 2+ and 3+ oxidation numbers. Titanium has one more $3d$ electron than scandium. Experiments show that it has the predicted 2+, 3+, and 4+ numbers. The trend continues across the fourth row. Vanadium has a maximum oxidation number of 5+, chromium 6+, and manganese 7+. Iron, with a configuration of $1s^2 2s^2 2p^6 3s^2 3p^6 4s^2 3d^6$, has oxidation numbers of 2+ and 3+. For iron to have oxidation numbers higher than 3+ would mean breaking up a half-full $3d$ sublevel. Recall that an atom with a half-full sublevel represents a particularly stable configuration.

Group 13 (IIIA) elements lose three electrons and have an oxidation number of 3+. Group 14 (IVA) may have a 2+ or 4+ oxidation number.

In Groups 15 (VA), 16 (VIA), and 17 (VIIA), there is a general tendency to gain electrons to complete the octet. The outside level is already more than half-filled. These elements show oxidation numbers of 3−, 2−, and 1− respectively. It is also possible for these elements to lose electrons and have positive oxidation numbers. The tendency to lose electrons increases as we move down a column.

PROBLEMS

3. Predict the oxidation numbers for the following elements.

a. Al	c. Cl	e. Mg	g. Na
b. N	d. Zn	f. S	h. Mn

4. Which electrons were gained or lost to complete the outer octet and produce the following ions?

a. K^+	c. Ga^{3+}	e. Sn^{4+}	g. Ca^{2+}
b. O^{2-}	d. P^{3-}	f. Br^-	h. Sc^{3+}

10:4   FIRST IONIZATION ENERGY

Some atoms tend to give up electrons and become positive ions. Other atoms tend to gain electrons and become negative ions. These atomic tendencies have a periodic nature.

The energy needed to remove an atom's most loosely held electron is called **first ionization energy.** It is measured in kilojoules per mole. A metal is characterized by a low first ionization energy. Nonmetals have high first ionization energies.

In any column or group, there is a gradual decrease in ionization energy as atomic number increases. The increased distance of the outer electrons from the nucleus and the **shielding effect** of the inner electrons tend to lower the ionization energy. Though it appears that the increased nuclear charge of an element with a greater atomic number would increase ionization energy, the lowering effects of increased distance and shielding are greater. Remember that the number of electrons in the outermost sublevel is the same for all elements in a column or group.

Ionization energy tends to increase as atomic number increases in any horizontal row or period. This increase is a result of the increasing nuclear charge. There are some deviations from this expected trend of increasing ionization energy. These deviations result from the factors listed in Table 10-1.

Table 10-1

Factors Affecting Ionization Energy
1. **Nuclear charge**—the larger the nuclear charge, the greater the ionization energy.
2. **Shielding effect**—the greater the shielding effect, the less the ionization energy.
3. **Radius**—the greater the distance between the nucleus and the outer electrons of an atom, the less the ionization energy.
4. **Sublevel**—an electron from a full or half-full sublevel requires additional energy to be removed.

It is possible to measure other (second, third, and so on) ionization energies of an atom. Ionization energy increases with the removal of each additional electron.

PROBLEM

5. Which atom in each of the following pairs would have the lower first ionization energy?

a. N, O	**d.** C, Ge	**g.** I, Sb
b. Te, Sn	**e.** Br, I	**h.** Al, N
c. Ne, F	**f.** Mg, Ca	**i.** F, S

CHAPTER REVIEW PROBLEMS

1. Within a group, does the radii of atoms increase or decrease as the atomic number increases?

2. Does the radii of atoms within a period increase or decrease as the atomic number increases?

3. In each of the following pairs of atoms, pick the one that is larger.

   a. Mg, Na   **c.** Al, B   **e.** F, N
   b. K, Ca   **d.** Br, Cl   **f.** Ne, Ar

4. In each of the following pairs of particles, pick the one that is smaller.

   a. Fe, Fe^{3+} **c.** Ac^{3+}, U^{3+} **e.** Mo^{6+}, Mo
   b. S^{2-}, S   **d.** Br^-, Se^{2-} **f.** As^{3-}, As

5. Predict the oxidation number of the following elements.

   a. Li   **d.** C   **g.** F
   b. Be   **e.** P   **h.** Ar
   c. B   **f.** O   **i.** K

6. Predict the oxidation numbers of the following elements.

   a. Rb   **c.** Pu   **e.** V
   b. Co   **d.** Bi   **f.** Ba

7. In a group, will the ionization energy tend to increase or decrease with increasing atomic number?

8. In a period, will the ionization energy tend to increase or decrease with increasing atomic number?

9. Do metals or nonmetals generally have lower ionization energies?

10. Carbon has a first ionization energy of 1086.5 kJ/mol. Predict whether the first ionization energies of the following elements will be more or less than that of carbon.

    a. helium   **c.** fluorine
    b. lithium   **d.** silicon

11. As the distance between the nucleus and the outer electrons of an atom increases, will the ionization energy increase or decrease?

12. As the shielding effect increases, will the ionization energy increase or decrease?

13. As the positive charge on an ion increases, will the ionization energy increase or decrease?

TYPICAL ELEMENTS

11

Elements in the same group on the periodic table have similar outer electron configurations. This arrangement gives them a similarity of properties and is the reason a group is sometimes called a family of elements. The similarity is particularly strong in Groups 1 (IA), 2 (IIA), 17 (VIIA), and 18 (VIIIA).

11:1 HYDROGEN

Hydrogen is a unique element and is thus a family by itself. The most abundant element in the universe, hydrogen is widely used in industry to make products as diverse as fertilizer, missile fuel, and margarine.

Hydrogen can react in four ways. It can lose its one electron to form the **hydrogen ion, H$^+$.** It can gain an electron as it forms the **hydride ion, H$^-$,** and combine with positive metal ions. Hydrogen can share electrons with most nonmetals. It can also act as a bridging atom between two atoms, such as boron.

11:2 REPRESENTATIVE METALS

Lithium, sodium, and potassium belong to Group 1 (IA), the alkali metals. These elements have low densities, are soft, and very reactive, forming 1+ ions. Reactivity increases as the atomic numbers of these metals increase. Their ionization energies become less because of the increased distance of the electrons from the nucleus and the shielding effect. Alkali metals form binary compounds with most nonmetals. Lithium is not typical of this group, since its reactions are more like magnesium, a Group 2 (IIA) element.

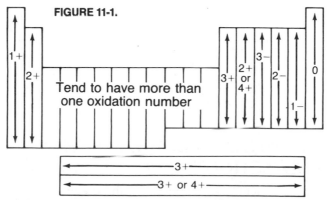

FIGURE 11-1.

Trends in Oxidation Numbers of the Elements

Group 2 (IIA) elements are known as alkaline earth metals. These elements are also reactive, and they form 2+ ions. Most compounds of these metals are soluble in water.

Aluminum, one of the Group 13 (IIIA) metals, is the most abundant metal in the earth's crust. It tends to share its three outer electrons, and is less reactive than the metals of Groups 1 (IA) and 2 (IIA).

11:3 REPRESENTATIVE NONMETALS

The elements of Group 14 (IVA) have atoms with four electrons in the outer level. These elements generally react by sharing electrons. Carbon is the first element in this group. The major part of carbon chemistry is classed as organic chemistry. **Catenation** occurs when carbon forms "chains" with other carbon atoms. Generally, compounds that do not contain carbon are called inorganic compounds. Different forms of the same element are called **allotropes.** Carbon has two allotropes: diamond and graphite.

Nitrogen and phosphorus differ greatly even though they are adjacent members of Group 15 (VA). Nitrogen occurs in oxidation states ranging from 3− through 5+. Phosphorus shows only 3−, 0, 3+, and 5+ oxidation states. Nitrogen gas, N_2, is very stable but many nitrogen compounds are relatively unstable. TNT, an explosive, is one example. Elemental phosphorus, solid at room temperature, occurs as P_4 molecules. White and red phosphorus are allotropes.

Oxygen, Group 16 (VIA), is the most plentiful element in the earth's crust. It gains two electrons to achieve a stable octet and forms O^{2-} ions. Metallic oxides generally react with water to form basic solutions. Nonmetallic oxides generally form acidic solutions when dissolved in water. Some oxides, called amphoteric oxides, can produce either acidic or basic solutions, depending on the other substances present. Ozone, O_3 is a highly reactive allotrope of oxygen. The chemistry of sulfur is similar to that of oxygen.

Group 17 (VIIA) is the highly reactive halogen (salt forming) family. These elements exist as diatomic molecules. They react either by forming 1− ions or by sharing electrons. Fluorine is the most reactive of all elements, because of its small radius and limited shielding effect.

In 1962, the first "inert" gas compound was synthesized. Since that time the gases of Group 18 (VIIIA) have been called the noble gases. Xenon, krypton, and radon compounds have been made. However, the noble gases are generally considered the most stable elements.

11:4 TRANSITION METALS, LANTHANIDES AND ACTINIDES

The transition metals ("B" groups) are those elements whose highest energy electrons are in d sublevels. The d electrons may be lost, one at a time, after the outer s electrons have been lost. The fourth period elements, titanium through zinc, are used primarily as structural metals. They can be used alone or as alloys. Chromium is a transition metal. It has multiple oxidation numbers. Because of its $4s^13s^5$ outer electron configuration, it is stable and resists corrosion. Zinc's behavior differs slightly from other transition elements due to a full d sublevel, $4s^23d^{10}$.

All of the lanthanides show 3+ as the most stable state. Neodymium, a soft reactive metal, is a typical example of the elements whose highest energy level electrons are in the $4f$ sublevel. The actinides are those elements whose highest energy level electrons are in the $5f$ sublevel. Curium, a silvery, hard metal of medium density is an example. It is reactive and highly toxic.

CHAPTER REVIEW PROBLEMS

Identify the false statements and correct them.

1. Group 2 (IIA) elements that form 2+ ions are known as alkali metals.
2. Graphite and diamond are isotopes of carbon.
3. The transition metals are those elements whose highest energy electrons are in the $4f$ sublevel.
4. The shielding effect blocks the attraction of the nucleus for outer electrons.
5. The tendency of carbon atoms to form long chains is called catenation.
6. When hydrogen gains one electron, it forms the hydrogen ion, H^+.
7. Organic chemistry is the chemistry of carbon compounds.
8. The family of elements having eight outer electrons, Group 18 (VIIIA), is called the halogens.
9. Amphoteric oxides react with water to form either acidic or basic solutions.
10. The most reactive elements on the periodic table are in Groups 2 (IIA) and 17 (VIIA).

CHEMICAL BONDING 12

12:1 BOND CHARACTER

The chemical bonds formed between atoms depend on two periodic properties: the electron configurations of the atoms and the attraction the atoms have for electrons. The relative tendency of an atom to attract electrons to itself when bonded with another atom is called **electronegativity.** Examine Table A-9 in the Appendix. It shows that the variation in electronegativity follows the same trend as ionization energies.

When two atoms transfer electrons, ions are produced. The electrostatic force that holds two ions together due to their differing charges is the **ionic bond.** Ionic compounds have high melting points, conduct electricity in the molten state, tend to be soluble in water, and usually crystallize as well-defined crystals.

If two elements combine by sharing electrons, they are said to form a **covalent bond.** The shared pair or pairs of electrons constitute a covalent bond. The resulting particle is called a **molecule.** Covalent compounds typically have low melting points, do not conduct electricity, and are brittle.

Electronegativity differences can be used to determine whether a bond is ionic or covalent. Use Table 12-1 to find the percent ionic or covalent character of a bond. As you can see, most bonds show some ionic and covalent character. The character of bonds is on a continuum. The value of 1.67 is generally used for convenience as a dividing point. Electronegativity differences less than 1.67 are considered mainly covalent; differences above 1.67 are considered mainly ionic.

Table 12-1

Character of Bonds									
Electronegativity Difference	0.00	0.65	0.94	1.19	1.43	1.67	1.91	2.19	2.54	3.03
Percent Ionic Character	0%	10%	20%	30%	40%	50%	60%	70%	80%	90%
Percent Covalent Character	100%	90%	80%	70%	60%	50%	40%	30%	20%	10%

Example 1

Classify as ionic or covalent the bond that forms between calcium and oxygen.

Solving Process:

From Table A-9 the electronegativity of calcium is found to be 1.04 and oxygen is 3.50.

$$\text{Electronegativity difference} = 3.50 - 1.04 = 2.46$$

Use Table 12-1 to determine the percent ionic character. The difference of 2.46 is between 70% and 80%. The bond is considered to be an ionic bond.

PROBLEMS

1. Classify the bonds between the following pairs of atoms as principally ionic or covalent.

   a. magnesium—chlorine   **d.** titanium—oxygen
   b. potassium—sulfur   **e.** copper—bromine
   c. cobalt—carbon   **f.** selenium—iodine

2. For each compound listed below, determine the character of the bond between the elements.

   a. NiO   **c.** $CaCl_2$ **e.** NaF
   b. BN   **d.** FeSi   **f.** Zn_3P_2

12:2   BOND LENGTH

The chemist makes use of four different types of radii—atomic, ionic, covalent, and van der Waals. Values for these radii can be found in your textbook and most chemical handbooks. We studied in Section 10:2 how ionic radii differ from atomic radii because of the loss or gain of electrons. Ionic radii are determined from ionic crystals. By adding the radii of two ions in a compound we may find their **internuclear distance** in a crystal.

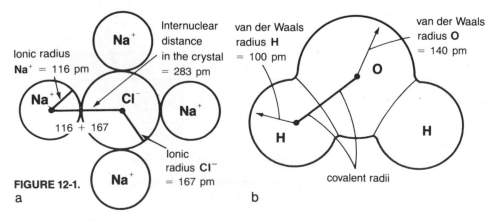

FIGURE 12-1.

The distance between nuclei along the bond axis is called the **bond length.** This length is not really fixed because the atoms vibrate as though the bond were a spring. Bond lengths are average values. The bond length is the sum of the covalent radii of the atoms in the bond.

A certain minimum distance must be maintained between atoms that are not bonded to each other. This limitation exists because the electron cloud of one atom repels the electron cloud of other atoms. The radius of the imaginary rigid shell of an atom is called the van der Waals radius. It is named for the Dutch physicist Johannes van der Waals.

PROBLEMS

Use Figures 12-2a and b to answer the following questions.

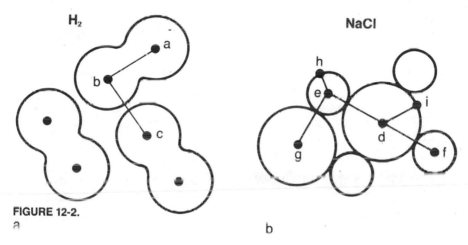

FIGURE 12-2.

a   b

3. What are the names for the following lines?

a. ab	**c.** di	**e.** df	**g.** eh
b. bc	**d.** de	**f.** eg	

4. What type of bonds does hydrogen have?

5. What type of bond exists between sodium and chlorine?

12:3 METALS

The properties of metals are not explained by ionic and covalent bonding theories. Metals conduct electricity, which indicates a ready source of electrons. Most metals have only one or two outer energy level electrons. These electrons are loosely held and readily move into the **conduction band** when an energy source is applied. Electrons are free to travel in the conduction band and are called **delocalized electrons.**

Metals differ from metalloids and nonmetals in that the energy gaps, the **forbidden zones,** in metals are very small, Figure 12-3. If sufficient energy is used the outer electrons in a semiconductor can be forced into the conduction band. The forbidden zone in nonmetals is too large an energy gap for electrons to pass over. For this reason, nonmetals are often referred to as insulators.

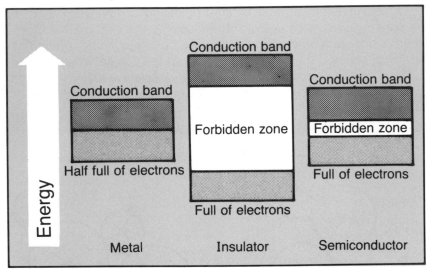

FIGURE 12-3.

CHAPTER REVIEW PROBLEMS

1. Use Table A-9 to predict which of the following bonds will be ionic or covalent.
   a. Ca—F   c. H—O
   b. S—O   d. K—Cl

2. Answer the following questions about trends on the periodic table with "increases" or "decreases."
   a. Within a family of elements, what happens to the atomic radii as the atomic number increases?
   b. Within a family of elements, what happens to the electronegativity as the atomic number increases?
   c. Within a period, what happens to the electronegativity as the atomic number increases?

3. Match the following characteristics with the correct bond type—ionic, covalent, or metallic.
   a. electrons transferred shared
   b. electrons delocalized
   c. electrons shared

MOLECULAR STRUCTURE 13

The structure of a substance determines its properties. It is, therefore, important to be able to predict the structure of molecules. Several theories have been proposed to explain the structure of molecules.

13:1 LEWIS ELECTRON DOT STRUCTURES

Being able to draw Lewis structures for polyatomic ions and molecules is very helpful in determining their structures. Guidelines for drawing these structures follow. Methane, CH_4, and the carbonate ion, CO_3^{2-}, are used as examples.

1. The first step is to decide what atoms are bonded together. The formula may suggest how the atoms are to be arranged. For those atoms given, the arrangements are

$$
\begin{array}{ccc}
& H & \\
H & C & H \quad \text{and} \\
& H &
\end{array}
\qquad
\begin{array}{c}
O \quad O \\
C \\
O
\end{array}
$$

   This choice is not always easy. For most binary covalent compounds and polyatomic ions, the central atom will be the atom that occurs once in the formula. For oxygen-containing acids, the hydrogens that are released from these compounds are bonded to oxygen. When in doubt, choose the most symmetrical atom arrangement.

2. Count the total number of outer level electrons in the ion or molecule. For CH_4, there are eight, four from carbon plus one from each of the four hydrogens. For CO_3^{2-} there are twenty-four, four from carbon, six from each of the three oxygens, plus the two added to give the ion a charge of 2−.

3. Place a pair of electrons (dots) between the central atom and each of the other atoms.

$$
\begin{array}{c}
H \\
H\!:\!\overset{\displaystyle ..}{\underset{\displaystyle ..}{C}}\!:\!H \\
H
\end{array}
\qquad
\begin{array}{c}
O \quad O \\
\cdot C \cdot \\
O
\end{array}
$$

4. Distribute the remaining outer electrons so that each atom has a filled outer energy level, usually an octet of electrons. Some exceptions are H, which has two, and B, which will have six.

83

Our structure for CH_4 above is complete. We have used all eight electrons in such a way that carbon has eight and each hydrogen has two. However, we must add electrons to the carbonate unit.

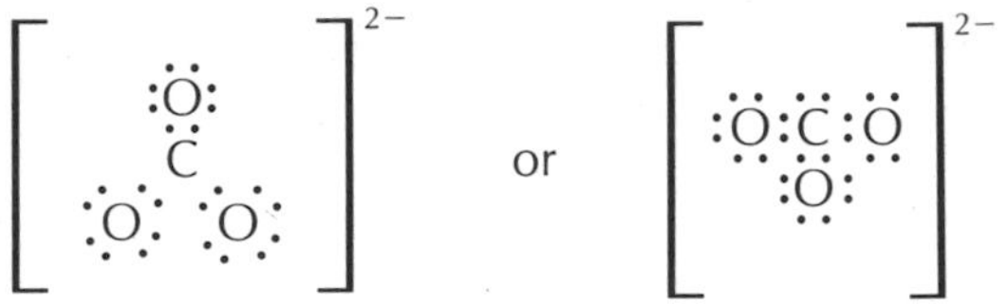

or

Neither structure meets the requirement of eight electrons around each atom. This leads to step 5.

5. When there are not enough electrons, make double or triple bonds. When there are extra electrons, place these on the central atom.

To have eight electrons on each atom, we move an additional pair of electrons between C and an O to create a double bond.

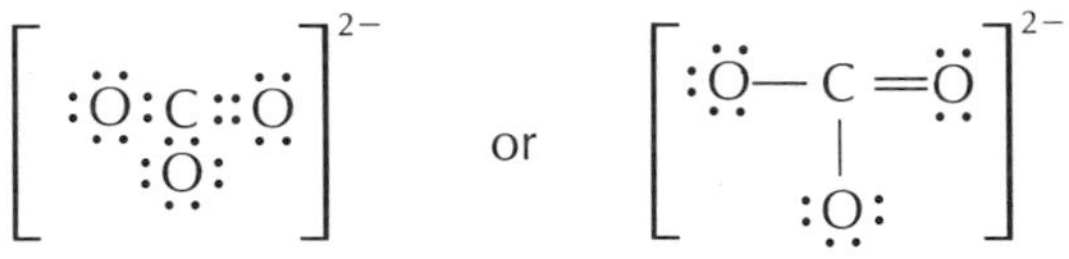

or

Thus, the unit contains 24 electrons arranged so that each atom has 8 electrons.

13:2   RESONANCE

The structure we have written for carbonate indicates one double and two single bonds. Double bonds are shorter than single bonds, but bond length measurements show that all three bonds are the same length. The values are intermediate between single and double. The Lewis structure doesn't match reality. We get around this problem by using a concept called **resonance** in which we represent a molecular structure as an average of two or more equivalent structures. For the carbonate ion, we write

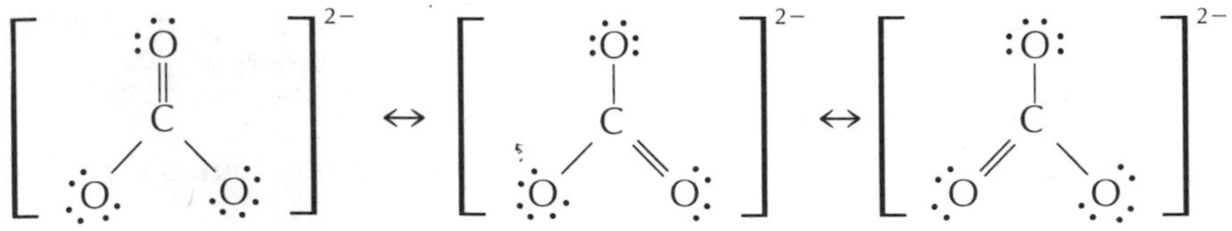

One carbonate ion exists. It has three bonds of equal length.

PROBLEMS

1. Predict a reasonable arrangement of atoms in the following.

    a. CO_2 **b.** BCl_3 **c.** NO_3^- **d.** H_3PO_4

2. Draw Lewis structures for each of the following.

a. H_2S **c.** NO_3^- **e.** CCl_4

b. NH_4^+ **d.** CO **f.** HCOOH (one H bonds to C, one to O)

3. Which of the structures in question 2 involve resonance?

13:3   OUTER LEVEL ELECTRON PAIR REPULSION

One theory of molecular geometry holds that the outer level electron pair charge clouds repel each other. Thus, *the electron pairs, shared or unshared, stay as far apart as possible to minimize repulsion.*

This theory explains why CO_2 is linear, H_2O is bent, or angular, and CH_4 is tetrahedral. See Table 13-1.

Table 13-1

Molecular Geometry			
Number of Electron Clouds	Electron Geometry	Hybridization at Central Atom (A) and Examples	Shape
2	:—A—: linear	sp (180°) $BeCl_2$ CO_2	
3	A trigonal planar	sp^2 (120°) BF_3 BCl_3	
4	A tetrahedral	sp^3 (109°28') CH_4 CCl_4	
5	A trigonal bipyramidal	sp^3d or dsp^3 (90°, 120°, 180°) PF_5 $AsCl_5$	
6	A octahedral	sp^3d^2 or d^2sp^3 (90°, 180°) SF_6 SeF_6	

Example 1

Predict the molecular structure of water, H_2O.

Solving Process:

The electron dot structure for water is $H \colon \overset{\cdot\cdot}{\underset{\cdot\cdot}{O}} \colon$.
H

There are four electron pairs on oxygen. When these electron pairs are as far apart as possible, their clouds will point to the corners of a tetrahedron. Thus, the two hydrogen atoms form an angular molecule with oxygen, as their electron clouds are bent away from the two unshared electron pairs.

In a regular tetrahedron the bond angles are 109.5° as they are in CH_4 and CCl_4, each of which contains four shared electron pairs. The H-O-H bond angle in water is 104.5°. This angle is caused by the two unshared pairs of electrons that spread their charge clouds over a larger volume. The repulsion between unshared pairs is greater than that between shared pairs.

13:4 HYBRID ORBITALS

Another theory explains molecular shape in terms of the formation of orbitals that are hybrids of s, p, and d orbitals. In this theory, bonding is viewed as an overlap of orbitals. The bonds between H and O in water are formed by the overlap of the half-filled s orbital in H and a half-filled p orbital in O.

To explain the bonding in compounds of beryllium, boron, carbon, and similar atoms, the idea of **hybrid orbitals** is used. For example, beryllium forms BeH_2. However, its electron configuration shows only paired outer electrons. The two Be—H bonds are accounted for by proposing the formation of two sp orbitals.

One of the $2s$ electrons is "promoted" to a $2p$ orbital, and two equivalent hybrid orbitals result. The two sp orbitals are directed in space to minimize repulsion. A linear structure results.

We predict sp^2 hybridization in boron that results in three orbitals in a triagonal planar arrangement, 120° bond angle. Carbon forms four sp^3 hybrid orbitals. These orbitals are directed in a tetrahedral arrangement, 109° bond angle.

Two different types of orbital overlap are observed. A bond formed by the direct overlap of two orbitals is called a **sigma bond (σ).** This type of overlap includes s-s, s-p, and p-p overlap in an end-to-end manner. When two p orbitals overlap sideways with their axes parallel, they form a **pi (π)**

bond. Single bonds can be considered as sigma bonds. A double bond is made up of one sigma bond and one pi bond. Molecules containing multiple bonds are usually more reactive than molecules containing only single bonds. A triple bond contains one sigma and two pi bonds.

13:5 MOLECULAR ORBITAL DIAGRAMS

Molecular orbital theory permits the study of the electron configuration of molecules in a manner similar to that of an atom's electron configuration. A molecular orbital is an area of high electron probability and has a definite energy.

As two hydrogen atoms collide, their s orbitals overlap to form a low energy molecular orbital called a bonding orbital. The law of conservation of energy requires that a high energy, antibonding orbital also be formed. The bonding orbital is designated σ_{1s} (sigma one ess), while the antibonding orbital is called σ^*_{1s}. The asterisk indicates an antibonding orbital.

The three p atomic orbitals are perpendicular to each other, one lying along each of the three axes. They are labeled p_x, p_y, and p_z. As noted before, p orbitals of different atoms can overlap side-to-side or end-to-end. If we label the ones that overlap end-to-end as p_x, the set of bonding and antibonding orbitals that form are σ_{p_x} and $\sigma^*_{p_x}$. The p_y and p_z orbitals are perpendicular to the p_x orbitals and overlap side to side, forming π-type molecular orbitals. These orbitals are π_{p_y} and $\pi^*_{p_y}$, and π_{p_z} and $\pi^*_{p_z}$.

Figure 13-1 shows the relative energies of these orbitals. The number of molecular orbitals formed equals the total number of atomic orbitals in the atoms combined. The electrons fill the lowest available orbitals first. The order of filling is

$$\sigma_{1s} < \sigma^*_{1s} < \sigma_{2s} < \sigma^*_{2s} < \pi_{2p_y} = \pi_{2p_z} < \sigma_{2p_x} < \pi^*_{2p_y}$$
$$= \pi^*_{2p_z} < \sigma^*_{2p_x}$$

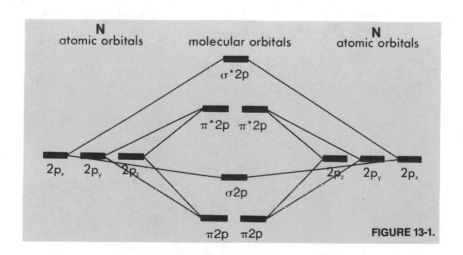

FIGURE 13-1.

A superscript is added to each orbital to indicate the number of electrons in the orbital. This notation is then referred to as the molecular orbital configuration. As with atomic electron configurations, electrons use unoccupied orbitals of the same energy before pairing up.

The number and strength of bonds that form between two atoms is measured by the **bond order.**

$$bond\ order = 1 = single\ bond$$
$$bond\ order = 2 = double\ bond$$
$$bond\ order = 3 = triple\ bond$$

The bond order can be calculated from the molecular orbital configuration. Subtract the number of electrons in antibonding orbitals from the number of electrons in bonding orbitals and divide the difference by two. A bond order of zero means no stable molecule exists.

Example 2

Use a molecular orbital diagram to write the molecular orbital configuration and compute the bond order for the nitrogen molecule, N_2.

Solving Process:

When the two nitrogen atoms combine, their atomic orbitals form the molecular orbitals shown in Figure 13-2. Each nitrogen atom has five outer

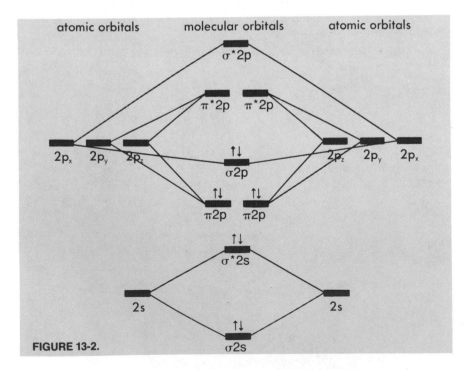

FIGURE 13-2.

electrons, $2s^2 2p^3$. Therefore, there would be ten electrons to place in molecular orbitals in the second energy level.

The molecular orbital configuration of N_2 is

$$(\sigma_{1s})^2 \, (\sigma^*_{1s})^2 \, (\sigma_{2s})^2 \, (\sigma^*_{2s})^2 \, (\pi_{2p_y})^2 \, (\pi_{2p_z})^2 \, (\sigma_{2p_x})^2$$

Since electrons in energy levels other than the outer level cancel, they can be omitted when calculating bond order.

$$\text{bond order} = \frac{\text{bonding} - \text{antibonding}}{2} = \frac{8 - 2}{2} = 3$$

Therefore, the N_2 molecule is stable and there is a triple bond between nitrogen atoms.

PROBLEM

4. For each of the following, complete a molecular orbital diagram, write the molecular orbital configuration, and determine the bond order.

    a. Li_2 b. Be_2 c. C_2

CHAPTER REVIEW PROBLEMS

1. How many electrons should be shown in Lewis structures of each of the following?

    a. HNO_3 c. O_2F_2 e. $POBr_3$
    b. CN^- d. CS_2 f. $C_2O_4^{2-}$

2. Draw Lewis structures for each of the following. Include all resonance structures.

    a. PH_3 d. NO^+ g. NH_3
    b. CS_2 e. CO_3^{2-} h. $SOCl_2$ (S is central atom)
    c. OH^- f. HCN i. PCl_5

3. Compare the C to O bond lengths in CO_2 and CO_3^{2-}.

4. Why is the N—H bond angle in NH_3 less than a tetrahedral angle of 109.5°?

5. Carbon uses four hybrid (sp^3) orbitals in the molecule, CH_4. Explain how these hybrid orbitals form.

6. Distinguish a sigma-bond from a pi-bond.

7. Predict the shape of the following using the electron pair repulsion model.

    a. BCl_3 c H_2S e. SiF_4
    b. MgI_2 d. CI_4 f. SCl_6

8. a. Write a molecular orbital diagram for He_2.
   b. Compute the bond order for He_2.
   c. Write the molecular orbital configuration for He_2.
   d. Would you expect an He_2 molecule to exist?

9. a. Write the molecular orbital diagram for the BN molecule.
   b. Compute the bond order for BN.
   c. Write the molecular orbital configuration for BN.
   d. Would you expect a BN molecule to exist?

POLAR MOLECULES

14

14:1 POLARITY

Most chemical bonds are neither 100% ionic nor 100% covalent. Atoms have different electron-attracting abilities, as measured by ionization energies and electronegativites. This difference results in unequal sharing of the bonding electrons, producing polar bonds and often polar molecules. A **polar bond** is one in which there is an uneven charge distribution. In the molecule HCl, for example, chlorine has a partial negative charge (δ^-) and hydrogen a partial positive charge (δ^+).

$$\overset{\delta^+}{H}\!-\!\overset{\delta^-}{Cl} \quad \text{or} \quad H\!\Rightarrow\!Cl$$

The electronegativity difference is $2.83 - 2.20 = 0.63$. The result is a polar bond, or dipole, and also a polar molecule. An arrow is used to represent a polar bond. The arrow points to the element with higher electronegativity.

Not all molecules having polar bonds are polar. Molecular geometry must be considered. If the polar bonds are arranged symmetrically, the polar effects cancel, as in CO_2, BCl_3, and CCl_4.

$$O\!\Lleftarrow\! C \!\Rrightarrow\! O$$

Unsymmetrical arrangements occur in H_2O and NH_3, producing polar molecules.

Many physical properties of molecules, such as melting and boiling points and solubility are affected by the degree of polarity of molecules.

Example 1

Determine the polarity of HCN and $SOCl_2$.

91

Solving Process:

Determine the molecular geometry by drawing Lewis structures and using the electron pair repulsion theory.

$$:\ddot{O}:\ddot{S}:\ddot{C}l:$$
$$:\ddot{C}l:$$

H : C : : : N :

linear   trigonal pyramid

Use electronegativities to determine bond polarity H = 2.20, C = 2.50, N = 3.07, S = 2.44, Cl = 2.83, O = 3.50. Electronegativity differences give these bond polarities:

$$H \rightarrow C \rightarrow N \qquad O \leftarrow S \rightarrow Cl$$
$$\downarrow$$
$$Cl$$

Since both arrangements are unsymmetrical, polar molecules result.

PROBLEMS

1. Which of the following bonds is most polar? In each bond, indicate the atom that carries the partial negative charge.

   a. H-I   **b.** P-I   **c.** As-Br   **d.** N-S

2. Which of the following molecules are polar?

   a. SO_2 **b.** $AsCl_3$ **c.** H_2Se **d.** SO_3

14:2   VAN DER WAALS FORCES

The attractive forces between molecules strongly influence their physical properties. Strong intermolecular attractions between molecules in solids and liquids affect the melting and boiling points of these substances. The stronger the forces, the higher these temperatures are. The chief forces of intermolecular attraction are dipole-dipole forces and London, or dispersion, forces. These forces are known as **van der Waals forces.**

Dipole-dipole forces exist between polar molecules. Dispersion forces are temporary dipoles in nonpolar molecules. These instantaneous dipoles are created as the movement of electrons shifts the electron density. The more electrons a molecule has the stronger the dispersion forces. In general, for molecules of approximately the same molecular mass, dipole-dipole forces are stronger than dispersion forces.

PROBLEMS

3. Compare the strength of intermolecular forces in methane, CH_4 (molecular mass = 16) and ammonia, NH_3 (molecular mass = 17).

4. List these molecules in order of increasing van der Waals forces: Br_2, F_2, Cl_2, I_2.

14:3 COMPLEX IONS

Some polar molecules, such as H_2O and NH_3, and some negative ions react with transition metal ions to form **complex ions** and coordination compounds. An example is $Fe(H_2O)_6^{2+}$, hexaaquairon(II) ion. The polar molecules and negative ions, called **ligands,** bond by donating a pair of electrons to the central atom. In the resulting bond, called a **coordinate covalent bond,** both electrons come from one atom. Thus, when a complex ion combines with an oppositely charged ion to form a neutral species, it is called a coordination compound. The cancer drug, diammine dichloroplatinum(II), $Pt(NH_3)_2Cl_2$, is a coordination compound.

14:4 NAMING COMPLEX IONS

In naming a complex ion, the ligands are named first, followed by the name of the central ion. Each type of ligand is preceded by a prefix designating the number of molecules or ions of that particular ligand present in the complex. The prefixes used are *di-*, *tri-*, *tetra-*, *penta-*, and *hexa-*.

Table 14-1

Some Common Ligands			
Ligand	**Name**	**Ligand**	**Name**
OH^-	hydroxo	$S_2O_3^{2-}$	thiosulfato
Br^-	bromo	$C_2O_4^{2-}$	oxalato
Cl^-	chloro	H_2O	aqua
F^-	fluoro	NH_3	ammino
I^-	iodo	CO	carbonyl
S^{2-}	thio	NO	nitrosyl
CN^-	cyano		

The ligands are named in alphabetical order. We disregard the prefix when determining the alphabetical order. If the complex as a whole possesses a negative charge, the name of the complex ion ends in *-ate*. If the central ion has more than one possible oxidation number, a Roman numeral in parentheses must follow the name of the central ion.

Table 14-2

Latin Stems Used in Some Metal Complexes			
Metal	**Latin Stem**	**Metal**	**Latin Stem**
copper	cuprate	lead	plumbate
gold	aurate	silver	argentate
iron	ferrate	tin	stannate

Example 2

Name the complex ion $FeCO(CN)_5^{3-}$.

Solving Process:

In the complex ion there are two ligands, CO, carbonyl, and CN^-, cyano. The carbonyl ligand is alphabetically named first. The cyano ligand is preceded by the prefix penta, followed by the name of the central ion. The ending on the word iron remains unchanged if the ion is positive, but in this example it is negative. The elements listed in Table 14-2 use the Latin stem when the ion is negative. Thus, iron becomes ferrate. Iron has more than one possible oxidation number, so its oxidation number is given in parentheses after its name. The name of the complex ion is written as one word. The name is

carbonylpentacyanoferrate(II) ion

PROBLEMS

5. Name the following complex ions. ·
   a. $AuCl_4^-$
   b. $Cr(NH_3)_3Cl^{2+}$
   c. $Cu(NH_3)_4^{2+}$
   d. HgI_4^{2-}
6. Write formulas for the following complex ions.
   a. hexaaquachromium(III)
   b. hexaamminecobalt(III)

CHAPTER REVIEW PROBLEMS

1. Use Table A-9 to arrange the following bonds in order of increasing polarity: H—O, H—H, H—Cl, H—S, H—Br, H—Ga. Indicate the atom in each bond that carries the partial negative charge.
2. Which of the following molecules are polar?
   a. CO
   b. $SiCl_4$
   c. $COCl_2$ (C is central atom)
   d. $HCBr_3$ (C is central atom)
3. Choose the substance in each of the following pairs that has the stronger intermolecular forces.
   a CH_4, CH_3Cl
   b. H_2, N_2
   c. $AsCl_3$, $AsBr_3$
   d. SO_2, SO_3
   e. H_2S, H_2Se
   f. CH_4, CCl_4
4. What two types of particles act as ligands?
5. How does a polar covalent bond differ from a nonpolar covalent bond?
6. What term is used to describe a particle that has ligands grouped around a central positive ion?
7. What type of molecules have polar bonds arranged in an asymmetrical pattern?

8. If two covalently bonded atoms have a large difference in electro-negativities, will the bond be polar or nonpolar?

9. Name the following complexes.

   a. $Zn(OH)_4^{2-}$ **b.** $Ag(S_2O_3)_2^{3-}$ **c.** $PbCl_4^{2-}$ **d.** $Ni(NH_3)_6^{2+}$

10. Write formulas for the following complex ions and predict their shapes.

    a. tetraammineiron(II) ion   **c.** diamminesilver ion
    b. hexaaquocopper(II) ion   **d.** hexahydroxostannate(IV) ion

11. The first complex ion synthesized in the laboratory was made in 1691 by the artist Dreisbach. This ion, $[Fe(CN)_6]^{4-}$, was used by the artist to make blue paints. What is the name of the ion?

12. If anhydrous $CuSO_4$ is dissolved in concentrated HCl(aq), $[CuCl_4]^{2-}$ ions form, causing the solution to turn yellow. A blue solution results when $CuSO_4$ is dissolved in water and $[Cu(H_2O)_4]^{2+}$ ions form. Name these two complex ions.

KINETIC THEORY

15

15:1 GAS PRESSURE

The effect on matter of temperature and pressure is described by the kinetic theory. The **kinetic theory** assumes that all matter is made up of very small particles that are in constant motion and undergo perfectly elastic collisions.

Gas molecules collide with each other billions of times per second. Gas molecules also strike the walls of their container. It is the number of collisions and the force of the collisions that cause gas pressure. **Pressure** is force per unit area. The scientific standard for pressure is defined in pascals. One pascal (Pa) is the pressure of 1 newton per square meter (N/m²). Normal air pressure at sea level is 101 325 Pa or 101.325 kilopascals (kPa).

An instrument called a **manometer** (mah NAHM uh tuhr) is used to measure pressure. There are two types of manometers. In the "open" type, air exerts pressure on the column of liquid on one arm of a U-tube. The gas being studied exerts pressure on the other arm. The difference in liquid level between the two arms is a measure of the gas pressure relative to the air pressure. The "closed" type has a vacuum above the liquid in one arm.

A **barometer** is a closed-arm manometer used to measure atmospheric pressure. Most barometers are calibrated to read millimeters of mercury (mm Hg). For converting units,

$$101.325 \text{ kPa} = 760 \text{ mm or } 1 \text{ kPa} = 7.50 \text{ mm Hg}$$

FIGURE 15-1.

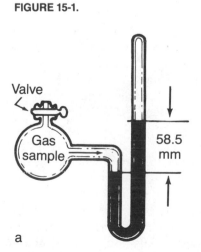

Valve

Gas sample

58.5 mm

a

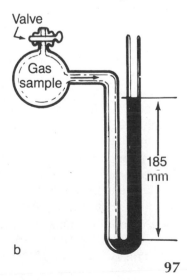

Valve

Gas sample

185 mm

b

97

Example 1

In Figure 15-1b, the closed arm of the manometer is filled with oxygen. Compute the pressure of the oxygen in kilopascals. The difference in mercury levels is 185 mm and the atmospheric pressure is 98.95 kPa.

Solving Process:

The mercury is higher in the arm open to the atmosphere. Thus, the pressure exerted by the O_2 must be greater than that of the air. As a result, we must add the pressure of the mercury to the air pressure to get the O_2 pressure. Before adding, however, we must convert the 185 mm difference in height to kilopascals.

$$\text{number of kPa} = \frac{185 \cancel{mm}}{} \left| \frac{1 \text{ kPa}}{7.50 \cancel{mm}} \right. = 24.7 \text{ kPa}$$

Now we can add the two pressures.

$$\text{pressure of } O_2 = 98.95 + 24.7 = 124 \text{ kPa}$$

Example 2

Suppose the difference in height of the two mercury levels in the closed manometer in Figure 15-1a is 58.5 mm. What is the pressure in kilopascals of the gas in the container?

Solving Process:

Since the column of mercury is 185 mm high and 7.50 mm of mercury equals 1 kPa, the pressure is

$$\text{pressure of gas} = \frac{58.5 \cancel{mm}}{} \left| \frac{1 \text{ kPa}}{7.50 \cancel{mm}} \right. = 7.80 \text{ kPa}$$

PROBLEMS

1. A closed manometer is filled with mercury and connected to a container of sulfur dioxide gas. The difference in the height of mercury in the two arms is 560 mm. What is the pressure of the SO_2 in kilopascals?

2. An open manometer is filled with mercury and connected to a container of hydrogen. The mercury level is 78.0 mm higher in the arm of the tube connected to the air. Air pressure is 100.7 kPa. What is the pressure of the hydrogen in kilopascals?

3. An open manometer is filled with mercury and connected to a container of nitrogen. The level of mercury is 26.0 mm higher in the arm of the tube connected to the container of nitrogen. Air pressure is 99.6 kPa. What is the pressure, in kilopascals, of the nitrogen?

4. A closed manometer is filled with mercury and connected to a container of argon gas. The difference in height of mercury in the two arms is 116.0 mm. What is the pressure, in kilopascals, of the argon?

15:2   TEMPERATURE

Kinetic energy is the energy of motion. A measure of that kinetic energy is **temperature.** The average kinetic energy of molecules or atoms in a gas is the same for all samples at a particular temperature. The temperature and mass of gas particles determines their average speed. At a given temperature, a particle with large mass will move more slowly than a particle with small mass.

Particle speed is directly related to changes in temperature. Since molecular motion of a gas decreases as the temperature decreases, it should be possible theoretically to lower the temperature to a point where all molecular motion ceases. This temperature, known as **absolute zero,** is −273.15°C.

Scientists have made a temperature scale based on absolute zero. It is known as the absolute, or **kelvin scale.** The kelvin (K) is the SI unit of temperature. The zero point of the kelvin scale is absolute zero. The divisions, or degrees, are the same size as those of the Celsius scale. Thus,

$$K = {}^\circ C + 273$$

PROBLEMS

5. Convert the following temperatures from Celsius to kelvin.
   a. 29°   b. −56°   c. 344°   d. −38°   e. 100°   f. 25°
6. Convert the following temperatures from kelvin to Celsius.
   a. 168   b. 255   c. 546   d. 300   e. 53   f. 273

CHAPTER REVIEW PROBLEMS

1. What is an instrument called that is used to measure gas pressure?
2. Which theory explains the effect of temperature and pressure on matter?
3. What name is used to describe a closed manometer that directly measures the absolute pressure of the atmosphere?
4. Theoretically, all molecular motion ceases at what temperature?
5. What is the standard pressure in kPa of air at sea level under normal conditions?
6. What is caused by the force and number of collisions that gas molecules have with the container's walls?
7. At the same temperature, which molecule will move faster, the lighter or heavier one?
8. An open manometer is filled with mercury and connected to a container of neon gas. The mercury level is 42.8 mm higher in the open arm. The barometric pressure is exactly 101.325 kPa. What is the pressure, in kilopascals, of the neon?

9. How does the amount of energy required to change the temperature 1 C° compare to that of one kelvin degree?

10. An open manometer is filled with mercury. The difference in the mercury level in the arms is 81.2 mm. The mercury level is higher in the gas sample arm. What is the pressure, in kilopascals, of the gas in the container if the air pressure is 95.6 kilopascals?

11. In a closed manometer assume that the height of the levels differs by 362 mm Hg. What is the pressure in kPa of the gas in the container?

12. Convert the following temperatures from one temperature scale to another as indicated.

   a. 516 K to °C   **c.** 26°C to K   **e.** 421°C to K
   b. 155°C to K   **d.** 14 K to °C   **f.** 373 K to °C

13. Suppose you have two vials at the same temperature, one containing sulfur dioxide, SO_2, and the other containing chlorine, Cl_2. When they are opened across the room from you, which would you expect to smell first?

SOLIDS 16

16:1 UNIT CELLS

The chemist classifies solids as either crystalline or amorphous. **Crystals** are rigid bodies that have flat faces meeting at definite angles and having sharp melting points. When a crystal is cut, it is said to cleave. The two resulting pieces will have the same flat faces and definite angles. **Amorphous solids** such as glass or paraffin do not have definite shapes. They soften and then melt over a wide temperature range. When a glass breaks, it is said to fracture, which results in curved or irregular surfaces.

The **unit cell** is the simplest repeating unit in a crystal. The space lattice is formed by stacking identical unit cells together to form one of seven crystal systems. These crystal systems are described in Table 16-1.

Different unit cells can form the same crystal shape. In Figure 16-1 we observe that the cubic crystal can be formed from simple cubic, face-centered cubic, or body centered cubic unit cells.

FIGURE 16-1.

Face-centered cubic

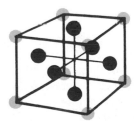

Cubic

Body-centered cubic

Table 16-1

	Lengths of the Unit Cell Axes	Angles Between the Unit Cell Axes	Crystal System
Seven Crystal Systems			
	all equal	all = 90°	cubic
	2 equal 1 unequal	all = 90°	tetragonal
	3 equal 1 unequal	1 = 90° 3 = 60°	hexagonal
	all equal	all ≠ 90°	rhombo-hedral
	all unequal	all = 90°	ortho-rhombic
	all unequal	2 = 90° 1 ≠ 90°	monoclinic
	all unequal	all ≠ 90°	triclinic

Most metals exhibit one of three types of crystal structure. Two of these arrangements are called closest packing structures. In hexagonal closest packing (HCP) and cubic closest packing (CCP or face-centered cubic), each metal atom has twelve neighboring atoms. The number of neighboring atoms or ions is called the coordination number. The atoms in HCP and CCP structures occupy 74% of the volume of the crystal. By comparison, simple cubic structures have coordination numbers of six with the atoms occupying 52% of the crystal volume.

The Group IA (1) as well as some other metals crystallize in the body-centered cubic (BCC) structure. For BCC structures the coordination number is eight and 68% of the volume is occupied by the atoms.

Some metals can be heat treated, or tempered, because the atoms change their packing as the temperature rises. In general, the trend is toward the HCP arrangement. A **polymorphous** substance has two or more crystal structures.

We must not assume that crystals have perfect order. There are defects in real crystals. Particles can be missing from their proper position; planes of particles can be misaligned. These defects are called dislocations. Sometimes a crystal is manufactured with a deliberate defect. For example, perfect crystals are "doped" to make semiconductors (transistors).

16:2 HYDRATES

A number of compounds called **hydrates** attract and hold water molecules in their crystal structure. The water is called **water of hydration** and may be removed by heating. The solid residue remaining after the water is removed is called the anhydrous material. **Anhydrous** means "without water."

In the formula of a hydrated compound, the number of water molecules involved is indicated by placing a raised dot after the anhydrous formula and writing the water formula with a coefficient if necessary. For example, $CuSO_4 \cdot 5H_2O$ is copper(II) sulfate pentahydrate. *Hydrate* means "water" and the Greek prefix *penta-* indicates the number of water molecules per formula unit of compound. For example:

Na_2CO_3	sodium carbonate
$Na_2CO_3 \cdot H_2O$	sodium carbonate monohydrate
$Na_2CO_3 \cdot 7H_2O$	sodium carbonate heptahydrate
$Na_2CO_3 \cdot 10H_2O$	sodium carbonate decahydrate

The ions of some anhydrous substances have such a strong attraction for water molecules that the dehydrated crystal will recapture and hold water molecules from the air. Such a substance is called a hygroscopic (hi gruh SKAHP ihk) substance. Some substances are so **hygroscopic** that they take up enough water from the air to dissolve and form a liquid solution. These substances are said to be **deliquescent** (del ih KWES uhnt). The opposite process can also occur. Water of hydration may be spontaneously released to the air. A substance that releases water molecules to the air from the crystal is said to be **efflorescent** (ef luh RES uhnt).

PROBLEMS

1. Name each of the following compounds.
   a. $MgCO_3$
   b. $MgCO_3 \cdot 3H_2O$
   c. $MgCO_3 \cdot 5H_2O$
   d. $Nd(CH_3COO)_3 \cdot H_2O$
   e. $Ni(CN)_2 \cdot 4H_2O$
   f. $Pr_2(CO_3)_3 \cdot 8H_2O$

2. Write formulas for each of the following compounds.
   a. calcium oxalate monohydrate
   b. cerium(III) bromate nonahydrate
   c. hydrogen bromide hexahydrate
   d. iron(II) oxalate dihydrate
   e. iron(III) oxalate pentahydrate
   f. lithium iodide trihydrate

CHAPTER REVIEW PROBLEMS

1. How is a crystal defined?

2. What is the simplest repeating unit in a crystal's geometric arrangement called?

3. What is the three-dimensional arrangement of unit cells repeated over and over in a definite arrangement called?

4. Each atom in a hexagonal closest packing arrangement is surrounded and touched by how many other atoms?

5. Almost all metals are packed into one of three kinds of unit cells. List the three most common unit cells for metals.

6. Do all natural crystals have perfect structures?

7. What term is used to describe the process of adding some impurities to crystals deliberately?

8. What term is used to describe a single substance that has two or more crystalline shapes?

9. Water molecules may be incorporated into the crystal structure. What do we call these crystals?

10. What is a substance called after the water of hydration has been removed?

11. Some crystals will recapture and hold water molecules from the air. What is such a substance called?

12. Some substances will absorb enough water from the air to dissolve and form a solution. What term is applied to these substances?

13. What term is used to describe a substance that releases water molecules to the air from the crystal?

14. How are the particles arranged in an amorphous solid?

15. What common substance is an excellent example of an amorphous material?

16. Name the following compounds.
    a. $NiCl_2 \cdot 6H_2O$
    b. $Mg(ClO_4)_2 \cdot 6H_2O$
    c. $Mg_3(PO_4)_2 \cdot 4H_2O$
    d. $Ca(NO_3)_2 \cdot 3H_2O$

17. Write the formula for the following hydrates.
    a. cobalt(II) chloride hexahydrate
    b. barium hydroxide octahydrate
    c. gallium(III) oxide monohydrate
    d. magnesium hydrogen arsenate heptahydrate

LIQUIDS 17

17:1 PHASE DIAGRAMS

The solid, liquid, and gas phases of a substance exist at different temperatures and pressures. The **phase diagram** is a convenient way to represent graphically the conditions at which a particular phase is stable.

Figure 17-1 is a phase diagram for CO_2, carbon dioxide. There are three lines that divide the diagram into solid, liquid, and gas regions. Each point on a line represents a temperature and pressure at which the two phases are in equilibrium. The normal boiling point and normal melting point occur where the equilibrium line is cut by the standard atmospheric pressure line 101.325 kPa. The **triple point** indicates the temperature and pressure at which all three phases are in equilibrium.

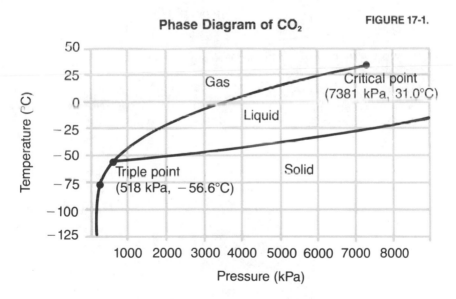

Phase Diagram of CO₂   FIGURE 17-1.

In a closed system, liquid and gaseous carbon dioxide can be in equilibrium. Above the critical temperature there is only one phase, gaseous carbon dioxide. The **critical temperature,** T_c, is the temperature above which no amount of pressure will liquefy the gas. At the critical temperature the minimum pressure necessary to liquefy the gas is called the **critical pressure,** P_c. A high critical temperature indicates that the attractive force between the particles is strong. Methyl chloride, CH_3Cl, has a $T_c = 144°C$

105

and P_c = 6685 kPa. It can be liquified by increasing the pressure. By compressing the gas the molecules come close enough that van der Waals forces can hold them together.

FIGURE 17-2.

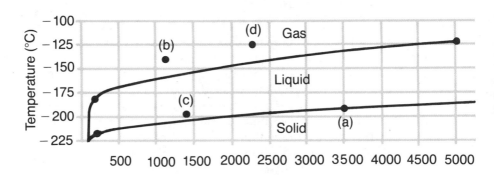

Phase Diagram for O₂

PROBLEMS

1. Using Figure 17-2, determine the following for oxygen.
   a. critical temperature   c. normal melting point
   b. critical pressure   d. normal boiling point
2. Using Figure 17-1, determine the state of matter that exists for CO_2 under the following conditions.
   a. 4000 kPa and −100°C   c. 3000 kPa and −25°C
   b. 1000 kPa and 10°C   d. 101.3 kPa and 0°C
3. What transition would occur at the labeled points on Figure 17-2 when the following changes occur?
   a. at point A if temperature increased
   b. at point B if temperature decreased
   c. at point C if pressure increased
   d. at point D if pressure decreased

17:2 ENERGY AND CHANGE OF STATE

When a substance is heated, the energy of its particles is increased. If the kinetic energy is increased, the result is an increase in the temperature of the substance. If the increase is in potential energy, the physical state of the substance will change. The change, or combination of changes, that will take place depends upon the starting temperature of the substance. Similar considerations can be applied to removing energy from (cooling) a substance.

The changes of state from solid to liquid and liquid to solid take place at the same temperature, which is labeled the **melting point** or **freezing point.** The changes from liquid to gas and gas to liquid take place at the same temperature, which is labeled the **boiling point** or **condensing point.** The amount of energy required for a state change depends on the nature and amount of a substance. If we use q to represent the quantity of energy needed to melt a substance, then

$$q = m(\Delta H_{fus})$$

where m is the mass of the substance and H_{fus} is a property of a substance called **enthalpy of fusion.** Similarly, to boil a substance, the relationship is

$$q = m(\Delta H_{vap})$$

where H_{vap} is a property of a substance called its **enthalpy of vaporization.** Table 17-1 lists the enthalpies of fusion and vaporization for several substances.

Table 17-1

Molar Enthalpies of Fusion and Vaporization for Some Substances (in kJ/mol)			
Fusion(H_{fus})		**Vaporization (H_{vap})**	
aluminum	10.71	aluminum	290.8
arsenic	27.7	benzene	30.8
gold	12.4	gold	324.4
indium	3.26	helium	0.084
iron	13.8	iron	350
steel	13.8	selenium	26.3
titanium	14.146	sodium	97.4
water	6.012	water	40.7

Example 1

How much energy is required to melt 86.3 g of iron at its melting point?

Solving Process:

The energy required for this phase change depends upon the mass, 86.3 g, and enthalpy of fusion, 13.8 kJ/mol. To make use of the H_{fus} value, the quantity of iron must be in units of moles. Thus, the solution is

$$q = mass \times enthalpy\ of\ fusion \times mole\ conversion$$

$$= \frac{86.3\ g\ Fe}{} \left| \frac{13.8\ kJ}{1\ mol\ Fe} \right| \frac{1\ mol\ Fe}{55.8\ g\ Fe} = 21.3\ kJ$$

The amount of energy required to change the temperature of a substance depends upon the amount and nature of the substance as well as the extent of the temperature change. The energy required is calculated by

$$q = m(\Delta T)C_p$$

where q is the energy added (or removed), m is the mass of the substance, ΔT is the change in temperature, and C_p is a property of the substance called its **specific heat.** Review Section 3:5 for an example problem.

You may be asked to do calculations that involve both temperature and state changes. For such problems, each step involving a temperature or state change is solved separately. The sum of the energy changes for all the steps is the solution to the problem. For example, suppose you are asked to start with a solid substance below its melting point and determine the energy required to change that substance to a gas above its boiling point. The following steps must be taken.

- **a.** heat the solid to its melting point
- **b.** melt the solid
- **c.** heat the liquid to its boiling point
- **d.** boil the liquid
- **e.** heat the gas to the required temperature

Example 2

How much energy is released when 42.5 g of aluminum vapor are cooled from 4750°C to 25.0°C?

freezing point = 660.0°C   boiling point = 2467°C
    H_{vap} = 291 kJ/mol H_{fus} = 10.7 kJ/mol
    $C_p(g)$ = 1.05 J/g·C° $C_p(l)$ = 0.869 J/g·C°
    $C_p(cr)$ = 0.903 J/g·C°

Solving Process:

It is often helpful in problems of this type to draw a graph to indicate the steps in changing the vapor to solid.

FIGURE 17-3.

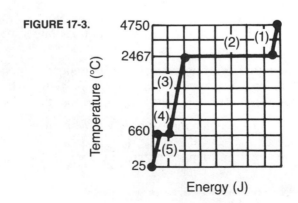

Step 1: Calculate the energy released as the Al gas is cooled to the condensing point, 2467°C. Convert joules to kilojoules so the units in each step will be the same.

$$q = m(\Delta T)C_p$$

$$= \frac{42.5\,g \mid 2283\,°C \mid 1.05\,J \mid 1\text{ kJ}}{g·°C \mid 1000\,J} = 102\text{ kJ}$$

Step 2: Calculate the energy released as the Al gas is condensed. You must convert grams of Al to moles because H_{vap} is given in kJ/mol.

$$q = mass \times mole\ conversion \times enthalpy\ of\ vaporization$$

$$= \frac{42.5\,g \mid 1\text{ mol} \mid 291\text{ kJ}}{27.0\,g \mid 1\text{ mol}} = 458\text{ kJ}$$

Step 3: Calculate the energy released as the liquid Al is cooled to the freezing point, 660.0°C.

$$q = \frac{42.5\,g \mid 1807\,°C \mid 0.869\,J \mid 1\text{ kJ}}{g·°C \mid 1000\,J} = 66.7\text{ kJ}$$

Step 4: Calculate the energy released as the liquid Al is frozen.

$$q = mass \times mole\ conversion \times enthalpy\ of\ vaporization$$

$$= \frac{42.5\,g \mid 1\text{ mol} \mid 10.7\text{ kJ}}{27.0\,g \mid 1\text{ mol}} = 16.9\text{ kJ}$$

Step 5: Calculate the energy released as the solid Al is cooled to 25.0°C.

$$q = \frac{42.5\,g \mid 635\,°C \mid 0.903\,J \mid 1\text{ kJ}}{g·°C \mid 1000\,J} = 24.4\text{ kJ}$$

The total energy released is the sum of all five steps.

$$102\text{ kJ} + 458\text{ kJ} + 66.7\text{ kJ} + 16.9\text{ kJ} + 24.4\text{ kJ} = 668\text{ kJ}$$

PROBLEMS

4. Compute the energy changes associated with the following transitions.
   a. melting 55.8 g Ti at 1666°C
   b. condensing 14.2 g H_2O at 100.0°C
   c. boiling 53.5 g C_6H_6, benzene, at 80.1°C
   d. freezing 27.3 g Al at 660°C
   e. melting 76.4 g Au at 1064°C

5. Compute the energy changes associated with the following transitions.
   a. heating 49.2 g acetic acid, CH_3COOH, from 24.1°C to 67.3°C
   b. heating 9.61 g toluene, $C_6H_5CH_3$, from 19.6°C to 75.0°C
   c. heating 2.47 g kerosene from 17.1°C to 46.7°C
   d. cooling 31.9 g chalk from 83.2°C to 55.5°C
   e. cooling 63.6 g glass from 95.5°C to 42.3°C

CHAPTER REVIEW PROBLEMS

1. In a closed, insulated system, ice is floating in water. The temperature is 0°C. Will all of the water freeze?

2. Water is boiling at 100°C. The hot plate's surface temperature is increased. Will the water now boil at a higher temperature?

3. Will a gas liquefy above the critical temperature when the pressure increases a large amount?

4. Are the vapor pressure of the liquid phase and the vapor pressure of the gas phase equal at the boiling point?

5. Are the attractive forces between the particles strong or weak when the vapor pressure of a substance is high?

6. Gas can be liquified when what temperature and pressure changes occur?

7. Using the phase diagram for compound x, Figure 17-4, answer the following questions.

   a. At what temperature does the vapor pressure of the solid equal atmospheric pressure?
   b. What is the temperature of the triple point?
   c. What is the critical temperature?
   d. What is the critical pressure?
   e. At what labeled point does boiling occur?
   f. At what point do solid and liquid phases exist in equilibrium?

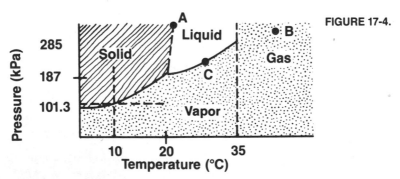

FIGURE 17-4.

Use Tables 17-1 and A-8 to answer the following questions.

8. How much energy is required to raise the temperature of 91.4 g solid steel from 25.0°C to 76.1°C?

9. How much energy is required to raise the temperature of 4.66 g kerosene from 10.9°C to 26.8°C?

10. How much energy is required to raise the temperature of 175 g H_2O from −11.0°C to 140.0°C?

11. If 100.0 g of pure water at 27°C are placed into an insulated flask, how many grams of ice at 0.0°C must be added to lower the temperature of the water to 5.0°C? (recall: energy lost = energy gained)

GASES 18

Air in a tire exerts pressure. A partially filled balloon will expand if it is placed over a hot radiator. In marked contrast to solids and liquids, gas volumes change noticeably with small changes in pressure and temperature. These changes were studied by experimenting with real gases and the relations obtained were reduced to equations that defined the behavior of gases. These equations, known as the gas laws, are valid only for an ideal gas. An **ideal gas** is one composed of particles with no attractive forces and no volume. Although ideal gases do not actually exist, they give good approximations in most situations for real gases.

18:1 BOYLE'S LAW

What is pressure? As gas molecules hit the walls of a container, the particles exert a force on the container. The number of collisions and the force of the collisions cause gas pressure. The standard unit for pressure is the pascal, which represents force per unit area. One pascal (Pa) is the pressure of one newton per square meter (N/m^2). Air pressure at sea level has been used as a scientific standard of pressure. However, this pressure changes with changing weather conditions. Normal air pressure at sea level is 101 325 Pa or 101.325 kilopascals (kPa).

A **barometer** is used to measure atmospheric pressure. Most barometers are calibrated in millimeters of mercury (mm Hg). For converting units, 101.325 kPa = 760 mm or 1 kPa = 7.50 mm Hg.

If the pressure on an ideal gas in a confined container is increased, the volume decreases. When the pressure is doubled, the new gas volume is half the original gas volume. If the pressure is decreased to half the original pressure, the new volume is double the old volume. Robert Boyle found that gas volume and pressure vary inversely. **Boyle's law** is *the volume of an enclosed gas varies inversely as the pressure, if the temperature remains constant.*

Our primary interest in solving Boyle's law problems is to find a new volume when the original volume and the change in pressure are known. The change in pressure can be represented by a pressure ratio. The new volume of a gas after a change in pressure at a constant temperature is calculated by

$$V_2 = V_1 \frac{P_1}{P_2}$$

where V_1 is the initial volume and P_1 is the initial pressure. The given values can be substituted into the equation or the changes in the gas volume can be visualized using Boyle's law.

The preferred volume unit is cubic meters (m^3). However, cubic decimeters (dm^3) and cubic centimeters (cm^3) are also used.

Mentally determine whether the new volume will be larger or smaller than the old volume and arrange the pressure ratio accordingly. If the new volume will be larger, multiply by a ratio that is greater than 1; if smaller, multiply by a ratio less than 1. The following points should be considered when solving Boyle's law problems.

1. A pressure increase decreases the volume, which means the pressure ratio should be less than 1.

2. A pressure decrease increases the volume, which means the pressure ratio should be greater than 1.

3. To calculate a new pressure when the old pressure and the volume change are known, use the relationship:

new pressure = old pressure × volume ratio

4. The volume and pressure vary inversely.

Example 1

If 425 cm^3 of oxygen are collected at a pressure of 9.80 kPa what volume will the gas occupy if the pressure is changed to 9.40 kPa?

Solving Process:

The pressure decreases from 9.80 to 9.40 kPa. The volume should increase according to Boyle's law. To have a volume increase, the pressure ratio must be greater than 1. The pressure ratio is

$$\frac{9.80 \text{ kPa}}{9.40 \text{ kPa}}$$

In calculations, use the relationship:

new volume = old volume × pressure ratio

$$= \frac{425 \text{ cm}^3}{} \left| \frac{9.80 \text{ kPa}}{9.40 \text{ kPa}} = 443 \text{ cm}^3 \right.$$

Example 2

Calculate the pressure of a gas that occupies a volume of 125 cm^3, if at a pressure of 95.0 kPa, it occupies a volume of 219 cm^3.

Solving Process:

The volume decreases from 219 cm^3 to 125 cm^3. The pressure must increase, so the volume ratio must be greater than 1, or

$$\frac{219 \text{ cm}^3}{125 \text{ cm}^3}$$

new pressure = old pressure × volume ratio

$$= \frac{95.0 \text{ kPa}}{} \left| \frac{219 \text{ cm}^3}{125 \text{ cm}^3} = 166 \text{ kPa} \right.$$

PROBLEMS

1. Correct the following gas volumes from the initial conditions to the new conditions (assume the temperature remains constant).
   a. 100.0 cm^3 oxygen at 10.50 kPa to 9.91 kPa
   b. 50.0 cm^3 hydrogen at 97.3 kPa to 101 000 Pa
   c. 500.0 cm^3 sulfur dioxide at 95.6 kPa to 101.3 kPa
   d. 150.0 cm^3 nitrogen at 101.30 kPa to 120.0 kPa
   e. 2.00 m^3 nitrogen at 158.0 kPa to 109.0 kPa
   f. 1.50 dm^3 neon at 98.2 kPa to 150 kPa

2. A flask containing 90.0 cm^3 of hydrogen was collected under a pressure of 97.5 kilopascals. At what pressure would the volume be 70.0 cm^3, assuming the temperature is kept constant?

3. A gas has a volume of 275 cm^3 when measured at a pressure of 9.80 × 10^4 Pa. If the temperature is not changed, what would the gas volume be at standard pressure?

4. A gas has a volume of 50.0 m^3 at standard pressure. Assuming no temperature change, what volume will the gas occupy
   a. if the pressure is doubled?
   b. if the pressure is tripled?
   c. if the original pressure is cut in half?

5. What is the volume occupied by 10.0 dm^3 of gas at standard pressure after it has been compressed at constant temperature to 500.0 kPa?

6. A gas is confined in a cylinder with a movable piston at one end. When the volume of the cylinder is 760.0 cm^3 the pressure of the gas is 125.0 kPa. When the cylinder volume is reduced to 450.0 cm^3, what is the pressure?

18:2   DALTON'S LAW OF PARTIAL PRESSURE

If a mixture consists of two or more gases, each gas exerts a partial pressure independently of the other gases present. The partial pressure of a gas in a mixture is the pressure that the gas would exert if it were the only gas in the container. The total pressure is equal to the sum of the individual gas pressures. **Dalton's law of partial pressure** can be stated as *the sum of the partial pressures of a mixture of gases is the total pressure exerted by the enclosed gases.*

In the chemistry laboratory, gases (such as oxygen, nitrogen, and hydrogen) bubble through water as they are collected. As a result, water vapor molecules exert a pressure along with the collected gas. The pressure of the dry gas can be found only by deducting the pressure due to water molecules. Vapor pressure depends upon the temperature. The warmer the gas, the greater the pressure of the water vapor. Table A-14 lists the vapor pressure of water at varying temperatures.

Example 3

A quantity of gas is collected over water at 10.0°C in a 125 cm³ vessel. The manometer indicates a pressure of 98.0 kPa. What volume would the dry gas occupy at standard pressure and 10.0°C?

Solving Process:

We must determine what part of the total pressure is due to water vapor. Table A-14 indicates that at 10.0°C, water has a vapor pressure of 1.2 kPa. To find the pressure of the collected gas:

$$P_{gas} = P_{total} - P_{water}$$

$$= 98.0 \text{ kPa} - 1.2 \text{ kPa}$$

$$= 96.8 \text{ kPa}$$

Since this pressure is less than standard, the gas would have to be compressed to change it to standard. The pressure ratio by which the volume is to be multiplied must be less than 1.

$$\text{new volume} = \frac{125 \text{ cm}^3}{} \left| \frac{96.8 \text{ kPa}}{101.3 \text{ kPa}} \right. = 119 \text{ cm}^3$$

PROBLEMS

7. Determine the partial pressure of oxygen collected over water if the temperature is 28°C and the total gas pressure is 98.74 kPa.

8. The partial pressure of helium is 13.5 kPa in a mixture of helium, oxygen, and methane gases. If the total pressure is 96.4 kPa and the partial pressure of oxygen is 29.3 kPa, what is the partial pressure of the methane gas?

9. A 79.9 cm³ sample of oxygen is collected by water displacement at 24°C. What volume would the gas occupy at standard pressure if the gas is collected originally at a pressure of 98.5 kPa?

10. In a series of laboratory experiments, different gases were collected over water at the indicated water temperature and pressure. Correct each volume to the volume the dry gas would occupy at standard pressure. The temperature is constant.

    a. 52.0 cm³ gas at 18°C and 94.5 kPa
    b. 75.0 cm³ gas at 23°C and 97.2 kPa
    c. 135 cm³ gas at 21°C and 98.4 kPa
    d. 225 cm³ gas at 27°C and 102.5 kPa

18:3   KELVIN TEMPERATURE

All gases (in contrast to solids and liquids) expand and contract at approximately the same rate. When a gas is heated, it expands by 1/273 of its volume at 0° Celsius for each temperature increase of one Celsius degree. When a gas is cooled, it contracts 1/273 of its volume at 0° Celsius for each Celsius degree the temperature is lowered.

No gas has ever been cooled to −273°C. All gases liquefy or solidify at temperatures higher than −273°C. The temperature −273°C is called absolute zero. It is written zero kelvin or 0 K. To convert from °C to K, add 273 to the Celsius temperature.

$$K = 273 + C°$$

Scientists have chosen 273 K (0°C) as a standard temperature for working with gases.

18:4 CHARLES'S LAW

If the temperature of an ideal gas increases, the volume increases, when the pressure remains constant. If the temperature of a gas decreases, the volume decreases. **Charles's law** can be stated as *the volume of a quantity of gas varies directly as the kelvin temperature, if the pressure remains constant.* Note that temperature must be expressed in kelvin.

It is possible to predict the new volume of a gas when the old volume and the temperature change are known. The temperature change is expressed as an absolute temperature ratio. The equation used to calculate the new volume is

new volume = old volume × kelvin temperature ratio

$$V_2 = V_1 \frac{T_2}{T_1}$$

The subscripts represent the initial and final conditions, as in the Boyle's law relationship. The following points should be considered when solving Charles's law problems.

1. An absolute temperature increase gives a volume increase, which means an absolute temperature ratio greater than 1.

2. An absolute temperature decrease gives a volume decrease, which means an absolute temperature ratio less than 1.

3. The new temperature in kelvins can be calculated when the initial kelvin temperature and new and old volumes are known:

    new temperature (K) = old temperature (K) × volume ratio

4. The kelvin temperature varies directly as the volume.

Example 4

What volume will a sample of nitrogen occupy at 28.0°C if the gas occupies a volume of 457 cm^3 at a temperature of 0.0°C? Assume the pressure remains constant.

Solving Process:
Convert the temperatures from Celsius to kelvin.

$$K = 273 + °C$$

$$K = 273 + 28.0°C = 301 \text{ K} \quad \text{and} \quad K = 273 + 0.0°C = 273 \text{ K}$$

A kelvin temperature increase (from 273 K to 301 K) will cause a volume increase. The kelvin temperature ratio must be greater than 1.

$$\frac{301 \text{ K}}{273 \text{ K}}$$

new volume = old volume × kelvin temperature ratio

$$= \frac{457 \text{ cm}^3}{} \left| \frac{301 \text{ K}}{273 \text{ K}} \right. = 504 \text{ cm}^3$$

Example 5

If a gas occupies a volume of 733 cm³ at 10.0°C, at what temperature, in °C, will it occupy a volume of 1225 cm³ if the pressure remains constant?

Solving Process:
An increase in volume (from 733 cm³ to 1225 cm³) indicates a temperature increase. The volume ratio must be greater than 1.

$$\frac{1225 \text{ cm}^3}{733 \text{ cm}^3}$$

$$T_2 = \frac{T_1}{} \left| \frac{V_2}{V_1} \right.$$

$$= \frac{283 \text{ K}}{} \left| \frac{1225 \text{ cm}^3}{733 \text{ cm}^3} \right. = 473 \text{ K}$$

Convert 473 K to °C.

$$°C = 473 \text{ K} - 273 = 200°C$$

PROBLEMS

11. A gas has a volume of 10.0 m³ at standard temperature. Assuming no pressure change, what volume will the gas occupy

    a. if the kelvin temperature is doubled?

    b. if the original kelvin temperature is halved?

12. Correct the following gas volumes from the initial conditions to the new conditions (assume that the pressure remains constant).

    a. 250.0 cm³ chlorine at 10.0°C to 60.0°C

    b. 75.0 cm³ hydrogen at 20.0°C to −10.0°C

    c. 100.0 cm³ oxygen at 27.0°C to standard temperature

    d. 300.0 cm³ nitrogen at 15.0°C to 38.0°C

    e. 2.30 dm³ nitrogen dioxide at standard temperature to 40.0°C

    f. 35.0 cm³ helium at 285 K to 92 K

13. A gas occupies a volume of 560 cm³ at a temperature of 120°C. To what temperature must the gas be lowered, if it is to occupy 400.0 cm³? Assume a constant pressure.

18:5   COMBINED GAS LAW

Boyle's and Charles's laws can be used together to form a combined gas law. This law can be used in a situation where both a pressure and a temperature change occur. A pressure ratio and a kelvin temperature ratio are needed to calculate the new volume.

new volume = old volume × pressure ratio × kelvin temperature ratio

Each ratio is considered independently in setting up the expression. You will want to construct a pressure-volume-temperature data table.

Value	Old conditions	New conditions	What happens to the gas volume?
Pressure			
Volume			
Temperature			

"What happens to the gas volume?" is answered with the word "decrease" or "increase," depending upon whether the pressure or temperature ratio is larger or smaller than 1.

The initials STP are often used in gas law problems. **STP** means standard temperature and pressure. The **standard pressure** for measuring gases is 101 325 Pa (101.325 kPa). For convenience in solving problems 101.3 kPa is used. **Standard temperature** is 0°C or 273 K. All temperature ratios must be expressed in kelvin.

Example 6

Calculate the volume of a gas at STP if 502 cm³ of the gas are collected at 29.7°C and 96.0 kPa.

Solving Process:

Organize the data given as shown and convert the Celsius temperatures to kelvins.

Value	Old conditions	New conditions	What happens to the gas volume?
P	96.0 kPa	101.3 kPa	decreases
V	502 cm³	?	?
T	302.7 K	273.2 K	decreases

new volume = old volume × pressure ratio × kelvin temperature ratio

$$= \frac{502 \text{ cm}^3}{1} \left| \frac{96.0 \text{ kPa}}{101.3 \text{ kPa}} \right| \frac{273.2 \text{ K}}{302.7 \text{ K}} = 429 \text{ cm}^3$$

Example 7

If 400.0 cm³ of oxygen are collected over water at 20.0°C, and the atmospheric pressure is 97.0 kPa, what is the volume of the dry oxygen at STP?

Solving Process:

Organize the data. Convert C° to K and correct the total pressure for water vapor pressure.

Note that the gas is not actually wet when it is collected over water. When a gas is collected over water, some of the water molecules inevitably escape from the liquid surface and form water vapor. The collected gas, therefore, contains both gas and water molecules. To find the pressure due to gas molecules, you must account for and deduct the pressure due to water vapor molecules.

Value	Old conditions	New conditions	What happens to the gas volume?
P	97.0 − 2.3 = 94.7 kPa	101.3 kPa	decreases
V	400.0 cm³	?	?
T	293 K	273 K	decreases

new volume = old volume × pressure ratio × kelvin temperature ratio

$$= \frac{400.0 \text{ cm}^3}{1} \left| \frac{94.7 \text{ kPa}}{101.3 \text{ kPa}} \right| \frac{273 \text{ K}}{293 \text{ K}} = 348 \text{ cm}^3$$

PROBLEMS

14. Convert the following gas volumes to the new conditions using the combined gas law.
    a. $5.00 × 10^2$ cm³ hydrogen at 20.0°C and 120 kPa to STP
    b. $2.50 × 10^2$ cm³ oxygen at 27°C and 95.0 kPa to STP
    c. $1.00 × 10^2$ cm³ chlorine at STP to 20.0°C and 98.0 kPa
    d. 140 cm³ hydrogen at 15°C and 110.0 kPa to 40.0°C and 94.5 kPa

15. The following gases are collected over water at the given conditions. Calculate the volume occupied by the dry gas at standard conditions.
    a. $2.00 × 10^2$ cm³ oxygen at 15°C and 94 000 Pa
    b. 125 cm³ hydrogen at 20.0°C and 97 500 Pa
    c. 50.0 cm³ nitrogen at 28°C and 99 500 Pa
    d. 325 cm³ oxygen at 25°C and 98.6 kPa

16. A gas occupied 550.0 cm^3 at a pressure of 9.95 × 10^4 Pa and a temperature of 21°C. Several days later it was measured at a pressure of 9.78 × 10^4 Pa and temperature of 15°C. What volume did the gas occupy under these new conditions?

17. A 47.0 cm^3 volume of nitrogen gas is collected over water at a water temperature of 18°C and a pressure of 98.5 kPa. What volume will the gas occupy at standard conditions?

18. An automobile tire has a pressure of 210.0 kPa at 20.0°C. What will be the tire pressure after driving, if the tire temperature rises to 35.0°C?

19. The respiratory rate for a person is about 15 breaths per minute. Assume that each average breath is about 510 cm^3 of air at 20.0°C and 99.5 kPa. What volume of air in cubic meters, corrected to standard conditions, does the individual breathe in one day?

18:6 GAS DENSITY

The volume of a gas changes with change in temperature or pressure. Specifically, if we increase the pressure on a gas we decrease the volume; thus, we would have a greater density. If we increase the temperature of a gas, the volume increases, and the density is lower. The density of a gas varies directly with the pressure and inversely with the temperature.

For convenience, gas density is usually expressed in grams per cubic decimeter. Using g/cm^3 would give very small numbers for gas densities. Remember that 1000 cm^3 equal 1 dm^3.

Example 8

If the density of oxygen is 1.43 g/dm^3 at standard pressure and temperature, what is the density of oxygen at 99.0 kPa and 27.0°C?

Solving Process:

The original density must be adjusted by a pressure ratio and a kelvin temperature ratio to the new conditions.

Value	Old conditions	New conditions	What happens to the density?
P ·	101.3 kPa	99.0 kPa	decreases
T	273 K	300.0 K	decreases
D	1.43 g/dm^3	?	?

The pressure decreases and the temperature increases. A temperature increase gives a density decrease. The pressure and temperature ratios are

$$\frac{99.0 \text{ kPa}}{101.3 \text{ kPa}} \qquad \frac{273 \text{ K}}{300.0 \text{ K}}$$

new density = old density × pressure ratio × temperature ratio

$$= \frac{1.43 \text{ g}}{\text{dm}^3} \left| \frac{99.0 \text{ kPa}}{101.3 \text{ kPa}} \right| \frac{273 \text{ K}}{300.0 \text{ K}} = 1.27 \text{ g/dm}^3$$

PROBLEMS

20. Sulfur dioxide has a density of 2.927 g/dm^3 at STP. What is its density at a pressure of 120.0 kPa and a temperature of 50.0°C?

21. A gas has a density of 3.472 g/dm^3 at STP. Determine its density at a pressure of 95.0 kPa and a temperature of 27.0°C.

22. A gas has a density of 2.851 g/dm^3 at STP. The pressure is dropped by 20.0 kPa in order to attempt to change the density to 2.000 g/dm^3. What must be the new temperature to achieve this lower density?

18:7 GAS DIFFUSION AND GRAHAM'S LAW

If a gas molecule having an odor is moving at 200 meters per second, why does it take several minutes before it is detected across the room? Although the molecules of a gas move in a straight line, they travel only a relatively short distance before colliding with another molecule. These collisions result in a time-consuming zig-zag path across the room. The dispersion of gases from an area of high concentration to an area of low concentration is called **diffusion.**

Effusion occurs when a gas passes through a small hole into a vacuum. In 1846 Thomas Graham discovered a relationship between molecular mass and effusion rate. **Graham's law** states that *the relative rate at which two gases at the same temperature and pressure will effuse varies inversely as the square root of the ratio of the molecular masses of the gases.*

Example 9

Calculate the ratio of rates of effusion of N$_2$ molecules to that of CO$_2$ molecules from the same container at the same temperature and pressure.

Solving Process:

The two rates of effusion vary inversely as the square root of the ratio of their molecular masses.

$$\frac{\text{rate N}_2}{\text{rate CO}_2} = \sqrt{\frac{\text{mass CO}_2}{\text{mass N}_2}}$$

The molecular mass of N$_2$ is 28.0 u. The molecular mass of CO$_2$ is 44.0 u. Substitute these masses into the equation.

$$\frac{\text{rate N}_2}{\text{rate CO}_2} = \sqrt{\frac{44.0}{28.0}} = \frac{1.25}{1}$$

The N$_2$ gas molecules effuse 1.25 times faster than the CO$_2$ molecules.

PROBLEMS

23. What is the ratio of the speed of hydrogen molecules to the speed of neon atoms when both gases are at the same temperature and pressure?

24. At a certain temperature, the velocity of chlorine molecules, Cl_2, is 0.0410 m/s. What is the velocity of sulfur dioxide molecules, SO_2, at the same temperature and pressure?

CHAPTER REVIEW PROBLEMS

1. Correct the following gas volumes from the initial conditions to the new conditions. Assume that the pressure or temperature is constant, if not given.

   a. 45.0 cm^3 at 49°C to −29°C
   b. 270.0 cm^3 at standard temperature to 25°C
   c. 75.0 cm^3 at standard pressure to 90.8 kPa
   d. 165 cm^3 at 75 000 Pa to 84 000 Pa
   e. 95.0 cm^3 at STP to 24°C and 91.5 kPa
   f. 1.50 dm^3 at STP to −15°C and 110.0 kPa
   g. 325 cm^3 at 30.0°C and 95.0 kPa to STP
   h. 240 cm^3 at 5°C and 92.0 kPa to 40.0°C and 105.0 kPa

2. Oxygen has a density of 1.429 g/dm^3 at STP. Which change will result in a greater change in density? What is the new density?

   a. decreasing the temperature from 0.0°C to −40.0°C
   b. increasing the pressure from 100.0 kPa to 114.5 kPa

3. What is the density of a gas at STP if its density is 1.75 g/dm^3 at 110.0 kPa and 45°C?

4. At STP, the density of a gas is 3.24 mg/cm^3. What is its density in g/dm^3 at 30.0°C and 95.0 kPa?

5. If the pressure on 100 cm^3 of a gas is doubled, what volume will the gas occupy, assuming no other changes?

6. The volume of a gas at a pressure of 90.0 kPa is doubled and the temperature remains constant. What is the final pressure exerted by the gas?

7. An unbreakable meteorological balloon is released from the ground. Ground level pressure is 98.5 kPa and the temperature is 18°C. The balloon contains 74.0 dm^3 of hydrogen gas. As the balloon ascends, the pressure drops to 7.0 kPa.

   a. What is the new volume of the balloon, assuming no temperature change?
   b. If a temperature drop of 79° occurs, what is the new volume of the balloon after the temperature change?
   c. Of the two factors, pressure and temperature, which had the greatest effect in changing the volume of the balloon?

8. If the temperature of a gas is 0°C and the temperature is changed so that the gas volume doubles, what is the new temperature of the gas?

9. A balloon will burst at a volume of 2.0 dm^3. If the gas in a partially filled balloon occupies 0.75 dm^3 at a temperature of 21°C and a pressure of 9.90 × 10^4 Pa, what is the temperature at which it will burst if the pressure is 1.01 × 10^5 Pa at the time it breaks?

10. What is the ratio of the speed of carbon monoxide, CO, molecules to that of nitrogen(II) oxide, NO, molecules when both gases are at the same temperature?

GASES AND THE MOLE 19

19:1 AVOGADRO'S PRINCIPLE AND MOLAR VOLUME

What is the relationship between the mass of a gas and its volume? **Avogadro's principle** states that *equal volumes of all gases, measured under the same conditions of pressure and temperature, contain the same number of particles*. It has been found experimentally that 1 mole of any gas at STP contains 6.02×10^{23} particles. This number of particles is called the **Avogadro constant**. One mole of any gas has a mass equal to its molecular mass. For example:

$$1 \text{ mole } N_2 = 28.0 \text{ g } N_2 = 6.02 \times 10^{23} \text{ molecules of } N_2$$
$$1 \text{ mole } CO_2 = 44.0 \text{ g } CO_2 = 6.02 \times 10^{23} \text{ molecules of } CO_2$$

The volume of one mole of a gas at STP is the molar volume of the gas. One mole of a gas at STP occupies 22.4 cubic decimeters (dm^3). This volume is the same for all gases at STP. The mass and volume of any gas are related as follows:

$$1 \text{ mole of any gas} = \text{molecular mass} = 22.4 \text{ dm}^3$$

Example 1

How many grams of carbon dioxide, CO_2, will occupy a volume of 500.0 cm^3 at STP?

Solving Process:

The conversion equalities are

$$1 \text{ mol } CO_2 = 22.4 \text{ dm}^3 \text{ CO}_2 \text{ (STP)}$$
$$1 \text{ mol } CO_2 = 44.0 \text{ g } CO_2$$

$$\text{grams CO}_2 = \frac{500.0 \text{ cm}^3 \text{ CO}_2}{} \left| \frac{1 \text{ dm}^3}{1000 \text{ cm}^3} \right| \frac{1 \text{ mol}}{22.4 \text{ dm}^3} \left| \frac{44.0 \text{ g CO}_2}{1 \text{ mol CO}_2} \right.$$

$$= 0.982 \text{ g}$$

PROBLEMS

Assume the volumes given are at STP unless other conditions are specified.

1. Calculate the number of moles contained in each of the following gas volumes.

   a. 5.00×10^4 cm^3 H$_2$ **d.** 15 000 cm^3 NH$_3$

   b. 1.000×10^3 cm^3 N$_2$ **e.** 2500 cm^3 O$_2$

   c. 6500 cm^3 SO$_2$ **f.** 2.000×10^3 cm^3 CO$_2$

2. Calculate the mass of each of the following volumes of gas.

   a. 20.0 m^3 CH$_4$ **d.** 0.300 m^3 N$_2$O

   b. 1500.0 cm^3 Cl$_2$ **e.** 3.0 m^3 N$_2$

   c. 70.0 cm^3 SO$_3$ **f.** 3500.0 cm^3 H$_2$S

3. Calculate the volume in dm^3 of each of the following.

   a. 4.0 mol Br$_2$ **e.** 2.50 mol NH$_3$

   b. 200.0 g H$_2$S   **f.** 50.0 g NO$_2$

   c. 25.5 g SO$_2$ **g.** 7.00 mol O$_2$

   d. 600.0 g Cl$_2$ **h.** 10.0 g HCl

19:2   IDEAL GAS EQUATION

The **ideal gas equation** combines the four physical variables (pressure, volume, temperature, and number of particles) for gases into one equation. Remember that an ideal gas is composed of point masses with no mutual attraction. All real gases deviate somewhat from the gas laws since the molecules of real gases occupy volume and attract one another.

The ideal gas equation is $PV = nRT$, where P is the pressure in kilopascals. V is the volume in cubic decimeters and T is the temperature in kelvin. The n represents the number of moles of a gas. With these units, the value of the constant R is 8.31 dm^3·kPa/mol·K. There are other values of R depending upon the units used to derive R.

We can use the ideal gas equation to determine the molecular mass (M) of a gas. The number of moles (n) of any species is equal to its mass (m) divided by the molecular mass (M). Thus, the ideal gas equation can also be written as

$$PV = nRT \quad \text{or} \quad PV = \frac{m}{M} RT \quad \text{or} \quad M = \frac{mRT}{PV}$$

Example 2

How many moles of gas will a 1250 cm^3 flask hold at 35.0°C and a pressure of 95.4 kPa?

Solving Process:

The ideal gas equation can be solved for the number of moles, *n*, of a substance.

$$PV = nRT \quad \text{or} \quad n = \frac{PV}{RT}$$

Before we can substitute the known values into the ideal gas equation, 35.0°C must be converted to 308.2 K. We get the following expression.

$$n = \frac{95.4 \text{ kPa}}{8.31 \frac{\text{dm}^3 \cdot \text{kPa}}{\text{mol} \cdot \text{K}}} \quad \frac{1250 \text{ cm}^3}{308.2 \text{ K}} \quad \frac{1 \text{ dm}^3}{1000 \text{ cm}^3} = 0.0466 \text{ mol}$$

$$\quad\quad\quad P \quad\quad\quad\quad V$$
$$\quad\quad\quad R \quad\quad\quad\quad T$$

The solution is 0.0466 mol. Note that all other units in the problem divide out.

Example 3

A flask has a volume of 258 cm³. A gas with mass 1.475 g is introduced into the flask at a temperature of 302.0 K and a pressure of 9.86×10^4 Pa. Calculate the molecular mass of the gas using the ideal gas equation.

Solving Process:

The number of moles, n, of a substance is equal to mass, m, divided by the molecular mass, M. Therefore, the ideal gas equation may be written

$$PV = \frac{mRT}{M}, \quad \text{or} \quad M = \frac{mRT}{PV}$$

$$M = \frac{1.475 \text{ g}}{9.86 \times 10^4 \text{ Pa}} \quad \frac{8.31 \text{ dm}^3 \cdot \text{kPa}}{\text{mol} \cdot \text{K}} \quad \frac{302.0 \text{ K}}{258 \text{ cm}^3} \quad \frac{1000 \text{ Pa}}{1 \text{ kPa}}$$

$$\frac{1000 \text{ cm}^3}{1 \text{ dm}^3} = 146 \text{ g/mol}$$

Remember that the units of volume, pressure, temperature, and quantity of gas must be consistent with the value of R.

PROBLEMS

4. What is the molecular mass of sulfur dioxide, SO_2, if 300.0 cm³ of the gas has a mass of 0.855 g at STP?

5. A sample of hydrogen iodide, HI, has a mass of 2.28 g and occupies 400.0 cm³ at STP. What is the molecular mass of this compound?

6. If 0.179 g of methane, CH_4, occupy 0.250 dm³, what is the molecular mass of methane if the volume is given at standard conditions?

7. From the volume, temperature, and pressure, calculate the number of moles for each gas listed using the ideal gas equation.
   a. 750.0 cm³ O_2 at 27°C and 99.0 kPa
   b. 3.00 dm³ CO_2 at −15°C and 103.0 kPa

8. Calculate the volume each gas will occupy under the conditions listed using the ideal gas equation.
   a. 3.00 mol H_2 at 24°C and 100.5 kPa
   b. 150.0 g Cl_2 at −12.5°C and 98.5 kPa
9. The density of a sample of phosphorus trifluoride, PF_3, is 3.90 g/dm³. What is the molecular mass of this gas at STP?

$$\left(\text{Hint: } D = \frac{m}{V} = \frac{MP}{RT}\right)$$

19:3   MASS-GAS VOLUME PROBLEMS

Many chemical reactions involve gases. It is often necessary to know the volume of gas involved with a known mass of material in a reaction. Problems of this type are similar to mass-mass problems, however one additional piece of information is needed. In mass-volume problems, mass is changed to moles of the desired substance and then converted to volume using the relationship:

1 mole of any gas = 22.4 dm³ of that gas at STP

The reverse calculation may also be done. Volume is changed to moles and moles are changed to mass.

Example 4

Calculate the volume of oxygen produced at STP by the decomposition of 10.0 g of potassium chlorate, $KClO_3$.

Solving Process:
Write the balanced equation.

$$2KClO_3(cr) \rightarrow 2KCl(cr) + 3O_2(g)$$

Start with the known mass of $KClO_3$ given in the problem and convert to volume of oxygen at STP.

	grams of given	convert to moles	mole ratio	
volume O_2 =	$\dfrac{10.0\ \text{g KClO}_3}{}$	$\dfrac{1\ \text{mol KClO}_3}{123\ \text{g KClO}_3}$	$\dfrac{3\ \text{mol O}_2}{2\ \text{mol KClO}_3}$	

$$\text{convert to } dm^3 \text{ of unknown}$$
$$\frac{22.4\ \text{dm}^3}{1\ \text{mol O}_2} = 2.73\ \text{dm}^3$$

Example 5

A student performs an experiment involving the reaction of magnesium metal with hydrochloric acid to form hydrogen gas. From the given data, calculate the mass of magnesium.

   1. volume of hydrogen gas formed   42.0 cm³

2. temperature of hydrogen   20.0°C

3. pressure   99.3 kPa

4. vapor pressure of water   2.3 kPa

5. pressure of dry hydrogen (99.3 − 2.3)   97.0 kPa

Solving Process:

Determine the volume of dry hydrogen at STP. Use the combined gas law.

$$\text{volume dry } H_2 = \frac{42.0 \text{ cm}^3 \text{ H}_2}{} \left| \frac{97.0 \cancel{kPa}}{101.3 \cancel{kPa}} \right| \frac{273.2 \cancel{K}}{293.2 \cancel{K}}$$

$$= 37.5 \text{ cm}^3$$

Use the volume of dry H_2 (37.5 cm³) and the molar volume to find the moles of hydrogen gas formed at STP.

$$\text{mol } H_2 = \frac{37.5 \cancel{\text{cm}^3 \text{ H}_2}}{} \left| \frac{1 \text{ mol } H_2}{22.4 \cancel{\text{dm}^3 \text{ H}_2}} \right| \frac{1 \cancel{\text{dm}^3}}{1000 \cancel{\text{cm}^3}}$$

$$= 1.67 \times 10^{-3} \text{ mol}$$

Write a balanced equation and use it to find the mass of magnesium.

$$Mg(cr) + 2HCl(aq) \rightarrow MgCl_2(aq) + H_2(g)$$

$$\text{mass Mg} = \frac{1.67 \times 10^{-3} \cancel{\text{mol } H_2}}{} \left| \frac{1 \cancel{\text{mol Mg}}}{1 \cancel{\text{mol } H_2}} \right| \frac{24.3 \text{ g Mg}}{1 \cancel{\text{mol Mg}}} = 0.0406 \text{ g}$$

PROBLEMS

Assume that all volumes are at STP.

10. How many cm³ of hydrogen are produced if 4.00 g zinc react with excess hydrochloric acid?

$$Zn(cr) + 2HCl(aq) \rightarrow ZnCl_2(aq) + H_2(g)$$

11. If excess chlorine gas reacts with a solution containing 20.0 g of potassium bromide, how many cubic centimeters of bromine gas can be produced?

$$2KBr(aq) + Cl_2(g) \rightarrow 2KCl(aq) + Br_2(g)$$

12. How many grams of copper(II) oxide can be reduced to copper metal with 10.0 dm³ of H_2?

$$CuO(cr) + H_2(g) \rightarrow Cu(cr) + H_2O(g)$$

13. Calculate the cm³ of oxygen that can be produced by the electrolysis of 5.00 g of water.

$$2H_2O(l) \rightarrow 2H_2(g) + O_2(g)$$

14. In the reaction between aluminum and oxygen, how many grams of aluminum are required to react with 5.00 dm³ of oxygen?

$$4Al(cr) + 3O_2(g) \rightarrow 2Al_2O_3(cr)$$

19:4   VOLUME-VOLUME PROBLEMS

It is possible to calculate the volume of a gas in a reaction when the volume of another gas in the reaction is known. Two methods can be used in solving these volume-volume problems. The first method is the same as the mass-mass or mass-volume method.

The steps are

Step 1. Convert the given volume to moles.

Step 2. From the balanced equation, convert the moles of given substance to moles of required substance.

Step 3. Convert the moles of required substance back to its volume.

In each case, the temperature and pressure must be taken into consideration. Two methods of solving for gas volume are given. The second method usually involves only an inspection and simple mental calculation. It can be used easily when the temperature and pressure remain constant.

Example 6

If 6.00 dm³ of oxygen are available to burn carbon disulfide, CS_2, how many dm³ of carbon dioxide are produced? The products of the combustion of carbon disulfide are carbon dioxide and sulfur dioxide.

Solving Process:

Balance the equation for this reaction.

$$CS_2(l) + 3O_2(g) \rightarrow CO_2(g) + 2SO_2(g)$$

Convert 6.00 dm³ O_2 to dm³ of CO_2.

$$\text{volume } CO_2 = \frac{6.00 \text{ dm}^3 \text{ } O_2}{} \left| \frac{1 \text{ mol } O_2}{22.4 \text{ dm}^3 \text{ } O_2} \right| \frac{1 \text{ mol } CO_2}{3 \text{ mol } O_2} \right|$$

$$\frac{22.4 \text{ dm}^3 \text{ } CO_2}{1 \text{ mol } CO_2} = 2.00 \text{ dm}^3$$

Therefore, 6.00 dm³ O_2 will produce 2.00 dm³ CO_2. Note that the changes to and from moles divide out.

Alternate Method: *Temperature and Pressure Constant*

The balanced equation indicates the relative number of moles of reactant and product. The coefficients also indicate the relative volumes of the gases at constant temperature and pressure. The relationship is a result of the principle stated in Avogadro's hypothesis: *equal volumes of gases at the same temperature and pressure contain the same number of particles.* If the gases are measured under the same conditions of temperature and pressure then 3 volumes O_2 : 1 volume CO_2 or 3 dm³ O_2 : 1 dm³ CO_2. The volume of CO_2 will be one-third the volume of O_2. Since the O_2 volume is 6.00 dm³, the CO_2 volume is 2.00 dm³. Conversion ratios could be used as follows.

$$\text{volume CO}_2 = \frac{6.00 \, \cancel{dm^3 \, O_2}}{} \left| \frac{1 \, dm^3 \, CO_2}{3 \, \cancel{dm^3 \, O_2}} \right.$$

$$= 2.00 \, dm^3$$

PROBLEMS

15. In the electrolysis of water, 75.0 cm³ of oxygen gas are produced. How many cm³ of hydrogen are produced?

$$2H_2O(l) \rightarrow 2H_2(g) + O_2(g)$$

16. If an electric discharge produces 20.0 cm³ of ozone, O_3, how many cubic centimeters of oxygen are required?

$$3O_2(g) \rightarrow 2O_3(g)$$

17. Ammonia can be produced by the Haber process. If 60.0 dm³ of NH_3 are produced, how many dm³ of hydrogen and nitrogen are necessary?

$$3H_2(g) + N_2(g) \rightarrow 2NH_3(g)$$

18. How many cm³ of chlorine gas are required to produce 50.0 cm³ of hydrogen chloride gas?

$$H_2(g) + Cl_2(g) \rightarrow 2HCl(g)$$

19. The residue from the complete decomposition of potassium chlorate is found to contain 1.80 g of potassium chloride. Determine the following:
    a. grams of $KClO_3$ originally present
    b. grams of oxygen produced
    c. cubic centimeters of oxygen at STP

19:5 LIMITING REACTANTS

Many reactions continue until one of the reactants is consumed. The reactant that is used up first is called the **limiting reactant.** The other reactant is said to be in *excess.* When discussing limiting reactants, we will deal only with nonreversible reactions. It is possible to determine whether a material is in excess or is deficient in a reaction by experiment or by calculation.

Limiting reactant problems are most easily solved by comparing the moles of the reactants present using the following steps.

Step 1. Write a balanced equation.

Step 2. Change both given quantities to moles.

Step 3. From the balanced equation, determine the moles of required substance that each given quantity will produce.

Step 4. Complete the problem using the quantity that yields the lesser amount of product. This reactant is the limiting reactant.

Example 7

If 40.0 g of H_3PO_4 react with 60.0 g of $MgCO_3$, calculate the volume of CO_2 produced at STP.

Solving Process:

Step 1. Write the balanced equation.

$$2H_3PO_4(aq) + 3MgCO_3(cr) \rightarrow Mg_3(PO_4)_2(cr) + 3CO_2(g) + 3H_2O(l)$$

Step 2. Change grams of reactant to moles of reactant.

$$\text{mol } H_3PO_4 = \frac{40.0 \text{ g } H_3PO_4}{} \left| \frac{1 \text{ mol } H_3PO_4}{98.0 \text{ g } H_3PO_4} \right. = 0.408 \text{ mol}$$

$$\text{mol } MgCO_3 = \frac{60.0 \text{ g } MgCO_3}{} \left| \frac{1 \text{ mol } MgCO_3}{84.3 \text{ g } MgCO_3} \right. = 0.712 \text{ mol}$$

Step 3. From the balanced equation determine the moles of CO_2 that will be produced by each reactant.

$$\text{mol } CO_2 = \frac{0.408 \text{ mol } H_3PO_4}{} \left| \frac{3 \text{ mol } CO_2}{2 \text{ mol } H_3PO_4} \right. = 0.612 \text{ mol}$$

$$\text{mol } CO_2 = \frac{0.712 \text{ mol } MgCO_3}{} \left| \frac{3 \text{ mol } CO_2}{3 \text{ mol } MgCO_3} \right. = 0.712 \text{ mol}$$

Step 4. Use the limiting reactant to complete the problem.

$$\text{volume } CO_2 = \frac{0.612 \text{ mol } CO_2}{} \left| \frac{22.4 \text{ dm}^3}{1 \text{ mol } CO_2} \right. = 13.7 \text{ dm}^3 \text{ at STP.}$$

Therefore, 40.0 g of H_3PO_4 will produce 13.7 dm^3 of CO_2 measured at standard temperature and pressure.

The same approach for finding limiting reactants can also be used in mass-mass or volume-volume problems.

PROBLEMS

20. If 20.0 g of NaOH react with 30.0 g of H_2SO_4 to produce Na_2SO_4, which reactant is limiting?

$$2NaOH(aq) + H_2SO_4(aq) \rightarrow Na_2SO_4(aq) + 2 H_2O(l)$$

21. If 5.00 g of copper metal react with a solution containing 20.0 g of $AgNO_3$ to produce silver metal, which reactant is limiting?

$$Cu(cr) + 2AgNO_3(aq) \rightarrow Cu(NO_3)_2(aq) + 2Ag(cr)$$

22. What reactant is limiting if 3.00 dm^3 of Cl_2 at STP react with a solution containing 25.0 g of NaBr to produce Br_2?

23. If 20.0 g of KOH react with 15.0 g of $(NH_4)_2SO_4$, calculate the dm^3 of NH_3 produced at STP.

24. Magnesium acetate can be prepared by a reaction involving 15.0 g of iron(III) acetate with either 10.0 g of $MgCrO_4$ or 15.0 g of $MgSO_4$. Which reaction will give the greatest yield of $Mg(CH_3COO)_2$? How many grams of $Mg(CH_3COO)_2$ will be produced?

$$2Fe(CH_3COO)_3(aq) + 3MgCrO_4(cr) \rightarrow$$
$$3Mg(CH_3COO)_2(aq) + Fe_2(CrO_4)_3(cr)$$

$$2Fe(CH_3COO)_3(aq) + 3MgSO_4(cr) \rightarrow$$
$$3Mg(CH_3COO)_2(aq) + Fe_2(SO_4)_3(cr)$$

19:6 NONSTANDARD CONDITIONS

Gas volume changes dramatically when pressure or temperature change. The molar volume is 22.4 dm^3 only at STP. If the experimental conditions are different from STP in a problem, it is still necessary to calculate the gas volume at STP.

The secret to success in these problems is to remember that the central step (moles of given to moles of unknown) must take place at STP. Thus, if you are given a volume of gas at other than STP, you must convert to STP before performing the moles to moles step in the solving process. On the other hand, if you are requested to find the volume of a gas at conditions other than STP, you must convert the volume after the moles to moles step.

Example 8

How many grams of ammonium sulfate must react with excess sodium hydroxide to produce 408 cm^3 of ammonia measured at 27°C and 98.0 kPa?

Solving Process:

Write the balanced equation.

$$(NH_4)_2SO_4(cr) + 2NaOH(aq) \rightarrow Na_2SO_4(aq) + 2NH_3(g) + 2H_2O(l)$$

Convert 408 cm^3 NH_3 at 27°C and 98.0 kPa to STP and then convert to g of $(NH_4)_2SO_4$. Since the temperature decreases, the volume decreases and the absolute temperature ratio is

$$\frac{273\ K}{300\ K}$$

Since pressure increases, volume decreases and the pressure ratio is

$$\frac{98.0\ kPa}{101.3\ kPa}$$

$$\text{mass}\ (NH_4)_2SO_4 = \frac{408\ cm^3\ NH_3}{} \cdot \frac{273\ K}{300\ K} \cdot \frac{98.0\ kPa}{101.3\ kPa} \cdot \frac{1\ mol\ NH_3}{22.4\ dm^3}$$

$$\cdot \frac{1\ mol\ (NH_4)_2SO_4}{2\ mol\ NH_3} \cdot \frac{132\ g\ (NH_4)_2SO_4}{1\ mol\ (NH_4)_2SO_4} \cdot \frac{1\ dm^3}{1000\ cm^3} = 1.06\ g$$

To produce 408 cm³ NH_3 at 27°C and 98.0 kPa, it is necessary to react 1.06 g $(NH_4)_2SO_4$ with excess sodium hydroxide.

Example 9

What volume of hydrogen collected over water at 27°C and 97.5 kPa is produced by the reaction of 3.00 g of Zn with an excess of sulfuric acid? The vapor pressure of water at 27°C is 3.6 kPa.

Solving Process:
Write the balanced equation.

$$Zn(cr) + H_2SO_4(aq) \rightarrow ZnSO_4(aq) + H_2(g)$$

The cubic decimeters of H_2 at STP must be converted to the conditions given in the problem. As the temperature is increased, the volume will increase, so the absolute temperature ratio is

$$\frac{300 \text{ K}}{273 \text{ K}}$$

As pressure is decreased volume will increase, so the pressure ratio is

$$\frac{101.3 \text{ kPa}}{97.5 \text{ kPa}}$$

This ratio must be corrected for the vapor pressure of water, which is 3.6 kPa at this temperature. The corrected ratio is

$$\frac{101.3 \text{ kPa}}{97.5 - 3.6 \text{ kPa}} \quad \text{or} \quad \frac{101.3 \text{ kPa}}{93.9 \text{ kPa}}$$

Convert from grams of Zn to cubic decimeters of dry H_2 at 27°C and 97.5 kPa. Then convert to cubic decimeters of H_2 at STP by using the absolute temperature and pressure ratios.

$$\text{volume } H_2 = \frac{3.00 \text{ g Zn}}{} \left| \frac{1 \text{ mol Zn}}{65.4 \text{ g Zn}} \right| \frac{1 \text{ mol } H_2}{1 \text{ mol Zn}} \left| \frac{22.4 \text{ dm}^3 H_2}{1 \text{ mol } H_2} \right|$$

$$\left| \frac{300 \text{ K}}{273 \text{ K}} \right| \frac{101.3 \text{ kPa}}{93.9 \text{ kPa}} = 1.22 \text{ dm}^3 H_2$$

Hence, 3.00 g Zn will react with excess H_2SO_4 to give 1.22 dm³ of H_2 measured at 27°C and 97.5 kPa over water.

PROBLEMS

25. If 14.7 g of sodium peroxide (Na_2O_2) react with water to produce sodium hydroxide and oxygen gas, how many dm³ of oxygen are produced at 22°C and 1.12×10^5 Pa?

26. How many dm³ of chlorine gas measured at 18.5°C and 98.0 kPa can be produced by the electrolysis of 62.3 g NaCl to give sodium metal and chlorine gas?

27. How many dm^3 of nitrogen measured at 21.5°C and 9.55 × 10^4 Pa are required to react with excess calcium carbide, CaC$_2$, to produce 100.0 g of calcium cyanamid, CaCN$_2$, and carbon?

28. How many grams of iron metal must react with excess steam to produce 10.0 dm^3 of hydrogen collected over water at 20.0°C and 9.90 × 10^4 Pa? The other product is iron(II,III) oxide, Fe$_3$O$_4$(Fe$_3$O$_4$ is actually FeO·Fe$_2$O$_3$).

CHAPTER REVIEW PROBLEMS

1. One mole of He has a mass of 4.0026 g and 1.000 dm^3 of He (at STP) has a mass of 0.1787 g. Calculate the molar volume of helium.

2. A sample of gas has a mass of 1.248 g and occupies 300.0 cm^3 at STP. What is the molecular mass of this gas?

3. From the volume, temperature, and pressure data given, calculate the number of moles and the mass in grams for each gas listed using the ideal gas equation.
   a. 2000.0 cm^3 NH$_3$ at 10.0°C and 105.0 kPa
   b. 5.00 dm^3 SO$_2$ at 21.0°C and 100.0 kPa

4. Calculate the volume each gas will occupy under the conditions listed using the ideal gas equation.
   a. 5.00 mol CH$_4$ at 27.0°C and 97.2 kPa
   b. 200.0 g NH$_3$ at 12.0°C and 104.5 kPa

5. What is the molecular mass of a gas if 5.75 g of the gas occupy a volume of 3.50 dm^3? The pressure was recorded as 9.525 × 10^4 Pa and the temperature is 52°C.

6. How many cubic centimeters of hydrogen at STP are produced by the reaction of 0.750 g of sodium metal with excess water?

$$2Na(cr) + 2H_2O(l) \rightarrow 2NaOH(aq) + H_2(g)$$

7. What mass of magnesium will react with excess hydrochloric acid to produce 5.00 × 10^2 cm^3 of H$_2$ at STP?

$$Mg(cr) + 2HCl(aq) \rightarrow MgCl_2(aq) + H_2(g)$$

8. When lead(II) sulfide is burned in air, lead(II) oxide and sulfur dioxide are produced. If 20.0 dm^3 of sulfur dioxide were produced, how many cubic decimeters of oxygen gas were required to react with the lead(II) sulfide?

$$2PbS(cr) + 3O_2(g) \rightarrow 2PbO(cr) + 2SO_2(g)$$

9. In a reaction involving carbon monoxide and iron(III) oxide, the products are iron metal and carbon dioxide. If 84.75 dm^3 of carbon dioxide are produced, how many dm^3 of carbon monoxide are required?

10. Calcium carbide (CaC$_2$) reacts with water to produce calcium hydroxide and acetylene (C$_2$H$_2$). What volume of the gas at STP could be produced from the reaction of 50.0 g of CaC$_2$ and 50.0 g of water?

11. Hydrogen burns to give water. If 200.0 cm³ of H_2 reacts with 150.0 cm³ of O_2, what volume of water vapor is produced? How many cubic centimeters of gas remain unreacted and what gas remains? Assume that all volumes are measured at any given temperature above the normal boiling point of water.

12. How many grams of sodium hydrogen carbonate, $NaHCO_3$, must be heated to produce 2.50 dm³ of carbon dioxide measured at 22.5°C and 97.5 kPa? The other products are sodium carbonate and water.

13. If 3.20 g of aluminum react with excess hydrochloric acid, how many cm³ of hydrogen collected over water at 20.0°C and 99.5 kPa are produced?

ENERGY AND DISORDER 20

20:1 ENTHALPY, ENTROPY, AND FREE ENERGY

All chemical changes are accompanied by changes in energy and the degree of disorder for the particles involved. The study of matter and energy interactions is called **thermodynamics.** Thermodynamic calculations can be kept simple if we reduce all variables to a set of standard conditions. These standards are 25°C, 100.0 kPa, and 1 molar solutions.

The variables of interest to the chemist studying the thermodynamics of chemical reactions include

H, the **enthalpy,** or heat content, of a substance

S, the **entropy,** or disorder, of a substance

G, the Gibbs **free energy,** or chemical potential, of a substance

The changes in these variables during a reaction is the difference between the values for the products and the reactants.

Chemists are interested in ΔH since if $\Delta H < 0$ the reaction is **exothermic,** that is, energy is given off. On the other hand if $\Delta H > 0$, the reaction is **endothermic,** that is, energy is taken in. The chief use of ΔS is as a step in determining ΔG. Of course, if $\Delta S > 0$ there is an increase in disorder and if $\Delta S < 0$ there is a decrease in disorder. ΔG is important because if $\Delta G < 0$ the reaction is spontaneous and if $\Delta G > 0$ the reaction is not spontaneous.

Enthalpy and free energy quantities are relative values compared to free elements defined as having zero enthalpy and zero free energy. The enthalpy and free energy of each substance are therefore represented by ΔH_f° and ΔG_f°, respectively. The superscript "$\circ$" designates standard conditions. The subscript "f" designates "of formation" since the formation of the substance from the free elements is the enthalpy or free energy. The reactants (in this case the free elements) would be equal to zero. At standard conditions, the equations become

$$\Delta H^\circ_{(reaction)} = \Sigma \Delta H_f^\circ{}_{(products)} - \Sigma \Delta H_f^\circ{}_{(reactants)}$$
$$\Delta G^\circ_{(reaction)} = \Sigma \Delta G_f^\circ{}_{(products)} - \Sigma \Delta G_f^\circ{}_{(reactants)}$$
$$\Delta S^\circ_{(reaction)} = \Sigma S^\circ_{(products)} - \Sigma S^\circ_{(reactants)}$$

Example 1

What is the enthalpy change for the following reaction?

$$Cl_2(g) + 2HBr(g) \rightarrow 2HCl(g) + Br_2(g)$$

135

Solving Process:

From Table A-10 of thermodynamic values in the Appendix, we find the following ΔH_f° values:

$$HBr = -36.4 \text{ kJ/mol}$$
$$HCl = -92.3 \text{ kJ/mol}$$

By definition, the enthalpy of formation for Cl_2 and Br_2 is 0.

$$\Delta H^\circ = \Sigma \Delta H_{f \text{ (products)}}^\circ - \Sigma \Delta H_{f \text{ (reactants)}}^\circ$$

$$\Delta H^\circ = \left[\frac{1 \text{ mol } Br_2}{\text{mol } Br_2} \cdot 0 \text{ kJ} + \frac{2 \text{ mol } HCl}{\text{mol } HCl} \cdot (-92.3) \text{ kJ} \right] -$$
$$\left[\frac{1 \text{ mol } Cl_2}{\text{mol } Cl_2} \cdot 0 \text{ kJ} + \frac{2 \text{ mol } HBr}{\text{mol } HBr} \cdot (-36.4) \text{ kJ} \right]$$

$$= -111.8 \text{ kJ}$$

The negative sign indicates that the products have less enthalpy, than the reactants. Thus, energy must have been released, and the reaction is exothermic.

Example 2

For the reaction

$$Ca(cr) + 2H_2O(l) \rightarrow Ca(OH)_2(cr) + H_2(g)$$
$$\Delta S^\circ = 25.7 \text{ J/K}$$

What is S° for $Ca(OH)_2(cr)$?

Solving Process:

From Table A-10 we find the following S° values:

$$Ca(cr) = 41.4 \text{ J/mol·K}$$
$$H_2O(l) = 69.9 \text{ J/mol·K}$$
$$H_2(g) = 131 \text{ J/mol·K}$$

$$\Delta S^\circ = \Sigma S_{\text{(products)}}^\circ - \Sigma S_{\text{(reactants)}}^\circ$$

$$25.7 \text{ J/K} = \left[\frac{1 \text{ mol } Ca(OH)_2 \cdot x}{} + \frac{1 \text{ mol } H_2 \cdot 131 \text{ J}}{\text{mol } H_2 \cdot K} \right] -$$
$$\left[\frac{1 \text{ mol } Ca \cdot 41.4 \text{ J}}{\text{mol } Ca \cdot K} + \frac{2 \text{ mol } H_2O \cdot 69.9 \text{ J}}{\text{mol } H_2O \cdot K} \right]$$

$$x = 75.9 \text{ J/mol·K}$$

PROBLEMS

1. Find ΔH° for the following reactions.
   a. $2KBr(cr) + H_2SO_4(l) \rightarrow K_2SO_4(cr) + 2HBr(g)$
   b. $Mg_3N_2(cr) + 6H_2O(l) \rightarrow 3Mg(OH)_2(cr) + 2NH_3(g)$
   c. $NH_4NO_3(cr) \rightarrow N_2O(g) + 2H_2O(l)$

2. Find $\Delta S°$ for the following reactions.

a. $Zn(NO_3)_2(aq) + 2NaOH(aq) \rightarrow Zn(OH)_2(cr) + 2NaNO_3(aq)$
b. $2NO_2(g) + H_2O(l) \rightarrow HNO_2(aq) + HNO_3(aq)$
c. $Mg(cr) + 2HNO_3(aq) \rightarrow Mg(NO_3)_2(aq) + H_2(g)$

20:2   SPONTANEOUS REACTIONS

An American chemist, J. Willard Gibbs, discovered the relationship among entropy, enthalpy, and free energy to be

$$\Delta G° = \Delta H° - T\Delta S°$$

where T is the absolute temperature. A **spontaneous reaction** is one in which ΔG is negative. Using tables of thermodynamic values we can predict whether a reaction is spontaneous at standard conditions. If a table includes values of $\Delta G_f°$, the $\Delta G°$ for the reaction can be calculated directly as in the previous section. $\Delta G°$ can also be calculated using $\Delta H°$, T, and $\Delta S°$.

Example 3

Is the following reaction spontaneous?

$$2H_2O_2(l) \rightarrow 2H_2O(l) + O_2(g)$$

Solving Process:
From the table of thermodynamic values in the Appendix, we obtain the following $\Delta G_f°$ values:

$$H_2O_2 = -120 \text{ kJ/mol}$$
$$H_2O = -237 \text{ kJ/mol}$$
$$O_2 = 0 \text{ kJ}$$

$$\Delta G° - \Sigma\Delta G°_{f(products)} \quad \Sigma\Delta G°_{f(reactants)}$$

$$\Delta G° = \left[\frac{2 \text{ mol } H_2O}{} \left| \frac{(-237) \text{ kJ}}{\text{mol } H_2O} + \frac{1 \text{ mol } O_2}{} \right| \frac{0 \text{ kJ}}{\text{mol } O_2} \right] -$$

$$\left[\frac{2 \text{ mol } H_2O_2}{} \left| \frac{(-120) \text{ kJ}}{\text{mol } H_2O_2} \right. \right]$$

$$= -234 \text{ kJ}$$

$\Delta G°$ is negative, so the reaction is spontaneous at standard conditions. Note, however, the term spontaneous tells us nothing about how long a reaction will take.

Example 4

Calculate the standard enthalpy of formation, $\Delta H_f°$, of iron(III) oxide at 298 K by the thermite welding process.

$$2Al(cr) + Fe_2O_3(cr) \rightarrow 2 Fe(cr) + Al_2O_3(cr)$$

Use thermodynamic values from Table A-10 and the following data for Fe(cr): $\Delta H_f^\circ = 0$ kJ/mol, $\Delta G_f^\circ = 0$ kJ/mol, and $S^\circ = 27.3$ J/mol·K.

Solving Process:

a. Since the enthalpy change for the thermite reaction is not given, we must calculate it from the relationship, $\Delta G^\circ = \Delta H - T\Delta S$. We must first calculate ΔG° and ΔS°. It is best to organize the data you will use from A-10 into a table.

	Reactants		$\rightarrow$	Products	
Value	**Fe_2O_3**	**2Al**		**2 Fe**	**Al_2O_3**
ΔH_f° (kJ/mol)	?	0		0	−1676
ΔG_f° (kJ/mol)	−742	0		0	−1582
ΔS° (J/mol K)	87.4	28.3		27.3	50.9

b. To find ΔG° use the following equation.

$$\Delta G^\circ_{(reaction)} = \Sigma\Delta G^\circ_{f\ (products)} - \Sigma\Delta G^\circ_{f\ (reactants)}$$

It is important to use the balanced chemical equation. Multiply each ΔG_f° by the number of moles from the balanced equation. Substitute these values into the equation used to determine ΔG°(reaction).

$$\Delta G^\circ = \left[\frac{1\ mol\ Al_2O_3}{}\ \middle|\ \frac{-1582\ kJ}{1\ mol\ Al_2O_3} + \frac{2\ mol\ Fe}{}\ \middle|\ \frac{0\ kJ}{1\ mol\ Fe}\right] -$$

$$\left[\frac{2\ mol\ Al}{}\ \middle|\ \frac{0\ kJ}{1\ mol\ Al} + \frac{1\ mol\ Fe_2O_3}{}\ \middle|\ \frac{-742\ kJ}{1\ mol\ Fe_2O_3}\right]$$

$$= -840\ kJ/mol$$

c. To find ΔS° use the equation

$$\Delta S^\circ_{(reaction)} = \Sigma S^\circ_{(products)} - \Sigma S^\circ_{(reactants)}$$

$$= \left[\frac{2\ mol\ Fe}{}\ \middle|\ \frac{27.3\ J/mol\cdot K}{1\ mol\ Fe} + \frac{1\ mol\ Al_2O_3}{}\ \middle|\ \frac{50.9\ J/mol\cdot K}{1\ mol\ Al_2O_3}\right] -$$

$$\left[\frac{1\ mol\ Fe_2O_3}{}\ \middle|\ \frac{87.4\ J/mol\cdot K}{1\ mol\ Fe_2O_3} + \frac{2\ mol\ Al}{}\ \middle|\ \frac{28.3\ J/mol\cdot K}{1\ mol\ Al}\right]$$

$$= -38.5\ J/mol\cdot K$$

d. To find ΔH° for this reaction, use $\Delta G^\circ = \Delta H^\circ - T\Delta S^\circ$ and solve for ΔH°. ($T = 298$ K)

$$\Delta H^\circ = \Delta G^\circ + T\Delta S^\circ$$

$$= -840\ kJ + \left(\frac{298\ K}{}\ \middle|\ \frac{-38.5\ J}{mol\cdot K}\ \middle|\ \frac{1\ kJ}{1000\ J}\right)$$

$$= -851\ kJ/mol$$

e. To find ΔH_f° for Fe_2O_3, substitute the $\Delta H^\circ_{(reaction)}$ into the equation

$$\Delta H^\circ_{(reaction)} = \Delta H^\circ_{f\,(products)} - \Delta H^\circ_{f\,(reactants)}$$

$$-851\ \frac{kJ}{mol} - \left[\frac{2\ \text{mol Fe}}{} \left| \frac{0\ kJ}{1\ \text{mol Fe}} + \frac{1\ \text{mol Al}_2O_3}{} \right| \frac{-1676\ kJ}{1\ \text{mol Al}_2O_3} \right] -$$

$$\left[\frac{1\ \text{mol Fe}_2O_3}{} \left| \frac{\Delta H_f^\circ}{1\ \text{mol Fe}_2O_3} + \frac{2\ \text{mol Al}}{} \right| \frac{0\ kJ}{1\ \text{mol Al}} \right]$$

$$= \left(-1676\ \frac{kJ}{mol} \right) - \Delta H_f^\circ$$

$$\Delta H_f^\circ = -825\ kJ/mol$$

Example 5

For the reaction

$$P_4O_{10}(cr) + 6H_2O(l) \rightarrow 4H_3PO_4(aq)$$
$$\Delta H^\circ = -424\ kJ$$
$$\Delta S^\circ - \quad 209\ J/K$$

Is the reaction spontaneous?

Solving Process:

The spontaneity of a reaction is indicated by ΔG and $\Delta G^\circ = \Delta H^\circ - T\Delta S^\circ$.

$$\Delta G^\circ = -424\ kJ - [(298\ K)(-209\ J/K)]$$
$$\Delta G^\circ = -424\ kJ + 62282\ J = \quad 424\ kJ + 62.3\ kJ$$
$$\Delta G^\circ = -362\ kJ$$

The reaction is spontaneous.

PROBLEMS

3. Find ΔG° for the following reactions and predict the spontaneity at standard conditions.
   a. $Ca(OH)_2(cr) + 2NH_4Cl(aq) \rightarrow CaCl_2(aq) + 2NH_3(g) + 2H_2O(l)$
   b. $2NaCl(cr) + H_2SO_4(l) \rightarrow Na_2SO_4(l) + 2HCl(g)$
   c. $CaCl_2(aq) + 2NaOH(aq) \rightarrow Ca(OH)_2(cr) + 2NaCl(aq)$
4. Predict the spontaneity of the following reactions at 298 K.
   a. $Sn(cr) + 4HNO_3(aq) \rightarrow SnO_2(cr) + 4NO_2(g) + 2H_2O(l)$, $(\Delta H^\circ = -192\ kJ$, $\Delta S^\circ = 887\ J/K)$
   b. $2N_2O_5(g) \rightarrow 4NO_2(g) + O_2(g)$, $(\Delta H^\circ = 110\ kJ$, $\Delta S^\circ = 839\ J/K)$
   c. $Mn(cr) + 2HCl(aq) \rightarrow MnCl_2(aq) + H_2(g)$, $(\Delta H^\circ = -221\ kJ$, $\Delta S^\circ = 79.7\ J/K)$
5. Calculate S° for H_2O (g) from the reaction that occurs when methane gas burns. $CH_4(g) + 2O_2(g) \rightarrow CO_2(g) + 2H_2O(g)$

6. Calculate ΔG_f° for H_2SO_4 from the neutralization reaction between the base, NaOH, and sulfuric acid, H_2SO_4. $2NaOH(aq) + H_2SO_4(aq) \rightarrow Na_2SO_4(aq) + 2H_2O(l)$

20:3 HESS'S LAW

Some reactions may be too slow, explosive, or have many side reactions making it impractical to measure directly the enthalpy of reaction. **Hess's Law** enables chemists to measure the enthalpy of a reaction that cannot be measured directly in the laboratory.

Enthalpy is a state function because it is independent of the reaction pathway. *The enthalpy change for a reaction is the sum of the enthalpy changes for a series of reactions that add up to the overall reaction.*

Example 6

What is the enthalpy of reaction for the oxidation of ethanol to acetic acid?

$$CH_3CH_2OH(l) + O_2(g) \rightarrow CH_3COOH(l) + H_2O(l)$$

The standard enthalpy of combustion of ethanol is measured in a calorimeter and found to be -1370 kJ/mol.

$$(\text{reaction 1}) \; CH_3CH_2OH(l) + 3O_2(g) \rightarrow 2CO_2(g) + 3H_2O(g)$$

The standard enthalpy of combustion of acetic acid is -874 kJ/mol.

$$(\text{reaction 2}) \; CH_3COOH(l) + 2O_2(g) \rightarrow 2CO_2(g) + 2H_2O(g)$$

Solving Process:

Since the desired reaction has CH_3CH_2OH on the left, leave reaction one as it is. The desired reaction has CH_3COOH on the right. Reaction 2 must be reversed before adding it to reaction 1.

$(1) \; CH_3CH_2OH + 3O_2 \rightarrow 2CO_2 + 3H_2O \quad \Delta H = -1370$ kJ/mol

$(2) \; 2CO_2 + 2H_2O \rightarrow CH_3COOH + 2O_2 \quad \Delta H = +874$ kJ/mol

Note that the sign on the enthalpy for the reversed equation has been changed. Now the two equations can be simplified and their enthalpies can be added to give

$$CH_3CH_2OH + O_2 \rightarrow CH_3COOH + H_2O \quad \Delta H = -496 \text{ kJ/mol}$$

PROBLEM

7. Calculate the enthalpy for the reaction given below.

$C_2H_4(g) + H_2(g) \rightarrow C_2H_6(g)$

Use the following data:

$$C_2H_6(g) + \tfrac{7}{2}O_2(g) \rightarrow 2CO_2(g) + 3H_2O(l) \quad \Delta H = -1560 \text{ kJ}$$
$$H_2(g) + \tfrac{1}{2}O_2(g) \rightarrow H_2O(l) \qquad\qquad \Delta H = -286 \text{ kJ}$$
$$2CO_2(g) + 2H_2O(l) \rightarrow C_2H_4(g) + 3O_2(g) \quad \Delta H = +1411 \text{ kJ}$$

CHAPTER REVIEW PROBLEMS

Use Table A-10 in the Appendix for thermodynamic data.

1. Find $\Delta G°$ for the following reactions and predict the spontaneity at standard conditions.
   a. $3Mg(cr) + N_2(g) \rightarrow Mg_3N_2(cr)$
   b. $3Cu(cr) + 8HNO_3(aq) \rightarrow 3Cu(NO_3)_2(aq) + 4H_2O(l) + 2NO(g)$

2. Find $\Delta H°$ for the following reactions.
   a. $2NO(g) + O_2(g) \rightarrow 2NO_2(g)$
   b. $4Zn(cr) + 9HNO_3(aq) \rightarrow 4Zn(NO_3)_2(aq) + NH_3(g) + 3H_2O(l)$

3. Find $\Delta S°$ for the following reactions.
   a. $4HBr(g) + O_2(g) \rightarrow 2H_2O(l) + 2Br_2(l)$
   b. $Cu(cr) + Ag_2SO_4(aq) \rightarrow CuSO_4(aq) + 2Ag(cr)$

4. Predict the spontaneity of the following reactions at 298 K using $\Delta G = \Delta H - T\Delta S$.
   a. $I_2(cr) + Cl_2(g) \rightarrow 2ICl(l)$ ($\Delta H° = -47.8$ kJ, $\Delta S° = -16.45$ J/K)
   b. $Na_2O(cr) + SiO_2(cr) \rightarrow Na_2SiO_3(cr)$ ($\Delta H° = -192$ kJ, $\Delta S° = -0.837$ J/K)

5. Calculate the enthalpy of reaction for the equation listed below.
   $$CuCl_2(cr) + Cu(cr) \rightarrow 2CuCl(cr)$$
   Use the following data.
   $$Cu(cr) + Cl_2(g) \rightarrow CuCl_2(cr) \quad \Delta H = -206 \text{ kJ}$$
   $$2Cu(cr) + Cl_2(g) \rightarrow 2CuCl(cr) \quad \Delta H = -136 \text{ kJ}$$

6. Calculate the enthalpy of formation of carbon dioxide from its elements.
   $$C(g) + 2O(g) \rightarrow CO_2(g)$$
   Use the following data.
   $$2O(g) \rightarrow O_2(g) \qquad\qquad \Delta H = -250 \text{ kJ}$$
   $$C(cr) \rightarrow C(g) \qquad\qquad \Delta H = +720 \text{ kJ}$$
   $$CO_2(g) \rightarrow C(cr) + O_2(g) \quad \Delta H = +390 \text{ kJ}$$

7. If $\Delta H = +66$ kJ for the reaction $Ca(OH)_2(cr) \rightarrow CaO(cr) + H_2O(l)$ what is $\Delta H_f°$ for $CaO(cr)$?

8. Calculate $\Delta H_f°$ for 1 mol of butane gas, C_4H_{10}, from the reaction that occurs when a butane gas lighter is used.
   $$2C_4H_{10}(g) + 13O_2(g) \rightarrow 8CO_2(g) + 10H_2O(g)$$

SOLUTIONS   21

21:1 SOLUTE—SOLVENT

A solution consists of a dissolved substance, the **solute,** and a dissolving medium, the **solvent.** A solution is a homogeneous mixture (has a constant composition throughout). A solute need not be a solid. It can be a gas, such as HCl in hydrochloric acid, or a liquid, such as the ethylene glycol in a car's cooling system If the solution contains two liquids, the liquid that is in the greater amount is called the solvent. The most common solvent is water.

Knowing the actual strength of a solution is more useful than knowing in general terms that it is dilute or concentrated. The concentration of solutions can be described quantitatively in many ways. Molarity, molality, and mole fraction are discussed in this chapter.

21:2 MOLARITY

A solution for which a precise concentration is known is called a **standard solution.** Its strength is often expressed in terms of **molarity.** A 1 molar solution contains 1 mole of solute dissolved in enough solvent (usually water) to make 1 cubic decimeter of solution.

$$molarity\ (M) = \frac{number\ of\ moles\ of\ solute}{cubic\ decimeters\ of\ solution}$$

Chemists express concentration in terms of molarity because they are interested in measuring a certain number of particles. One mole of sodium chloride, NaCl, is 58.5 grams. If 58.5 grams of NaCl are dissolved in enough water to make 1 cubic decimeter of solution, the solution is a 1M solution of NaCl. Similarly, if 2 moles of NaCl (117.0 grams) are dissolved in enough water to make 1 cubic decimeter of solution, the solution is a 2M solution. Fifty cubic centimeters of a solution with a 2M concentration and 500 cubic centimeters of the same solution will have the same concentration, 2M. The total number of particles changes when the volume is changed but the concentration of particles (the number of particles per unit volume) does not change.

Example 1

Calculate the molarity of a 1500 cubic centimeter solution that contains 200.0 g of $MgCl_2$.

Solving Process:

The problem requires the calculation of molarity. Molarity is moles of solute per (divided by) dm^3 of solution. Therefore, the data concerning solute is placed in the numerator, and the data concerning the solution in the denominator. The solute data in the numerator is then converted to moles, and the solution data in the denominator to dm^3.

$$\text{molarity} = \frac{200.0 \text{ g } MgCl_2}{1500 \text{ cm}^3} \left| \frac{1 \text{ mol } MgCl_2}{95.3 \text{ g } MgCl_2} \right| \frac{1000 \text{ cm}^3}{1 \text{ dm}^3}$$

$$= 1.4 \text{ mol/dm}^3 = 1.4M$$

Example 2

How many cubic centimeters of a $1.50M$ sulfuric acid solution can be made using 36.0 g of sulfuric acid?

Solving Process:

Convert grams of sulfuric acid to moles of sulfuric acid. The moles of H_2SO_4 can be converted to dm^3 of H_2SO_4 using the concentration. Finally, volume is converted to cubic centimeters.

$$\frac{\text{volume of}}{\text{solution}} = \frac{36.0 \text{ g } H_2SO_4}{} \left| \frac{1 \text{ mol } H_2SO_4}{98.1 \text{ g } H_2SO_4} \right| \frac{1 \text{ dm}^3}{1.50 \text{ mol } H_2SO_4} \right|$$

$$\frac{1000 \text{ cm}^3}{1 \text{ dm}^3} = 245 \text{ cm}^3$$

Example 3

Calculate the mass of solute required to make 750 cubic centimeters of a $2.50M$ sodium chloride solution.

Solving Process:

Convert the volume of solution to moles using the given concentration. The $2.50M$ solution contains 2.50 mol $NaCl/dm^3$ solution. Convert the moles of NaCl to grams of NaCl, using the formula mass of NaCl.

$$\frac{\text{grams of}}{\text{solute}} = \frac{750 \text{ cm}^3}{} \left| \frac{1 \text{ dm}^3}{1000 \text{ cm}^3} \right| \frac{2.50 \text{ mol } NaCl}{1 \text{ dm}^3} \right| \frac{58.5 \text{ g } NaCl}{1 \text{ mol } NaCl}$$

$$= 110 \text{ g } NaCl$$

PROBLEMS

1. Calculate the molarity of the following solutions.
   a. 825 cm³ that contains 30.0 g of acetic acid (CH_3COOH)
   b. 2050 cm³ that contains 49.0 g of phosphoric acid (H_3PO_4)
   c. 1.50 dm³ that contains 102 g of potassium hydroxide

2. How many cubic decimeters of solution can be made from each of the following?
   a. a 2.00M solution using 80.0 g sodium hydroxide
   b. a 0.500M solution using 80.0 g sodium hydroxide
   c. a 6.00M solution using 126 g nitric acid

3. Calculate the mass of solute in the following solutions.
   a. 750.0 cm³ of $CaCl_2$ solution that is 0.500M
   b. 3000.0 cm³ of a KOH solution that is 2.50M
   c. 250.0 cm³ of a Na_2SO_4 solution that is 2.00M

21:3 MOLALITY

Some properties of a solution depend only on the number of particles, not on the type of particles. These properties are called **colligative properties.** The number of particles in a mass of solvent can affect the boiling or freezing point of the solvent. Molality is used in place of molarity when dealing with colligative properties. **Molality (m)** is the number of moles of solute per 1000 grams or 1 kilogram of solvent. A one molal (1 m) solution contains one mole of solute in each 1 kilogram of solvent. A two molal (2 m) solution contains two moles of solute dissolved in each kilogram of solvent.

Example 4

Calculate the molality of a solution made by dissolving 45.0 g of glucose, $C_6H_{12}O_6$, in 500.0 g of water.

Solving Process:

Convert grams of glucose to moles of glucose. The molality expression gives the number of moles of solute per kilogram of solvent (water). The molecular mass of glucose is 180.0 g.

$$\text{molality} = \frac{45.0 \text{ g } C_6H_{12}O_6}{500.0 \text{ g } H_2O} \left| \frac{1000 \text{ g } H_2O}{1 \text{ kg } H_2O} \right| \frac{1 \text{ mol } C_6H_{12}O_6}{180.0 \text{ g } C_6H_{12}O_6}$$

$$= \frac{0.500 \text{ mol}}{1 \text{ kg } H_2O} = 0.500m$$

Example 5

Calculate the mass of ethanol that must be dissolved in 750.0 g of water to make a 2.00m solution.

Solving Process:

The concentration unit 2.00m can be written as

$$\frac{2.00 \text{ mol CH}_3\text{CH}_2\text{OH}}{1000 \text{ g H}_2\text{O}}$$

To obtain the mass of CH_3CH_2OH, multiply the mass of water by the concentration unit and then convert to grams of ethanol by using the molecular mass of the solute, 46.1 grams.

$$\text{mass of solute} = \frac{750.0 \text{ g H}_2\text{O}}{} \left| \frac{2.00 \text{ mol CH}_3\text{CH}_2\text{OH}}{1000 \text{ g H}_2\text{O}} \right| \frac{46.1 \text{ g CH}_3\text{CH}_2\text{OH}}{1 \text{ mol CH}_3\text{CH}_2\text{OH}}$$

$$= 69.2 \text{ g CH}_3\text{CH}_2\text{OH}$$

PROBLEMS

4. Calculate the molality of the following solutions.
   a. 1.50 mol $NaCH_3COO$ dissolved in 750.0 g of water
   b. 3.00 mol H_2SO_4 dissolved in 1250.0 g of water
   c. 50.0 g acetic acid, CH_3COOH, dissolved in 500.0 g of water
5. Determine the grams of solute required to prepare the following solutions.
   a. 3.00m solution of KOH containing 1500.0 g of water
   b. 0.500m solution CH_3COOH containing 750.0 g of water
6. Calculate the grams of water required to make a 0.500m solution that contains 20.0 g of NaCl.

21:4   MOLE FRACTION

Another way to express solution concentration is mole fraction. The mole fraction (X) of a substance in a solution is defined as the moles of substance divided by the moles of solution (sum of moles of solute + moles of solvent).

$$X = \frac{moles\ solute}{(moles\ of\ solute\ +\ moles\ of\ solvent)}$$

The sum of the mole fractions of all the components of a solution equals one.

Example 6

What are the mole fractions of glucose and water in a solution made of 7.59 g of glucose, $C_6H_{12}O_6$, dissolved in 125 g of water?

Solving Process:
The molecular mass of glucose is 180.0 g. Find the moles of glucose.

$$\text{mol glucose} = \frac{7.59 \text{ g } C_6H_{12}O_6}{} \left| \frac{1 \text{ mol } C_6H_{12}O_6}{180.0 \text{ g } C_6H_{12}O_6} = 0.0422 \text{ mol} \right.$$

The molecular mass of H_2O is 18.0 u. Find the moles of water.

$$\text{mol } H_2O = \frac{125 \text{ g } H_2O}{} \left| \frac{1 \text{ mol } H_2O}{18.0 \text{ g } H_2O} = 6.94 \text{ mol} \right.$$

Determine the mole fraction of $C_6H_{12}O_6$.

$$\text{mol fraction} = \frac{\text{mol solute}}{(\text{mol solute} + \text{mol solvent})}$$

$$= \frac{0.0422 \text{ mol}}{(0.0422 + 6.94) \text{ mol}} = \frac{0.0422}{6.98} = 0.006\ 05$$

Determine the mole fraction of H_2O.

$$\text{mol fraction} = \frac{6.94}{6.98} = 0.994$$

If one multiplies the mole fraction by 100, you have the mole percent. In the above problem 99.4% of the molecules in the solution are H_2O.

PROBLEMS

Calculate the mole fraction for each component in the following solutions.
7. 22.5 g CH_3CH_2OH in 1.00×10^2 g H_2O
8. 39.5 g $C_6H_5CH_3$, toluene, in 1.5×10^2 g C_6H_6, benzene.

CHAPTER REVIEW PROBLEMS

1. Calculate the molarity of the following solutions.
   a. 500.0 cm³ that contains 82.0 g calcium nitrate
   b. 250.0 cm³ that contains 50.0 g copper(II) sulfate pentahydrate
   c. 1000.0 cm³ that contains 116 g sodium carbonate heptahydrate
2. Calculate the mass of solute in the following solutions.
   a. 250.0 cm³ of $Na_2SO_4 \cdot 7H_2O$ solution that is 2.00M
   b. 1.500 dm³ of KH_2PO_4 solution that is 0.240M
   c. 2500.0 cm³ of a HNO_3 solution that is 4.00M

3. How many cubic decimeters of solution can be made from each of the following?

   a. a 0.100M solution using 117 g sodium chloride
   b. a 1.00M solution using 50.0 g copper(II) sulfate pentahydrate
   c. a 0.200M solution using 200.0 g sodium sulfide

4. How many grams of lead(II) acetate, $Pb(CH_3COO)_2$, must be used to make 500.0 cm^3 of a solution that is to contain 10.0 mg/cm^3 of lead ion? What is the molarity of this solution?

5. Calculate the molality of the following solutions.

   a. 15.0 g ethanol dissolved in 250.0 g water
   b. 10.0 g glucose, $C_6H_{12}O_6$, dissolved in 500.0 g water
   c. 1.204 × 10^{24} molecules CH_3COOH dissolved in 1500.0 g water

6. Determine the grams of solute required to prepare each of the following solutions.

   a. 2.50m solution of $C_6H_{12}O_6$ containing 2000.0 g water
   b. 1.25m solution of NaCl containing 250.0 g water

7. Determine the mass of ethylene glycol, $C_2H_4(OH)_2$, which must be dissolved in 2500.0 g water to make a 4.00m solution.

8. Calculate the mole fraction of methanol, CH_3OH, when 3.20 g of methanol are dissolved in 4.61 g of ethanol, CH_3CH_2OH.

9. A laboratory experiment requires 0.100M $Pb(NO_3)_2$. How many grams of $Pb(NO_3)_2$ are needed to make 175 cm^3 of the solution?

10. A teacher needs to prepare 15 sets of solutions for a chemistry lab. Each set must have 70.0 cm^3 of 0.200M $FeSO_4·7H_2O$. What mass of $FeSO_4·7H_2O$ is required to prepare enough solution for the class?

COLLIGATIVE AND COLLOIDAL PROPERTIES

22

22:1 MOLES OF SOLUTE

When a solute is dissolved in a solvent, the vapor pressure of the solvent is reduced. The amount of the reduction depends upon the number of solute particles in a given amount of solvent. Since both the freezing point and boiling point of a liquid depend on its vapor pressure, introduction of a solute into a solvent will change the solvent's freezing and boiling points. The freezing point of the solvent is lowered by the addition of the solute. The addition of a solute also increases the boiling point of a solvent.

The change in freezing point and boiling point varies directly as the concentration of solute particles. One mole or 6.02×10^{23} particles of a molecular solute dissolved in 1000 grams of water (a 1 molal solution) lowers the freezing point of the water by 1.853 C°. This temperature interval (1.853 C°) is the **molal freezing point constant** for water. One mole of the ionic solute, NaCl, contains 2 moles of solute particles (1 mole Na^+ and 1 mole Cl^-). Thus, the freezing point of the water is lowered by 2×1.853 C°.

One mole of a molecular solute dissolved in 1000 grams of water (a 1 molal solution) raises the boiling point of the water by 0.515 C°. This temperature interval is called the **molal boiling point constant** for water. One mole of the ionic substance $BaCl_2$ contains 3 moles of solute particles (1 mole Ba^{2+} and 2 moles Cl^-). The boiling point of the water is raised by 3×0.515 C°.

Both neutral molecules and electrically charged ions change the boiling and freezing points of a solution. Pure substances that act as solvents have fixed boiling and freezing points. Unless otherwise stated, the solvent used is water. Other solvents can be used, but each solvent has a different and characteristic molal freezing point depression constant and molal boiling point elevation constant. See Table A-12 in the Appendix for other values.

Boiling point and freezing point constants for water can be used to calculate

1. the freezing point of the solution
2. the boiling point of the solution
3. the molecular mass of the solute from the freezing point or the boiling point

22:2   FREEZING POINT CALCULATIONS

The freezing point of a solution can be calculated from the mass or the moles of the solute dissolved in a known mass of water. Or, if the freezing point is known, the concentration of the solution can be calculated. The conversion ratio used is

$$\frac{1m \text{ concentration}}{1.853 \text{ C}°}$$

This constant relates the freezing point depression for water to the molal concentration.

Example 1

Calculate the freezing point of a solution containing 5.70 g of sugar, $C_{12}H_{22}O_{11}$, in 50.0 g water.

Solving Process:

Convert grams of solute per gram of water to moles of solute per kilogram of water (molality). Then multiply by the conversion ratio to obtain the change in freezing point.

$$\text{change in freezing point} = \frac{5.70 \text{ g } C_{12}H_{22}O_{11}}{50.0 \text{ g } H_2O} \left| \frac{1000 \text{ g } H_2O}{1 \text{ kg } H_2O} \right.$$

$$\left. \frac{1 \text{ mol}}{342 \text{ g } C_{12}H_{22}O_{11}} \right| \frac{1.853 \text{ C}°}{1m} = 0.618 \text{ C}°$$

To determine the freezing point of the solution, subtract the change in freezing point from 0°C, the freezing point of water.

$$\text{freezing point} = 0°C - 0.618 \text{ C}° = -0.618°C$$

PROBLEMS

1. Calculate the freezing point of a solution that contains 30.0 g sodium acetate, $NaCH_3COO$, dissolved in 250.0 g water.
2. Calculate the freezing point if 46.0 g glycerol, $C_3H_5(OH)_3$, are dissolved in 500.0 g water.

22:3   BOILING POINT CALCULATIONS

These calculations are similar to the calculations involving the freezing point of water solutions. The ratio used is $1m$ concentration/0.515 C°.

Example 2

Calculate the boiling point of a solution containing 5.70 g sugar, $C_{12}H_{22}O_{11}$, dissolved in 50.0 g water.

Solving Process:

Use the molal boiling point constant of 0.515 C° to calculate the change in boiling point.

$$\text{change in boiling point} = \frac{5.70 \text{ g } C_{12}H_{22}O_{11}}{50.0 \text{ g } H_2O} \left| \frac{1000 \text{ g } H_2O}{1 \text{ kg } H_2O} \right| \frac{1 \text{ mol}}{342 \text{ g } C_{12}H_{22}O_{11}}$$

$$\left| \frac{0.515 \text{ C}°}{1 \text{ m}} = 0.172 \text{ C}° \right.$$

Add the change in boiling point to the boiling point of water 100°C.

$$\text{boiling point} = 100°C + 0.172 \text{ C}° = 100.172°C$$

Example 3

How many grams of a molecular substance (molecular mass 50.0) must be added to 500.0 g water to have a boiling point of 101.56°C?

Solving Process:

Start with the change in boiling point (1.56 C°) and convert to molal concentration.

$$\text{molality} = \frac{1.56 \text{ C}°}{} \left| \frac{1 m}{0.515 \text{ C}°} = 3.03 m \right.$$

Convert to grams of solute.

$$\text{mass of solute} = \frac{500.0 \text{ g } H_2O}{} \left| \frac{3.03 \text{ mol}}{1000 \text{ g } H_2O} \right| \frac{50.0 \text{ g}}{1 \text{ mol}} = 75.8 \text{ g}$$

PROBLEMS

3. Determine the boiling points of the following solutions.
   a. 16.0 g calcium chloride, $CaCl_2$, dissolved in 250.0 g H_2O
   b. 23.0 g copper(II) sulfate, $CuSO_4$, dissolved in 250.0 g H_2O
   c. 30.0 g silver nitrate, $AgNO_3$, dissolved in 250.0 g H_2O
4. How many grams of NaCl must be dissolved in 500.0 g water to raise the boiling point to 101.51°C?
5. How many grams of ethylene glycol, $C_2H_4(OH)_2$, must be dissolved in 2000.0 g H_2O to lower the freezing point to −29.75°C?

22:4 MOLECULAR MASS CALCULATIONS

The molecular mass of a solute can be determined by changes in the freezing point or boiling point. The freezing point method is more practical because of the greater temperature interval involved. It also can be more accurately measured since the boiling point is changed more by atmospheric pressure than the freezing point.

First, determine the molality of the solute from the freezing or boiling point data. Second, determine the grams per mole (molecular mass) from the calculated molality and the concentration given.

Example 4

If 3.25 g of a molecular substance are dissolved in 125.0 g H_2O, what is the molecular mass of the solute if the solution freezes at $-0.930°C$?

Solving Process:
Calculate the molality of the solution using the freezing point change.

$$\text{molality} = \frac{0.93°C}{} \left| \frac{1m}{1.853°C} \right. = 0.50m$$

Convert from grams solute per grams water to grams per mole by using the concentration determined in the first step.

$$\text{molecular mass} = \frac{3.25 \text{ g solute}}{125.0 \text{ g } H_2O} \left| \frac{1000 \text{ g } H_2O}{0.50 \text{ mol solute}} \right. = 52 \text{ g/mol}$$

PROBLEMS

6. What is the molecular mass of glucose if 22.6 g gives a freezing point of $-0.93°C$ when dissolved in 250.0 g H_2O?

7. If 21.3 g of sodium nitrate, $NaNO_3$, are dissolved in 1.00×10^3 g H_2O, the freezing point is $-0.93°C$. What is the molecular mass of the solute?

8. When 92.0 g of a molecular compound were dissolved in 1000.0 g H_2O, the freezing point of the solution was lowered to $-3.72°C$. Determine the molecular mass of this compound.

22:5 OSMOTIC PRESSURE

Semipermeable membranes will allow solvent molecules to pass through them, but not larger solute molecules. When two solutions having the same solvent are separated by such a membrane, the solvent will move from the higher solvent concentration to the lower solvent concentration through the membrane. The pressure required to stop the flow is called the **osmotic pressure.** Since osmotic pressure depends on the solute concentration, not on the nature of the substance, it is a colligative property.

A solution's osmotic pressure Π (pi) is related to the molar concentration. This relationship is expressed in the equation

$$\Pi = MRT.$$

Where Π is the osmotic pressure, M is the molarity of the solution, R is the ideal gas constant, and T is the kelvin temperature.

Example 5

What osmotic pressure would be exerted by a solution that is 1.67M at 22.0°C?

Solving Process:

Since the units of R are dm³·kPa/mol·K, we will express our molarity as 1.67 mol/1.00 dm³.

$$\Pi = MRT$$

$$= \frac{1.67 \text{ mol}}{1.00 \text{ dm}^3} \left| \frac{8.31 \text{ dm}^3 \cdot \text{kPa}}{\text{mol} \cdot \text{K}} \right| \frac{295 \text{ K}}{} = 4.09 \times 10^3 \text{ kPa}$$

PROBLEMS

9. What osmotic pressure would be exerted by a solution that is 2.75M at 30.5°C?

10. What is the osmotic pressure of the solution in which 75.9 g of solute with molecular mass of 3722 g/mol are dissolved in enough water to make 1.10 dm³ of solution at 25°C?

CHAPTER REVIEW PROBLEMS

Use the constants from Table A-12 to solve the following.

1. What are the freezing and boiling points of a solution that contains 10.0 g naphthalene, $C_{10}H_8$, dissolved in 50.0 g benzene?

2. What are the freezing and boiling points of a solution that contains 23.0 g $MgSO_4$ dissolved in 250.0 g H_2O?

3. How many grams of an organic compound (molecular mass 75.0) must be dissolved in 500.0 g acetic acid to lower the freezing point of the solution to 0.00°C?

4. Determine the grams of an organic compound (molecular mass 125) which must be dissolved in 750.0 g cyclohexane to raise the boiling point of the resulting solution to 88.46°C.

5. If the freezing point of a solution containing 0.258 g of a substance dissolved in 40.0 g benzene is 5.20°C, what is the molecular mass of the substance?

6. What is the molecular mass of an organic compound if 16.0 g of the compound when dissolved in 225.0 g nitrobenzene increased the boiling point by 8.56 C°?

7. Calculate the osmotic pressure at 30.0°C of an aqueous solution containing 12.7 g of sucrose, $C_{12}H_{22}O_{11}$, in 150.0 cm³ of solution.

8. What osmotic pressure would be exerted by a 5.75 × 10⁻²M solution at 25.0°C?

9. Chemical analysis of an organic compound gives the following results: C 69.50%, H 7.25%, O 23.25%. When 1.58 grams of this compound were dissolved in 30.0 g benzene, it gave a freezing point depression of 1.95 C°. What is the molecular mass and the molecular formula of this compound?

10. Chemical analysis of an organic compound gave the following results: C 55.00%, H 2.75%, N 12.80%, O 29.40%. When 1.270 grams of this compound were dissolved in 35.00 g cyclohexane the boiling point was elevated by 0.464 C°. What are the molecular mass and the molecular formula of this compound?

REACTION RATE AND CHEMICAL EQUILIBRIUM 23

In the previous chapters we have assumed that the reactions have gone to completion. Reactions tend to go to completion because of the formation of a gas (e.g., CO_2, SO_2), a precipitate (e.g., $AgCl$, $PbSO_4$), or a slightly ionized substance (e.g., H_2O, HF). Formation of these or similar species causes the ions from the initial reactants to be removed from the reaction.

$$2KClO_3(cr) \rightarrow 2KCl(cr) + 3O_2(g)$$
(formation of a gas)

$$Na^+(aq) + F^-(aq) + H^+(aq) + Cl^-(aq) \rightarrow Na^+(aq) + Cl^-(aq) + HF(aq)$$
(formation of a slightly ionized substance, hydrofluoric acid)

$$AgNO_3(aq) + NaCl(aq) \rightarrow NaNO_3(aq) + AgCl(cr)$$
(formation of a precipitate)

23:1 REVERSIBLE REACTIONS

It has been determined experimentally that the conversion of some reactants to products is incomplete, regardless of the reaction time. Initially the reactants are present at a definite concentration. As the reaction proceeds, the reactant concentration decreases as the product is produced. However, a point is reached at which the reactant concentration levels off and becomes constant. The concentration levels for the reactants and products no longer change. A state of **chemical equilibrium** is established.

An example of a reaction that can proceed in either direction is the equilibrium system involving nitrogen, hydrogen, and ammonia gases. The reversible reaction is written as

$$N_2(g) + 3H_2(g) \underset{reverse}{\overset{forward}{\rightleftarrows}} 2NH_3(g) + energy$$

A reversible chemical reaction is in chemical equilibrium when the rates of the opposing reactions are equal and the overall concentrations remain constant. Thus a state of chemical equilibrium is considered to be dynamic.

155

23:2   REACTION RATE

The study of chemical kinetics involves the variables that affect reaction rates. The **reaction rate** is a measurement of the increase of product or decrease of reactant in $mol/dm^3 \cdot s$. The factors that can change the rate at which product is produced are reactant concentration, temperature, surface area, catalyst, and nature of reactants.

The rate can be calculated by using the rate law expression. The rate law expression relates rate of a chemical reaction to concentration of reactants. For the reaction $A + B \rightarrow$ products, the general form of the rate law is

$$rate = k[A]^x [B]^y$$

The **specific rate constant,** k, is a proportionality constant that relates rate and concentration. The exponents x and y give the reaction order with respect to that reactant. These exponents must be determined experimentally. The sum of the exponents in a rate law expression gives the overall order of a reaction.

The rate law expression is determined experimentally. A series of reactions is run in which the concentration of one reactant is varied while the other reactant's concentration remains fixed. The effect can be seen by observing any change in the rate of product formation. The concentration is expressed in mol/dm^3 and is indicated by brackets [ ].

Example 1

Nitrogen(II) oxide reacts with oxygen gas to produce nitrogen(IV) oxide. What is the rate law expression?

$$2NO(g) + O_2(g) \rightarrow 2NO_2(g)$$

Trial	Initial [NO]	Initial [O$_2$]	Initial rate of formation of NO$_2$
1	0.015	0.010	0.0041 mol/dm$^3 \cdot$s
2	0.030	0.010	0.0164 mol/dm$^3 \cdot$s
3	0.015	0.020	0.0082 mol/dm$^3 \cdot$s

Solving Process:

By comparing Trial 1 with Trial 2 we observe that the concentration of NO has doubled while the concentration of O_2 remains constant. The rate increases four times. The rate law is second order with respect to NO. In the same way, compare Trial 1 to Trial 3. The concentration of NO remains constant while the concentration of O_2 doubles. The rate doubles, indicating that the rate law is first order with respect to O_2. The rate law expression is predicted to be

$$rate = k[NO]^2[O_2]$$

PROBLEMS

Use the following data to answer questions 1-3 for the reaction

$$NO_2(g) + O_2(g) \rightarrow 2N_2O_5(g)$$

Trial	Initial [NO$_2$]	Initial [O$_2$]	Initial rate of formation of N$_2$O$_5$
1	0.025	0.011	3.1 × 10^{-4} mol/dm^3·s
2	0.025	0.022	6.2 × 10^{-4} mol/dm^3·s
3	0.050	0.011	6.2 × 10^{-4} mol/dm^3·s

1. Write the rate law expression for the reaction.
2. Calculate the rate constant.
3. Use the rate law expression and calculated value of k to compute the initial rate of formation of N$_2$O$_5$ if the initial concentrations of NO$_2$ and O$_2$ were each 0.030M.

23:3 LE CHATELIER'S PRINCIPLE AND REACTANTS

Sometimes, systems initially at equilibrium are subjected to an outside influence or stress. Concentration, pressure, and temperature changes affect equilibrium because they produce a stress. **Le Chatelier's principle** states: *If a system in equilibrium is subjected to a stress, the equilibrium will shift in an attempt to reduce the stress.* To see how these variables affect the equilibrium, consider the reaction between nitrogen and hydrogen to form ammonia.

It more reactant is added to the system in equilibrium, the reaction shifts to the right (the product side) and more product is formed. For example, in the ammonia equation

$$N_2(g) + 3H_2(g) \rightleftarrows 2NH_3(g) + energy$$

the addition of N$_2$ puts a stress on the system. The system can relieve the stress by consuming N$_2$. The system shifts to the right to consume N$_2$, and in the process, produces more NH$_3$. If a reactant is removed, the reaction shifts to the left. In the ammonia synthesis, if we remove some H$_2$, the system can relieve the stress by producing H$_2$. When the system shifts left to replace the missing H$_2$, it also produces more N$_2$ and consumes NH$_3$.

Pressure affects only gaseous equilibrium systems. As pressure on the reactant gases is increased, the reaction shifts toward the side with the least volume. In the ammonia synthesis, an increase of pressure would shift the equilibrium to the right. In the process of shifting, four particles (N$_2$ + 3H$_2$) are converted to two particles (2NH$_3$). The number of particles colliding is thereby reduced, which also reduces the pressure. Lowering the pressure relieves the stress.

If temperature is increased, the reaction shifts in such a way that the endothermic reaction is favored. In the ammonia synthesis, the reaction from left to right is exothermic, while the reaction from right to left is endothermic. Consequently, a rise in temperature will shift the reaction to the left.

PROBLEM

4. For the following gaseous equilibrium reactions, indicate what happens to the equilibrium position (shift to right or left) when the indicated stress or condition change occurs.

a. remove NH_3 gas   **b.** decrease pressure

$$N_2 + 3H_2 \rightleftarrows 2NH_3 + \textit{energy}$$

c. decrease temperature   **d.** add a catalyst

$$CO_2 + H_2 + \textit{energy} \rightleftarrows CO + H_2O$$

e. increase SO_2 concentration **f.** increase temperature

$$2SO_2 + O_2 \rightleftarrows 2SO_3 + \textit{energy}$$

g. increase temperature   **h.** increase CO concentration

$$CO_2 + C + \textit{energy} \rightleftarrows 2CO$$

i. decrease pressure   **j.** remove N_2O_4

$$N_2O_4 + \textit{energy} \rightleftarrows 2NO_2$$

k. increase H_2 concentration   **l.** increase pressure

$$H_2 + Cl_2 \rightleftarrows 2HCl + \textit{energy}$$

m. decrease O_2 concentration   **n.** add catalyst

$$N_2 + O_2 + \textit{energy} \rightleftarrows 2NO$$

23:4   EQUILIBRIUM CONSTANT

Consider the reaction

$$N_2 + 3H_2 \rightleftarrows 2NH_3$$

The rate law expressions for the forward and reverse reactions obtained from experimental data are

the rate of forward reaction $= k_f[N_2][H_2]^3$

the rate of reverse reaction $= k_r[NH_3]^2$

At equilibrium, the two rates are equal.

$$k_f[N_2][H_2]^3 = k_r[NH_3]^2$$

Solving for the constants, k_f/k_r, gives a new constant termed the equilibrium constant, K_{eq}.

$$K_{eq} = \frac{[\text{products}]}{[\text{reactants}]} = \frac{[NH_3]^2}{[N_2][H_2]^3}$$

Note that the coefficients from the balanced equation are used as exponents in the expression for the equilibrium constant. Remember that for rate law expressions, the exponents must be determined experimentally.

There is a unique value of K_{eq} for each reaction and for each temperature. At equilibrium, if K_{eq} is much greater than 1, the products are favored. If the K_{eq} is much less than 1, the reactants are favored.

Example 2

What is the equilibrium constant, K_{eq}, for the following reaction if the equilibrium concentrations at 25°C are $[N_2O_4] = 0.0450M$ and $[NO_2] = 0.0161M$?

$$N_2O_4(g) \rightleftarrows 2NO_2(g)$$

Solving Process:

$$K_{eq} = \frac{[NO_2]^2}{[N_2O_4]} = \frac{[0.0161]^2}{[0.0450]}$$

$$= 0.005\ 76$$

The low value indicates that at equilibrium most of the oxygen and nitrogen will be in the form N_2O_4.

Example 3

What is the equilibrium concentration of NO in the following reaction if the equilibrium concentration of N_2 and O_2 are each $0.72M$ and at 25°C $K_{eq} = 4.6 \times 10^{-31}$? The equation for the reaction is

$$N_2(g) + O_2(g) \rightleftarrows 2NO(g)$$

Solving Process:

$$K_{eq} = \frac{[NO]^2}{[N_2][O_2]}$$

$$4.6 \times 10^{-31} = \frac{[x]^2}{[0.72][0.72]}$$

$$x^2 = 2.4 \times 10^{-31}$$

$$x = 4.9 \times 10^{-16}M$$

PROBLEMS

5. Determine the equilibrium constant for the following reaction if the equilibrium concentrations of $[N_2O_4] = 1.50 \times 10^{-3}$ and $[NO_2] = 0.571$.

$$N_2O_4(g) \rightleftarrows 2NO_2(g)$$

6. For the reaction $2SO_2(g) + O_2(g) \rightleftarrows 2SO_3(g)$, the equilibrium concentrations of the sulfur oxides are $[SO_2] = 2.00$ and $[SO_3] = 10.0$. What is the concentration of the oxygen when the K_{eq} is 800.0 for the reaction?

7. Write the equilibrium constant expression for the following reactions.
   a. $CO(g) + 2H_2(g) \rightleftarrows CH_3OH(g)$
   b. $CO(g) + 3H_2(g) \rightleftarrows CH_4(g) + H_2O(g)$
   c. $4NH_3(g) + 3O_2(g) \rightleftarrows 2N_2(g) + 6H_2O(g)$
   d. $2CO(g) + O_2(g) \rightleftarrows 2CO_2(g)$

8. Bromine, Br_2, reacts with nitrogen(II) oxide, NO, to form nitrosyl bromide, NOBr, according to the equation

$$Br_2(g) + 2NO(g) \rightleftarrows 2NOBr(g)$$

At equilibrium, the concentration of $[Br_2] = 0.214M$, $[NOBr] = 0.0667M$, and $[NO] = 0.428M$. Calculate the value of K_{eq} at 68°C.

9. The equilibrium constant for the reaction

$$4H_2(g) + CS_2(g) \rightleftarrows CH_4(g) + 2H_2S(g)$$

at 755°C is 0.246. What is the equilibrium concentration of H_2S if at equilibrium the concentration of $[CH_4] = 0.001\ 08M$, $[H_2] = 0.0316M$, and $[CS_2] = 0.0898M$?

23:5 GIBBS FREE ENERGY AND EQUILIBRIUM

The free energy change, ΔG, of a reaction was used in Chapter 20 to predict if a reaction would be spontaneous ($\Delta G < 0$). A spontaneous reaction would be expected to go to completion. The reactants would be almost completely converted to products. We would expect the value of the equilibrium constant to be large. The mathematical relationship between ΔG and K_{eq} is

$$\Delta G = -RT(\ln K_{eq})$$

In the expression, R is the universal gas constant, T is the absolute temperature, and $\ln$ is the base of natural logarithms.* Natural logarithms can be found using any scientific calculator.

Example 4

For the reaction $2NO(g) + Br_2(g) \rightleftarrows 2NOBr(g)$ at 115.5°C the equilibrium constant is 1.774. What is the ΔG for this reaction? $R = 0.008\ 31$ kJ/mol·K

Solving Process:

$$\Delta G = -RT(\ln K_{eq})$$
$$= -(0.008\ 31)(388.5)(\ln 1.774)$$
$$= -1.85\ kJ/mol$$

Example 5

What is the value of the equilibrium constant for the reaction $PCl_3(g) + Cl_2(g) \rightleftarrows PCl_5(g)$ at 27.8°C when $\Delta G = -55.1$ kJ?

Solving Process:

Solving the equation $\Delta G = -RT(\ln K_{eq})$ for K_{eq} we find that

$$\ln K_{eq} = \frac{\Delta G}{-RT}$$

$$= \frac{-55.1\ kJ}{-(0.008\ 31)(300.8)}$$

*Expressed in terms of common logarithms the equation becomes $\Delta G = -2.30RT\ (\log K_{eq})$.

Use the $\boxed{e^x}$ key or $\boxed{INV}$ $\boxed{lnx}$ to take the antiln of 22.0.

$$K_{eq} = 3.74 \times 10^9$$

The equilibrium constant is so large that we assume all the reactant has been converted to product.

PROBLEMS

10. Calculate the ΔG at 727°C for the reaction $2SO_2(g) + O_2(g) \rightleftarrows 2SO_3(g)$. The K_{eq} is 4.17×10^{-2}.
11. At 188°C, ΔG for the reaction $PCl_5(g) \rightleftarrows PCl_3(g) + Cl_2(g)$ is 2.97 kJ/mol. Calculate the value of the equilibrium constant.

CHAPTER REVIEW PROBLEMS

1. Write equilibrium constant expressions, K_{eq}, for each of the following reactions.
   a. $2NO_2(g) \rightleftarrows N_2O_4(g)$
   b. $2H_2(g) + CO(g) \rightleftarrows CH_3OH(g)$
   c. $4NO(g) + 6H_2O(g) \rightleftarrows 5O_2(g) + 4NH_3(g)$
   d. $2H_2S(g) + CH_4(g) \rightleftarrows 4H_2(g) + CS_2(g)$
2. The following initial rate data for the reaction $A + B \rightarrow C$ were obtained. Write the rate law for the reaction.

Trial	[A] in mol/dm^3	[B]	Initial rate in mol/dm^3·s
1	0.15	0.15	3×10^{-2}
2	0.15	0.30	3×10^{-2}
3	0.30	0.30	1.2×10^{-1}

3. A reaction has the rate law, $Rate = k[A][B]^2$. If the numerical value of $k = 2.5 \times 10^{-2}(dm^3)^2/mol^2 \cdot s$, what is the rate when the concentration of A is 0.20M and the concentration of B is 0.30M?
4. The thermal decomposition of ethylene oxide, C_2H_4O, produces methane, CH_4, and carbon monoxide, CO.

$$C_2H_4O(g) \rightleftarrows CH_4(g) + CO(g)$$

The following data was collected at 725 K.

Trial	Initial [C$_2$H$_4$O] in mol/dm^3	Initial rate in mol/dm^3·s
1	0.001 412	3.451×10^{-5}
2	0.002 824	6.902×10^{-5}

   a. Write the rate law for the reaction.
   b. Calculate the value of the specific rate constant.
5. Ammonia can be converted to the high nitrogen content fertilizer urea, NH_2CONH_2, according to the equation

$$CO_2(aq) + 2NH_3(aq) \rightleftarrows NH_2CONH_2(aq) + H_2O(l) + \textit{energy}$$

Indicate whether the equilibrium shifts left or right when the indicated stress or condition change occurs.

a. remove urea, NH_2CONH_2
b. increase CO_2 concentration
c. increase temperature
d. add catalyst

6. Industries manufacture methanol, CH_3OH, by the reaction

$$2H_2(g) + CO(g) \rightleftarrows CH_3OH(g)$$

The equilibrium constant is 10.42 at 479.0 K. What is the equilibrium concentration of methanol vapor if the equilibrium concentration of $[H_2] = 0.4578M$ and $[CO] = 0.2289M$?

7. What is the equilibrium constant, K_{eq}, for the reaction $H_2(g) + Br_2(g) \rightleftarrows 2HBr(g)$ if the equilibrium concentrations at 381°C are $[H_2] = 0.0821M$, $[Br_2] = 0.0433M$, and $[HBr] = 0.357M$?

8. What is the value of the equilibrium constant for the catalyzed reaction $2SO_2(g) + O_2(g) \rightleftarrows 2SO_3(g)$ at 25.0°C when ΔG for the reaction is -142 kJ?

9. Calculate ΔG for the reaction $Ag(NH_3)_2^+(aq) \rightleftarrows Ag^+(aq) + 2NH_3(aq)$ at 325 K. The K_{eq} is 5.29×10^{-16}.

ACIDS, BASES, AND SALTS 24

24:1 ACID-BASE THEORIES

Several definitions have been proposed for acids and bases. Depending upon the situation, each definition has its advantages and disadvantages. Three acid-base theories are Arrhenius, Brønsted-Lowry, and Lewis.

The **Arrhenius theory** is the oldest approach to acid-base theory. It is adequate for most introductory chemistry concepts. The theory explains acids and bases by the concept of ion formation. An acid ionizes in solution to produce hydrogen ions, H^+. For example, hydrochloric acid ionizes in one step.

$$HCl \rightarrow H^+ + Cl^-$$

Sulfuric acid, a polyprotic compound, ionizes in two steps.

$$H_2SO_4 \rightarrow H^+ + HSO_4^-$$
$$HSO_4^- \rightarrow H^+ + SO_4^{2-}$$

A base ionizes or dissociates in solution to produce hydroxide ions, OH^-.

$$NaOH \rightarrow Na^+ + OH^-$$

The Arrhenius theory accounts for the characteristic properties of acids and bases.

Brønsted and Lowry expanded the definition of a base to include any substance that would accept a proton. An acid is defined as a proton donor. The products that result from an acid-base reaction are called the conjugate acid and the conjugate base.

$$\underset{\text{acid}}{HF(aq)} + \underset{\text{base}}{HCO_3^-(aq)} \rightleftarrows \underset{\text{conjugate acid}}{H_2CO_3(aq)} + \underset{\text{conjugate base}}{F^-(aq)}$$

The conjugate base is the particle that remains after a proton is donated by an acid. The conjugate acid is formed when a base accepts a proton from an acid. The hydrogen carbonate ion, HCO_3^-, behaves as a base but does not contain ionizable hydroxide.

The **Lewis** definition of acids and bases is the broadest of the three theories. Lewis defined an acid as an electron-pair acceptor and a base as

163

an electron-pair donor. This definition includes reactions that contain neither hydrogen nor hydroxide ions. Molecules as well as ions can be treated
as acids or bases. Consider the reaction

$$Na_2O + SO_3 \rightarrow Na_2SO_4$$

Sodium is a spectator ion. Using the Lewis electron dot symbols

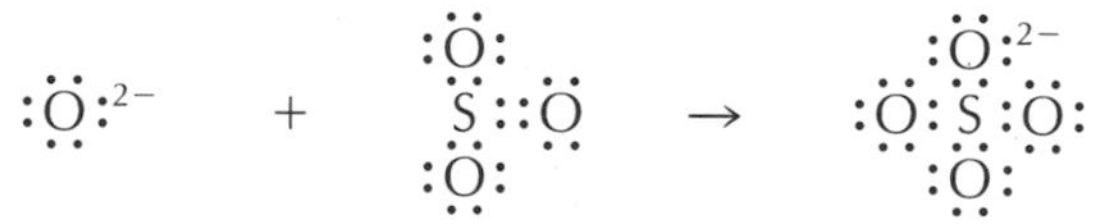

base	acid
electron-pair donor	electron-pair acceptor

The oxide ion can donate the electron pair to the SO_3 molecule.

PROBLEMS

1. Identify the acid, base, conjugate acid, and conjugate base in the following reactions.
   a. $HCN(aq) + SO_4^{2-}(aq) \rightarrow HSO_4^-(aq) + CN^-(aq)$
   b. $CH_3COO^-(aq) + H_2S(aq) \rightarrow CH_3COOH(aq) + HS^-(aq)$
2. Identify the Lewis acid and Lewis base in the following reactions.
   a. $Al^{3+} + 6H_2O \rightarrow Al(H_2O)_6^{3+}$
   b. $2NH_3 + Ag^+ \rightarrow Ag(NH_3)_2^+$

24:2 NAMING ACIDS AND SALTS

Water solutions of binary hydrides form acids. The stem derived from
the hydride is given a prefix *hydro-* and a suffix *-ic* and is followed by the
word *acid*. The binary hydride HCl is called hydrogen chloride as a gas,
but as an aqueous solution it is called hydrochloric acid.

Table 24-1

Binary Acids		
Formula	**Name**	**Anion**
HF(aq)	hydrofluoric acid	F^-, fluoride ion
HCl(aq)	hydrochloric acid	Cl^-, chloride ion
HBr(aq)	hydrobromic acid	Br^-, bromide ion
H_2S(aq)	hydrosulfuric acid	S^{2-}, sulfide ion

Many common acids contain only oxygen, hydrogen, and a nonmetallic ion or a polyatomic ion. Such acids are called **oxyacids**. The suffixes
-ous and *-ic* indicate the oxidation state of the atom bound to the oxygen
and hydrogen. The *-ous* suffix indicates a lower oxidation state. Table
24-2 lists common acids and anions.

Table 24-2

Acids Containing Oxygen			
Formula	**Name**	**Anion**	
$HClO_4$	perchloric acid	ClO_4^-	perchlorate
$HClO_3$	chloric acid	ClO_3^-	chlorate
$HClO_2$	chlorous acid	ClO_2^-	chlorite
$HClO$	hypochlorous acid	ClO^-	hypochlorite
HNO_3	nitric acid	NO_3^-	nitrate
HNO_2	nitrous acid	NO_2^-	nitrite
H_2SO_4	sulfuric acid	SO_4^{2-}	sulfate
H_2SO_3	sulfurous acid	SO_3^{2-}	sulfite
CH_3COOH	acetic acid	CH_3COO^-	acetate
H_2CO_3	carbonic acid	CO_3^{2-}	carbonate
H_3PO_4	phosphoric acid	PO_4^{3-}	phosphate
$H_2C_2O_4$	oxalic acid	$C_2O_4^{2-}$	oxalate

In a neutralization reaction an acid reacts with a base to form a salt and H_2O. The reaction goes to completion since a molecular compound (water) is formed. The water is only slightly ionized. For practical purposes, the water does not react again.

$$H_2SO_4 + 2NaOH \rightarrow Na_2SO_4 + 2H_2O$$
$$\text{Acid} \quad \text{Base} \quad \text{Salt} \quad \text{Water}$$

The other compound formed is called a salt. **Salts** are crystalline solids. A salt contains the positive ion of a base and the negative ion of an acid. In addition to common salts such as $NaCl$ and Na_2SO_4, another group of salts, termed acid salts, contain hydrogen, $NaHSO_4$, sodium hydrogen sulfate; K_2HPO_4, potassium monohydrogen phosphate; KH_2PO_4, potassium dihydrogen phosphate.

Salts may be soluble or insoluble in water. The common solubility rules are indicated in Table A-11 in the Appendix.

PROBLEMS

3. Name the following acids.

a. HCl
b. HNO_3
c. H_2SO_4
d. H_3PO_4
e. $HClO_3$
f. CH_3COOH
g. HNO_2
h. $HClO$
i. H_2SO_3
j. H_2CO_3
k. $HClO_2$
l. $HClO_4$

4. Name the following salts. Include the name of the acid from which the salt is obtained.

a. $NaClO_3$
b. $Fe(ClO_4)_2$
c. NH_4BrO_3
d. $Mg(IO_3)_2$
e. MnI_2
f. $Ba(NO_3)_2$
g. $PbCl_2$
h. $Hg(BrO_3)_2$
i. $ZnSO_4$
j. $Ca(ClO)_2$

5. Write formulas for each salt and write the formula of the acid from which the salt can be obtained.

a. ammonium sulfate
b. barium hypochlorite
c. lithium chlorate
d. cobalt(II) sulfite

e. mercury(I) bromate
f. chromium(III) nitrate
g. magnesium chloride
h. potassium perchlorate

24:3   STRENGTHS OF ACIDS AND BASES

A strong acid such as hydrochloric acid exists in solution as ions.

$$H_2O(l) + HCl(g) \rightarrow H_3O^+(aq) + Cl^-(aq)$$

The concentration of H_3O^+ ions determines the strength of an Arrhenius acid. When a weak acid dissolves in water, an equilibrium is established between the molecular form and the ionic form of the substance.

$$H_2O(l) + CH_3COOH(l) \rightleftarrows H_3O^+(aq) + CH_3COO^-(aq)$$

The reverse reaction is favored. As a result, there is a small concentration of ions. The amount of ionization is directly related to acid strength.

Strong bases, such as sodium hydroxide, also dissolve in water to form ions.

$$NaOH(cr) \rightarrow Na^+(aq) + OH^-(aq)$$

When $NH_3(g)$, a weak base, dissolves in water, few ions are produced.

$$H_2O(l) + NH_3(g) \rightleftarrows NH_4^+(aq) + OH^-(aq)$$

About 99% of the $NH_3(g)$ remains in the molecular form. As with acids, the amount of ionization is directly related to base strength.

24:4   NET IONIC EQUATIONS

When an aqueous solution of silver nitrate is added to an aqueous solution of zinc chloride, a white precipitate, silver chloride, forms.

$$2AgNO_3(aq) + ZnCl_2(aq) \rightarrow 2AgCl(cr) + Zn(NO_3)_2(aq)$$

The equation above shows all the substances as molecules even though three of them are actually existing as ions in solution. The equation would be more accurate if it were written in ionic form.

$$2Ag^+(aq) + 2NO_3^-(aq) + Zn^{2+}(aq) + 2Cl^-(aq) \rightarrow$$
$$2AgCl(cr) + Zn^{2+}(aq) + 2NO_3^-(aq)$$

You will notice that some ions appear in the same form on both the reactant and product sides. These ions, called **spectator ions,** do not take part in the reaction. Spectator ions can be subtracted from both sides of the equation to leave the **net ionic equation.**

$$2Ag^+(aq) + 2Cl^-(aq) \rightarrow 2AgCl(cr)$$

We divide each coefficient by two to reduce the net ionic equation to its final form.

$$Ag^+(aq) + Cl^-(aq) \rightarrow AgCl(cr)$$

The net ionic equation shows that mixing any solution of silver ions with any solution of chloride ions will produce the precipitate AgCl.

The following rules are used to write net ionic equations.

Rule 1. The binary acids HCl, HBr, and HI are strong and are written in ionic form. All others are weak, and are written in molecular form.

Rule 2. The number of oxygen atoms in a strong ternary acid exceeds the number of hydrogen atoms by two or more. Strong acids are written in ionic form.

Rule 3. The second and subsequent ionizations of polyprotic acids are always weak, even if the original acid is strong. Weak acids are written in molecular form.

Rule 4. Group IA (1) and IIA (2) metal hydroxides are strong bases and are written in ionic form. All other hydroxides are written in molecular form.

Rule 5. Soluble salts are written in ionic form. Insoluble salts are written in molecular form. Use Table A-11 to determine the solubility of a salt.

Rule 6. Oxides are written in molecular form.

Rule 7. Gases are written in molecular form.

Example 1

Write the net ionic equation for the following reaction.

zinc metal + hydrochloric acid $\rightarrow$ zinc chloride + hydrogen gas

Solving Process:

Rule 1: HCl is a strong acid (ionic).

Rule 5: $ZnCl_2$ is soluble (ionic).

Rule 7: H_2 gas is molecular.

(a) Write the balanced molecular equation.

$$Zn(cr) + 2HCl(aq) \rightarrow ZnCl_2(aq) + H_2(g)$$

(b) Write the ionic equation.

$$Zn(cr) + 2H^+(aq) + 2Cl^-(aq) \rightarrow Zn^{2+}(aq) + 2Cl^-(aq) + H_2(g)$$

(c) Determine the net ionic equation by subtracting out any spectator ions.

$$Zn(cr) + 2H^+(aq) \rightarrow Zn^{2+}(aq) + H_2(g)$$

PROBLEM

6. Write the net ionic equation for each word equation.

   a. sodium + water $\rightarrow$ sodium hydroxide + hydrogen

b. phosphoric acid + magnesium hydroxide →
magnesium phosphate + water
c. barium chloride + sodium sulfate →
sodium chloride + barium sulfate
d. magnesium hydroxide + ammonium phosphate →
magnesium phosphate + ammonia + water
e. iron(III) bromide + ammonium sulfide →
iron(III) sulfide + ammonium bromide

24:5   IONIZATION CONSTANT

When ionic compounds are dissolved in water the ions separate from each other in a process called **dissociation.** Many molecular compounds, when dissolved in water, react with the water to produce ions in a process called **ionization.**

It is assumed that strong electrolytes dissociate completely. A $0.1M$ solution of a strong acid, such as HCl, contains $0.1M$ hydronium ions. Similarly, a $0.5M$ solution of a strong base, such as NaOH, contains $0.5M$ hydroxide ions. However, the ionization of weak electrolytes, such as the weak acids CH_3COOH, HNO_2, H_2SO_3, and the only common weak base, $NH_3(aq)$, is not complete.

Weak acids and weak bases ionize, in general, as follows (HA represents a weak acid and B represents a weak base)

$$HA + H_2O \rightleftarrows H_3O^+ + A^- \quad B + H_2O \rightleftarrows BH^+ + OH^-$$

The ionization of weak electrolytes occurs only to a small extent before equilibrium is established. An equation that allows you to determine the concentration of each substance at equilibrium is called an equilibrium expression.

The equilibrium expression for ionization involves the concentration of the products multiplied together and divided by the concentration of the reactants. All of these concentrations are in moles per dm^3 and are thus placed in brackets [ ]. Assuming the reaction $A + 2B \rightleftarrows C + 3D$, the constant K is

$$K_{eq} = \frac{[products]}{[reactants]} = \frac{[C][D]^3}{[A][B]^2}$$

Note that the individual concentrations of B and D are raised to the second and third powers. The numbers 2 and 3 come from the coefficients in front of B and D, respectively, in the balanced equation. The equilibrium expression for the ionization equation of a weak acid or a weak base is

$$K_{eq} = \frac{[H_3O^+][A^-]}{[HA][H_2O]} \qquad K_{eq} = \frac{[BH^+][OH^-]}{[B][H_2O]}$$

The concentration of the water is essentially constant (55.6M). Multiplying both sides of the equation by [H_2O] produces a new constant expression called an **ionization constant.** The expression for the weak acid ionization constant is

$$K_a = \frac{[H_3O^+][A^-]}{[HA]}$$

The expression for the weak base ionization constant is

$$K_b = \frac{[BH^+][OH^-]}{[B]}$$

Example 2

Calculate the [OH^-] of a 0.500M solution of aqueous ammonia. The K_b of NH_3 is 1.74×10^{-5}.

Solving Process:

From the ionization equation, $NH_3 + H_2O \rightleftarrows NH_4^+ + OH^-$, write the ionization constant expression of ammonium hydroxide.

$$K_b = \frac{[NH_4^+][OH^-]}{[NH_3]}$$

Let [NH_4^+] = [OH^-] = x. [NH_3] is slightly less than the 0.500M by the concentration of the [NH_4^+]

$$1.74 \times 10^{-5} = \frac{x^2}{0.500 - x}$$

Because K_a is 10^{-5} and [NH_3] is $5 \times 10^{-1}M$, the difference is greater than three orders of magnitude. Thus, $0.500 - x \approx 0.500$.

$$1.74 \times 10^{-5} = \frac{x^2}{0.500}$$
$$x^2 = (1.74 \times 10^{-5})(0.500) = 8.70 \times 10^{-6}$$
$$x = \sqrt{8.85 \times 10^{-6}} = 2.95 \times 10^{-3}$$

Therefore, x = [NH_4^+] = [OH^-] = $2.95 \times 10^{-3}M$.

To check your answer you can use a process called iteration. To iterate, substitute your value for x, 2.95×10^{-3}, to obtain the value for [NH_3]. Then solve for [NH_4^+] and [OH^-].

$$x^2 = (1.74 \times 10^{-5})(0.500 - 2.95 \times 10^{-3})$$
$$x^2 = 8.65 \times 10^{-6}$$
$$x = 2.94 \times 10^{-3}M$$

The answer for x is similar for both processes and can be considered correct.

Example 3

Determine the experimental ionization constant of an acetic acid solution if 0.100 mole of acetic acid is dissolved in enough water to make 1.00 dm^3 of solution in which [H$_3$O$^+$] equals 0.001 35 mol/dm^3.

Solving Process:

The ionization equation is

$$CH_3COOH + H_2O \rightleftarrows H_3O^+ + CH_3COO^-$$

The ionization constant, K_a, for the acetic acid is

$$K_a = \frac{[H_3O^+][CH_3COO^-]}{[CH_3COOH]}$$

The concentration of the hydronium ion and the acetate ion both equal 0.001 35M. The molecular acetic acid has a concentration of [0.100 − 0.001 35M]. Substitute the value into the K_a expression and solve.

$$K_a = \frac{[0.001\ 35][0.001\ 35]}{[0.100 - 0.001\ 35M]} = 1.85 \times 10^{-5}$$

PROBLEMS

7. Determine the ionization constant for each of the weak electrolytes.
   a. a 0.001 00M acetic acid solution with [H$_3$O$^+$] = 1.27 × 10^{-4}M.
   b. a 0.0070M aqueous ammonia solution with [OH$^-$] = 3.46 × 10^{-4}M.
   c. a 0.100M hydrogen cyanide solution with [H$_3$O$^+$] = 7.85 × 10^{-6}M.
8. Determine the concentration of all substances in a flask that contains 1.00M CH$_3$COOH. The K_a is 1.75 × 10^{-5}.

24:6   PERCENT OF IONIZATION

When weak acids or bases dissolve in water, they ionize slightly. Most of the acid or base remains in the molecular form. The amount of original acid or base that ionizes is expressed as the percent of ionization.

$$\% \ ionization = \frac{[amount\ ionized]}{[original\ acid\ or\ base]} \times 100$$

The percent of ionization is used as an indicator of acid or base strength. The stronger acids usually have a higher percent of ionization.

If the percent ionization of the weak electrolyte is known, the K_a or the K_b can be calculated if the concentration of the solution is given.

Example 4

If an acetic acid solution has an initial concentration of 0.0800M and is 1.50% ionized, determine the experimental K_a of the CH$_3$COOH.

Solving Process:

If the initial $[CH_3COOH]$ concentration is 0.0800, the $[H_3O^+]$ and the $[CH_3COO^-]$ can be obtained by multiplying the concentration by the percent ionization.

$$[H_3O^+] = [CH_3COO^-] = (0.0800)(0.0150) = 0.001\ 20M$$

At equilibrium $[CH_3COOH] = 0.0800 - 0.001\ 20 = 0.0788M$.

From the ionization equation $CH_3COOH + H_2O \rightleftarrows H_3O^+ + CH_3COO^-$ write the K_a expression. Substitute and solve for K_a.

$$K_a = \frac{[H_3O^+][CH_3COO^-]}{[CH_3COOH]} = \frac{[1.20 \times 10^{-3}]^2}{[7.88 \times 10^{-2}]} = \frac{1.44 \times 10^{-6}}{7.88 \times 10^{-2}} = 1.83 \times 10^{-5}$$

Example 5

If the K_a of hydrofluoric acid is 6.61×10^{-4} and the HF solution has an initial concentration of 0.150M, calculate the percent of ionization.

Solving Process:

From the ionization equation determine the amount ionized by solving the K_a expression for x.

$$HF + H_2O \rightleftarrows H_3O^+ + F^-$$

$$K_a = \frac{[H_3O^+][F^-]}{[HF]} = \frac{[x][x]}{[0.150]}$$

The [HF] is assumed to be 0.150 instead of 0.150 − x, as x is a very small number. Substitute the K_a value and solve for x:

$$6.61 \times 10^{-4} = \frac{[x][x]}{[0.150]}$$

$$x^2 = 9.92 \times 10^{-5}$$

$$x = 9.96 \times 10^{-3}M$$

Check your answer using iteration.

$$x^2 = (6.61 \times 10^{-4})(0.150 - 9.96 \times 10^{-3})$$
$$x^2 = 9.26 \times 10^{-5}$$
$$x = 9.62 \times 10^{-3}$$

Since there is a difference between your two values for x, continue to iterate until your value for x does not change.

$$x^2 = (6.61 \times 10^{-4})(0.150 - 9.62 \times 10^{-3})$$
$$x = 9.63 \times 10^{-3}$$

Now that you have a corrected value for x, continue to solve for percent of ionization.

$$\% \ ionization = \frac{[amount \ ionized]}{[original \ acid]} \times 100$$

$$= \frac{9.63 \times 10^{-3}M}{0.150M} \times 100 = 6.42\%$$

PROBLEMS

9. Find the experimental ionization constants of the following weak electrolytes.

    a. $0.100M$ HF   8.50% ionized

    b. $0.500M$ CH_3COOH 1.88% ionized

    c. $0.0130M$ CH_3CH_2COOH 3.70% ionized

    d. $0.200M$ $HAsO_2$ 0.005 50% ionized

10. If the K_a of chlorous acid, $HClO_2$, is 1.1×10^{-2}, calculate the percent of ionization of a $0.225M$ solution.

11. Calculate the percent of ionization of a $0.125M$ hypoiodous acid (HIO) solution. The K_a is 2.29×10^{-11}.

24:7 COMMON ION EFFECT

In the previous problems it was assumed that the ionization process occurred in pure water. If, however, a common ion provided by an electrolyte is present, the calculations are slightly different.

Consider the ionization of acetic acid in pure water.

$$CH_3COOH + H_2O \rightleftarrows H_3O^+ + CH_3COO^-$$

The concentrations of the $[H_3O^+]$ and the $[CH_3COO^-]$ are the same, since both ions come from the same source that yields one ion of each when the acid ionizes.

If some sodium acetate is added, the concentration of the $[CH_3COO^-]$ increases because there are two sources of acetate ion, and one of the sources (the $NaCH_3COO$) is completely ionized. According to Le Chatelier's principle (an equilibrium reaction shifts so as to relieve a stress), the $[H_3O^+]$ decreases sharply as the reverse reaction toward the molecular acid occurs and the acetic acid concentration increases. The K_a value remains constant.

Example 6

Determine the H_3O^+ concentration in a solution of CH_3COOH that is $0.100M$ if enough $NaCH_3COO$ is added to make the solution $2.00M$ with respect to the CH_3COO^-. The K_a of CH_3COOH is 1.75×10^{-5}.

Solving Process:

$$CH_3COOH + H_2O \rightleftarrows H_3O^+ + CH_3COO^-$$

Let $[H_3O^+] = x$ and we know $[CH_3COO^-] = 2.00$.

Also $[CH_3COOH] = 0.100 - x \cong 0.100$.

$$K_a = \frac{[H_3O^+][CH_3COO^-]}{[CH_3COOH]}$$

$$1.75 \times 10^{-5} = \frac{x(2.00)}{(0.100)}$$

$$= \frac{(1.75 \times 10^{-5})(0.100)}{(2.00)} = 8.75 \times 10^{-7}M$$

The $[H_3O^+]$ in a solution that is 2.00M in acetate ion and 0.100M in CH_3COOH is $8.75 \times 10^{-7}M$. The $[H_3O^+]$ in a pure 0.100M CH_3COOH solution is $1.32 \times 10^{-3}M$. The concentration of the $[H_3O^+]$ has decreased sharply after adding the sodium acetate.

PROBLEMS

12. What is the hydronium ion concentration in a solution 0.0875M HClO and 0.0550M NaClO? Refer to Table A-13 for the K_a.

13. If it is necessary to reduce the concentration of the $[H_3O^+]$ to 2.00 × $10^{-4}M$, what must be the concentration of the $[CH_3COO^-]$ in a 0.400M solution of acetic acid? The K_a is 1.75×10^{-5}.

24:8 POLYPROTIC ACIDS

A number of polyprotic acids ionize to form one H_3O^+ ion in each step of the ionization. Thus a polyprotic acid has several ionization constants, with each constant relating to the ionization of that particular step.

Phosphoric acid (H_3PO_4), a triprotic acid, has three different ionization constants.

$$H_3PO_4 + H_2O \rightleftarrows H_3O^+ + H_2PO_4^- \quad K_1 = \frac{[H_3O^+][H_2PO_4^-]}{[H_3PO_4]}$$

$$= 7.08 \times 10^{-3}$$

$$H_2PO_4^- + H_2O \rightleftarrows H_3O^+ + HPO_4^{2-} \quad K_2 = \frac{[H_3O^+][HPO_4^{2-}]}{[H_2PO_4^-]}$$

$$= 6.31 \times 10^{-8}$$

$$HPO_4^{2-} + H_2O \rightleftarrows H_3O^+ + PO_4^{3-} \quad K_3 = \frac{[H_3O^+][PO_4^{3-}]}{[HPO_4^{2-}]}$$

$$= 4.17 \times 10^{-13}$$

The smaller the value of K, the weaker the acid. For any polyprotic acid, the first ionization constant is always considerably larger than the second; the second ionization constant is greater than the third. Each successive ionization leaves the negative polyatomic ion with greater attraction for the remaining hydrogen ion or ions and, therefore, each successive ionization is less likely to occur than the preceding ionizations.

For the previous problems in this chapter, it was assumed that the concentration of the ionized species was very small compared to the concentration of the molecular species. This assumption is correct for slightly ionized acids and bases in aqueous solution which are not too dilute. However, for medium strength electrolytes, this simplifying assumption cannot be made. For these electrolytes, it is necessary to use the quadratic equation or iteration.

Example 7

Determine the hydronium ion concentration for the first ionization of a phosphoric acid, H_3PO_4, solution which is $0.0100M$. The K_a of H_3PO_4 is 7.08×10^{-3}.

Solving Process:

From the equation, $H_3PO_4 + H_2O \rightleftarrows H_3O^+ + H_2PO_4^-$, obtain the expression for the equilibrium constant.

$$K_a = \frac{[H_3O^+][H_2PO_4^-]}{[H_3PO_4]}$$

Since $[H_3O^+] = [H_2PO_4^-]$, both can equal x. Also, at equilibrium, $[H_3PO_4] = 0.0100 - x$. (In previous problems, $0.0100 - x$ was assumed to be 0.0100. This assumption cannot be made for medium strength electrolytes.) Substitute the values into the K_a expression.

$$7.08 \times 10^{-3} = \frac{[x][x]}{[0.0100 - x]}$$

Rearrange and obtain

$$x^2 + 7.08 \times 10^{-3} x + (-7.08 \times 10^{-5}) = 0$$

The rearrangement has the quadratic form $ax^2 + bx + c = 0$. If a, b, and c are coefficients, the roots can be obtained by substituting into the quadratic equation.

$$x = \frac{-b \pm \sqrt{b^2 - 4ac}}{2a}$$

where $a = 1$; $b = 7.08 \times 10^{-3}$; and $c = -7.08 \times 10^{-5}$.

$$x = \frac{-7.08 \times 10^{-3} \pm \sqrt{(7.08 \times 10^{-3})^2 - 4(1)(-7.08 \times 10^{-5})}}{2(1)}$$

$$= \frac{-7.08 \times 10^{-3} \pm 8.58 \times 10^{-2}}{2}$$

$$= +0.005\,59 \text{ and } -0.0464 \text{ mol/dm}^3$$

A negative concentration (-0.0464) has no meaning in chemistry. The correct answer is $0.005\,59M$. Obviously $0.005\,59M$ is not negligible compared to the original concentration of $0.0100M$. This problem can be solved using iteration. However, you would need to iterate 18 times to obtain your final answer. You should still check your answer using iteration.

$$x^2 = (7.08 \times 10^{-3})(0.0100 - 5.59 \times 10^{-3})$$
$$x = 5.59 \times 10^{-3}M$$

PROBLEM

14. The second ionization of a $0.100M$ sulfuric acid solution is

$$HSO_4^- + H_2O \rightarrow H_3O^+ + SO_4^{2-}$$

The K_a is 1.02×10^{-2}. Calculate the hydronium ion concentration by:
a. making the false assumption that x can be neglected compared to $0.100M$.
b. solving by using the quadratic equation.

CHAPTER REVIEW PROBLEMS

1. Define an acid according to the following theories.
   a. Arrhenius theory
   b. Brønsted-Lowry theory
   c. Lewis theory
2. Name the following acids.
   a. HBr
   b. HNO_2
   c. H_2SO_4
   d. H_2S
   e. H_3PO_3
   f. $HClO_3$
   g. HI
   h. CH_3COOH
   i. H_3AsO_4
   j. HIO_3
   k. H_2SiO_3
   l. H_2CO_3
3. Write formulas for the following. Identify each as acid, base, or salt.
   a. magnesium hydroxide
   b. hydrochloric acid
   c. zinc nitrate
   d. sulfurous acid
   e. sodium hypochlorite
   f. potassium hydroxide
4. Label the acid, base, conjugate acid, and conjugate base in the following reactions.
   a. $HSO_4^-(aq) + Cl^-(aq) \rightarrow SO_4^{2-}(aq) + HCl(aq)$
   b. $OH^-(aq) + CH_3COOH(aq) \rightarrow CH_3COO^-(aq) + H_2O(l)$

5. Identify the Lewis acid and Lewis base in the reaction of Ni^{2+} with four water ligands.

$$Ni^{2+}(aq) + 4H_2O(l) \rightarrow Ni(H_2O)_4^{2+}(aq)$$

6. Apply the rules for writing the net ionic equations to these reactions.
   a. sodium hydroxide + hydrochloric acid → sodium chloride + water
   b. potassium metal + water → potassium hydroxide + hydrogen gas
   c. silver nitrate + sodium chloride → sodium nitrate + silver chloride

7. Using Table A-13, determine the molar concentration of all substances in a 1.000 dm^3 volumetric flask filled with a water solution containing 1.750 moles of boric acid, H_3BO_3.

8. Calculate the hydronium ion concentration in a 0.045M HIO solution. Refer to Table A-13 for K_a.

9. What is the value of K_b for $NH_3(aq)$ if a 0.1250M solution has the following equilibrium concentrations: $[NH_4^+] = [OH^-] = 1.478 \times 10^{-3}M$, $[NH_3] = 0.1235M$?

10. Determine the first ionization constant for 0.0285M H_2CO_3 solution with $[H_3O^+] = 1.11 \times 10^{-4}M$.

11. Find the experimental ionization constant for a 0.0535M HClO solution that ionizes 2.35%.

12. Calculate the percent ionization of a 0.075M HCN solution. Refer to Table A-13 for K_a.

13. Calculate the $[H_3O^+]$ in a solution that is 1.125M CH_3COOH if enough $NaCH_3COO$ is added to make the solution 0.5005M with respect to the CH_3COO^-. Refer to Table A-13 for K_a.

14. Use the quadratic equation to calculate the $[H_3O^+]$ in a 0.750M $CH_2ClCOOH$ solution. Refer to Table A-13 for K_a.

$$CH_2ClCOOH(aq) + H_2O(l) \rightarrow H_3O^+(aq) + CH_2ClCOO^-(aq)$$

SOLUTIONS OF ELECTROLYTES 25

25:1 SOLUBILITY PRODUCT CONSTANT

Most insoluble ionic solids are actually soluble in water to a limited extent. These solids dissociate slightly in water. The compound silver chloride dissociates slightly in water to give silver ions, Ag^+, and chloride ions, Cl^-. An equilibrium is established in the saturated solution between the solid and the ions in the solution. The equation for this equilibrium is

$$AgCl(cr) \rightleftarrows Ag^+(aq) + Cl^-(aq)$$

The above equation can be represented mathematically by a constant, K_{eq}, called the **equilibrium constant.** By definition, this constant is equal to the concentration of the products in moles per dm^3 divided by the concentration of the reactants in moles per dm^3. The concentration of each ion is raised to a power that is equal to the coefficient of the ion in the balanced equation. This constant can be expressed as follows.

$$K_{eq} = \frac{[products]}{[reactants]} = \frac{[Ag^+][Cl^-]}{[AgCl]}$$

The concentration of a pure solid such as AgCl is a constant. Since both terms, [AgCl] and K_{eq}, are constants, they can be multiplied together to form a new constant, which is termed the **solubility product constant,** K_{sp}.

$$[Ag^+][Cl^-] = K_{eq}[AgCl] = K_{sp}$$

The solubility product constant, K_{sp}, is the product of the concentrations of the ions in a saturated solution raised to the power of their coefficients in the balanced equation. For example, the expression of the solubility product for $PbCl_2$ would be

$$PbCl_2 \rightleftarrows Pb^{2+} + 2Cl^-$$
$$K_{sp} = [Pb^{2+}][Cl^-]^2$$
ion product

Using the equation for K_{sp}, it is possible to calculate the solubility of a salt if its K_{sp} is known, or to calculate the K_{sp} from the solubility. The K_{sp} is an experimental value and depends on the temperature, as does K_{eq}. The solubility of a salt expressed in moles per cubic decimeter is the molar solubility of the salt.

Example 1

A 1.00 dm^3 saturated solution of AgCl is evaporated to dryness and the residue is equivalent to 1.34×10^{-5} mole. What is the experimental K_{sp} of the silver chloride?

Solving Process:

The equation for the system is $AgCl \rightleftarrows Ag^+ + Cl^-$. Therefore, in a saturated solution of AgCl, 1.34×10^{-5} mole AgCl gives 1.34×10^{-5} mole Ag^+ and 1.34×10^{-5} mole Cl^-. The solubility product expression for AgCl is

$$K_{sp} = [Ag^+][Cl^-]$$

Since the concentration in moles per dm^3 is given, substitute this value directly into the equation.

$$K_{sp} = [1.34 \times 10^{-5}][1.34 \times 10^{-5}] = 1.80 \times 10^{-10}$$

Example 2

If the K_{sp} of AgCl is 1.78×10^{-10}, determine the solubility of AgCl in grams per dm^3.

Solving Process:

From the equation $AgCl \rightleftarrows Ag^+ + Cl^-$, note that the concentration of Ag^+ is equal to the concentration of Cl^-. Let the Ag^+ concentration be equal to x:

$$[Ag^+] = [Cl^-] = x$$

Substitute this value into the K_{sp} equation:

$$[Ag^+][Cl^-] = x^2 = K_{sp} = 1.78 \times 10^{-10}$$

$$x^2 = 1.78 \times 10^{-10}$$

$$x = \sqrt{1.78 \times 10^{-10}} = 1.33 \times 10^{-5} M$$

The molar solubility, x, is 1.33×10^{-5} mole per dm^3. In grams per dm^3 it is

$$\text{molar solubility} = \frac{1.33 \times 10^{-5} \text{ mol AgCl}}{1 \text{ dm}^3} \left| \frac{144 \text{ g AgCl}}{1 \text{ mol AgCl}} \right.$$

$$= 1.92 \times 10^{-3} \text{ g AgCl/dm}^3$$

A useful application of the K_{sp} data is to determine if precipitation will occur when a salt and a solution or when two solutions are mixed. Precipitation takes place only when the ion product exceeds the K_{sp}.

$$\left. \begin{array}{l} \text{ion product} < K_{sp} \\ \text{ion product} = K_{sp} \end{array} \right\} \qquad \text{no precipitate will form}$$

$$\text{ion product} > K_{sp} \qquad \qquad \text{precipitate will form}$$

Remember that if the final solution is formed by mixing two solutions it is necessary to consider dilution. Each solute is diluted when the other solution is added.

Example 3

Will precipitation occur when 50.0 cm³ of a $3.00 \times 10^{-2}M$ $Pb(NO_3)_2$ solution is added to 50.0 cm³ of $2.00 \times 10^{-3}M$ KCl? The K_{sp} of $PbCl_2$ is 1.62×10^{-5}.

Solving Process:

Assume that no change in volume occurs when the two solutions are mixed and that the final volume will be 100.0 cm³. First calculate the concentration of ions in the mixture as if they do not react. The Pb^{2+} concentration, because of a twofold dilution, is $1.50 \times 10^{-2}M$. The Cl^- concentration, because of a twofold dilution, is $1.00 \times 10^{-3}M$. Use these new concentrations of Pb^{2+} and Cl^- to calculate the ion product and determine if it exceeds the K_{sp}.

The equation for equilibrium of a saturated solution is

$$PbCl_2 \rightleftarrows Pb^{2+} + 2Cl^-$$

Therefore, on substitution the ion product becomes

$$[Pb^{2+}][Cl^-]^2 = [1.50 \times 10^{-2}][1.00 \times 10^{-3}]^2 = 1.50 \times 10^{-8}$$

Since 1.50×10^{-8} is smaller than the K_{sp} of $PbCl_2$(1.62×10^{-5}), precipitation does not occur. The solution is unsaturated.

PROBLEMS

From the solubilities, determine the experimental value of the K_{sp} for each of the following compounds.

1. AgI 2.88×10^{-6} g/1.00 dm³
2. $BaCO_3$ 7.00×10^{-5} mol/dm³
3. CaF_2 0.0170 g/1.00 dm³
4. $Pb(OH)_2$ 4.20×10^{-6} mol/dm³
5. SrF_2 1.22×10^{-2} g/100 cm³
6. $Pb(IO_3)_2$ 2.30 mg/100 cm³

Calculate the molar solubility of the following compounds from their K_{sp} values.

7. CuS 6.31×10^{-36}
8. SrC_2O_4 1.58×10^{-7}
9. $Al(OH)_3$ 1.26×10^{-33}
10. PbI_2 7.08×10^{-9}
11. Determine the solubility in g/dm³ of the compounds listed in Problems 8 and 10.

Determine if precipitation would occur in the following cases. (Use Table A-15 for K_{sp} values.)

12. 25.0 cm^3 of $6.00 \times 10^{-6}M$ $Sr(NO_3)_2$ is mixed with 25.0 cm^3 of 4.00 $\times 10^{-7}M$ H_3PO_4. K_{sp} of $Sr_3(PO_4)_2$ is 4.07×10^{-28}.

13. 100.0 cm^3 of a $5.00 \times 10^{-3}M$ $Ba(NO_3)_2$ is mixed with 100.0 cm^3 of $2.00 \times 10^{-2}M$ NaF.

14. 50.0 cm^3 of $6.0 \times 10^{-4}M$ $AgNO_3$ is mixed with 50.0 cm^3 of $5.0 \times 10^{-4}M$ K_2CrO_4.

25:2   IONIZATION OF WATER: THE pH SCALE

Pure water ionizes slightly into hydronium and hydroxide ions:

$$H_2O(l) + H_2O(l) \rightleftarrows H_3O^+(aq) + OH^-(aq)$$

It has been found by experiment that one dm^3 of pure water contains only one ten millionth of a mole of hydronium ions and one ten millionth of a mole of hydroxide ions. A substance that contains more hydronium ions than hydroxide ions is acidic; a substance that contains more hydroxide ions than hydronium ions is basic. A neutral substance such as pure water contains an equal number of hydronium ions and hydroxide ions. The ions are in equilibrium in pure water when the concentration of hydronium ions is 1.00×10^{-7} mol/dm^3 and the hydroxide ion concentration is also 1.00×10^{-7} mol/dm^3.

$H_2O + H_2O$	$\rightleftarrows$	H_3O^+	$+$	OH^-
1 dm^3 water	*at equilibrium*	*1.00×10^{-7} mol*		*1.00×10^{-7} mol*
(55.6 mol)	*contains*	*hydronium ions*		*hydroxide ions*

We can now write the equilibrium expression for water with the information just given and find an equilibrium constant for water.

$$2H_2O \rightleftarrows H_3O^+ + OH^-$$

$$K_{eq} = \frac{[H_3O^+][OH^-]}{[H_2O][H_2O]}$$

Since the ionization of water is very small in comparison with the total concentration of water (55.6M)*, the concentration of water can be assumed to remain constant. If the concentration of water is constant, we can multiply both sides of the equation by this constant without destroying the relationship.

$$[H_2O]^2 \times (K_{eq}) = [H_2O]^2 \times \left(\frac{[H_3O^+][OH^-]}{[H_2O]^2} \right)$$

---

*You may wonder where the 55.6M came from. We are working with one dm^3 of water that has a mass of 1000 g. You know that one mole of water has a mass of 18.0 g. Therefore, one dm^3 of water must contain

$$\frac{1000 \text{ g}}{18.0 \text{ g/mol}} = 55.6 \text{ mol water.}$$

Since both $[H_2O]$ and K_{eq} are constants, their product will also be constant. We call this constant the ion product constant of water and denote it by the symbol K_w. The ion product constant for water has been found to be 1.00×10^{-14} at room temperature.

$$K_w = [H_3O^+][OH^-] = 1.00 \times 10^{-14}$$

Note that when

$$[H_3O^+] = 1.00 \times 10^{-1}, \text{ the } [OH^-] = 1.00 \times 10^{-13}$$
$$[H_3O^+] = 1.00 \times 10^{-13}, \text{ the } [OH^-] = 1.00 \times 10^{-1}$$
$$[H_3O^+] = 1.00 \times 10^{-7}, \text{ the } [OH^-] = 1.00 \times 10^{-7}$$

This simple relationship has been used to construct the pH scale, which is used to indicate how acidic or basic a solution is. The pH scale ranges from 0 to 14. A pH of 7 is neutral; a pH below 7 is acidic; and a pH above 7 is basic.

The pH scale indicates the hydronium ion concentration. Another related scale, the pOH scale, is used to indicate the hydroxide ion concentration. Note that as the pH increases, the pOH decreases and the product, $[H_3O^+] \times [OH^-]$, is always 1.00×10^{-14}. If you know the pH, simply subtract the pH value from 14 to change to the pOH scale.

$$pH + pOH = 14$$

K_w is a constant for all dilute aqueous solutions. Although the concentrations of H_3O^+ and OH^- may change when substances are added to water, the product of $[H_3O^+]$ and $[OH^-]$ remains the same

$$K_w = [H_3O^+][OH^-] = 1.00 \times 10^{-14}$$

If an acid is added to a solution, the $[H_3O^+]$ increases and the $[OH^-]$ decreases. If a base is added, the $[OH^-]$ increases and $[H_3O^+]$ decreases. Even in solutions that are acidic and contain a very large number of hydronium ions, a very small number of hydroxide ions exist.

To work problems involving pH and pOH, you must translate from these two scales back to concentration of moles per dm^3. If you wish to prepare a solution of a specific pH, you must also know how many moles of hydronium ion must be present per dm^3. For the simpler problems, you will have no difficulty if you thoroughly understand the definitions of pH, pOH, $[H_3O^+]$ and $[OH^-]$. For the more complex problems, you must be able to manipulate logarithms and exponents using a scientific calculator.

We will use a neutral solution to show the relationship between the symbols and their relation to exponents and logarithms. A neutral solution contains 1.00×10^{-7} moles of hydronium ions per dm^3 and 1.00×10^{-7} moles of hydroxide ions per dm^3.

$$[H_3O^+] = 1.00 \times 10^{-7} \qquad pH = 7$$
$$[OH^-] = 1.00 \times 10^{-7} \qquad pOH = 7$$

Note that the pH and pOH are simply the exponents of the ion concentrations without the negative signs. To translate into mathematical form, we must introduce logarithms because we are dealing with exponents.

$$pH = -\log [H_3O^+] \qquad pOH = -\log [OH^-]$$

Logs are used because they are exponents of ten and it is convenient to deal with hydronium ion concentrations in terms of powers of ten and scientific notation. (See the Appendix B for a discussion on logs.)

Example 4

What is the pH of a solution that contains 1.00×10^{-4} mol H_3O^+/dm^3?
Solving Process:

$$
\begin{aligned}
pH &= -\log [H_3O^+] \\
&= -\log (1.00 \times 10^{-4}) = -(\log 1.00 + \log 10^{-4}) \\
&= -[0.0000 + (-4)] = 4.00
\end{aligned}
$$

Example 5

Find the pH and pOH of a solution that contains 0.003 50 mol H_3O^+/dm^3.
Solving Process:

Method I: Using Log Tables

$$
\begin{aligned}
pH &= -\log [H_3O^+] \\
&= -\log (3.50 \times 10^{-3}) = -(\log 3.50 + \log 10^{-3}) \\
&= -[0.5441 + (-3)] = 2.46
\end{aligned}
$$

Method II: Using a Calculator

$$
\begin{aligned}
pH &= -\log [H_3O^+] \\
&= -\log (3.50 \times 10^{-3})
\end{aligned}
$$

Enter the concentration into the display of a scientific calculator. Press the key labeled $\boxed{\text{LOG}}$.
Press $\boxed{+/-}$ to change the sign.

$$pH = 2.46$$

Solve for the pOH:

$$
\begin{aligned}
pH + pOH &= 14.00 \\
pOH &= 14.00 - 2.46 = 11.54
\end{aligned}
$$

Example 6

Calculate the $[H_3O^+]$ of a solution that has a pH of 3.70.
Solving Process:

Method I: Using Log Tables

$$
\begin{aligned}
pH &= -\log [H_3O^+] \\
-3.70 &= \log [H_3O^+]
\end{aligned}
$$

Because the logarithm table does not give the mantissa for negative numbers, -3.70 is expressed as a positive mantissa and a negative characteristic, $0.3000 - 4$. From the log table, the antilog of 0.3000 is 2.00. The antilog of -4 is 10^{-4}.

$$0.3000 - 4 = \log [H_3O^+]$$
$$2.00 \times 10^{-4} M = [H_3O^+]$$

Method II: Using a Calculator

Enter the pH into the calculator's display. Change its sign by pressing $\boxed{+/-}$.

Take the antilog by pressing $\boxed{\text{INV}}$ then $\boxed{\text{LOG}}$, or use the $\boxed{Y^x}$ by entering $10 \boxed{Y^x}$ with $x = -$pH.

$$2.00 \times 10^{-4} M = [H_3O^+]$$

Example 7

What is the $[OH^-]$ and the $[H_3O^+]$ of a solution if the pOH is 4.40?

Solving Process:

$$pOH = -\log [OH^-]$$
$$-4.40 = \log [OH^-]$$

Method I: Using Log Tables

Because the logarithm table does not give the mantissa for negative numbers, -4.4 is expressed as $0.6000 - 5$. From the log table, antilog 0.6000 $= 3.98$.

$$0.6000 - 5 = \log [OH^-]$$
$$3.98 \times 10^{-5} = [OH^-]$$

Method II: Using a Calculator

Enter the pOH into the calculator's display. Change its sign by pressing $\boxed{+/-}$

Take the antilog by pressing $\boxed{\text{INV}}$ then $\boxed{\text{LOG}}$, or use the $\boxed{Y^x}$ by entering $10 \boxed{Y^x}$ with $x = -$pOH.

$$3.98 \times 10^{-5} M = [OH^-]$$

To solve for the $[H_3O^+]$, substitute into the equation.

$$[H_3O^+] \times [OH^-] = 1.00 \times 10^{-14}$$

$$[H_3O^+] = \frac{1.00 \times 10^{-14}}{[OH^-]}$$

$$= \frac{1.00 \times 10^{-14}}{3.98 \times 10^{-5}}$$

$$= 2.51 \times 10^{-10} M$$

PROBLEMS

15. Calculate the pH and pOH of solutions with these concentrations.
    a. 0.000 10 mole H_3O^+ per dm^3
    b. 0.018 mole OH^- per dm^3
    c. 1.62×10^{-5} mole OH^- per dm^3
    d. 4.09×10^{-2} mole H_3O^+ per dm^3

16. Calculate the $[H_3O^+]$ of the following solutions.
    a. pH = 3.72   b. pH = 6.65   c. pOH = 12.0   d. pH = 8.2

17. Calculate the $[OH^-]$ of the following solutions.
    a. pOH = 11.0   b. pH = 4.25   c. pOH = 8.5   d. pH = 2.9

18. Calculate the pH and the pOH of solutions having the following concentrations. Assume 100% ionization. Remember that 1 mole of H_2SO_4 produces 2 moles of H_3O^+ ion.

    a. 0.0025M NaOH   d. 0.048M HCl
    b. 0.0025M H_2SO_4 e. 0.032M KOH
    c. 0.075M H_2SO_4 f. 0.000 17M NaOH

19. The pH of human blood is 7.4. What is the $[H_3O^+]$?

20. What is the $[H_3O^+]$ in a ripe red tomato that has a pH of 4.2?

25:3 BUFFERS

One use of the common ion effect (Chapter 24) is in buffering a solution. A solution is buffered if it resists change in its hydronium or hydroxide ion concentration when either of these ions is added.

A solution containing a weak acid or base and its completely ionized salt will act as a buffer. An example is a solution of acetic acid, CH_3COOH and sodium acetate, $NaCH_3COO$. Another example is aqueous ammonia, $NH_3(aq)$ and ammonium chloride, NH_4Cl.

In a solution of CH_3COOH and $NaCH_3COO$ there are a large quantity of CH_3COO^- ions, a large quantity of CH_3COOH molecules, and a small quantity of H_3O^+ ions. The Na^+ is a spectator ion and does not take part in the buffering. Any completely ionized acetate salt, such as KCH_3COO would work just as well. If an acid such as HNO_3 were added to the buffer, the H_3O^+ of the acid reacts with part of the CH_3COO^- to form more CH_3COOH. The following equation indicates only those ions actually involved in the reaction.

$$H_3O^+ + CH_3COO^- \rightarrow CH_3COOH + H_2O$$
$$\text{from the} \qquad \text{from the}$$
$$\text{acid} \qquad \text{salt}$$

The reaction tends to restore the original H_3O^+ concentration.

If a base, such as KOH, is added, the OH^- reacts with the CH_3COOH in a neutralization reaction.

$$CH_3COOH + OH^- \rightarrow H_2O + CH_3COO^-$$

from the acid   from the base

If the concentrations of the weak acid and its salt or the weak base and its salt are varied, the H_3O^+ concentration of the solution can be fixed within broad limits. The calculations are the same as those illustrated in Section 24:7.

Consider a buffer solution consisting of sodium acetate and acetic acid. Most of the acetate ion is furnished by the soluble salt. The equation for K_a can be modified to determine $[H_3O^+]$.

$$K_a = \frac{[H_3O^+][CH_3COO^-]}{[CH_3COOH]} = \frac{[H_3O^+][salt]}{[acid]}$$

$$[H_3O^+] = K_a \frac{[acid]}{[salt]}$$

The pH can be calculated using $[H_3O^+]$, as in the following example.

Example 8

A buffer solution contains 0.500 mole per dm^3 each of acetic acid and sodium acetate. Determine the pH of the solution. The K_a of the acetic acid is 1.75×10^{-5}.

Solving Process:

Method I: Using Log Tables

$$[H_3O^+] = K_a \frac{[acid]}{[salt]} = \frac{[1.75 \times 10^{-5}][0.500]}{[0.500]} = 1.75 \times 10^{-5}M$$

$$pH = -\log H_3O^+ = -\log(1.75 \times 10^{-5})$$
$$= -(\log 1.75 + \log 10^{-5})$$
$$= -[0.2430 + (-5)]$$
$$pH = 4.76$$

Method II: Using the Calculator

Enter the concentration into the display of a scientific calculator. Press the key labeled $\boxed{LOG}$: Press $\boxed{+/-}$ to change the sign.

$$pH = 4.76$$

PROBLEMS

21. A buffer solution contains 0.133 mol/dm^3 of acetic acid and 0.215 mol/dm^3 sodium acetate. Determine the pH of the solution. The K_a of acetic acid is 1.75×10^{-5}.

22. Blood contains the H_2CO_3, $NaHCO_3$ buffer system. Calculate the pH of a blood sample that contains 0.001 34M H_2CO_3 and 0.0250M

$NaHCO_3$. The K_a for the first ionization of H_2CO_3 is 4.37×10^{-7}.

$$H_2O(l) + H_2CO_3(aq) \rightleftarrows H_3O^+(aq) + HCO_3^-(aq)$$

25:4 TITRATIONS

Titration is an experimental procedure in which a standard solution is used to determine the concentration of an unknown solution. A **standard solution** is one of known concentration. The titration involves the gradual addition of one solution to another until the solute in the first solution has completely reacted with the solute in the second solution. This point is called the equivalence point (same as stoichiometric point). The equivalence point is detected using an indicator. The point at which the indicator changes color is called the endpoint of the titration.

The most common titrations involve the reaction of an acid solution with a basic solution. The reaction of the acid and base is termed a **neutralization.** The products of this reaction are a salt and water.

$$acid + base \rightarrow salt + water$$

The three types of titration reactions are: (1) an acid with a base to give a soluble salt and water, (2) a soluble salt with a second soluble salt to give a precipitate, and (3) an oxidizing material with a reducing material.

The reaction between a strong acid (e.g., HCl or HNO_3) and a strong base (e.g., $NaOH$) gives salts (e.g., $NaCl$ or $NaNO_3$). Since these salts are products of strong acids and strong bases, the resulting solution is neutral.

For a strong acid/strong base titration, the pH at the equivalence point is 7; but only a small amount of reagent causes a major pH change. The titration curve for the neutralization reaction is shown in Figure 25-1a. Curves can be produced using a pH meter connected to a chart recorder. The indicator selected should change color in the pH range from about 4 to 10. Phenolphthalein is usually used since it is easy to detect visually a slight pink color from a colorless liquid.

Reaction between a strong acid (HCl, HNO_3, or H_2SO_4) and a weak base (NH_3) also produces salts (NH_4Cl, NH_4NO_3, or $(NH_4)_2SO_4$). These salts hydrolyze to form slightly acidic solutions. The titration curve for this reaction is shown in Figure 25-1b. Methyl orange can be used as an indicator because of the low pH region in which it changes color.

The reaction between a weak acid (CH_3COOH) and a strong base ($NaOH$) gives a salt ($NaCH_3COO$). Such salts hydrolyze to give a slightly basic solution. The titration curve for this reaction is shown in Figure 25-1c. Any indicator changing color in the higher pH ranges could be used, but phenolphthalein is most frequently used.

The concentration of the acid and basic solutions will change the position of the curves only slightly (especially at the start and completion of the titration) in relation to the pH.

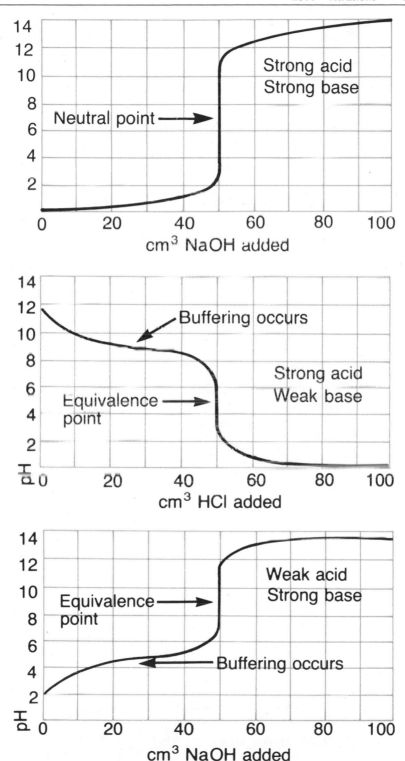

Example 9

If 20.0 cm^3 of a 0.300M solution of NaOH is required to neutralize completely 30.0 cm^3 of a sulfuric acid solution, what is the molarity of the H$_2$SO$_4$ solution?

Solving Process:

(a) First write the balanced equation.

$$2NaOH + H_2SO_4 \rightarrow Na_2SO_4 + 2H_2O$$

(b) Since the concentration of the base is given, determine the moles of NaOH.

$$\text{number of moles} = \frac{20.0 \text{ cm}^3}{} \left| \frac{0.300 \text{ mol NaOH}}{1.00 \text{ dm}^3} \right| \frac{1 \text{ dm}^3}{1000 \text{ cm}^3}$$

$$= 0.006\ 00 \text{ mol NaOH}$$

(c) From the coefficients of the balanced equation, 2 moles of base are required for reaction with 1 mole of acid.

$$\text{number of moles} = \frac{0.006\ 00 \text{ mol NaOH}}{} \left| \frac{1 \text{ mol H}_2\text{SO}_4}{2 \text{ mol NaOH}} \right.$$

$$= 0.003\ 00 \text{ mol H}_2\text{SO}_4$$

(d) Determine the molarity of the acid.

$$\text{molarity} = \frac{0.003\ 00 \text{ mol H}_2\text{SO}_4}{30.0 \text{ cm}^3} \left| \frac{1000 \text{ cm}^3}{1 \text{ dm}^3} \right.$$

$$= 0.100 \text{ mol H}_2\text{SO}_4/\text{dm}^3$$

Example 10

What volume of 0.500M HNO$_3$ is required to neutralize 25.0 cm^3 of a 0.200M NaOH solution?

Solving Process:

(a) The balanced equation is

$$HNO_3 + NaOH \rightarrow NaNO_3 + H_2O$$

(b) Since the concentration of the base is given, determine the moles of NaOH.

$$\text{mol NaOH} = \frac{25.0 \text{ cm}^3 \text{ soln}}{} \left| \frac{0.200 \text{ mol NaOH}}{1.00 \text{ dm}^3 \text{ soln}} \right| \frac{1 \text{ dm}^3}{1000 \text{ cm}^3}$$

$$= 0.005\ 00 \text{ mol}$$

(c) From the coefficients of the balanced equation, 1 mole of acid will react completely with 1 mole of base.

$$0.005\ 00 \text{ mol NaOH} = 0.005\ 00 \text{ mol HNO}_3$$

(d) Therefore

$$\text{volume} = \frac{0.005\ 00\ \cancel{mol\ HNO_3}}{} \left| \frac{\cancel{1.00\ dm^3\ soln}}{0.500\ \cancel{mol\ HNO_3}} \right| \frac{1000\ cm^3}{\cancel{1\ dm^3}}$$

$$= 10.0\ cm^3\ soln$$

PROBLEMS

23. Calculate the unknown quantity for the complete neutralization of the following.

	Acid		Base	
	concentration	*volume*	*concentration*	*volume*
a.	0.250M HCl	30.00 cm³	? NaOH	25.00 cm³
b.	0.500M H₂SO₄	?	0.750M KOH	20.00 cm³
c.	? HNO₃	15.00 cm³	1.50M NH₃	25.00 cm³
d.	0.400M HNO₃	35.00 cm³	0.800M NaOH	?

24. What is the molarity of a NaOH solution if 25.00 cm³ is required to completely neutralize 40.00 cm³ of a 1.50M solution of H₂SO₄?

25. Calculate the cm³ of a 0.600M solution of HNO₃ necessary to neutralize 28.55 cm³ of a 0.450M solution of KOH.

26. A titration of 15.00 cm³ of household ammonia, NH₃(aq), required 38.57 cm³ of 0.780M HCl. Calculate the molarity of the ammonia.

25:5 TITRATIONS WITH NORMAL SOLUTIONS

Another quantitative expression for the concentration of solutions is **normality**. A 1N solution contains one equivalent mass of solute per dm³ of solution.

$$\text{normality } (N) = \frac{number\ of\ equivalents\ of\ solute}{dm^3\ of\ solution}$$

An equivalent is that quantity of a substance that provides 1 mole of charge. Consider these three substances.

$$NaNO_3 \rightarrow Na^+ + NO_3^-$$
$$Na_2SO_4 \rightarrow 2Na^+ + SO_4^{2-}$$
$$Na_3PO_4 \rightarrow 3Na^+ + PO_4^{3-}$$

$NaNO_3$ contains 1 equivalent per mole; Na_2SO_4 contains 2 equivalents; and Na_3PO_4 contains 3 equivalents. The equivalent masses of these substances are

$$NaNO_3 \qquad \frac{85.0\ g}{1\ mol} \times \frac{1\ mol}{1\ eq} = 85.0\ g/eq$$

$$Na_2SO_4 \qquad \frac{142.1\ g}{1\ mol} \times \frac{1\ mol}{2\ eq} = 71.05\ g/eq$$

$$Na_3PO_4 \qquad \frac{164.0\ g}{1\ mol} \times \frac{1\ mol}{3\ eq} = 54.67\ g/eq$$

Titration problems can also be solved using the concentration expression normality and substituting into a mathematical equation.

Consider a reaction between a $1.00N$ HCl solution and a $1.00N$ NaOH solution. It is necessary to add equal volumes of the acid and base to have a complete reaction. An equal number of H_3O^+ ions and OH^- ions react to produce water. The other product, NaCl, is a salt of a strong acid and a strong base. The resulting solution is neutral.

The equivalent mass of a substance is that mass of material that will produce one mole of charge. One equivalent mass of hydrogen ions will react with one equivalent mass of hydroxide ions. An equal number of equivalents of acid and equivalents of base will react completely to form a salt.

$$normality = \frac{number\ of\ equivalents\ of\ solute}{1\ dm^3\ of\ solution}$$

$$\frac{eq\ acid}{1\ dm^3\ solution}\ \bigg|\ dm^3\ acid = \frac{eq\ base}{1\ dm^3\ solution}\ \bigg|\ dm^3\ base$$

On substitution:

$$normality\ acid \times volume\ acid = normality\ base \times volume\ base$$

or

$$N_a \times V_a = N_b \times V_b$$

If any three values are known, the fourth value can be calculated. For the factors to be equivalent, both volume terms must be in the same unit.

Acids or bases with one reacting hydrogen ion or hydroxide ion per formula unit contain 1 equivalent per mole. Acids or bases with two reacting hydrogen ions or hydroxide ions contain 2 equivalents per mole. Examples of the relationship between molarity and normality are

one reacting ion	HCl	$2.00M$ HCl	$= 2.00N$ HCl
(1 eq = 1 mol)	NaOH	$0.300M$ NaOH	$= 0.300N$ NaOH
two reacting ions	H_2SO_4	$0.750M\ H_2SO_4$	$= 1.50N\ H_2SO_4$
(2 eq = 1 mol)			

Example 11

If $20.0\ cm^3$ of a $3.00N$ solution of NaOH are required to neutralize $30.0\ cm^3$ of a sulfuric acid solution, what is the normality of the H_2SO_4?

Solving Process:

$$equivalents\ of\ acid = equivalents\ of\ base$$
$$N_a \times V_a = N_b \times V_b$$

Change cm^3 to dm^3 and then substitute:

$$N_a = \frac{3.00N}{0.0300\,dm^3}\bigg|\frac{0.0200\,dm^3}{}$$

$$= 2.00N$$

Example 12

How many grams of KOH are required to neutralize completely 200.0 cm^3 of a 4.00N solution of HNO$_3$?

Solving Process:

For neutralization to be complete, the number of equivalents of acid must be equal to the number of equivalents of base. First, calculate the number of equivalents of acid. Then convert this answer to grams of KOH.

$$\text{equivalents HNO}_3 = \frac{1.00 \text{ eq } HNO_3}{1\,dm^3}\bigg|\frac{0.200\,dm^3}{} = 0.800 \text{ eq}$$

equivalents acid = equivalents base

$$\text{mass KOH} = \frac{0.800 \text{ eq KOH}}{}\bigg|\frac{1 \text{ mol KOH}}{1 \text{ eq KOH}}\bigg|\frac{56.1 \text{ g KOH}}{1 \text{ mol KOH}} = 44.9 \text{ g}$$

PROBLEMS

27. What is the normality and the molarity of a phosphoric acid solution if 25.00 cm^3 of the solution is necessary to completely react with 30.00 cm^3 of a 0.500N KOH solution?

28. In a laboratory experiment involving the neutralization of vinegar using 0.500N NaOH, the following data was collected.

	Volume of vinegar	**Volume of base**
Trial 1	10.00 cm^3	17.59 cm^3
Trial 2	15.27 cm^3	28.39 cm^3
Trial 3	20.14 cm^3	36.58 cm^3

Calculate:

a. the normality of the vinegar in each trial
b. the grams of acetic acid per dm^3 of vinegar

CHAPTER REVIEW PROBLEMS

1. Given the following solubilities, determine the K_{sp} for each compound.
   a. Bi$_2$S$_3$ 1.70×10^{-15} mol/dm^3
   b. Ca$_3$(PO$_4$)$_2$ 3.92×10^{-6} mol/dm^3

2. Calculate the molar solubility for the following compounds using the K_{sp} values given.
   a. Ag$_2$S 6.31×10^{-50}
   b. BaCrO$_4$ 2.00×10^{-10}

3. Determine the mass of calcium fluoride, CaF$_2$, that will dissolve in 100.0 dm^3 of water. Assume that there is no volume change. K_{sp} of CaF$_2$ is 2.69×10^{-11}.

4. Determine if a precipitate of silver chromate, Ag_2CrO_4, will form when 100.0 cm³ of 0.100M $AgNO_3$ are added to 100.0 cm³ of 0.350M K_2CrO_4. K_{sp} of Ag_2CrO_4 is 9.00×10^{-12}.

5. If a solution contains $1.00 \times 10^{-2}M$ chloride ions and $1.00 \times 10^{-3}M$ iodide ions, which will precipitate first, AgCl or AgI, if a solution of $AgNO_3$ is added one drop at a time? The K_{sp} of AgCl is 1.56×10^{-10}; K_{sp} of AgI is 1.50×10^{-16}.

6. The approximate pH of some common substances is listed. Calculate the pOH, the $[H_3O^+]$, and the $[OH^-]$.

   a. vinegar   2.9   **e.** soft drink   3.0
   b. orange   3.5   **f.** tomato   4.2
   c. rainwater 6.2   **g.** egg   7.8
   d. seawater   8.5   **h.** milk of magnesia   10.5

7. The approximate pH of some common chemical solutions is listed. Calculate the pOH, the $[H_3O^+]$, and the $[OH^-]$.

   a. 0.1M HCl   1.00   **d.** 0.1M H_2SO_4 1.20
   b. 0.1M CH_3COOH 2.90   **e.** 0.1M $NaHCO_3$ 8.40
   c. 0.1M NH_3(aq)   11.10   **f.** 0.1M NaOH   13.00

8. What is the pH of a buffer solution that contains 0.159 mol/dm³ acetic acid and 0.195 mol/dm³ sodium acetate? The K_a for acetic acid is 1.76×10^{-5}.

9. How many cm³ of 0.500M NaOH are necessary to neutralize completely 20.00 cm³ of each of the following acids?

   a. 0.150M HNO_3 **c.** 0.220M HCl
   b. 0.250M H_2SO_4 **d.** 0.450M H_3PO_4

10. In a laboratory experiment, 20.00 cm³ of NH_3(aq) solution is titrated to the methyl orange endpoint using 15.65 cm³ of a 0.200M HCl solution. What is the concentration of the aqueous ammonia solution?

11. How many cm³ of 0.750M sulfuric acid are needed to neutralize completely 20.00 cm³ of 0.427M NaOH solution?

12. What volume of 0.250N H_3PO_4 is required to neutralize 30.00 cm³ of a 0.0500N $Ba(OH)_2$ solution?

13. Determine the normality and the molarity of a sulfuric acid solution if 30.00 cm³ is used to neutralize 40.00 cm³ of a 0.500N KOH solution.

14. If 1.25 grams of pure $CaCO_3$ required 25.50 cm³ of a hydrochloric acid solution for complete reaction, calculate the normality of the acid.

15. A common constituent of the "hardness" of water is calcium carbonate. The amount of $CaCO_3$ is determined in the laboratory by titration with a standard acid such as HCl, producing water and CO_2. A laboratory technician titrated a 100.0 cm³ sample of water containing $CaCO_3$ with 0.100N HCl and found that 15.20 cm³ of acid were needed to reach the endpoint. Calculate the mass of $CaCO_3$ contained in exactly one dm³ of the water.

OXIDATION-REDUCTION

26

26:1 OXIDATION NUMBERS

In most of the equations considered in previous chapters one species displaces another species that is similarly charged. Double displacement reactions such as the neutralizations are common examples. The species are ionic and retain the same charge as reactants and products.

$$2NaOH(aq) + H_2SO_4(aq) \rightarrow Na_2SO_4(aq) + 2HOH(l)$$

$$2Na^+(aq) + 2OH^-(aq) + 2H^+(aq) + SO_4^2 (aq)$$
$$\rightarrow 2Na^+(aq) + SO_4^{2-}(aq) + 2H_2O(l)$$

An oxidation-reduction reaction or **redox reaction** involves a change in the charges of the ions. Reactions such as synthesis and single displacement are oxidation-reduction reactions since there have been changes in the charges.

Oxidation number is the charge that an atom *appears* to have when both electrons in a bond are assigned to the more electronegative atom. Without knowledge of electron bond formulas, the oxidation states of an atom may be assigned from the following rules.

1. All free elements are assigned an oxidation number of zero. Thus, hydrogen in H_2, oxygen in O_2, and phosphorus in P_4, all have an oxidation number of zero.

2. The oxidation number of a monatomic ion is equal to the charge on the ion.
   a. Group IA (1) elements form only 1+ ions.
   b. Group IIA (2) elements form only 2+ ions.
   c. Halogen elements have a 1− oxidation number except in interhalogen compounds.

3. In practically all hydrogen-containing compounds, the oxidation number of hydrogen is 1+. The exception occurs with the metal hydrides, in which the oxidation number of hydrogen is 1−.

4. The oxidation number of oxygen in compounds is generally 2−. The exceptions are the peroxides, in which the oxidation number is 1−, and in oxygen difluoride, OF_2, where oxygen has an oxidation number of 2+.

5. All oxidation numbers that are assigned must be consistent with the conservation of charge. For neutral particles, the oxidation numbers of all atoms must add up to zero. For a polyatomic ion, the oxidation numbers of the atoms must add up to the charge on the polyatomic ion. Review the following examples.

	hydrogen	oxygen	sulfur	Total Charge
sulfuric acid	$2(1+)$ +	$4(2-)$ +	?	= 0
H_2SO_4	oxidation number of S = 6+			
sulfite ion		$3(2-)$ +	?	= 2-
SO_3^{2-}	oxidation number of S = 4+			

PROBLEM

1. In the following, give the oxidation number for the indicated atoms.
   a. Al in Al_2O_3
   b. S in $Na_2S_2O_3$
   c. Mn in MnO_4^-
   d. Cl in ClO_3^-
   e. Fe in $FeCl_3$
   f. Cr in $Cr_2O_7^{2-}$
   g. C in K_2CO_3
   h. N in NO_3^-

26:2 HALF-REACTIONS

Oxidation is the process by which electrons are removed from atoms or ions. **Reduction** is the process by which electrons are added to atoms or ions. Oxidation and reduction must occur at the same time in a reaction, and the number of electrons lost must equal the number gained.

A redox equation can be separated into an oxidation half-reaction and a reduction half-reaction. The method of balancing oxidation-reduction equations is to balance separately the oxidation half-reaction and the re-duction half-reaction. The two half-reactions are added to obtain the bal-anced equation for the total reaction.

Use the following general approach to balance redox reactions.

1. Write the separate half-reactions.
2. Balance the electrons using oxidation numbers.
3. Balance the atoms in each half-reaction as follows:
   a. Balance all atoms with the use of coefficients, except hydrogen and oxygen atoms.
   b. Add enough water (H_2O) to the side deficient in oxygen to balance the oxygen.
   c. Add sufficient hydrogen ion (H^+) to the side deficient in hydrogen to balance the hydrogen.
4. Multiply the half-reactions by small whole numbers to balance the electrons.
5. Add the two half-reactions and subtract any duplications on either side of the equation.

Example 1

Write a balanced oxidation-reduction equation for the following reaction.

$$MnO_4^- + H_2SO_3 \rightarrow Mn^{2+} + HSO_4^- + H_2O$$

Solving Process:

Separate the reaction into two half-reactions. Balance the half-reactions separately. The reduction half-reaction is

$$MnO_4^- \rightarrow Mn^{2+}$$

The first step in balancing the half-reaction is to indicate the number of electrons gained or lost. In the reduction half-reaction being considered here, the manganese has an oxidation number 7+ before the reaction and 2+ after the reaction. Thus manganese must gain 5 electrons.

$$MnO_4^- + 5e^- \rightarrow Mn^{2+}$$

The next step is to balance all elements other than oxygen and hydrogen. In the reaction above, one manganese atom appears on each side of the equation. The equation is balanced with respect to maganese atoms, the only element present in addition to oxygen. No change is needed to balance the manganese.

Next oxygen should be balanced. You may assume that all the oxidation-reduction reactions in this book take place in water solution. Thus, oxygen atoms are always available in the form of water molecules.

$$MnO_4^- + 5e^- \rightarrow Mn^{2+} + 4H_2O$$

Finally the hydrogen atoms must be balanced. Hydrogen is available in water molecules but using water to balance hydrogen atoms would throw the oxygen atoms out of balance. If you note that the solution is acidic (H_2SO_3 is one of the reactants) then you will realize that H^+ ions will be abundant in the solution and can be used to balance the hydrogen atoms.

$$MnO_4^- + 8H^+ + 5e^- \rightarrow Mn^{2+} + 4H_2O$$

The reduction half-reaction is now balanced.

The oxidation half-reaction must now be balanced. The sulfur atoms change oxidation number from 4+ to 6+, and they lose two electrons each.

$$H_2SO_3 \rightarrow HSO_4^- + 2e^-$$

Again use the available H_2O and H^+ to balance the half-reaction with respect to oxygen and hydrogen.

$$H_2SO_3 + H_2O \rightarrow HSO_4^- + 2e^- + 3H^+$$

Before the two half-reactions can be combined to give the overall equation, the coefficients of the electrons must be adjusted so that the same number of electrons are lost as are gained. The manganese half-reaction requires five electrons while the sulfur half-reaction produces two. The least common multiple of five and two is ten, so the reduction half-reaction is multiplied by two and the oxidation half-reaction by five.

Reduction half-reaction $\times$ 2

$$2MnO_4^- + 16H^+ + 10e^- \rightarrow 2Mn^{2+} + 8H_2O$$

Oxidation half-reaction $\times$ 5

$$5H_2SO_3 + 5H_2O \rightarrow 5HSO_4^- + 10e^- + 15H^+$$

Adding the two half-reactions and eliminating the electrons that appear in equal numbers on both sides gives

$$2MnO_4^- + H^+ + 5H_2SO_3 \rightarrow 2Mn^{2+} + 5HSO_4^- + 3H_2O$$

Reactions of the oxidation-reduction type can also take place in basic solution. Balance these just as you would an acidic reaction and then add sufficient hydroxide ions (OH^-) to each side to change all H^+ ions to H_2O molecules. Remember that the same number of hydroxide ions must be added to each side of the reaction.

Example 2

Write a balanced oxidation-reduction equation for the following reaction.

$$NO_2 + OH^- \rightarrow NO_2^- + NO_3^-$$

Solving Process:

Note that nitrogen is both oxidized and reduced in this reaction.

Reduction	Oxidation

Skeleton

$$NO_2 \rightarrow NO_2^- \qquad\qquad\qquad NO_2 \rightarrow NO_3^-$$

Balance electrons

$$NO_2 + e^- \rightarrow NO_2^- \qquad\qquad\qquad NO_2 \rightarrow NO_3^- + e^-$$

Nitrogen atoms are balanced

Balance oxygen

$$NO_2 + e^- \rightarrow NO_2^- \qquad\qquad\qquad H_2O + NO_2 \rightarrow NO_3^- + e^-$$

Balance hydrogen

(same) $\qquad\qquad H_2O + NO_2 \rightarrow NO_3^- + 2H^+ + e^-$

Convert to basic solution

(same) $\qquad\qquad H_2O + NO_2 + 2OH^- \rightarrow NO_3^- + 2H_2O + e^-$

Eliminate the excess water molecules on both sides

$$NO_2 + 2OH^- \rightarrow NO_3^- + H_2O + e^-$$

The number of electrons in each half-reaction is the same, so they may be added directly. The nitrogen dioxide molecules appearing in each half-reaction are combined in the final equation just as the electrons appearing on each side are eliminated.

$$2NO_2 + 2OH^- \rightarrow NO_2^- + NO_3^- + H_2O$$

PROBLEMS

Balance the following oxidation-reduction equations. All reactions take place in an acidic solution unless otherwise indicated.

2. $Cr(cr) + Sn^{4+}(aq) \rightarrow Cr^{3+}(aq) + Sn^{2+}(aq)$

3. $Al(cr) + H^{+}(aq) \rightarrow Al^{3+}(aq) + H_2(g)$

4. $Zn(cr) + Ag^{+}(aq) \rightarrow Zn^{2+}(aq) + Ag(cr)$

5. $NO_3^{-}(aq) + S(cr) \rightarrow NO_2(g) + H_2SO_4(aq)$

6. $Br_2(l) + SO_3^{2-}(aq) \rightarrow Br^{-}(aq) + SO_4^{2-}(aq)(basic)$

7. $Fe^{2+}(aq) + MnO_4^{-}(aq) \rightarrow Mn^{2+}(aq) + Fe^{3+}(aq)$

8. $Cu(cr) + SO_4^{2-}(aq) \rightarrow Cu^{2+}(aq) + SO_2(g)$

9. $Cu(cr) + NO_3^{-}(aq) \rightarrow Cu^{2+}(aq) + NO(g)$

10. $MnO_4^{-}(aq) + S^{2-}(aq) \rightarrow Mn^{2+}(aq) + S(cr)$

11. $CuS(cr) + NO_3^{-}(aq) \rightarrow Cu^{2+}(aq) + NO_2(g) + S(cr)$

12. $NO_2(g) + ClO^{-}(aq) \rightarrow NO_3^{-}(aq) + Cl^{-}(aq)(basic)$

13. $Fe^{2+}(aq) + Cr_2O_7^{2-}(aq) \rightarrow Fe^{3+}(aq) + Cr^{3+}(aq)$

14. $MnO_4^{-}(aq) + Cl^{-}(aq) \rightarrow Mn^{2+}(aq) + Cl_2(g)$

15. $IO_3^{-}(aq) + H_2S(g) \rightarrow I_2(g) + SO_3^{2-}(aq)(basic)$

16. $H_2SeO_3(aq) + Br^{-}(aq) \rightarrow Se(cr) + Br_2(g)$

17. $BrO_3^{-}(aq) + MnO_2(cr) \rightarrow Br^{-}(aq) + MnO_4^{-}(aq)(basic)$

18. $H_2S(g) + NO_3^{-}(aq) \rightarrow S(cr) + NO(g)$

CHAPTER REVIEW PROBLEMS

1. Give the oxidation number for the following.

    a. Te in TeO_2 **d.** P in PO_4^{3-}

    b. Cl in $HClO_2$ **e.** Sb in Sb_2O_5

    c. N in N_2O **f.** I in IO_3^{-}

Balance the following oxidation-reduction equations. All reactions take place in an acidic solution unless otherwise indicated.

2. $AsH_3(g) + ClO_3^{-}(aq) \rightarrow H_3AsO_4(aq) + Cl^{-}(aq)$

3. $HNO_2(aq) + I^{-}(aq) \rightarrow NO(g) + I_2(g)$

4. $MnO_4^{-}(aq) + H_2O_2(aq) \rightarrow Mn^{2+}(aq) + O_2(g)$

5. $MnO_2(cr) + ClO_3^{-}(aq) \rightarrow MnO_4^{-}(aq) + Cl^{-}(aq)(basic)$

6. $Br_2(l) \rightarrow Br^{-}(aq) + BrO_3^{-}(aq)(basic)$

7. $N_2O_4(aq) + Br^{-}(aq) \rightarrow NO_2^{-}(aq) + BrO_3^{-}(aq)(basic)$

8. $H_2PO_2^{-}(aq) + SbO_2^{-}(aq) \rightarrow HPO_3^{2-}(aq) + Sb(cr)(basic)$

9. $CrO_2^{-}(aq) + ClO^{-}(aq) \rightarrow CrO_4^{2-}(aq) + Cl^{-}(aq)(basic)$

10. $Cu(OH)_2(cr) + HPO_3^{2-}(aq) \rightarrow Cu_2O(cr) + PO_4^{3-}(aq)$

11. $HS^{-}(aq) + IO_3^{-}(aq) \rightarrow I^{-}(aq) + S(cr)$

12. $N_2O(g) + ClO^{-}(aq) \rightarrow Cl^{-}(aq) + NO_2^{-}(aq)(basic)$

13. $H_2SO_3(aq) + MnO_2(cr) \rightarrow SO_4{}^{2-}(aq) + Mn^{2+}(aq)$

14. $IO_4{}^-(aq) + I^-(aq) \rightarrow I_2(g)$

15. $CrO_4{}^{2-}(aq) + I^-(aq) \rightarrow Cr^{3+}(aq) + I_2(g)$

ELECTRO-
CHEMISTRY

27

27:1 REDUCTION POTENTIAL AND REACTION PREDICTION

Redox reactions can be used to generate electricity or can be produced by electricity. The study of these electrochemical changes is called **electrochemistry.**

Oxidation is the loss of electrons. A substance that acquires electrons from other substances easily is called an oxidizing agent. It is an oxidizing agent because it causes other substances to be oxidized. By convention, a series of half-reactions, termed the standard reduction potential table, is set up with the best oxidizing agent at the bottom left position. (See Table A-16 in the Appendix.) Each half-reaction has a characteristic reduction potential ($E°$) that is compared to a standard reference half-reaction.

$$2H^+(aq) + 2_e^- \rightarrow H_2(g)$$

This reaction is assumed to have a reduction potential of 0.000 volt (V) at 25°C, 101 325 kPa pressure and 1 molar H^+. Fluorine, F_2, is at the bottom of the list because it shows the greatest tendency to acquire electrons and become the fluoride ion. The fluoride ion is a very weak reducing agent since F^- does not readily give up its electrons.

The lithium ion, Li^+, is a weak oxidizing agent, as it does not readily gain electrons. However, the lithium atom easily gives up electrons, so it is a strong reducing agent.

A large positive potential indicates a great tendency for the reaction to occur. Fluorine gas will proceed readily to fluoride ion, since the potential is +2.87 volts. For all practical purposes, fluoride ion will not go to fluorine gas. Lithium ion will not proceed spontaneously to lithium metal since the potential is negative, −3.04 volts.

The potentials given in Table A-16 apply when the half-reaction takes place in the forward direction. In the reverse direction, the sign of the voltage is reversed. The E° values do not depend upon the number of electrons transferred.

Use the table to see if two half-reactions will react by adding the half-reaction potentials. It is necessary to balance the chemical quantities and the number of electrons, but no adjustment need be made in potential values. The potential is the ease with which certain electrons per atom or

199

ion are lost. Potentials are dependent on temperature, pressure, and concentration. Keep in mind that the given potential applies to the forward reaction. For the reverse direction, the sign of the potential is reversed.

Example 1

The following equation represents copper metal placed in a colorless silver ion solution.

$$Cu(cr) + 2Ag^+(aq) \rightarrow Cu^{2+}(aq) + 2Ag(cr)$$

Solving Process:

Write the half-reactions and obtain each voltage from the reduction potential table. Remember that the sign of the voltage may be reversed. Balance the electrons and add.

$$
\begin{array}{ll}
Cu \rightarrow Cu^{2+} + 2e^- & -0.340 \text{ V} \\
\underline{2Ag^+ + 2e^- \rightarrow 2Ag} & \underline{+0.7991 \text{ V}} \\
Cu + 2Ag^+ \rightarrow Cu^{2+} + 2Ag & +0.459 \text{ V}
\end{array}
$$

Since the voltage is positive, this reaction should occur spontaneously. Spontaneous does not mean instantaneous. A reaction occurs spontaneously when it occurs without additional energy such as heat or light. Note that the reverse reaction does not take place.

$$
\begin{array}{ll}
Cu^{2+} + 2e^- \rightarrow Cu & +0.340 \text{ V} \\
\underline{2Ag \rightarrow 2Ag^+ + 2e^-} & \underline{-0.7991 \text{ V}} \\
\text{No reaction} & -0.459 \text{ V}
\end{array}
$$

This reaction does not occur spontaneously since the voltage is negative.

PROBLEM

1. Calculate the potential in volts for each of the following reactions.
   a. $Cr(cr) + Ni^{2+}(aq) \rightarrow Cr^{2+}(aq) + Ni(cr)$
   b. $Al(cr) + H^+(aq) \rightarrow Al^{3+}(aq) + H_2(g)$
   c. $Br_2(l) + I^-(aq) \rightarrow Br^-(aq) + I_2(cr)$
   d. $Fe^{2+}(aq) + MnO_4^-(aq) \rightarrow Fe^{3+}(aq) + Mn^{2+}(aq)$
   e. $Cl_2(g) + Sn^{2+}(aq) \rightarrow Cl^-(aq) + Sn^{4+}(aq)$
   f. $Hg(l) + Hg^{2+}(aq) \rightarrow Hg_2^{2+}(aq)$

27:2 VOLTAIC CELLS

Chemists refer to a battery as an electrochemical cell. It consists of electrodes in contact with an electrolyte. An electric current is produced when the two half-cells are physically separated but electrically connected and electrons move through an external circuit. This process occurs spontaneously in a **voltaic** or **galvanic cell.** The voltaic cell is usually made of two half-cells connected by a salt bridge. The salt bridge completes the internal circuit by allowing ions to migrate between the cells. A porous ceramic cup can serve the same purpose as the salt bridge.

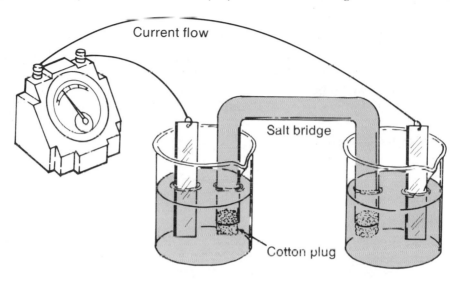

A convenient notation is used to represent a particular voltaic cell. The nickel-cadmium cell pictured above is represented by $Cd|Cd^{2+}||Ni^{2+}|Ni$. In this form the anode (oxidation half-cell) is written on the left. The cathode (reduction half-cell) is written on the right. The salt bridge connecting the two half-cells is represented by the two parallel vertical lines. The single line between Cd and Cd^{2+} represents the phase boundary between the solid Cd electrode and the solution (electrolyte).

Example 2

Consider the following electrochemical cell.

$$Li|Li^+||Ag^+|Ag$$

Use Table A-16 in the Appendix to help you analyze the cell.

Solving Process:

From Table A-16 find the two reduction half-reactions, and their E° value.

$$Li^+ + e^- \rightarrow Li, \ -3.040 \text{ V}$$
$$Ag^+ + e^- \rightarrow Ag, \ +0.7991 \text{ V}$$

The lower positive voltage indicates which half-reaction is written in reverse order. The sign on the voltage is also changed. The oxidation half-reaction is

$$Li \rightarrow Li^+ + e^-, \ \ +3.040 \text{ V}$$

This reaction occurs at the anode. Here the Li electrode loses both electrons and mass as it dissolves to form the Li^+ cation. Lithium metal is the reducing agent. The electrons leave the Li electrode and travel through the external circuit to the Ag electrode.

The reduction half-reaction is

$$Ag^+ + e^- \rightarrow Ag, \quad +0.7991 \text{ V}$$

This reaction occurs at the cathode. The cathode gains both electrons and mass. The silver cations migrate to the cathode, gain an electron, and plate out as silver metal. The Ag^+ is the oxidizing agent. The theoretical voltage on the meter would be

$$3.040 \text{ V} + 0.7991 \text{ V} = +3.839 \text{ V}$$

PROBLEMS

Use Table A-16 to help you answer questions 2 and 3.

2. Refer to the electrochemical cell below to answer each of the following questions.

$$Zn|Zn^{2+}||Pb^{2+}|Pb$$

   a. At which electrode does oxidation occur?
   b. Which electrode is the cathode?
   c. Electrons will flow from which electrode?
   d. Which electrode will gain in mass?
   e. What is the oxidizing agent?
   f. Write the half-reaction for the zinc half-cell.
   g. What is the theoretical voltage on the meter?

3. Refer to the electrochemical cell below to answer each of the following questions.

$$Al|Al^{3+}||Au^{3+}|Au$$

   a. At which electrode does reduction occur?
   b. Which electrode is the anode?
   c. Which electrode will lose in mass?
   d. To which electrode will the cations migrate?
   e. What is the reducing agent?
   f. Write the half-reaction for the gold half-cell.
   g. What is the theoretical voltage on the meter?

27:3   FARADAY'S LAWS

Electrochemistry is the study of the relationship between chemical change and electric energy. Michael Faraday experimented extensively to determine the relationship between electric charge and chemical energy. The following statements are known as Faraday's laws.

1. The mass of an element released at the electrode during electrolysis varies directly as the quantity of electricity that is passed through a solution.

2. The quantity of different elements that can be deposited by the same amount of electricity depends on the equivalent masses of these elements. Chemists measure the quantity of electrons in moles. Electricity is measured in coulombs (C). One coulomb is the quantity of electricity in one ampere (A) flowing for one second. The relationship of all these quantities is

$$1 \text{ mole } e^- = 96\,500 \text{ coulomb} = 1 \text{ ampere·second}$$

Thus 96 500 coulombs passing through molten Al_2O_3 will liberate 1/3 of an equivalent mass of aluminum (27.0 g) and 1/2 of an equivalent mass of oxygen (16.0 g).

$$96\,500 \text{ C} = 9.0 \text{ g Al} = 1/3 \text{ mol Al} = 6.02 \times 10^{23} \ e^-$$
$$96\,500 \text{ C} = 8.0 \text{ g O} = 1/2 \text{ mol O} = 6.02 \times 10^{23} \ e^-$$

Example 3

How many grams of aluminum will be deposited if 31 500 coulombs of electricity pass through an aluminum nitrate solution?

Solving Process:

Begin with the balanced equation for the reaction.

$$Al^{3+} + 3e^- \rightarrow Al$$

Convert coulombs to moles of electrons, to moles, to grams.

$$\text{grams Al} = \frac{31\,500 \text{ C}}{} \left| \frac{1 \text{ mol } e^-}{96\,500 \text{ C}} \right| \frac{1 \text{ mol Al}}{3 \text{ mol } e^-} \left| \frac{27.0 \text{ g Al}}{1 \text{ mol Al}} \right. = 2.91 \text{ g}$$

Example 4

If 10.0 amperes of current flow for 20.0 minutes through a solution of copper(II) nitrate, how many moles of copper are deposited?

Solving Process:

$$Cu^{2+} + 2e^- \rightarrow Cu$$

$$\text{mol Cu} = \frac{10.0 \text{ A}}{} \left| \frac{20.0 \text{ min}}{} \right| \frac{60 \text{ s}}{1 \text{ min}} \left| \frac{1 \text{ C}}{\text{A·s}} \right| \frac{1 \text{ mol } e^-}{96\,500 \text{ C}} \left| \frac{1 \text{ mol Cu}}{2 \text{ mol } e^-} \right.$$

$$= 0.0622 \text{ mol Cu}$$

Example 5

Calculate the mass of silver metal that can be deposited if a 5.12 A current is passed through a silver nitrate solution for 2.00 hours. The equation for the reaction is $Ag^+ + e^- \rightarrow Ag$.

Solving Process:

Obtain ampere·seconds by converting hours to seconds and multiplying by the number of amperes given. Convert ampere·seconds to coulombs. Finally change to moles of electrons, to moles, to grams.

$$\text{grams Ag} = \frac{5.12\,A}{} \left| \frac{2.00\,h}{} \right| \frac{60\,min}{1\,h} \left| \frac{60\,s}{1\,min} \right| \frac{1\,C}{A\cdot s}$$

$$\frac{1\,mol\,e^-}{96\,500\,C} \left| \frac{1\,mol\,Ag}{1\,mol\,e^-} \right| \frac{108\,g\,Ag}{1\,mol\,Ag} = 41.3\,g$$

Example 6

How many cubic decimeters of chlorine gas measured at STP are released by the passage of 8.12 amperes for 2.00 hours through molten magnesium chloride?

Solving Process:

The equation would be $2Cl^- \rightarrow Cl_2 + 2e^-$.

$$\text{volume Cl}_2 = \frac{8.12\,A}{} \left| \frac{2.00\,h}{} \right| \frac{60\,min}{1\,h} \left| \frac{60\,s}{1\,min} \right| \frac{1\,C}{A\cdot s}$$

$$\frac{1\,mol\,e^-}{96\,500\,C} \left| \frac{1\,mol\,Cl_2}{2\,mol\,e^-} \right| \frac{22.4\,dm^3\,Cl_2}{1\,mol\,Cl_2} = 6.79\,dm^3\,Cl_2$$

PROBLEMS

4. How many seconds are required to deposit 2.51 g Fe on an object using 15.4 A of current passing through an iron(III) nitrate solution? The equation for the reaction is $Fe^{3+} + 3e^- \rightarrow Fe$.

5. How many amperes are required to deposit 0.504 g Fe in 40.0 minutes by passing a current through a solution of iron(II) acetate?

6. Calculate the current required to liberate 5.60 dm³ Cl_2 at STP in 2.00 hours in the electrolysis of molten NaCl.

7. During the operation of a lead storage battery, the reaction at the two electrodes is as follows:

cathode $PbO_2 + 4H^+ + SO_4^{2-} + 2e^- \rightarrow PbSO_4 + 2H_2O$

anode $Pb + SO_4^{2-} \rightarrow PbSO_4 + 2e^-$

How much PbO_2 (in grams) is used when a current of 50.0 A in 1 hour is withdrawn from the battery?

CHAPTER REVIEW PROBLEMS

1. Calculate the positive or negative potential for each equation. Determine if the reactions will occur.

   a. $Ni(cr) + Cu^{2+}(aq) \rightarrow Ni^{2+}(aq) + Cu(cr)$
   b. $Cl^-(aq) + Br_2(l) \rightarrow Cl_2(g) + Br^-(aq)$
   c. $Cu(cr) + H^+(aq) \rightarrow Cu^{2+}(aq) + H_2(g)$
   d. $Mn(cr) + Co^{2+}(aq) \rightarrow Mn^{2+}(aq) + Co(cr)$
   e. $Zn^{2+}(aq) + Pb(cr) \rightarrow Zn(cr) + Pb^{2+}(aq)$

2. Determine the theoretical voltage for the following electrochemical cell.

$$Mn|Mn^{2+}||Fe^{2+}|Fe$$

3. Write the half-reaction that occurs at the anode in the following electrochemical cell.

$$Cr|Cr^{2+}||Sn^{2+}|Sn$$

4. How many moles of electrons are required to produce a 5.00 A current for 2.00 hours?

5. If 3.00 moles of electrons are required in producing 10.0 A of current, how many seconds are required?

6. What mass of copper is produced if 10 000.0 A·s pass through a copper(II) nitrate solution?

7. Calculate the grams of zinc deposited if 5.00 moles of electrons pass through a zinc acetate solution.

8. Using 2.50 moles of electrons how many grams of cadmium metal will be deposited from a cadmium sulfate solution?

9. If 193 000 coulombs of electricity pass through a silver nitrate solution, how many grams of silver metal are produced?

10. In the electrolysis of molten NaCl, how many moles of sodium metal are produced if 20.0 A of current flowing for 8.00 hours are used?

11. If it is necessary to deposit 1.50 g Ag on an object, how many seconds must 5.00 A of electricity flow through a solution of silver nitrate?

12. How many amperes of electricity flowing for 30.0 minutes are required to deposit 0.250 g Fe from an iron(III) nitrate solution?

NUCLEAR CHEMISTRY

28

28:1 TYPES OF RADIATION

The reactions studied in preceding chapters involved alterations in the electronic structure of atoms. In chemical reactions, the atom's nucleus remains unchanged. In contrast, nuclear reactions change nuclei of atoms. The number of protons and/or neutrons in the nuclei may increase or decrease. One element may be converted into another element. Nuclear reactions are accompanied by a change in energy. The amount of energy involved is many times greater than the energy associated with chemical reactions.

Radioactive elements such as uranium, radium, and polonium have unstable nuclei. Particles are emitted from unstable nuclei as they undergo a process called **radioactive decay.** The decay process continues until a stable element is formed. Stable nuclei do not give off particles of radiation.

Radioactive elements may occur naturally in the earth, as in the case of uranium, radium, and polonium. Normally stable elements can be made radioactive in the laboratory by bombarding them with high speed neutrons or charged particles.

Naturally occurring radioactive material produces three types of radiation. Alpha and beta radiation are made up of particles. Gamma rays are quanta of energy.

Alpha particles (α) are positively charged helium nuclei, each consisting of 2 protons and 2 neutrons. Each particle can be represented by the symbol $_2^4He$, in which the 2 represents the number of protons and the 4 represents the mass number.

Beta particles (β) are electrons represented by the symbol $_{-1}^0e$. The atomic number of each particle is -1 and the mass number is zero. Electrons do not exist in the nucleus as such but are produced when a neutron decays to form a proton.

$$_0^1n \rightarrow \, _1^1H + \, _{-1}^0e$$

When beta rays are emitted, the mass number of the nucleus remains the same, but the neutron/proton ratio is reduced.

Gamma rays (γ) possess neither mass nor charge but are quanta of energy similar to highly energetic X rays. Gamma rays are emitted when changes in the nucleus produce an excess of energy. Gamma radiation does not change the mass number or atomic number of the nucleus. The

207

emission of excess energy brings the nucleus to a less excited, more stable state. Gamma rays travel at the speed of light.

Other types of radioactive particles can be emitted when nuclei are bombarded with charged particles or high-speed neutrons and made artificially radioactive. Examples of these particles include the following:

$^{1}_{1}H$ is a proton or hydrogen atom with $A = 1$ and $Z = 1$

$^{2}_{1}H$ is a deuteron or hydrogen isotope with $A = 2$ and $Z = 1$

$^{1}_{0}n$ is a neutron with $A = 1$ and $Z = 0$ (no electric charge)

$^{0}_{+1}e$ is a positron with $A = 0$ and $Z = 1$

$^{0}_{0}\upsilon$ is a neutrino with $A = 0$ and $Z = 0$

28:2 BALANCING NUCLEAR EQUATIONS

In balancing nuclear equations, two rules must be followed.

1. The sum of the mass numbers on the left side and the right side of the equation must be equal.

2. The sum of the electric charges on the left side and the right side of the equation must be equal.

Radioactive particles given off during nuclear reactions are included in these equations in order to balance them.

Example 1

Complete the following nuclear equation.

$$^{208}_{84}Po \rightarrow \; ? \; + \; ^{4}_{2}He$$

Solving Process:

(a) Find the mass number of the unknown product. We know that the mass number is conserved in a nuclear reaction.

mass no. of 4 + mass no. of ? = 208
mass no. of ? = 208 − mass no. of 4
= 204

(b) Find the charge of the unknown product. We know that electric charge is conserved in a nuclear equation.

charge of 2 + charge of ? = 84
charge of ? = 84 − charge of 2
= 82

(c) Determine the identity of the unknown product and complete the nuclear equation. Turn to the periodic table and find which nuclide has an 82+ charge. This nuclide is lead, Pb. Thus, the completed nuclear equation is

$$^{208}_{84}Po \rightarrow \; ^{204}_{82}Pb \; + \; ^{4}_{2}He$$

PROBLEMS

1. Using the periodic table, write nuclear symbols for the isotopes.
   a. lead-208
   b. lead-210
   c. uranium-235
   d. carbon-14
   e. helium-5
   f. potassium-40
   g. lithium-8
   h. uranium-238

2. Complete and balance the following equations.
   a. $^{7}_{3}Li + ^{1}_{1}H \rightarrow ^{4}_{2}He + ?$
   b. $^{3}_{1}H + ^{2}_{1}H \rightarrow ? + ^{1}_{0}n$
   c. $^{14}_{6}C \rightarrow ^{14}_{7}N + ?$
   d. $^{9}_{4}Be + ^{4}_{2}He \rightarrow ^{12}_{6}C + ?$
   e. $^{14}_{7}N + ^{4}_{2}He \rightarrow ? + ^{0}_{+1}e$
   f. $^{26}_{12}Mg + ^{1}_{0}n \rightarrow ? + ^{0}_{+1}e$
   g. $^{59}_{27}Co + ^{2}_{1}H \rightarrow ? + ^{0}_{+1}e$

3. In a portion of the uranium decay series, lead-214 decays to bismuth-214 by beta emission. The bismuth-214 decays to polonium-214 by beta emission. The polonium-214 decays to lead-210 by alpha emission. Write balanced nuclear equations to represent these three steps.

28:3   HALF-LIFE

In a nuclear reaction, one element is changed into another element when there is a change in the number of protons in the nucleus. This process, called **transmutation,** can be natural or artificial. Transmutation continues until a stable element, whose nucleus is not radioactive, is produced. The time required for half of a sample of a radioactive isotope to decay is termed its **half-life.** Half-lives of some isotopes are only a fraction of a second. For others, the half-life may be millions or billions of years.

Table 28-1

Half-Life and Decay Mode of Selected Nuclides		
Nuclide	Half-Life	Decay Mode
$^{3}_{1}I$	12.26 years	β^-
$^{6}_{2}He$	0.797 seconds	β^-
$^{14}_{6}C$	5730 years	β^-
$^{19}_{8}O$	29.1 seconds	β^- and γ
$^{26}_{14}Si$	2.1 seconds	β^+ and γ
$^{60}_{26}Fe$	3×10^5 years	β^-
$^{71}_{30}Zn$	2.4 minutes	β^- and γ
$^{84}_{34}Se$	3.2 minutes	β^-
$^{212}_{82}Pb$	10.6 hours	β^- and γ
$^{210}_{84}Po$	138.40 days	α
$^{227}_{92}U$	1.3 minutes	α and γ
$^{235}_{92}U$	7.1×10^8 years	α and γ
$^{238}_{92}U$	4.51×10^9 years	α and γ
$^{236}_{94}Pu$	2.85 years	α and γ
$^{242}_{94}Pu$	3.79×10^5 years	α

The half-life of one isotope of zinc, $^{71}_{30}$Zn, is 2.4 minutes. Suppose we begin with 10.0 g of this isotope. At the end of 2.4 minutes, 5.0 g $^{71}_{30}$Zn would remain. The rest of the 10.0 g sample would have decayed to gallium. At the end of another 2.4 minutes, 2.5 g $^{71}_{30}$Zn would remain. After the third 2.4 minutes, the original 10.0 g sample would contain 1.25 g of the zinc isotope. The other 8.75 g $^{71}_{30}$Zn would have decayed to gallium.

Example 2

Cobalt-60 is used in cancer radiation therapy. If you start with 4.516×10^8 atoms of $^{60}_{27}$Co, how much time will pass before the amount is reduced to 1.764×10^6 atoms? The half-life is 5.26 years.

Solving Process:

(a) Divide the original amount by the present amount to obtain a ratio of atoms.

$$\frac{4.516 \times 10^8 \text{ atoms}}{1.764 \times 10^6 \text{ atoms}} = \frac{256 \text{ original atoms}}{1 \text{ remaining atom}}$$

(b) Determine the number of half-lives, where n is the number of half-lives.

$$2^n = 256$$
$$n(\log 2) = \log 256$$
$$n = \frac{\log 256}{\log 2}$$
$$= 8 \text{ half-lives}$$

(c) Calculate the amount of time that will pass.

$$\text{elapsed time} = \frac{5.26 \text{ y}}{\text{half-life}} \left| \frac{8 \text{ half-lives}}{} \right. = 42.1 \text{ years}$$

Example 3

Strontium-90 is present in nuclear fallout. Because it is in the same family as calcium, it can be found in milk and later, bones. If you start with 1.94×10^{17} atoms of $^{90}_{38}$Sr, how many atoms will remain after 140.5 years? The half-life of $^{90}_{38}$Sr is 28.1 years.

Solving Process:

number of remaining atoms = number of original atoms $\times 1/2^n$

(a) Divide 140.5 years by 28.1 years to find the number of half-lives.

$$\frac{140.5 \text{ y}}{28.1 \text{ y/half-life}} = 5.00 \text{ half-lives}$$

(b) To determine the ratio of remaining atoms to original atoms, use $1/2^n$ where n is the number of half-lives.

$$\frac{\text{remaining atoms}}{\text{original atoms}} = \frac{1}{2^n} = \frac{1}{2^5} = \frac{1}{32}$$

Only one atom remains for every 32 original atoms.

(c) Multiply the original number of atoms by 1/32.

$$(1.94 \times 10^{17} \text{ atoms})(1/32) = 6.06 \times 10^{15} \text{ atoms}$$

Thus after 140.5 years, 6.06×10^{15} atoms of radioactive $^{90}_{38}Sr$ remain.

PROBLEMS

4. The half-life of $^{71}_{30}Zn$ is 2.4 minutes. How long will it take for a sample of zinc-71 to decay to 1/16 its original mass?

5. A radioactive tracer, sodium-24, is used to study circulatory problems. If you start with 5.85×10^{23} atoms, how many atoms will remain after 12.0 days? The half-life of $^{24}_{11}Na$ is 4.0 days

6. Some patients with thyroid disorders receive radioactive iodine-131. The half-life of $^{131}_{53}I$ is 8.07 days. If you start with 7.73×10^{12} atoms, how much time will pass before the amount is reduced to 7.55×10^9 atoms?

CHAPTER REVIEW PROBLEMS

1. Complete the following nuclear equations. Indicate the new element formed during these reactions. Name the nuclear particle emitted.

   a. $^{22}_{11}Na \rightarrow ? + ^{0}_{-1}e$

   b. $^{66}_{29}Cu \rightarrow ? + ^{0}_{-1}e$

   c. $^{208}_{84}Po \rightarrow ? + ^{4}_{2}He$

   d. $^{27}_{14}Si \rightarrow ? + ^{0}_{+1}e$

2. Complete the following nuclear equations.

   a. $^{27}_{13}Al + ^{2}_{1}H \rightarrow ? + ^{4}_{2}He$

   b. $? + ^{1}_{0}n \rightarrow ^{42}_{19}K + ^{4}_{2}He$

   c. $^{63}_{29}Cu + ^{1}_{1}H \rightarrow ^{63}_{30}Zn + ?$

   d. $^{1}_{0}n + ? \rightarrow ^{136}_{53}I + ^{96}_{39}Y + 4^{1}_{0}n$

3. Batteries used in heart pacemakers contain plutonium-238. If your original sample contains 2.57×10^9 atoms of $^{238}_{94}Pu$, how much time will pass before the amount is reduced to 5.02×10^6 atoms. The half-life is 27.1 years.

4. Carbon-14 has a half-life of 5730 years and is used for radioactive dating. Assume we started with 2.18×10^{17} atoms of $^{14}_{6}C$ in a wood sample obtained from a wooden beam from an ancient tomb. There are 1.21×10^{17} atoms remaining. How old can we assume the wooden beam to be?

5. Promethium-147 has a half-life of 2.5 years and is used to paint luminous dials. If a sample originally contains 9.72×10^{23} atoms of $^{147}_{61}\text{Pm}$, how many atoms will remain after 10.0 years?

CLASSES OF ORGANIC COMPOUNDS

29

29:1 HYDROCARBONS

Organic compounds are compounds that contain carbon atoms linked together in chains or rings. **Hydrocarbons** are compounds that contain carbon and hydrogen. They are the simplest organic compounds. Hydrocarbons may be grouped into families. In some of these families, all the carbon-carbon bonds are single bonds. These compounds are said to be **saturated.** In other families, the compounds contain double or triple bonds and are **unsaturated.**

29:2 ALKANES

Alkanes are saturated hydrocarbons conforming to the general formula C_nH_{2n+2}, where n is a whole number equal to the number of carbon atoms. The alkane series is also termed the methane or paraffin series. The simplest alkanes are

CH_4
methane

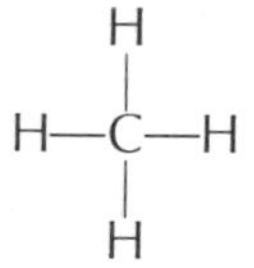

$$H-\underset{\underset{H}{|}}{\overset{\overset{H}{|}}{C}}-H$$

CH_3CH_3
ethane

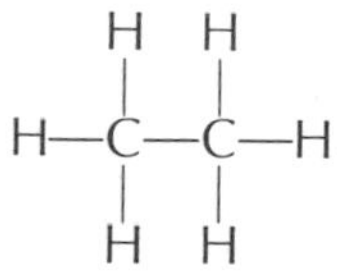

$$H-\underset{\underset{H}{|}}{\overset{\overset{H}{|}}{C}}-\underset{\underset{H}{|}}{\overset{\overset{H}{|}}{C}}-H$$

$CH_3CH_2CH_3$
propane

$$H-\underset{\underset{H}{|}}{\overset{\overset{H}{|}}{C}}-\underset{\underset{H}{|}}{\overset{\overset{H}{|}}{C}}-\underset{\underset{H}{|}}{\overset{\overset{H}{|}}{C}}-H$$

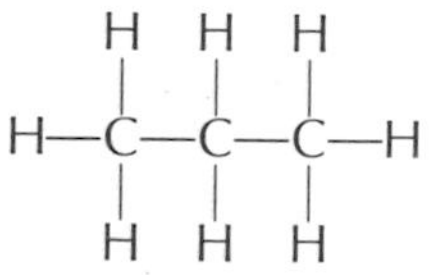

The first formula is a condensed structural formula. The second formula is an expanded structural formula.

Table 29-1 lists the stem name for each number of carbon atoms in a continuous chain or ring. It also gives some information about the alkanes of low molecular mass.

213

Table 29-1

	Alkane	Condensed Structural	Chemical	Number of
Stem Name	Name	Formula (unbranched)	Formula	Isomers
meth-	methane	CH_4	CH_4	1
eth-	ethane	CH_3CH_3	C_2H_6	1
prop-	propane	$CH_3CH_2CH_3$	C_3H_8	1
but-	butane	$CH_3(CH_2)_2CH_3$	C_4H_{10}	2
pent-	pentane	$CH_3(CH_2)_3CH_3$	C_5H_{12}	3
hex-	hexane	$CH_3(CH_2)_4CH_3$	C_6H_{14}	5
hept-	heptane	$CH_3(CH_2)_5CH_3$	C_7H_{16}	9
oct-	octane	$CH_3(CH_2)_6CH_3$	C_8H_{18}	18
non-	nonane	$CH_3(CH_2)_7CH_3$	C_9H_{20}	35
dec-	decane	$CH_3(CH_2)_8CH_3$	$C_{10}H_{22}$	75

Alkanes

With C_4H_{10}, the carbon atoms may be connected to give two different structural formulas. These two arrangements are **isomers.** Isomers have the same chemical formula but different structural formulas.

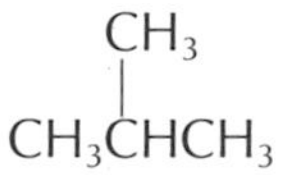

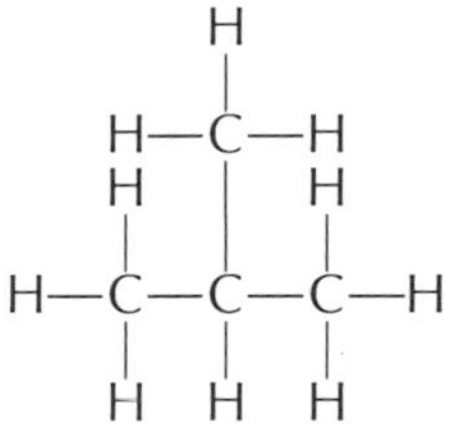

29:3 RULES FOR NAMING HYDROCARBONS

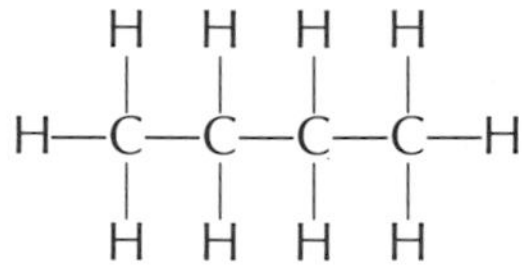

The following rules are used to name hydrocarbons.

1. Pick the longest continuous chain of carbon atoms and determine its name.

2. Number the carbon atoms in the chain beginning at the end that will give the lowest possible numbers for the different attached hydrocarbon groups.

3. Name the hydrocarbon groups attached to the longest chain by adding -yl to the stem name. Indicate the point of attachment by the number of the carbon atom to which the group is attached. Common group names are methyl, —CH_3, and ethyl, —CH_2CH_3.

For example, consider the following compound.

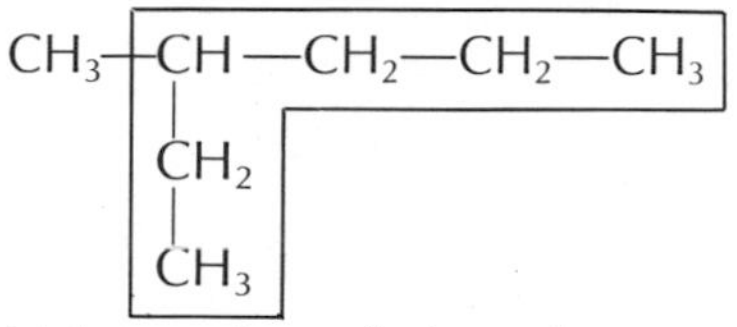

$$CH_3-\boxed{CH-CH_2-CH_2-CH_3}$$
$$\ \ \ \ \ \ \ \ \ \ |$$
$$\ \ \ \ \ \ \ CH_2$$
$$\ \ \ \ \ \ \ \ |$$
$$\ \ \ \ \ \ \ CH_3$$

The longest chain, which consists of six carbon atoms, is enclosed in a box. A chain of six carbon atoms is termed *hexane*. The carbon atoms in the longest chain are numbered in such a way as to give the lowest number possible to the attached group. At position 3 the attached group is termed *methyl*. The name of the compound is 3-methylhexane. Note that position numbers are separated from the name by hyphens.

The C_4H_{10} isomers we discussed previously are named butane and 2-methylpropane. The following are the isomers of pentane.

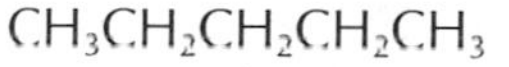

$$CH_3CH_2CH_2CH_2CH_3$$
pentane

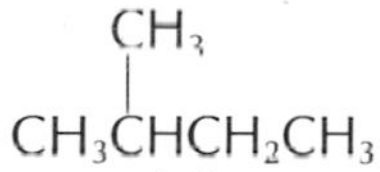

$$CH_3CHCH_2CH_3$$
(with CH_3 above)
2-methylbutane

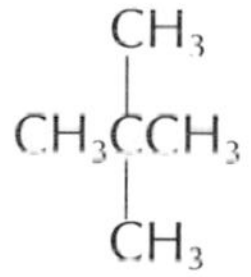

$$CH_3CCH_3$$
(with CH_3 above and CH_3 below)
2,2-dimethylpropane

Note that the position numbers are separated from each other by commas. The following are the isomers of hexane.

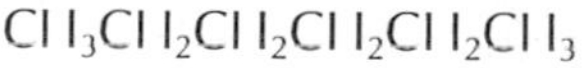

$$CH_3CH_2CH_2CH_2CH_2CH_3$$
hexane

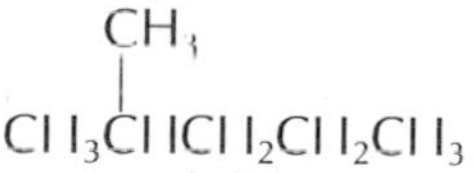

$$CH_3CHCH_2CH_2CH_3$$
(with CH_3 above)
2-methylpentane

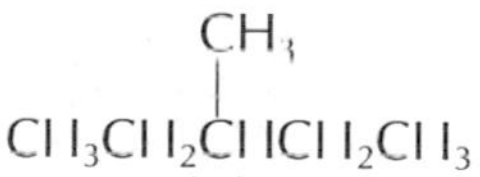

$$CH_3CH_2CHCH_2CH_3$$
(with CH_3 above)
3-methylpentane

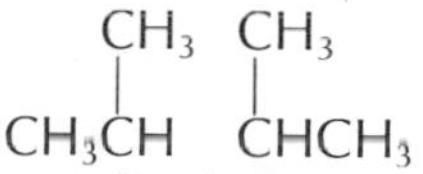

$$CH_3CH \quad CHCH_3$$
(with CH_3 above each)
2,3-dimethylbutane

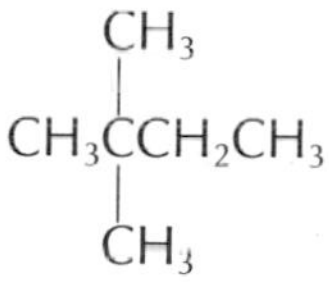

$$CH_3CCH_2CH_3$$
(with CH_3 above and CH_3 below)
2,2-dimethylbutane

4. When two or more groups are attached to a compound, the groups are named in alphabetical order. Consider the following example.

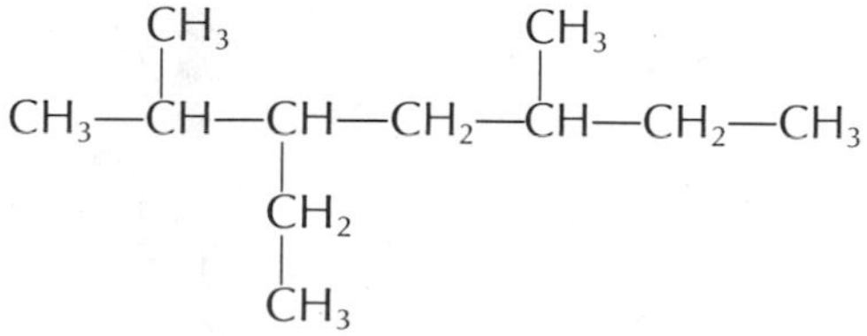

$$CH_3-CH-CH-CH_2-CH-CH_2-CH_3$$
(with CH_3 above the 2nd and 5th carbons)
$$\ \ \ \ \ \ \ \ \ \ |$$
$$\ \ \ \ \ \ \ CH_2$$
$$\ \ \ \ \ \ \ \ |$$
$$\ \ \ \ \ \ \ CH_3$$

3-ethyl-2,5-dimethylheptane

The longest continuous chain of carbon atoms is named heptane. The branched groups are ethyl and methyl. Since there are two methyl groups the prefix *di-* is used to indicate this number.

PROBLEMS

1. Name the following hydrocarbons.

a.
$$CH_3-CH_2-\overset{\overset{\displaystyle CH_3}{|}}{C}H-\overset{\overset{\displaystyle CH_2}{|}}{\underset{\underset{\displaystyle CH_3}{|}}{C}}H-CH_3$$

e.
$$CH_3-\overset{\overset{\displaystyle CH_3}{|}}{C}H-\overset{\overset{\displaystyle CH_2}{|}}{\underset{\underset{\displaystyle CH_3}{|}}{C}}H-\overset{\overset{\displaystyle CH_2}{|}}{C}H-CH_3$$

b.
$$CH_3-\overset{\overset{\displaystyle CH_3}{|}}{\underset{\underset{\displaystyle CH_3}{|}}{C}}{-}\overset{\overset{\displaystyle CH_2}{|}}{\underset{}{C}}H-CH_3$$

f.
$$CH_3-CH_2-\overset{\overset{\displaystyle CH_3}{|}}{C}H-\overset{\overset{\displaystyle CH_2}{|}}{\underset{\underset{\displaystyle CH_3}{|}}{C}}H-\overset{\overset{\displaystyle CH_2}{|}}{C}H-CH_3$$

c.
$$CH_3-\overset{\overset{\displaystyle CH_3}{|}}{\underset{\underset{\displaystyle CH_2}{|}}{C}}-CH_3$$
$$\underset{\underset{\displaystyle CH_3}{|}}{}$$

g.
$$CH_3-\overset{\overset{\displaystyle CH_2}{|}}{\underset{}{C}}H-\overset{}{C}H-CH_3$$

d.
$$CH_3-CH_2-\overset{\overset{\displaystyle CH_2-CH_2-CH_3}{|}}{\underset{\underset{\displaystyle CH_2-CH_3}{|}}{C}}-CH_2-CH_3$$

h.
$$CH_3-CH-\overset{\overset{\displaystyle CH_2-CH_3}{|}}{C}H-CH_3$$

2. Name the following hydrocarbons.

a. $CH_3CH_2CH_2\overset{\overset{\displaystyle CH_3}{|}}{C}HCH_3$

b. $CH_3\overset{\overset{\displaystyle CH_3}{|}}{C}HCH_2CH_3$

c. $CH_3\overset{\overset{\displaystyle CH_3}{|}}{\underset{\underset{\displaystyle CH_2CH_3}{|}}{C}}HCHCH_3$

d. $CH_3CH_2CHCH_2CH_3$
$$\underset{\underset{\displaystyle CH_3}{|}}{\overset{\overset{\displaystyle CH_2}{|}}{}}$$

e. $CH_3\overset{\overset{\displaystyle CH_3}{|}}{C}HCH_2\overset{\overset{\displaystyle CH_3}{|}}{C}HCH_3$

f. $CH_3\overset{\overset{\displaystyle CH_3}{|}}{C}H\ CHCH_2CH_3$
$$\underset{\underset{\displaystyle CH_3}{|}}{}$$

g. 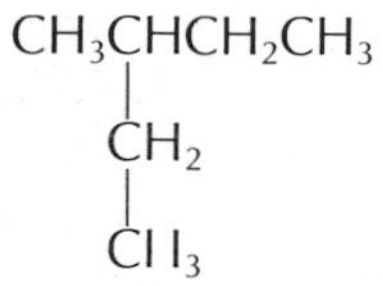 $CH_3CHCH_2CH_3$
  |
  CH_2
  |
  CH_3

CH_3
|
CH_2
|
h. 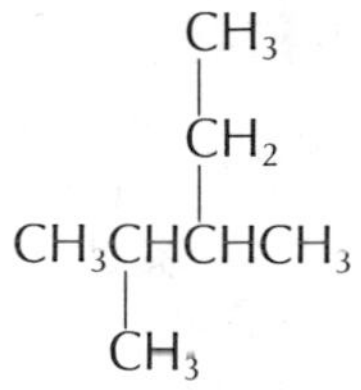 $CH_3CHCHCH_3$
    |
    CH_3

3. Listed below are the condensed structural formulas or names of the nine isomers of heptane, C_7H_{16}. Write either the formula or name for each.

a. $CH_3CH_2CH_2CH_2CH_2CH_2CH_3$

  CH_3 CH_3
  | |
b. 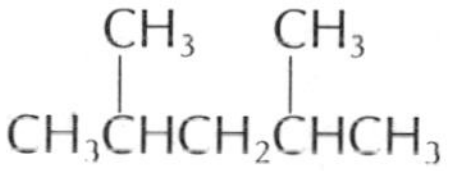 $CH_3CHCH_2CHCH_3$

    CH_3 CH_3
    | |
c. 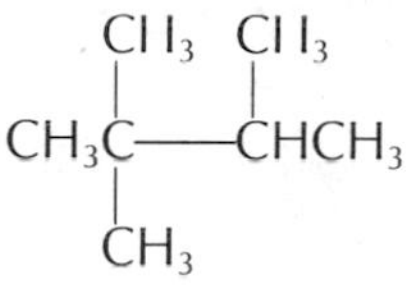 CH_3C——$CHCH_3$
    |
    CH_3

d. 2,3-dimethylpentane

e. 3,3-dimethylpentane

CH_3
|
f. 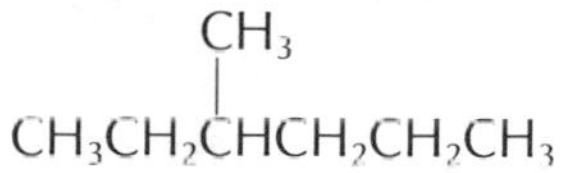 $CH_3CH_2CHCH_2CH_2CH_3$

  CH_3
  |
g. 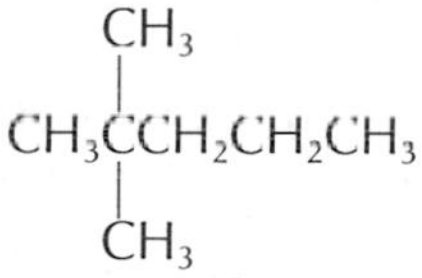 $CH_3CCH_2CH_2CH_3$
  |
  CH_3

h. 2-methylhexane

i. 3-ethylpentane

29:4 CYCLOALKANES

The cycloalkanes are saturated ring compounds having the general formula $C_n H_{2n}$. The following are some examples of cycloalkanes:

C_3H_6
cyclopropane

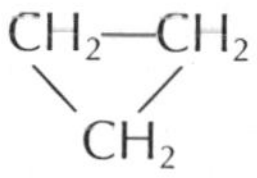

CH_2—CH_2
  \   /
   CH_2

C_5H_{10}
methlycyclobutane

CH_2—CH—CH_3
| |
CH_2—CH_2

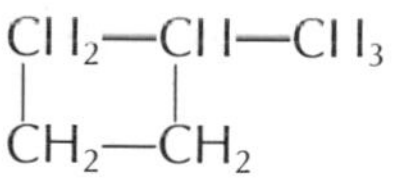

C_4H_8
cyclobutane

CH_2—CH_2
| |
CH_2—CH_2

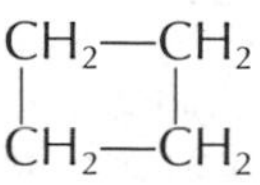

C_4H_8
methylcyclopropane

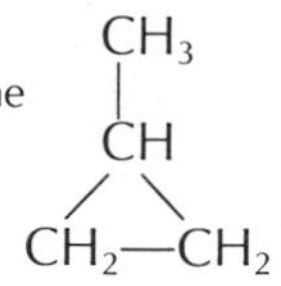

CH_3
|
CH
/ \
CH_2—CH_2

C_5H_{10}
cyclopentane

CH_2
/ \
CH_2 CH_2
| |
CH_2—CH_2

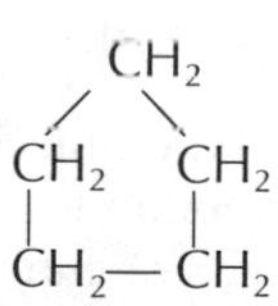

C_5H_{10}
1,1-dimethylcyclopropane

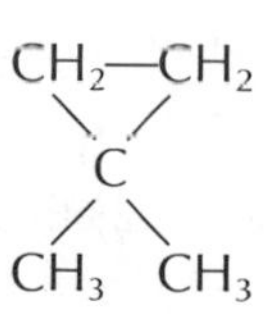

CH_2—CH_2
  \   /
   C
  / \
CH_3 CH_3

29:5   ALKENES

Alkenes are unsaturated compounds containing one double bond and having the general formula C_nH_{2n}. The -*ene* ending indicates a double bond. The position of the double bond is indicated by using the lower number of the two carbon atoms that the double bond joins. In compounds containing branched groups, the numbering of the double bond takes precedence. Note the following examples.

$$CH_2{=}CH_2 \qquad CH_3CH{=}CH_2 \qquad CH_3CH{=}CHCH_3$$
ethene   propene   2-butene

$$CH_3CH_2\overset{\overset{\textstyle CH_3}{|}}{C}{=}CH_2 \qquad\qquad CH_3\overset{\overset{\textstyle }{}}{C}HCH{=}CH_2$$
2-methyl-1-butene   3-methyl-1-butene

with CH_3 group below the CH carbon.

If a compound contains more than one double bond, the numbers of double bonds are noted with a Greek prefix preceding the -*ene* ending. For example,

$$CH_2{=}CHCH_2CH{=}CH_2 \qquad CH_2{=}CHCH{=}CH_2 \qquad CH_2{=}C{=}CHCH_2CH_3$$
1,4-pentadiene   1,3-butadiene   1,2-pentadiene

29:6   ALKYNES

Alkynes contain a triple bond and have the general formula C_nH_{2n-2}. They are named by replacing the -*ane* of the corresponding saturated hydrocarbon with -*yne*, except for the first compound in the series, for which the common name is used.

$$HC{\equiv}CH \qquad\qquad CH_3{-}C{\equiv}C{-}CH_3$$
acetylene   2-butyne
(ethyne)

Table 29-2

Hydrocarbon Summary			
Family	**Formula**	**Prefix or Suffix**	**Type of Compound**
alkanes	C_nH_{2n+2}	-ane	single bonds, saturated
cycloalkanes	C_nH_{2n}	cyclo-	ring structure, saturated
alkenes	C_nH_{2n}	-ene	double bond, unsaturated
alkynes	C_nH_{2n-2}	-yne	triple bond, unsaturated

29:7   AROMATIC HYDROCARBONS

All aromatic hydrocarbons contain one or more rings of carbon atoms held together by delocalized electrons. The compounds are named as derivatives of basic ring systems. Consider the ring structure of benzene. All positions on the benzene ring are equivalent.

benzene

Thus, only one monosubstituted compound is possible. The following are examples of monosubstituted aromatic hydrocarbons.

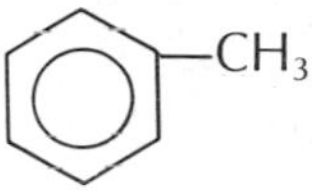

methylbenzene
(toluene)

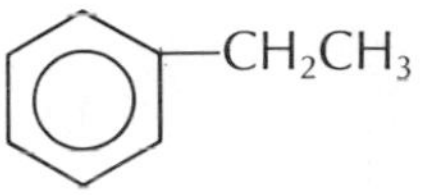

ethylbenzene

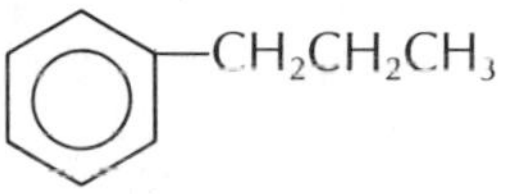

propylbenzene

For two substituents on the benzene ring three positions are possible. These positions may be designated by numbers or names, although the use of numbers is more correct.

position number	name
1,2	ortho- (o-)
1,3	meta- (m-)
1,4	para- (p-)

Disubstituted aromatic hydrocarbons include the following.

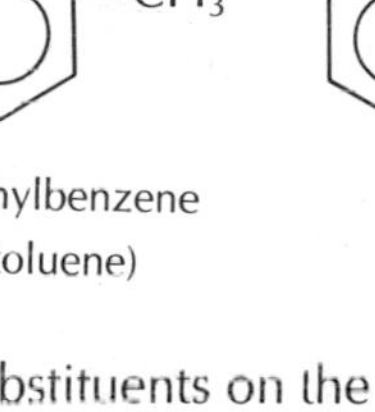

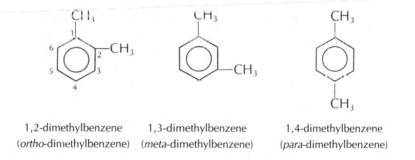

1,2-dimethylbenzene | 1,3-dimethylbenzene | 1,4-dimethylbenzene
(ortho-dimethylbenzene) | (meta-dimethylbenzene) | (para-dimethylbenzene)

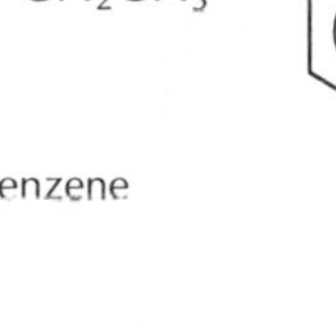

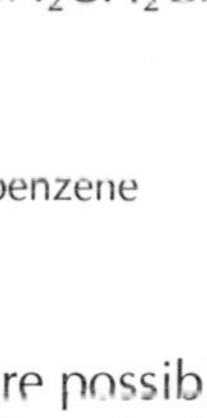

Thousands of compounds are derived from benzene or other ring systems. These other rings may be considered to be fused benzene rings. Two examples of fused rings are naphthalene, $C_{10}H_8$, and anthracene, $C_{14}H_{10}$.

naphthalene   anthracene

The radical —C_6H_5, which is the benzene ring with one less hydrogen, is termed the **phenyl radical.** Note the following examples.

CH₃CHCH₂CH₃

phenyl radical   ethylbenzene   2-phenylbutane
                                (phenylethane)

2-acetyloxybenzoic acid   styrene
(acetylsalicyclic acid or aspirin)

2,4,6-trinitrotoluene   dichlorodiphenyltrichloroethane
(TNT)   (DDT)

PROBLEMS

4. Name the compounds represented by the following formulas.

a. $CH_3CH{=}CHCH_2CH_3$ **c.**   **e.**

b.   **d.**   **f.** $CH{\equiv}CCH_3$

5. Draw the structural formulas for the following:
   a. 3-heptyne   **d.** 1,3-butadiene
   b. cyclopentene   **e.** 1-ethyl-2-methylbenzene
   c. 3-phenyl-2,2-dimethylhexane **f.** 2,4-dimethyl-2-pentene

29:8   HALOGEN DERIVATIVES OF HYDROCARBONS

By replacing a hydrogen atom with a halogen atom (—F, *fluoro;* —Cl, *chloro;* Br, *bromo;* and —I, *iodo*) on a hydrocarbon, additional isomers are possible. When naming these alkyl halides, the longest chain must contain the halogen-bearing carbon that is given the lowest possible number. For example,

$$CH_3CH_2CH_2Cl$$
1-chloropropane

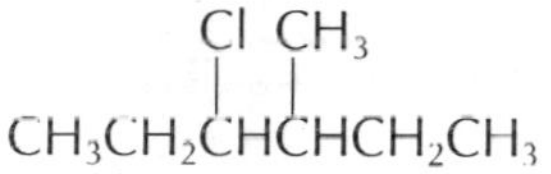

$$CH_3CH_2\overset{\underset{\displaystyle |}{Cl}}{C}H\overset{\underset{\displaystyle |}{CH_3}}{C}HCH_2CH_3$$
3-chloro-4-methylhexane

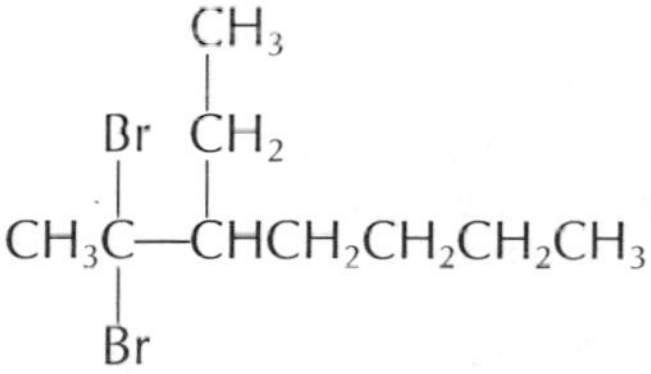

$$CH_3\overset{\underset{\displaystyle |}{Br}}{C}\overset{\underset{\displaystyle |}{CH_2}}{-}CHCH_2CH_2CH_2CH_3$$
2,2-dibromo-3-ethylheptane

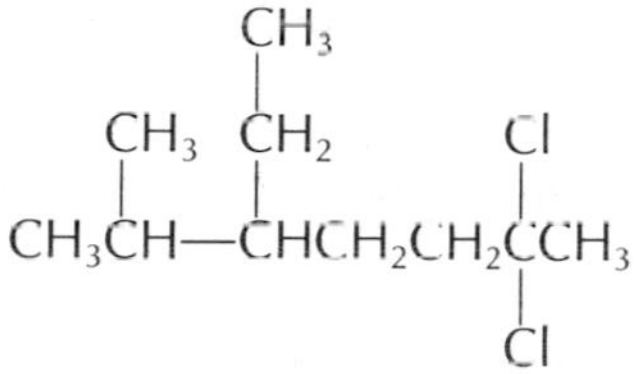

$$CH_3\overset{\underset{\displaystyle |}{CH_3}}{C}H\overset{\underset{\displaystyle |}{CH_2}}{-}CHCH_2CH_2\overset{\underset{\displaystyle |}{Cl}}{C}CH_3$$
2,2-dichloro-5-ethyl-6-methylheptane

1,4-dibromobenzene

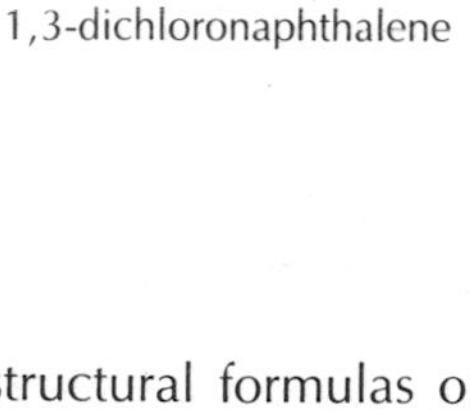

1,3-dichloronaphthalene

PROBLEMS

6. Listed below are the condensed structural formulas or the names of the eight isomers of $C_5H_{11}Cl$. Write either the formula or the name for each.

a. $CH_3CH_2CH_2CH_2CH_2Cl$

b. 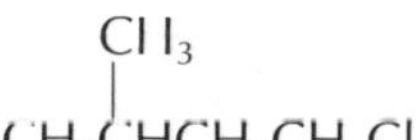 $CH_3\overset{\underset{\displaystyle |}{Cl\,I_3}}{C}HCH_2CH_2Cl$

c. 2-chloropentane

d. 2-chloro-2-methylbutane

e. 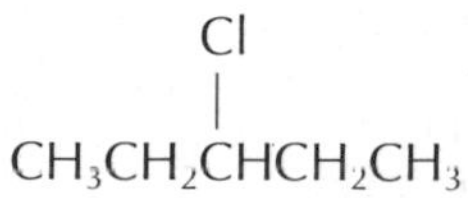 $CH_3CH_2\overset{\underset{\displaystyle |}{Cl}}{C}HCH_2CH_3$

f. 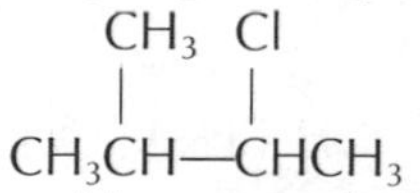 $CH_3\overset{\underset{\displaystyle |}{CH_3}}{C}H-\overset{\underset{\displaystyle |}{Cl}}{C}HCH_3$

g. 1-chloro-2-methylbutane

h. 1-chloro-2,2-dimethylpropane

7. Name the following compounds.

a. $CH_3CH_2\underset{\underset{\underset{CH_3}{|}}{\overset{\displaystyle CH_2}{|}}}{\overset{\displaystyle CH_3}{\underset{|}{C}}}CH_2CH_2Br$

h. $CH_3\underset{\overset{|}{\underset{}{\displaystyle}}}{\overset{\displaystyle CH_3}{\underset{|}{C}H}}CH{=}CHCH_3$

i. $CH_3\overset{\displaystyle CH_3}{\underset{|}{C}}{=}\overset{\displaystyle CH_3}{\underset{|}{C}}CH_2CH_3$

b. $CH_2{=}CH\overset{\displaystyle CH_3}{\underset{|}{C}H}CH{=}CH_2$

j. $CH_2{=}\overset{\displaystyle CH_3}{\underset{|}{C}}CH_2\overset{\displaystyle CH_3}{\underset{|}{C}}{=}CH_2$

c. $CH_2{=}CH\overset{\displaystyle CH_3}{\underset{\underset{CH_3}{|}}{\underset{|}{C}}}CH_3$

k. $CH_2{=}\overset{\displaystyle CH_3}{\underset{|}{C}}{-}\overset{\displaystyle CH_3}{\underset{\underset{CH_3}{|}}{\underset{|}{C}}}{-}CH{=}CHCH_3$

d. C_6H_5Cl

e. $CH_3CH{=}CHCH_2CH_3$

f. $CH_3\overset{\displaystyle CH_3}{\underset{|}{C}}{=}CHCH_3$

g. $CH_3CH_2CH{=}CH_2$

l.

8. Draw structural formulas for the following.

a. 3-heptene
b. 2-methylnaphthalene
c. trichloromethane
d. 2-chloro-3-phenylhexane
e. 1,3-cyclopentadiene
f. toluene (methylbenzene)
g. 1,4-dibromobenzene
h. 2-bromo-3-methyl-2-butene

29:9   HYDROXY COMPOUNDS

The hydroxy compounds, or alcohols, have a **hydroxyl group,** —OH, attached to the alkyl group. They are named by dropping the -e of the alkane series and adding -ol. If the hydroxyl group is attached to an aromatic group, the compound is called a **phenol.** Consider the following examples.

CH_3OH
methanol

CH_3CH_2OH
ethanol

$CH_3CH_2CH_2OH$
1-propanol

$CH_3\underset{\underset{OH}{|}}{C}HCH_3$
2-propanol

$CH_3CH_2CH_2CH_2OH$
1-butanol

$CH_3\underset{\underset{OH}{|}}{C}HCH_2CH_3$
2-butanol

$CH_3\underset{\underset{CH_3}{|}}{C}HCH_2OH$
2-methyl-1-propanol

$CH_3\overset{\displaystyle CH_3}{\underset{\underset{OH}{|}}{\underset{|}{C}}}CH_3$
2-methyl-2-propanol

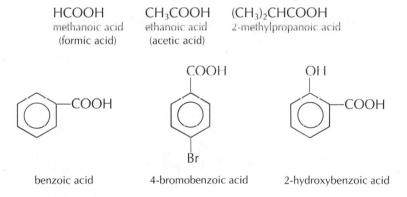

phenol   3-bromophenol   2-hydroxynaphthalene
                                       (2-naphthol)

29:10   CARBOXYLIC ACIDS

All organic acids have the functional group

$$-C{\overset{\displaystyle O}{\underset{\displaystyle OH}{\Big\langle}}}$$

which is called the **carboxyl group.** The carboxylic acid group is usually written as —COOH. The carbon of this group is considered the first carbon of the chain in naming compounds. The -e in the chain name is dropped and -*oic* plus the word *acid* is added. The common names are given in parenthesis.

HCOOH   CH$_3$COOH   (CH$_3$)$_2$CHCOOH
methanoic acid   ethanoic acid   2-methylpropanoic acid
(formic acid)   (acetic acid)

benzoic acid   4-bromobenzoic acid   2-hydroxybenzoic acid

29:11   ALDEHYDES

The functional group characteristic of aldehydes is

$$-C{\overset{\displaystyle O}{\underset{\displaystyle H}{\Big\langle}}}$$

These compounds are named by dropping the *-e* and adding *-al* to the chain name. The aldehyde carbon is given the number 1 in naming.

$HCHO$	CH_3CHO	CH_3CH_2CHO
methanal (formaldehyde)	ethanal	propanal

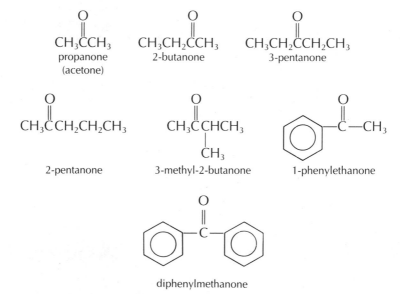

$CH_3CH_2CH_2CHO$	$(CH_3)_2CHCHO$	
butanal	2-methylpropanal	benzaldehyde

29:12 KETONES

Ketones contain the functional group

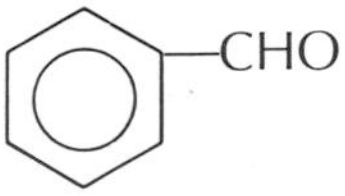

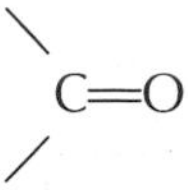

These compounds have the ending *-one*. The functional group is given the lowest possible number.

$CH_3\overset{\overset{O}{\|}}{C}CH_3$	$CH_3CH_2\overset{\overset{O}{\|}}{C}CH_3$	$CH_3CH_2\overset{\overset{O}{\|}}{C}CH_2CH_3$
propanone (acetone)	2-butanone	3-pentanone

$CH_3\overset{\overset{O}{\|}}{C}CH_2CH_2CH_3$	$CH_3\overset{\overset{O}{\|}}{C}\underset{\underset{CH_3}{\|}}{CH}CH_3$	
2-pentanone	3-methyl-2-butanone	1-phenylethanone

diphenylmethanone

29:13 ESTERS

Esters contain the group

$$-\overset{\overset{O}{\|}}{C}-O-$$

and are formed from organic acids. The *-ic* of the acid name is dropped and the ending *-ate* is added. The alkyl group replacing the hydrogen atom in the carboxyl group is named first as a separate word.

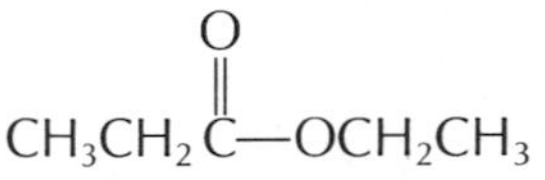

ethyl propanoate

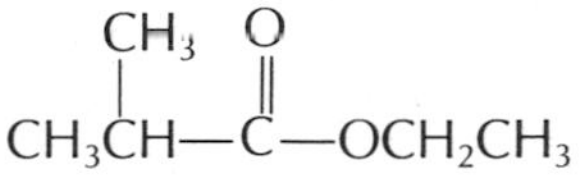

ethyl 2-methylpropanoate

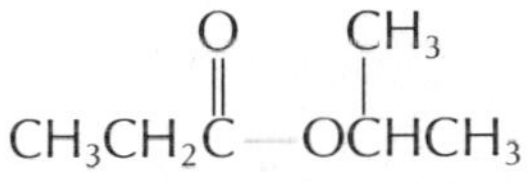

2-methylethyl propanoate

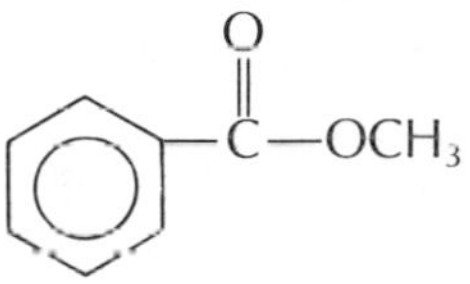

methyl benzoate

29:14 ETHERS

Ethers have the general formula R—O—R in which an oxygen atom is joined to two separate hydrocarbon groups. Ethers are named as *oxy*-derivatives of hydrocarbons.

$$CH_3—O—CH_2CH_3 \qquad CH_3CH_2CH_2—O—CH_2CH_3 \qquad CH_3—O—C_6H_5$$

methoxyethane

1-ethoxypropane

methoxybenzene

Table 20 3

Organic Compounds Containing Oxygen			
Compound	**General Formula***	**Characteristic Group**	**Ending**
Alcohol	R—OH	—OH	*-ol*
Carboxylic Acid	R—C(=O)—OH	—C(=O)—OH	*-oic acid*
Aldehyde	R—C(=O)—H	—C(=O)—H	*-al*
Ketone	R—C(=O)—R	—C(=O)—	*-one*
Ester	R—C(=O)—O—R	—C(=O)—O—	*-yl -oate*
Ether	R—O—R	—O—	*-oxy-*
*R represents any alkyl group such as -CH$_3$, methyl; -CH$_3$CH$_2$, ethyl; etc.			

29:15   NITROGEN CONTAINING COMPOUNDS

Amines are organic compounds containing nitrogen. Amines are derivatives of ammonia. One, two, or three of the hydrogens in ammonia can be replaced with an alkyl group. General formulas for amines are

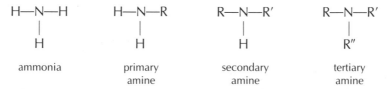

| ammonia | primary
amine | secondary
amine | tertiary
amine |

Nitrogen group substituted chains should be numbered so that the carbon attached to the nitrogen has the lowest possible number. The following table lists other classes of nitrogen containing organic compounds.

Table 29-4

Organic Compounds Containing Nitrogen		
Compound	**General Formula***	**Example**
Amines	$R-NH_2$	$CH_3CH_2NH_2$ ethanamine
Amides	$\begin{matrix} O \\ \parallel \\ R-C-NH_2 \end{matrix}$	CH_3CONH_2 ethanamide
Amino acids	$\begin{matrix} NH_2 \\ \mid \\ G-CH-COOH \end{matrix}$	$CH_3CH(NH_2)COOH$ alanine (2-aminopropanoic acid)
Nitriles	$R-C\equiv N$	$CH_3CH_2CH_2CN$ butanenitrile
Nitro compounds	$R-NO_2$	$C_6H_5NO_2$ nitrobenzene

*R represents any alkyl group such as $-CH_3$, methyl; CH_3CH_2-, ethyl and so on. G can represent a group made up of elements other than just carbon and hydrogen.

CHAPTER REVIEW PROBLEMS

1. Write structural formulas for the following compounds.
   a. 2-chlorobutane
   b. 2-butene
   c. 2-ethyl-3-methyl-1-butanol
   d. 3,3-dimethylbutanoic acid
   e. 2,5,5-trimethyl-4-heptone
   f. 1,8-nonadiyne
   g. 1,3-diiodobenzene
   h. ethoxybenzene
   i. 1-butanol
   j. 3-methyl-2-pentene

k. 2-ethyl-4-methylpentanal
l. 3-ethyl-2,4-dimethyl-3-hexanol
m. 5-chloro-3-ethyl-2-methylheptanoic acid
n. 2-phenylbutane
o. 7-bromo-2-naphthol
p. 4-bromobenzoic acid

2. Name the following organic compounds.

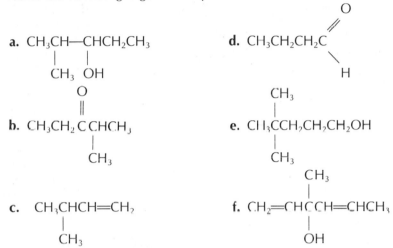

a. $CH_3CH—CHCH_2CH_3$
          | |
         CH_3 OH

b. $CH_3CH_2CCHCH_3$ (with O double bonded to C above, and CH_3 below)

c. $CH_3CHCH=CH_2$
          |
         CH_3

d. $CH_3CH_2CH_2C$ (with O double bonded and H)

e. $CH_3CCH_2CH_2CH_2OH$ (with CH_3 above and CH_3 below)

f. $CH_2=CHCCH=CHCH_3$ (with CH_3 above and OH below)

3. Name the following organic compounds.

a. $CH_3CH_2CHCH_2Cl$
              |
             CH_3

b. $CH_3C——CHCH_2Br$ (with CH_3 above, CH_3 and CH_3 below)

c. 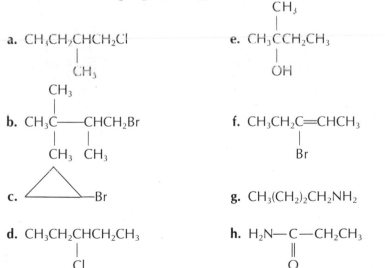 —Br

d. $CH_3CH_2CHCH_2CH_3$
              |
             Cl

e. $CH_3CCH_2CH_3$ (with CH_3 above and OH below)

f. $CH_3CH_2C=CHCH_3$
                  |
                 Br

g. $CH_3(CH_2)_2CH_2NH_2$

h. $H_2N—C—CH_2CH_3$ (with O double bonded below)

4. Each of the following formulas can be written as two compounds with different functional groups. Write the structural formulas, name the compounds, and identify the functional groups.
   a. C_2H_6O **b.** C_3H_6O **c.** C_5H_{10}

5. Draw structural formulas for the following.

a. ethanal
b. 2-butanone
c. 2-methyl-2-propanol
d. ethanoic acid
e. trimethanamine
f. propene
g. 2-pentyne

h. cyclobutane
i. cyclohexanamine
j. 2-aminopentane
k. 1,4-nitrophenol
l. 1,3-nitrobenzoic acid
m. ethanenitrile
n. propenoic acid

ORGANIC REACTIONS AND BIOCHEMISTRY 30

30:1 TYPES OF ORGANIC REACTIONS

In order to simplify your study of the thousands of organic reactions, a few main types are presented. By understanding these few reactions, you can predict the products of many organic reactions.

An **oxidation reaction** occurs when oxygen atoms are added to or hydrogen atoms are removed from a hydrocarbon molecule. Oxygen gas is a very strong oxidizer. When O_2 reacts with most hydrocarbons at high temperatures, H_2O and CO_2 are produced.

Example 1

Complete and balance. (Assume complete oxidation.)

$$C_4H_{10} + O_2 \rightarrow$$

Solving Process:

In a complete oxidation reaction, the products are CO_2 and H_2O. Add these to the product side and balance the equation.

$$2C_4H_{10} + 13O_2 \rightarrow 8CO_2 + 10H_2O$$

A **substitution reaction** occurs when a part of a reactant molecule is substituted for a hydrogen atom on a hydrocarbon molecule. All of the hydrogens of an alkane can be substituted. Thus, many unwanted products are formed in addition to the desired product. The hydrogen atoms of benzene, an aromatic, usually undergo substitution also.

Example 2

Complete the following substitution reaction.

$+ Br_2 \rightarrow$

Solving Process:

Each angle of the benzene hexagon represents a hydrogen bonded to a carbon atom. The bromine molecule breaks into two atoms in the presence of a catalyst. One Br atom is substituted for the hydrogen atom. The hydrogen combines with the other Br atom.

$$\text{⬡} + Br_2 \rightarrow \text{⬡—Br} + HBr$$

An **addition reaction** occurs when a reactant is added to each atom of a carbon-carbon multiple bond. Alkenes are more reactive than alkanes because of the double bond. Some reactants add to the double bond. Under certain conditions an alkene can add to another alkene to form chains called **polymers.** Alkynes can add to form polymers, also.

Example 3

What is the product of the following addition reaction?

$$CH_3—C≡C—CH_3 + 2Cl_2 \rightarrow$$

Solving Process:

Chlorine will add to the triple bond.

$$CH_3—C≡C—CH_3 + 2Cl_2 \rightarrow CH_3—\underset{\underset{Cl}{|}}{\overset{\overset{Cl}{|}}{C}}—\underset{\underset{Cl}{|}}{\overset{\overset{Cl}{|}}{C}}—CH_3$$

In the previous example, atoms were added to the triple bond. It is also possible to remove certain atoms to form double or triple bonds in an **elimination reaction.** In one type of elimination reaction a hydrogen atom from one carbon atom and a hydroxyl group from an adjacent carbon atom are removed, a double bond is formed in the original molecule, and a water molecule is formed. The H_2SO_4 acts as a dehydrating agent.

$$H—\underset{\underset{H}{|}}{\overset{\overset{H}{|}}{C}}—\underset{\underset{OH}{|}}{\overset{\overset{H}{|}}{C}}—\underset{\underset{H}{|}}{\overset{\overset{H}{|}}{C}}—H \xrightarrow{H_2SO_4} H—\underset{\underset{H}{|}}{\overset{\overset{H}{|}}{C}}—\overset{\overset{H}{|}}{C}=\overset{\overset{H}{|}}{C}—H + H_2O$$

2-propanol
(isopropyl alcohol)   propene   water

H_2O, HCl, and HNO_2 are often products of elimination reactions.

Example 4

Predict the products that will be formed in this elimination reaction.

$$CH_3-\underset{\underset{\displaystyle CH_3}{|}}{\overset{\overset{\displaystyle Cl}{|}}{C}}-\underset{\underset{\displaystyle H}{|}}{\overset{\overset{\displaystyle H}{|}}{C}}-CH_3 \rightarrow$$

Solving Process:

On two adjacent carbon atoms there are hydrogen and chlorine atoms. These atoms are eliminated to form HCl. The products are

$$CH_3-\underset{\underset{\displaystyle CH_3}{|}}{\overset{\overset{\displaystyle Cl}{|}}{C}}-\underset{\underset{\displaystyle H}{|}}{\overset{\overset{\displaystyle H}{|}}{C}}-CH_3 \rightarrow HCl + CH_3-\underset{\underset{\displaystyle CH_3}{|}}{C}=\underset{\underset{\displaystyle H}{|}}{C}-CH_3$$

When a carboxylic acid is mixed with an alcohol and heated, an ester is formed. This type of reaction is an **esterification reaction.** Flavor enhancers and perfumes are mixtures of esters and other substances.

Example 5

An apple scent can be produced by reacting methanol and butanoic acid. Complete the reaction.

$$CH_3-CH_2-CH_2-\overset{\overset{\displaystyle O}{\|}}{C}-OH + CH_3-OH \rightarrow$$

Solving Process:

The —OH from the carboxylic acid (R-COOH) will combine with the —H from the alcohol (R—OH) to form water. The two remaining parts of the molecules combine to form the ester

$$(R-\overset{\overset{\displaystyle O}{\|}}{C}-O-R')$$

$$CH_3CH_2CH_2\overset{\overset{\displaystyle O}{\|}}{C}-OH + CH_3-OH \rightarrow CH_3CH_2CH_2\overset{\overset{\displaystyle O}{\|}}{C}-O-CH_3 + H_2O$$

The reaction of a carboxylic acid and an alcohol is reversible. When an ester reacts with water to form a carboxylic acid and an alcohol, the process is called **hydrolysis.** The hydrolysis reaction will go to completion in the presence of a base. The products will be an alcohol and the metallic salt of the carboxylic acid (soap). **Saponification** (Latin for soap) is the hydrolysis of an ester in the presence of a base.

$$CH_2-O-\overset{\overset{\displaystyle O}{\|}}{C}-C_{17}H_{35}$$

$$CH-O-\overset{\overset{\displaystyle O}{\|}}{C}-C_{17}H_{35} + 3NaOH \rightarrow CH-OH + 3C_{17}H_{35}COO^-Na^+$$

$$CH_2-O-\overset{\overset{\displaystyle O}{\|}}{C}-C_{17}H_{35}$$

$$CH_2-OH$$
$$CH-OH$$
$$CH_2-OH$$

ester   +   base   →   alcohol   +   salt (soap)

PROBLEMS

Complete and balance the following equations.

1. $C_3H_8 + O_2 \rightarrow$ (oxidation reaction)

2. $CH_2{=}CH_2 + Br_2 \rightarrow$ (addition reaction)

3. ⬡ $+ Cl_2 \rightarrow$ (substitution reaction)

4.
$$CH_3-CH_2-CH_2-\overset{\overset{\displaystyle OH}{|}}{C}H-CH_3 \rightarrow \text{(elimination reaction)}$$

5.
$$CH_3-CH_2-\overset{\overset{\displaystyle O}{\|}}{C}-OH + CH_3-CH_2-OH \rightarrow \text{(esterification reaction)}$$

30:2 BIOMOLECULES

Twenty-one chemical elements have been found in living systems. These elements combine to form four groups of biomolecules: proteins, carbohydrates, lipids, and nucleic acids.

Proteins are polymers made of **amino acids.** A protein may contain 30 to several thousand amino acid units linked together. The sequence of the amino acids composing the protein determines the properties. Five amino acids can be arranged in 120 possible sequences. The chemical properties of a protein also depend upon the way in which the polymer chain is folded and coiled. The polar and nonpolar side chains help determine the characteristic twists and folds.

Molecules that have the general formula $C_x(H_2O)_y$ are called **carbohydrates.** They are important to living systems because they are used to provide energy and raw materials for cellular activity. They are also used to provide structure to plants (cellulose) and insects (chitin).

Monosaccharides are simple sugars that can link together to form polymers called polysaccharides. Cellulose is a polysaccharide that has a molecular mass in the millions. Plants store sugars in the form of starch, while animals form the polysaccharide glycogen. Carbohydrate storage provides the organism's energy reserves.

A biological substance that is more soluble in nonpolar organic solvents than in water is a **lipid.** Fats, oils, steroid hormones, and some vitamins are lipids.

Vegetable oils contain unsaturated fatty acids. Unsaturated fats contain double bonds and are generally liquids at room temperature. Animal fats are saturated and are usually solids at room temperature.

Fats are esters formed from glycerol and three fatty acids. Fatty acids are long chain carboxylic acids having 12 to 20 carbon atoms in the chain.

Nucleic acids are vital to plants and animals. They control cell metabolism and transfer genetic information. Nucleic acids are polymers of **nucleotides.** A nucleotide has three parts: a nitrogen base, a sugar, and a phosphate group. The general structure of a nucleotide consists of a phosphate group bonded to a sugar (5 carbons) which is bonded to an organic base.

$$PO_4^{3-}-CH_2$$

a nucleotide

The five organic bases most often found in nucleotides are adenine, cytosine, guanine, thymine, and uracil.

Recall that the sequence of amino acids in a protein determines its properties. In the same way, the sequence of nucleotides determines the properties of the nucleic acid.

Two nucleic acids are present in the cells, ribonucleic acid (RNA) and deoxyribonucleic acid (DNA). Genetic information is transferred from one generation to the next by DNA. RNA aids in making chemicals such as enzymes.

CHAPTER REVIEW PROBLEMS

1. Predict the product of the reaction between 2-butene and hydrogen iodide.

Complete and balance the equation for the following four reactions.

2. bromine + ethene

3. preparation of pentyl methanoate

4. complete oxidation of ethane

5. elimination of water from 1-pentanol

6. What is the principal function of DNA in the organism?
7. A nucleotide is composed of what three substances?
8. Soap is produced in what type of chemical reaction?
9. Proteins are polymers of what substances?
10. Why are carbohydrates important to living systems?
11. What is the difference between a saturated and an unsaturated fat?
12. What term is used to describe a lipid that contains double bonds?

APPENDIX A

DATA TABLES

Table A-1

SI Base Units		
Quantity	**Name**	**Symbol**
Length	meter	m
Mass	kilogram	kg
Time	second	s
Electric current	ampere	A
Thermodynamic temperature	kelvin	K
Amount of substance	mole	mol
Luminous intensity	candela	cd

Table A-2

SI Prefixes				
Prefix	**Symbol**	**Meaning**	**Multiplier (Numerical)**	**Multiplier (Exponential)**
			Greater than 1	
tera	T	trillion	**1 000 000 000 000	10^{12}
giga	G	billion	1 000 000 000	10^9
mega	M	million	1 000 000	10^6
*kilo	k	thousand	1 000	10^3
hecto	h	hundred	100	10^2
deka	da	ten	10	10^1
			Less than 1	
*deci	d	tenth	0.1	10^{-1}
*centi	c	hundredth	0.01	10^{-2}
*milli	m	thousandth	0.001	10^{-3}
*micro	μ	millionth	0.000 001	10^{-6}
*nano	n	billionth	0.000 000 001	10^{-9}
pico	p	trillionth	0.000 000 000 001	10^{-12}
femto	f	quadrillionth	0.000 000 000 000 001	10^{-15}
atto	a	quintillionth	0.000 000 000 000 000 001	10^{-18}

*These prefixes are commonly used in this book and should be memorized.
**Spaces are used to group digits in long numbers. In some countries, a comma indicates a decimal point. Therefore, commas will not be used.

Table A-3

Greek Alphabet					
Greek letter	**Greek name**	**English equiv- alent**	**Greek letter**	**Greek name**	**English equiv- alent**
A α	alpha	ä	N ν	nu	n
B β	beta	b	Ξ ξ	xi	ks
Γ γ	gamma	g	O o	omicron	o
Δ δ	delta	d	Π π	pi	p
E ε	epsilon	e	P ρ	rho	r
Z ζ	zeta	z	Σ σ	sigma	s
H η	eta	ā	T τ	tau	t
Θ θ	theta	th	Υ υ	upsilon	ü,ōō
I ι	iota	ē	Φ φ	phi	f
K κ	kappa	k	X χ	chi	h
Λ λ	lambda	l	Ψ ψ	psi	ps
M μ	mu	m	Ω ω	omega	ō

Table A-4

Common Physical Constants
Absolute Zero = $-273.15°C$ = 0 K
Atmospheric pressure (standard): 1 atm = 1.013 25 Pa = 760 mm Hg
Avogadro constant: N_0 = 6.022 17 $\times$ 10^{23} per mole
Charge of the electron: e = $-1.602\ 19 \times 10^{-19}$ coulomb
Faraday constant: F = 96 486.7 C/mol e$^-$
Ideal gas constant: R = 8.314 51 J/mol·K
Enthalpy of fusion of ice: 334 J/g
Enthalpy of vaporization of water: 2260 J/g
Mass of electron: m_e = 9.109 53 $\times$ 10^{-31} kg = 5.49 $\times$ 10^{-4} u
Mass of neutron: m_n = 1.6754 95 $\times$ 10^{-27} kg = 1.00867 u
Mass of proton: m_p = 1.673 265 $\times$ 10^{-27} kg = 1.00728 u
Molar gas volume: 22.4136 dm^3 (STP)
Planck constant: h = 6.626 08 $\times$ 10^{-34} J/Hz (J·s)
Speed of light in vacuum: c = 2.997 925 $\times$ 10^8 m/s

Table A-5

Symbols and Abbreviations	
α = rays from radioactive materials, helium nuclei	K_b = ionization constant (base)
	K_{eq} = equilibrium constant
β = rays from radioactive materials, electrons	K_{sp} = solubility product constant
	kg = kilogram
γ = rays from radioactive materials, high-energy quanta	M = molarity
	m = mass, molality
Δ = change in	m = meter (*length*)
λ = wavelength	mol = mole (*amount*)
ν = frequency	min = minute (*time*)
Π = osmotic pressure	N = newton (*force*)
A = ampere (*electric current*)	N_A = Avogadro constant
Bq = becquerel (*nuclear disintegration*)	n = number of moles
°C = Celsius degree (*temperature*)	P = pressure, power
C = coulomb (*quantity of electricity*)	Pa = pascal (*pressure*)
c = speed of light	p = momentum
cd = candela (*luminous intensity*)	q = heat
C_p = specific heat	R = gas constant
D = density	S = entropy
E = energy, electromotive force	Sv = sievert (*absorbed radiation*)
F = force, Faraday	s = second (*time*)
G = free energy	T = temperature
g = gram (*mass*)	U = internal energy
H = enthalpy	u = atomic mass unit
Hz = hertz (*frequency*)	V = volume
h = Planck's constant	V = volt (*electromotive force*)
h = hour (*time*)	v = velocity
J = joule (*energy*)	W = watt (*power*)
K = kelvin (*temperature*)	w = work
K_a = ionization constant (acid)	x = mole fraction

Table A-6

Oxidation Numbers of Monatomic Ions		

1+	2+	3+
cesium, Cs^+	barium, Ba^{2+}	aluminum, Al^{3+}
copper(I), Cu^+	beryllium, Be^{2+}	antimony(III), Sb^{3+}
hydrogen, H^+	cadmium, Cd^{2+}	bismuth(III), Bi^{3+}
indium(I), In^+	calcium, Ca^{2+}	boron, B^{3+}
lithium, Li^+	chromium(II), Cr^{2+}	cerium(III), Ce^{3+}
potassium, K^+	cobalt(II), Co^{2+}	cobalt(III), Co^{3+}
rubidium, Rb^+	copper(II), Cu^{2+}	chromium(III), Cr^{3+}
silver, Ag^+	iridium(II), Ir^{2+}	gallium(III), Ga^{3+}
sodium, Na^+	iron(II), Fe^{2+}	indium(III), In^{3+}
thallium(I), Tl^+	lead(II), Pb^{2+}	iridium(III), Ir^{3+}
	magnesium, Mg^{2+}	iron(III), Fe^{3+}
	manganese(II), Mn^{2+}	phosphorus(III), P^{3+}
	mercury(II), Hg^{2+}	rhodium(III), Rh^{3+}
	nickel(II), Ni^{2+}	thallium(III), Tl^{3+}
	platinum(II), Pt^{2+}	titanium(III), Ti^{3+}
	strontium, Sr^{2+}	uranium(III), U^{3+}
	tin(II), Sn^{2+}	vanadium(III), V^{3+}
	titanium(II), Ti^{2+}	
	tungsten(II), W^{2+}	
	vanadium(II), V^{2+}	
	zinc, Zn^{2+}	
	zirconium(II), Zr^{2+}	

4+		5+	
cerium(IV), Ce^{4+}	titanium(IV), Ti^{4+}	antimony(V), Sb^{5+}	
germanium(IV), Ge^{4+}	tin(IV), Sn^{4+}	bismuth(V), Bi^{5+}	
iridium(IV), Ir^{4+}	tungsten(IV), W^{4+}	phosphorus(V), P^{5+}	
lead(IV), Pb^{4+}	uranium(IV), U^{4+}	tungsten(V), W^{5+}	
platinum(IV), Pt^{4+}	vanadium(IV), V^{4+}	uranium(V), U^{5+}	
thorium(IV), Th^{4+}	zirconium(IV), Zr^{4+}	vanadium(V), V^{5+}	

1−	2−	3−	4−
bromide, Br^-	oxide, O^{2-}	nitride, N^{3-}	carbide, C^{4-}
chloride, Cl^-	selenide, Se^{2-}	phosphide, P^{3-}	
fluoride, F^-	sulfide, S^{2-}		
hydride, H^-			
iodide, I^-			

Table A-7

Charges of Common Polyatomic Ions	
1+ ammonium, NH_4^+	**2+** mercury(I), Hg_2^{2+}

1−	**2−**
acetate, CH_3COO^-	carbonate, CO_3^{2-}
amide, NH_2^-	chromate, CrO_4^{2-}
azide, N_3^-	dichromate, $Cr_2O_7^{2-}$
benzoate, $C_6H_5COO^-$	hexachloroplatinate(IV), $PtCl_6^{2-}$
bromate, BrO_3^-	hexafluorosilicate, SiF_6^{2-}
chlorate, ClO_3^-	molybdate, MoO_4^{2-}
cyanide, CN^-	oxalate, $C_2O_4^{2-}$
formate, $HCOO^-$	peroxide, O_2^{2-}
hydroxide, OH^-	peroxydisulfate, $S_2O_8^{2-}$
hypochlorite, ClO^-	selenate, SeO_4^{2-}
hypophosphite, $H_2PO_2^-$	silicate, SiO_3^{2-}
iodate, IO_3^-	sulfate, SO_4^{2-}
metaphosphate, PO_3^-	sulfite, SO_3^{2-}
nitrate, NO_3^-	tartrate, $C_4H_4O_6^{2-}$
nitrite, NO_2^-	tellurate, TeO_4^{2-}
perchlorate, ClO_4^-	tetraborate, $B_4O_7^{2-}$
periodate, IO_4^-	thiosulfate, $S_2O_3^{2-}$
permanganate, MnO_4^-	tungstate, WO_4^{2-}
peroxyborate, BO_3^-	
thiocyanate, SCN^-	**3−**
vanadate, VO_3^-	arsenate, AsO_4^{3-}
	citrate, $C_6H_5O_7^{3-}$
	hexacyanoferrate(III), $Fe(CN)_6^{3-}$
	phosphate, PO_4^{3-}
	4−
	hexacyanoferrate(II), $Fe(CN)_6^{4-}$
	diphosphate, $P_2O_7^{4-}$

Table A-8

Specific Heat Values (in $J/g \cdot C°$)								
Substance	C_p	**Substance**	C_p	**Substance**	C_p
Al	0.9025	CH_3CH_2OH	2.4194	$LiNO_3$	1.21
AlF_3	0.8948	CH_3COOH	2.05	$MgCO_3$	0.8957
As	0.3289	Fe	0.4494	$Mg(OH)_2$	1.321
Au	0.12905	glass	0.753	$MgSO_4$	0.8015
BeO	1.020	He	5.1931	Na_2CO_3	1.0595
CaC_2	0.9785	HI	0.22795	PCl_3	0.874
$CaSO_4$	0.7320	$H_2O(cr)$	2.06	SiC	0.6699
CCl_4	0.85651	$H_2O(l)$	4.18	SiO_2	0.7395
C_6H_6	1.74	$H_2O(g)$	2.02	Sn	0.2274
C_6H_{14}	2.26	ICl	0.661	steel(cr)	0.4494
C_6H_5Br	0.989	In(cr)	0.2407	steel(l)	0.719
$C_6H_5CH_3$	1.80	In(l)	0.216	Ti	0.5226
CCl_3CCl_3	0.728	K_2CO_3	0.904	$TiCl_4$	0.76535
chalk	0.920	kerosene	2.09	ZnS	0.469
CH_3COCH_3	2.18				

Table A-9

Electronegativities and First Ionization Energies

Legend:
- Top number = Ionization energy (kJ/mol)
- Bottom number = Electronegativity

1	2	3	4	5	6	7	8	9	10	11	12	13	14	15	16	17	18
1312 H 2.20																	**2372 He** —
520 Li 0.97	**900 Be** 1.47											**801 B** 2.01	**1087 C** 2.50	**1402 N** 3.07	**1314 O** 3.50	**1681 F** 4.10	**2081 Ne** —
496 Na 1.01	**738 Mg** 1.23											**578 Al** 1.47	**787 Si** 1.74	**1012 P** 2.06	**1000 S** 2.44	**1256 Cl** 2.83	**1521 Ar** —
419 K 0.91	**590 Ca** 1.04	**631 Sc** 1.20	**658 Ti** 1.32	**650 V** 1.45	**653 Cr** 1.56	**717 Mn** 1.60	**759 Fe** 1.64	**758 Co** 1.70	**737 Ni** 1.75	**745 Cu** 1.75	**906 Zn** 1.66	**579 Ga** 1.82	**784 Ge** 2.02	**1010 As** 2.20	**939 Se** 2.48	**1140 Br** 2.74	**1351 Kr** —
403 Rb 0.89	**550 Sr** 0.99	**616 Y** 1.11	**659 Zr** 1.22	**664 Nb** 1.23	**685 Mo** 1.30	**702 Tc** 1.36	**711 Ru** 1.42	**720 Rh** 1.45	**805 Pd** 1.35	**731 Ag** 1.42	**868 Cd** 1.46	**558 In** 1.49	**708 Sn** 1.72	**834 Sb** 1.82	**869 Te** 2.01	**1008 I** 2.21	**1170 Xe** —
376 Cs 0.86	**503 Ba** 0.97	**524 *Lu** 1.14	**675 Hf** 1.23	**761 Ta** 1.33	**733 W** 1.40	**760 Re** 1.46	**839 Os** 1.52	**888 Ir** 1.55	**868 Pt** 1.44	**890 Au** 1.42	**1006 Hg** 1.44	**589 Tl** 1.44	**716 Pb** 1.55	**703 Bi** 1.67	**812 Po** 1.76	**917 At** 1.96	**1037 Rn** —
— Fr 0.86	**509 Ra**** 0.97																

Lanthanides (*):

538 *La 1.08	**565 Ce** 1.08	**556 Pr** 1.07	**530 Nd** 1.07	**536 Pm** 1.07	**543 Sm** 1.17	**547 Eu** 1.01	**592 Gd** 1.11	**564 Tb** 1.10	**572 Dy** 1.10	**581 Ho** 1.10	**589 Er** 1.11	**596 Tm** 1.11	**603 Yb** 1.06

Actinides (**):

666 **Ac 1.00	**671 Th** 1.01	**— Pa** 1.14	**587 U** 1.30	**— Np** 1.29	**560 Pu** 1.25	**579 Am** —	**— Cm** —	**— Bk** —	**— Cf** —	**— Es** —	**— Fm** —	**— Md** —	

Table A-10

Thermodynamic Properties (25°C, 100.000 kPa)		
$\Delta H_f°$ in kJ/mol $\Delta G_f°$ in kJ/mol $S°$ in J/mol·K (concentration of aqueous solutions is 1M)		
Substance	$\Delta H_f°$	$\Delta G_f°$	$S°$
Ag(cr)	0	0	42.55
Ag_2SO_4(aq)	−698	−590	33.1
Al(cr)	0	0	28.33
Al_2O_3(cr)	−1675.7	−1582.3	50.92
Br_2(g)	30.9	3.1	245.4
Br_2(l)	0	0	152.231
CH_4(g)	−74.81	−50.72	186.264
C_2H_4(g)	52.26	68.15	219.56
C_2H_6(g)	−84.7	−32.9	229
C_4H_{10}(g)	−125	−15.7	310
CO_2(g)	−393.509	−394.359	213.74
Ca(cr)	0	0	41.42
$CaCl_2$(aq)	−878	−815	54.8
CaO(cr)	−635	−604	38.2
$Ca(OH)_2$(cr)	−986.09	−898.49	77.41
Cl_2(g)	0	0	223
Cu(cr)	0	0	33.1
$Cu(NO_3)_2$(aq)	−350	−157	193
$CuSO_4$(aq)	−679	−844	109
Fe(cr)	0	0	27.3
Fe_2O_3(cr)	−824.2	−742.2	87.40
H(g)	217.965	203	114.713
H_2(g)	0	0	130.684
HBr(g)	−36.40	−53.45	198.695
HCl(g)	−92.307	−95.299	186.908
HCl(aq)	−167.159	−131.228	56.5
HNO_2(aq)	−119	−55.6	46.1
HNO_3(aq)	−207	−111	53.3
H_2O(l)	−285.830	−237.129	69.91
H_2O(g)	−241.818	−228.572	188.825
H_2O_2(l)	−186	−120.35	109.6
H_3PO_4(aq)	−1279.0	−1119.1	110.50
H_2SO_4(l)	−814	−690	139
H_2SO_4(aq)	−909.27	−744.53	20.1
KBr(cr)	−393.798	−380.66	95.90
K_2SO_4(aq)	−1409	—	—
Mg(cr)	0	0	32.5
Mg_3N_2(cr)	−461	−422	88
$Mg(NO_3)_2$(aq)	−875	−677	175
$Mg(OH)_2$(cr)	−925	−834	63.1

(table continued on next page)

Substance	$\Delta H_f°$	$\Delta G_f°$	$S°$
$N_2(g)$	0	0	191.61
$NH_3(g)$	−46.11	−16.45	192.45
$NH_4Cl(aq)$	−300	−211	170
$NH_4NO_3(cr)$	−366	−184	151
$NO(g)$	90.25	86.55	210.761
$NO_2(g)$	+33.18	51.31	240.06
$N_2O(g)$	82.05	104.20	219.85
$NaCl(cr)$	−411.153	−384.138	72.13
$NaCl(aq)$	−446	−372	207
$NaNO_3(aq)$	−447.48	−373	205
$NaOH(aq)$	−427	−379	64.5
$Na_2SO_4(aq)$	−1387.08	−1270.16	149.58
$O_2(g)$	0	0	205.138
$P_4O_{10}(cr)$	−2984.0	−2697.7	228.86
$Zn(cr)$	0	0	41.63
$Zn(NO_3)_2(aq)$	−569	−370	181
$Zn(OH)_2(cr)$	−642	−554	81.2

Table A-11

Solubility Rules*

You will be working with water solutions, and it is helpful to have a few rules concerning what substances are soluble in water. The more common rules are listed below.

1. All common salts of the Group IA elements and ammonium ion are soluble.
2. All common acetates and nitrates are soluble.
3. All binary compounds of Group VIIA elements (other than F) with metals are soluble except those of silver, mercury(I), and lead.
4. All sulfates are soluble except those of barium, strontium, lead, calcium, silver, and mercury(I).
5. Except for those in Rule 1, carbonates, hydroxides, oxides, sulfides, and phosphates are insoluble.

*A substance is considered soluble if more than 3 g of the substance dissolve in 100 cm³ of water.

Table A-12

Molal Freezing and Boiling Point Constants (in C° kg/mol)				
Substance	Freezing point (°C)	Molal freezing point constant	Boiling point (°C)	Molal boiling point constant
Acetic Acid	16.66	3.90	117.90	2.530
Benzene	5.533	5.12	80.100	2.53
Camphor	178.75	37.7	207.42	5.611
Cyclohexane	6.54	20.0	80.725	2.75
Nitrobenzene	5.76	6.852	210.8	5.24
Phenol	40.90	7.40	181.839	3.60
Water	0.00	1.853	100.00	0.515

Table A-13

Ionization Constants			
Substance	Ionization Constant	Substance	Ionization Constant
$HCOOH$	1.77×10^{-4}	H_2O_2	1.78×10^{-12}
CH_3COOH	1.75×10^{-5}	H_3PO_4	7.08×10^{-3}
$CH_2ClCOOH$	1.36×10^{-3}	$H_2PO_4^-$	6.31×10^{-8}
$CHCl_2COOH$	5.50×10^{-2}	HPO_4^{2-}	4.17×10^{-13}
CCl_3COOH	3.02×10^{-1}	H_3PO_3	6.31×10^{-2}
$HOOCCOOH$	5.36×10^{-2}	$H_2PO_3^-$	2.00×10^{-7}
$HOOCCOO^-$	5.35×10^{-5}	H_3PO_2	5.89×10^{-2}
CH_3CH_2COOH	1.34×10^{-5}	H_2S	1.07×10^{-7}
C_6H_5COOH	6.25×10^{-5}	HS^-	1.26×10^{-13}
$(C_6H_5)_2CHCOOH$	1.15×10^{-4}	HSO_4^-	1.02×10^{-2}
H_3AsO_4	6.03×10^{-3}	H_2SO_3	1.29×10^{-2}
$H_2AsO_4^-$	1.05×10^{-7}	HSO_3^-	6.17×10^{-8}
H_3BO_3	5.75×10^{-10}	$HSeO_4^-$	2.19×10^{-2}
$H_2BO_3^-$	1.82×10^{-13}	H_2SeO_3	2.29×10^{-3}
HBO_3^{-2}	1.58×10^{-14}	$HSeO_3^-$	5.37×10^{-9}
H_2CO_3	4.37×10^{-7}	$HBrO$	2.51×10^{-9}
HCO_3^-	4.68×10^{-11}	$HClO$	2.88×10^{-8}
HCN	6.17×10^{-10}	HIO	2.29×10^{-11}
H_2CrO_4	1.82	NH_3	1.74×10^{-5}
$HCrO_4^-$	1.26×10^{-6}	H_2NNH_2	8.71×10^{-7}
HF	6.61×10^{-4}	H_2NOH	8.91×10^{-9}
HNO_2	7.24×10^{-4}		

Table A-14

Vapor Pressure of Water			
Temperature (°C)	Pressure (kPa)	Temperature (°C)	Pressure (kPa)
0	0.6	26	3.4
5	0.9	27	3.6
8	1.1	28	3.8
10	1.2	29	4.0
12	1.4	30	4.2
14	1.6	35	5.6
16	1.8	40	7.4
18	2.1	50	12.3
20	2.3	60	19.9
21	2.5	70	31.2
22	2.6	80	47.3
23	2.8	90	70.1
24	3.0	100	101.3
25	3.2		

Table A-15

Solubility Product Constants (at 25°C)			
Substance	K_{sp}	Substance	K_{sp}
AgBr	5.01×10^{-13}	CuS	6.31×10^{-36}
AgBrO$_3$	5.25×10^{-5}	FeC$_2$O$_4$	3.16×10^{-7}
Ag$_2$CO$_3$	8.13×10^{-12}	Fe(OH)$_3$	3.98×10^{-38}
AgCl	1.70×10^{-10}	FeS	6.31×10^{-10}
Ag$_2$CrO$_4$	1.12×10^{-12}	Hg$_2$SO$_4$	7.41×10^{-7}
Ag$_2$Cr$_2$O$_7$	2.00×10^{-7}	Li$_2$CO$_3$	2.51×10^{-2}
AgI	8.32×10^{-17}	MgCO$_3$	3.47×10^{-8}
AgSCN	1.00×10^{-12}	MgC$_2$O$_4$	8.57×10^{-5}
Al(OH)$_3$	1.26×10^{-33}	MgF$_2$	6.46×10^{-9}
Al$_2$S$_3$	2.00×10^{-7}	MnCO$_3$	1.82×10^{-11}
BaCO$_3$	5.13×10^{-9}	NiCO$_3$	6.61×10^{-9}
BaCrO$_4$	1.17×10^{-10}	NiS	3.16×10^{-19}
BaF$_2$	1.05×10^{-6}	PbCl$_2$	1.62×10^{-5}
BaSO$_4$	1.10×10^{-10}	PbI$_2$	7.08×10^{-9}
CaCO$_3$	2.88×10^{-9}	Pb(IO$_3$)$_2$	3.24×10^{-13}
CaSO$_4$	9.12×10^{-6}	SrCO$_3$	1.10×10^{-10}
CdS	7.94×10^{-27}	TlBr	3.39×10^{-6}
Cu(IO$_3$)$_2$	7.41×10^{-8}	ZnCO$_3$	1.45×10^{-11}
CuC$_2$O$_4$	2.29×10^{-8}	Zn(OH)$_2$	1.20×10^{-17}
Cu(OH)$_2$	2.19×10^{-20}	ZnS	1.58×10^{-24}

Table A-16

Standard Reduction Potentials (at 25°C, 101.325 kPa, 1M)	
Half-Reaction	**E° (Volts)**
$Li^+ + e^- \rightarrow Li$	−3.040
$K^+ + e^- \rightarrow K$	−2.924
$Cs^+ + e^- \rightarrow Cs$	−2.92
$Ba^{2+} + 2e^- \rightarrow Ba$	−2.92
$Ca^{2+} + 2e^- \rightarrow Ca$	−2.84
$Na^+ + e^- \rightarrow Na$	−2.713
$Am^{3+} + 3e^- \rightarrow Am$	−2.38
$Mg^{2+} + 2e^- \rightarrow Mg$	−2.356
$Ce^{3+} + 3e^- \rightarrow Ce$	−2.34
$H_2 + 2e^- \rightarrow 2H^-$	−2.25
$Pu^{3+} + 3e^- \rightarrow Pu$	−2.03
$Be^{2+} + 2e^- \rightarrow Be$	−1.97
$Al^{3+} + 3e^- \rightarrow Al$	−1.676
$SiF_6^{2-} + 4e^- \rightarrow Si + 6F^-$	−1.20
$Mn^{2+} + 2e^- \rightarrow Mn$	−1.18
$OCN^- + H_2O + 2e^- \rightarrow CN^- + 2OH^-$	−0.97
$Cr^{2+} + 2e^- \rightarrow Cr$	−0.91
$2H_2O + 2e^- \rightarrow H_2 + 2OH^-$	−0.828
$Zn^{2+} + 2e^- \rightarrow Zn$	−0.7626
$Ga^{3+} + 3e^- \rightarrow Ga$	−0.529
$U^{4+} + e^- \rightarrow U^{3+}$	−0.52
$H_3PO_3 + 2H^+ + 2e^- \rightarrow H_3PO_2 + H_2O$	−0.50
$2CO_2 + 2H^+ + 2e^- \rightarrow H_2C_2O_4$	−0.475
$NO_2^- + H_2O + e^- \rightarrow NO + 2OH^-$	−0.46
$Fe^{2+} + 2e^- \rightarrow Fe$	−0.44
$Eu^{3+} + 3e^- \rightarrow Eu$	−0.43
$Cr^{3+} + e^- \rightarrow Cr^{2+}$	−0.424
$2H^+(10^{-7}M) + 2e^- \rightarrow H_2$	−0.414
$Cd^{2+} + 2e^- \rightarrow Cd$	−0.4025
$PbSO_4 + 2e^- \rightarrow Pb + SO_4^{2-}$	−0.3505
$Co^{2+} + 2e^- \rightarrow Co$	−0.277
$Ni^{2+} + 2e^- \rightarrow Ni$	−0.257
$Sn^{2+} + 2e^- \rightarrow Sn$	−0.1316
$Pb^{2+} + 2e^- \rightarrow Pb$	−0.1251
$AgCN + e^- \rightarrow Ag + CN^-$	−0.02
$2H^+ + 2e^- \rightarrow H_2$	0.000
$UO_2^{2+} + e^- \rightarrow UO_2^+$	0.06
$S + 2H^+ + 2e^- \rightarrow H_2S$	0.14

Weak Oxidizing Agents/Strong Reducing Agents → (left margin)

Strong Oxidizing Agents/Weak Reducing Agents → (right margin)

(table continued on next page)

Half-Reaction	E° (Volts)
$Sn^{4+} + 2e^- \rightarrow Sn^{2+}$	0.154
$SO_4^{2-} + 4H^+ + 2e^- \rightarrow SO_2(aq) + 2H_2O$	0.158
$Cu^{2+} + e^- \rightarrow Cu^+$	0.159
$AgCl + e^- \rightarrow Ag + Cl^-$	0.22
$Hg_2Cl_2 + 2e^- \rightarrow 2Hg + 2Cl^-$	0.27
$UO_2^{2+} + 4H^+ + 2e^- \rightarrow U^{4+} + 2H_2O$	0.27
$Cu^{2+} + 2e^- \rightarrow Cu$	0.340
$Fe(CN)_6^{3-} + e^- \rightarrow Fe(CN)_6^{4-}$	0.36
$Cu^+ + e^- \rightarrow Cu$	0.520
$I_2 + 2e^- \rightarrow 2I^-$	0.5355
$Hg_2SO_4 + 2e^- \rightarrow 2Hg + SO_4^{2-}$	0.62
$2HgCl_2 + 2e^- \rightarrow Hg_2Cl_2 + 2Cl^-$	0.63
$O_2 + 2H^+ + 2e^- \rightarrow H_2O_2$	0.695
$Fe^{3+} + e^- \rightarrow Fe^{2+}$	0.771
$Hg_2^{2+} + 2e^- \rightarrow 2Hg$	0.7960
$Ag^+ + e^- \rightarrow Ag$	0.7991
$NO_3^- + 2H^+ + e^- \rightarrow NO_2 + H_2O$	0.80
$O_2 + 4H^+(10^{-7}M) + 4e^- \rightarrow 2H_2O$	0.82
$Hg^{2+} + 2e^- \rightarrow Hg$	0.8535
$ClO^- + H_2O + 2e^- \rightarrow Cl^- + 2OH^-$	0.90
$2Hg^{2+} + 2e^- \rightarrow Hg_2^{2+}$	0.9110
$NO_3^- + 3H^+ + 2e^- \rightarrow HNO_2 + H_2O$	0.957
$NO_3^- + 4H^+ + 3e^- \rightarrow NO(g) + 2H_2O$	0.96
$Pd^{2+} + 2e^- \rightarrow Pd$	0.99
$Br_2 + 2e^- \rightarrow 2Br^-$	1.0652
$MnO_2 + 4H^+ + 2e^- \rightarrow Mn^{2+} + 2H_2O$	1.23
$O_2 + 4H^+ + 4e^- \rightarrow 2H_2O$	1.229
$2HNO_2 + 4H^+ + 4e^- \rightarrow N_2O + 3H_2O$	1.27
$Cl_2 + 2e^- \rightarrow 2Cl^-$	1.35828
$Au^{3+} + 2e^- \rightarrow Au^+$	1.36
$Cr_2O_7^{2-} + 14H^+ + 6e^- \rightarrow 2Cr^{3+} + 7H_2O$	1.36
$PbO_2 + 4H^+ + 2e^- \rightarrow Pb^{2+} + 2H_2O$	1.46
$2ClO_3^- + 12H^+ + 10e^- \rightarrow Cl_2 + 6H_2O$	1.47
$HClO + H^+ + 2e^- \rightarrow Cl^- + H_2O$	1.49
$MnO_4^- + 8H^+ + 5e^- \rightarrow Mn^{2+} + 4H_2O$	1.51
$Au^{3+} + 3e^- \rightarrow Au$	1.52
$MnO_4^- + 4H^+ + 3e^- \rightarrow MnO_2 + 2H_2O$	1.70
$H_2O_2 + 2H^+ + 2e^- \rightarrow 2H_2O$	1.763
$Co^{3+} + e^- \rightarrow Co^{2+}$	1.92
$S_2O_8^{2-} + 2e^- \rightarrow 2SO_4^{2-}$	1.96
$O_3 + 2H^+ + 2e^- \rightarrow O_2 + H_2O$	2.075
$F_2 + 2e^- \rightarrow 2F^-$	2.87
$F_2 + 2H^+ + 2e^- \rightarrow 2HF$	3.053

Left margin (bottom to top): → Weak Oxidizing Agents/Strong Reducing Agents

Right margin (top to bottom): → Strong Oxidizing Agents/Weak Reducing Agents

APPENDIX B

LOGARITHMS

A logarithm or log is an exponent. We will work with exponents given in terms of base 10.

$$N = b^x$$

$$\text{number} = \text{base}^{\text{exponent or logarithm}}$$

$$100 = 10^{2.0000}$$

For the log 2.000, the part of the numeral to the left of the decimal point is the characteristic. The part to the right of the decimal point is the mantissa.

$$\text{Log } 100 = 2.000$$

characteristic   mantissa

Example 1

Find the log of 657.

Solving Process:

(a) Write the number in scientific notation, 6.57×10^2.

(b) Look in the table under the column (N). Find the first two digits, (65).

(c) Look to the right and find the mantissa that is in the vertical column under the third digit of the number (7). It is .8176.

(d) From the scientific notation, write the power of ten as the characteristic, to the left of the decimal point.

(e) Write the four digits from the table as the mantissa to the right of the characteristic and the decimal point, 2.8176.

Thus $657 = 10^{2.8176}$ or log $657 = 2.8176$.

When given a logarithm and asked to find the number it represents, we use the table to find the first three digits for the number. We use the characteristic to determine where to locate the decimal point with respect to these digits.

Example 2

Given the logarithm 2.8176, find the number it represents (antilog).

Solving Process:

(a) In the log table, find the mantissa that is closest to .8176.

(b) We find by looking under the column (N) that this mantissa corresponds to 65. The third digit is found at the top of the column in which the mantissa appears, 7. (657)

(c) Write the three digits (657) in scientific notation, 6.57×10^x.

(d) The characteristic will be the power of ten.

$$\text{antilog } 2.8176 = 6.57 \times 10^2 \text{ or } 657$$

Example 3

Find the log 0.00657.

Solving Process:

(a) Write the number in scientific notation, 6.57×10^{-3}.

(b) Look in the table under the column N for the first two digits, 6.5, and to the right in the column under the third digit, 7, for the mantissa. Note that the mantissa is always a positive number, .8176.

(c) From the scientific notation, we get the negative characteristic, -3.

(d) Add the negative characteristic and the positive mantissa $(-3.0000) + (+.8176) = 2.1824$. This value is more commonly represented as 7.8176-10. However, the negative logarithm -2.1824 is more useful in pH calculations.

Example 4

Find the antilog of -2.1824.

Solving Process:

(a) We ask ourselves what number would we add to the next, lesser integer, $-3.$, to get the log -2.1824. It would be 0.8176.

$$\begin{array}{r} -3.0000 \\ \text{subtract} \quad -2.1824 \\ \hline 0.8176 \end{array}$$

We know that logarithm tables do not give mantissas for negative numbers. So, we have changed the -2.1824 into the sum of a negative characteristic and a postive mantissa. The characteristic is always the next negative number. The positive mantissa was determined by asking ourselves what positive number would we add to the negative characteristic to get -2.1824.

$$-2.1824 = -3. + 0.8176$$

(b) Antilog -2.1824 = antilog $-3.$ $\times$ antilog 0.8176

We know the antilog of $-3.$ is 10^{-3}. From the table, we find that the antilog $0.8176 = 6.57$. Therefore the antilog of $-2.1824 = 6.57 \times 10^{-3}$.

Table B-1

Logarithms of Numbers									
N	0	1	2	3	4	5	6	7	8	9
10	0000	0043	0086	0128	0170	0212	0253	0294	0334	0374
11	0414	0453	0492	0531	0569	0607	0645	0682	0719	0775
12	0792	0828	0864	0899	0934	0969	1004	1038	1072	1106
13	1139	1173	1206	1239	1271	1303	1335	1367	1399	1430
14	1461	1492	1523	1553	1584	1614	1644	1673	1703	1732
15	1761	1790	1818	1847	1875	1903	1931	1959	1987	2014
16	2041	2068	2095	2122	2148	2175	2201	2227	2253	2279
17	2304	2330	2355	2380	2405	2430	2455	2480	2504	2529
18	2553	2577	2601	2625	2648	2672	2695	2718	2742	2765
19	2788	2810	2833	2856	2878	2900	2923	2945	2967	2989
20	3010	3032	3054	3075	3096	3118	3139	3160	3181	3201
21	3222	3243	3263	3284	3304	3324	3345	3365	3385	3404
22	3424	3444	3464	3483	3502	3522	3541	3560	3579	3598
23	3617	3636	3655	3674	3692	3711	3729	3747	3766	3784
24	3802	3820	3838	3856	3874	3892	3909	3927	3945	3962
25	3979	3997	4014	4031	4048	4065	4082	4099	4116	4133
26	4150	4166	4183	4200	4216	4232	4249	4265	4281	4298
27	4314	4330	4346	4362	4378	4393	4409	4425	4440	4456
28	4472	4487	4502	4518	4533	4548	4564	4579	4594	4606
29	4624	4639	4654	4669	4683	4698	4713	4728	4742	4757
30	4771	4786	4800	4814	4829	4843	4857	4871	4886	4900
31	4914	4928	4942	4955	4969	4983	4997	5011	5024	5038
32	5051	5065	5079	5092	5105	5119	5132	5145	5159	5172
33	5185	5198	5211	5224	5237	5250	5263	5276	5289	5302
34	5315	5328	5340	5353	5366	5378	5391	5403	5416	5428
35	5441	5453	5465	5478	5490	5502	5514	5527	5539	5551
36	5563	5575	5587	5599	5611	5623	5635	5647	5658	5670
37	5682	5694	5705	5717	5729	5740	5752	5763	5775	5786
38	5798	5809	5821	5832	5843	5855	5866	5877	5888	5899
39	5911	5922	5933	5944	5955	5966	5977	5988	5999	6010
40	6021	6031	6042	6053	6064	6075	6085	6096	6107	6117
41	6128	6138	6149	6160	6170	6180	6191	6201	6212	6222
42	6232	6243	6253	6263	6274	6284	6294	6304	6314	6325
43	6335	6345	6355	6365	6375	6385	6395	6405	6415	6425
44	6435	6444	6454	6464	6474	6484	6493	6503	6513	6522
45	6532	6542	6551	6561	6571	6580	6590	6599	6609	6618
46	6628	6637	6646	6656	6665	6675	6684	6693	6702	6712
47	6721	6730	6739	6749	6758	6767	6776	6785	6794	6803
48	6812	6821	6830	6839	6848	6857	6866	6875	6884	6893
49	6902	6911	6920	6928	6937	6946	6955	6964	6972	6981
50	6990	6998	7007	7016	7024	7033	7042	7050	7059	7067
51	7076	7084	7093	7101	7110	7118	7126	7135	7143	7152
52	7160	7168	7177	7185	7193	7202	7210	7218	7226	7235
53	7243	7251	7259	7267	7275	7284	7292	7300	7308	7316
54	7324	7332	7340	7348	7356	7364	7372	7380	7388	7396

N	0	1	2	3	4	5	6	7	8	9
55	7404	7412	7419	7427	7435	7443	7451	7459	7466	7474
56	7482	7490	7497	7505	7513	7520	7528	7536	7543	7551
57	7559	7566	7574	7582	7589	7597	7604	7612	7619	7627
58	7634	7642	7649	7657	7664	7672	7679	7686	7694	7701
59	7709	7716	7723	7731	7738	7745	7752	7760	7767	7774
60	7782	7789	7796	7803	7810	7818	7825	7832	7839	7846
61	7853	7860	7868	7875	7882	7889	7896	7903	7910	7917
62	7924	7931	7938	7945	7952	7959	7966	7973	7980	7987
63	7993	8000	8007	8014	8021	8028	8035	8041	8048	8055
64	8062	8069	8075	8082	8089	8096	8102	8109	8116	8122
65	8129	8136	8142	8149	8156	8162	8169	8176	8182	8189
66	8195	8202	8209	8215	8222	8228	8235	8241	8248	8254
67	8261	8267	8274	8280	8287	8293	8299	8306	8312	8319
68	8325	8331	8338	8344	8351	8357	8363	8370	8376	8382
69	8388	8395	8401	8407	8414	8420	8426	8432	8439	8445
70	8451	8457	8463	8470	8476	8482	8488	8494	8500	8506
71	8513	8519	8525	8531	8537	8543	8549	8555	8561	8567
72	8573	8579	8585	8591	8597	8603	8609	8615	8621	8627
73	8633	8639	8645	8651	8657	8663	8669	8675	8681	8686
74	8692	8698	8704	8710	8716	8722	8727	8733	8739	8745
75	8751	8756	8762	8768	8774	8779	8785	8791	8797	8802
76	8808	8814	8820	8825	8831	8837	8842	8848	8854	8859
77	8865	8871	8876	8882	8887	8893	8899	8904	8910	8915
78	8921	8927	8932	8938	8943	8949	8954	8960	8965	8971
79	8976	8982	8987	8993	8998	9004	9009	9015	9020	9025
80	9031	9036	9042	9047	9053	9058	9063	9069	9074	9079
81	9085	9090	9096	9101	9106	9112	9117	9122	9128	9133
82	9138	9143	9149	9154	9159	9165	9170	9175	9180	9186
83	9191	9196	9201	9206	9212	9217	9222	9227	9232	9238
84	9243	9248	9253	9258	9263	9269	9274	9279	9284	9289
85	9294	9299	9304	9309	9315	9320	9325	9330	9335	9340
86	9345	9350	9355	9360	9365	9370	9375	9380	9385	9390
87	9395	9400	9405	9410	9415	9420	9425	9430	9435	9440
88	9445	9450	9455	9460	9465	9469	9474	9479	9484	9489
89	9494	9499	9504	9509	9513	9518	9523	9528	9533	9538
90	9542	9547	9552	9557	9562	9566	9571	9576	9581	9586
91	9590	9595	9600	9605	9609	9614	9619	9624	9628	9633
92	9638	9643	9647	9652	9657	9661	9666	9671	9675	9680
93	9685	9689	9694	9699	9703	9708	9713	9717	9722	9727
94	9731	9736	9741	9745	9750	9754	9759	9763	9768	9773
95	9777	9782	9786	9791	9795	9800	9805	9809	9814	9818
96	9823	9827	9832	9836	9841	9845	9850	9854	9859	9863
97	9868	9872	9877	9881	9886	9890	9894	9899	9903	9908
98	9912	9917	9921	9926	9930	9934	9939	9943	9948	9952
99	9956	9961	9965	9969	9974	9978	9983	9987	9991	9996

ANSWERS TO PROBLEMS

CHAPTER 1 ──────────────────

PROBLEMS

1. d
2. c
3. a
4. b
5. c

6. a
7. a
8. b
9. b

CHAPTER REVIEW PROBLEMS

1. a
2. c
3. b
4. c
5. d
6. a
7. a
8. the effects of temperature and pressure on the percent yield of NH_3

9. pressure
10. percent NH_3
11. kPa
12. 10
13. 25%
14. 98%
15. 63%
16. 300°C

CHAPTER 2 ──────────────────

PROBLEMS

1. a. 4, ±0.001 g
   b. 3, ±0.001 kg
   c. 3, ±0.1 mL
   d. 2, ±100 m
   e. 2, ±0.001 g
   f. 4, ±0.01 g
   g. 3, ±0.001 cm
   h. 2, ±0.0001 g
   i. 3, ±0.0001 cm^3
   j. 5, ±0.001 cm
   k. 4, ±0.01 cm^3
   l. 4, ±0.0001 m
   m. 4, ±0.001 g
   n. 4, ±0.01 cm
   o. 7, ±1 g
2. a. 29 cm
   b. 32.9 g
   c. 7.16 m
   d. 0.181 g

3. a. 11.21 km
   b. 7.3 g
   c. 200 m
   d. 13.31 cm
4. a. 9.8 cm^2
   b. 2.4 m^2
   c. 0.0007 m^2
   d. 16 km^2
   e. 32 dm^3
   f. 64 cm^3
5. a. 56 cm
   b. 1.6
   c. 0.27 dm^2
   d. 8.08 m
   e. 2.32
   f. 30 g/cm^3

6. a. 750 000 mg
   b. 0.0015 km
   c. 86 400 s
   d. 520 m
   e. 0.065 kg
   f. 0.000 75 g
7. 800.0 g, $7.82
8. 523.1 km/hr
9. 0.915 m^3
10. 455 min.
11. 1.6×10^{-5} light years
12. a. 3×10^{-5} cm
    b. 8×10^6 g
    c. 5.5×10^7 m
    d. 2×10^{-3} g
    e. 7×10^{-6} m
    f. 6.5×10^4 km

13. a. 1.4×10^{-6} cm^2
    b. 2.1 m^2
    c. 2.00 g/cm^3
    d. 4.61×10^{-2} km
    e. 8.2×10^5 cm^3
    f. 3.0×10^3
    g. 3.0000×10^4 m/s
    h. 1×10^6 m^3
14. 1.40 g/cm^3
15. 11 g/cm^3
16. 1.40 g/dm^3
17. 22.0 cm^3
18. 120 g
19. 306.2 g

CHAPTER REVIEW PROBLEMS

1. 1000 cm/s
2. a. 3.50×10^2 cm
   b. 0.065 kg
   c. 5.2×10^5 mm
   d. 8140 cm^3
3. (lab)(mess)
4. a. 2   f. 1
   b. 3   g. 5
   c. 4   h. 3
   d. 2   i. 7
   e. 3   j. 2

5. 3470 cm^2
6. 4.1 g/cm^3
7. 390 m^3
8. 4.6×10^6 cm^3
9. 20 m/s
10. 9000 cm^3
11. a. 25.0 cm^3
    b. 16.4 cm^3
    c. 24.0 cm^3
12. 445 g, iron heavier

CHAPTER 3

PROBLEMS

1. a. solution
   b. element
   c. compound
   d. compound
   e. element
   f. compound
   g. solution
   h. heterogeneous mixture
   i. element
   j. heterogeneous mixture
   k. compound
   l. element

2. Properties
   a. chemical
   b. physical
   c. physical
   d. chemical
   e. physical
   f. physical
   g. physical
   h. chemical
   i. physical
   j. physical
   k. chemical
   l. physical

3. Changes
   a. physical
   b. chemical
   c. chemical
   d. physical
   e. chemical
   f. physical
   g. chemical
   h. physical

4. 93 300 J
5. 95 700 J
6. 2630 J
7. 15.5°C
8. 2.50 J/g·C°

CHAPTER REVIEW PROBLEMS

1. 4360 J
2. 1.29×10^3 J
3. 54.1 J
4. 647 J

5. 1590 J
6. 17.54°C
7. 0.4823 J/g·C°
8. 322 000 J

CHAPTER 4 ⎯⎯⎯⎯⎯⎯⎯⎯⎯⎯⎯⎯⎯⎯⎯

PROBLEMS

1. a. Cu
   b. Bi
   c. Nb
   d. Mg
   e. Ta
   f. Al
2. a. copper
   b. potassium
   c. lithium
   d. calcium
   e. sodium
   f. magnesium
3. a. LiF
   b. LiCl
   c. LiBr
   d. LiI
   e. Li_2O
   f. Li_2S
   g. CaF_2
   h. $CaCl_2$
   i. $CaBr_2$
   j. $Ca(OH)_2$
   k. CaO
   l. CaS

4. a. NaCN
   b. NaOH
   c. $NaBrO_3$
   d. $NaCH_3COO$
   e. $Ba(CN)_2$
   f. $Ba(OH)_2$
   g. BaO
   h. $BaSO_4$
5. a. $Ba(N_3)_2$
   b. $ZnMoO_4$
   c. $CsClO_4$
   d. $Al_2(SiO_3)_3$
   e. BP
   f. Ag_3N
   g. CdC_2O_4
   h. KSCN
   i. $Ca_3(PO_2)_2$
   j. $Al_2(SiF_6)_3$
6. a. $CaSO_4$
   b. $NaNO_3$
   c. $KClO_4$
   d. $Al_2(SO_4)_3$
   e. $KClO_3$
   f. $MgSO_3$

g. $LiNO_2$
h. $NaClO_2$
i. $(NH_4)_2Cr_2O_7$
j. $NaNO_2$

7. a. sodium sulfide
   b. lithium oxide
   c. magnesium bromide
   d. aluminum nitride
   e. calcium fluoride
   f. potassium iodide
   g. magnesium sulfate
   h. calcium hypochlorite
   i. barium nitrite

8. a. magnesium hydroxide
   b. calcium oxide
   c. lithium acetate
   d. zinc chloride
   e. sodium phosphide
   f. potassium selenide
   g. ammonium magnesium phosphate
   h. potassium nitrite
   i. potassium sodium carbonate

9. a. sodium sulfate
   b. silver nitrate
   c. zinc dichromate
   d. ammonium acetate
   e. potassium perchlorate
   f. ammonium chlorate
   g. calcium oxalate
   h. barium carbonate
   i. sodium dihydrogen phosphate

10. a. $MnCl_3$
    b. $FeBr_3$
    c. $CrBr_3$
    d. $SnCl_4$
    e. $MnBr_2$
    f. SnO_2
    g. Cr_2O_3
    h. PbO
    i. Mn_2O_7
    j. Hg_2O

11. a. titanium(II) chloride
    b. titanium(IV) bromide
    c. copper(I) chloride

d. lead(II) iodide
e. tin(IV) chloride
f. antimony(V) oxide
g. chromium(VI) oxide
h. manganese(II,III) oxide
i. titanium(IV) oxide
j. lead(II) oxide
k. bismuth(V) fluoride
l. nickel(II) bromide
m. copper(II) bromide
n. lead(II) chloride
o. chromium(III) fluoride

12. a. iron(III) sulfate
    b. chromium(II) hydroxide
    c. mercury(I) chlorate
    d. iron(II) perchlorate
    e. manganese(II) sulfate
    f. mercury(II) iodate
    g. lead(II) chlorite
    h. copper(II) acetate
    i. copper(I) sulfate
    j. cobalt(II) sulfate

13. a. $Cu(ClO_3)_2$
    b. Bi_2Te_3
    c. $Mn_2(SO_4)_3$
    d. $Fe(NO_3)_3$
    e. $Sn(NO_3)_4$
    f. $Cr_2(SO_4)_3$
    g. $Fe(OH)_2$
    h. $Cu_3(PO_4)_2$
    i. $Hg_2(NO_2)_2$
    j. $Pb(NO_3)_2$

14. a. Cl_2O
    b. ClO_2
    c. CS_2
    d. ClF_3
    e. Cl_2O_7
    f. SF_6

15. a. carbon dioxide
    b. nitrogen dioxide
    c. sulfur trioxide
    d. phosphorus trichloride
    e. nitrogen monoxide
    f. diphosphorus pentoxide

16. a. CH
    b. CH
    c. CH_2O
    d. C_2H_5
    e. P_2O_5
    f. SO_3
    g. NO_2
    h. NO_2
    i. $AgC_2H_2O_3$
    j. KS_2

17. a. 5
    b. 1
    c. 6
    d. 1
    e. 2
    f. 12

18. a. 14H, 7O
    b. 6N, 24H, 2P, 8O
    c. 8Al, 12O
    d. 3Cu, 3S, 12O

CHAPTER REVIEW PROBLEMS

1. a. $NaNO_2$
   b. Na_2CO_3
   c. Na_2SO_4
   d. KOH
   e. KNO_3
   f. K_2SO_3
   g. K_3PO_4
   h. CdC_2O_4
   i. $CdCO_3$
   j. $CdSO_4$
   k. $Cd_3(PO_4)_2$
   l. $AlBr_3$
   m. $Al(NO_3)_3$
   n. Al_2S_3

2. a. $Mg(NO_3)_2$
   b. $MgSO_4$
   c. $MgCO_3$
   d. $BaBr_2$
   e. $Ba(NO_3)_2$
   f. $BaSO_4$
   g. FeO
   h. $Fe(OH)_2$
   i. $FeCO_3$
   j. $FeSO_4$
   k. $FePO_4$
   l. $FeBr_3$

3. a. $SrCl_2$
   b. $Sr(OH)_2$
   c. $Sr(NO_3)_2$
   d. $SrSO_3$
   e. SrS
   f. $Fe_2(SO_4)_3$
   g. $FePO_4$
   h. $HgBr_2$
   i. $HgCO_3$
   j. HgS

4. a. sodium nitrate
   b. sodium sulfite
   c. sodium phosphate
   d. potassium nitrite
   e. potassium carbonate
   f. potassium sulfate
   g. cadmium bromide
   h. cadmium nitrate
   i. cadmium sulfite
   j. cadmium sulfide
   k. aluminum chloride
   l. aluminum hydroxide

5. a. magnesium nitrite
   b. magnesium sulfite
   c. magnesium phosphate
   d. barium nitrite
   e. barium sulfite
   f. barium carbonate
   g. aluminum sulfate
   h. aluminum phosphate
   i. iron(II) bromide
   j. iron(II) nitrate
   k. iron(II) sulfite
   l. iron(II) sulfide

6. a. barium phosphate
   b. strontium bromide
   c. strontium nitrate

d. strontium carbonate
e. strontium sulfate
f. strontium phosphate
g. iron(III) chloride
h. iron(III) nitrate
i. iron(III) sulfide
j. mercury(II) chloride
k. mercury(II) nitrate
l. mercury(II) sulfate

7. a. $NaOH$
b. $HgSO_4$
c. $Ca(ClO)_2$
d. $Pb_3(PO_4)_2$
e. $Al(ClO_3)_3$
f. $(NH_4)_2S$
g. Cu_2CO_3
h. Hg_2S
i. $Pb(CH_3COO)_2$
j. MnO_2
k. $MnSO_4$
l. Ag_2O
m. $Zn(NO_3)_2$
n. $Cr_2(SO_3)_3$
o. $(NH_4)_2Cr_2O_7$
p. Fe_2O_3

8. a. sodium acetate
b. nickel(II) nitrate
c. mercury(I) chloride
d. tin(II) phosphate
e. chromium(II) hydroxide
f. zinc chlorate
g. magnesium bromide
h. copper(I) azide
i. calcium hydride
j. barium nitrite
k. manganese(II) sulfide
l. tin(IV) nitrate
m. ammonium sulfate
n. lead(II) oxide
o. potassium cyanide

9. a. $Mg(NO_3)_2$
b. $AgCH_3COO$
c. $Ba(ClO_4)_2$
d. KNO_2

e. $(NH_4)_2SO_4$
f. $(NH_4)_2Cr_2O_7$
g. $BaMoO_4$
h. $Zn(SCN)_2$

10. a. iron(II) sulfate
b. ammonium chlorate
c. iron(II) acetate
d. copper(II) chromate
e. magnesium nitrate
f. aluminum phosphate
g. sodium sulfite
h. calcium chlorite
i. ammonium carbonate
j. silver chromate
k. barium phosphate
l. potassium perchlorate

11. a. $ZnSiF_6$
b. Sb_2S_5
c. Bi_2Te_3
d. TiI_4
e. NiF_2
f. MnO_2
g. PbO_2
h. $CaC_4H_4O_6$
i. HgO
j. Co_2O_3

12. a. zinc thiocyanate
b. antimony(V) oxide
c. titanium(II) oxide
d. indium(III) phosphide
e. manganese(III) oxide
f. chromium(III) acetate

13. a. C_3H_7
b. CO_2
c. NF_2
d. $C_3H_6Cl_2$
e. $C_5H_{10}O_2$
f. $PNCl_2$

14. a. 5
b. 9
c. 3
d. 6
e. 1
f. 4

CHAPTER 5

PROBLEMS

1. a. 98.1 u   e. 131 u
    b. 40.0 u   f. 213 u
    c. 80.0 u   g. 1350 u
    d. 233 u   h. 64.1 u
2. 180 u
3. a. 6.02 g
    b. 69.0 g
    c. 137 g
    d. 209 g
4. a. 2.02 mol
    b. 0.0992 mol
    c. 0.269 mol
    d. 0.150 mol
5. a. 1.20×10^{24} atoms
    b. 1.20×10^{24} atoms
    c. 1.81×10^{24} ions
    d. 1.20×10^{24} molecules
6. a. 23.0 g   c. 87.7 g
    b. 61.0 g   d. 5.73 g
7. a. 1.00M
    b. 0.250M
    c. 1.21M
8. a. 41.6 g
    b. 421 g
    c. 71.0 g
9. a. 1.00 dm^3
    b. 4.00 dm^3
    c. 0.737 dm^3
10. a. 30.0% O, 70% Fe
    b. 6.90% O, 93.1% Ag
    c. 7.37% O, 92.6% Hg
    d. 41.1% S, 58.9% Na
11. 32.4% Na
12. urea 46.7% N
    ammonia 82.4% N
13. a. 14.3% Na
    b. 9.97% S
    c. 69.6% O
    d. 55.9% H_2O
14. a. mono = 31.1% Ca
    di   = 27.3% Ca
    hexa = 18.3% Ca
    b. mono = 14.0% H_2O
    di   = 24.5% H_2O
    hexa = 49.3% H_2O
15. a. 15.3% H_2O experimental
    b. 84.72% $BaCl_2$
    c. 3% error
16. a. FeS
    b. MnS
    c. $K_2Cr_2O_7$
17. a. Na_2SO_4
    b. $Na_2S_2O_3$
18. a. FeO
    b. Fe_3O_4
    c. Fe_2O_3
19. a. P_2O_3, P_4O_6
    b. P_2O_5, P_4O_{10}
20. N_2O_4
21. a. $CoCl_2 \cdot 6H_2O$
    b. $Pb(CH_3COO)_2 \cdot 3H_2O$
    c. $NiSO_4 \cdot 6H_2O$
    d. $CaSO_4 \cdot 2H_2O$
22. $MgHPO_4 \cdot 3H_2O$

CHAPTER REVIEW PROBLEMS

1. a. 256 u   f. 149 u
    b. 381 u   g. 106 u
    c. 198 u   h. 129 u
    d. 666 u   i. 58.5 u
    e. 108 u
2. 121 u
3. 132 u
4. a. 204 g
    b. 108 g
    c. 221 g
    d. 911 g
    e. 778.7 g
    f. 131 g

5. a. 2.875 mol
   b. 1.001 mol
   c. 5.246 mol
   d. 0.499 mol
   e. 0.128 mol
   f. 0.484 mol
6. a. 3.00×10^{23} Ca atoms
   b. 2.01×10^{24} CO_2 molecules
   c. 1.20×10^{24} H_2S molecules
   d. 7.53×10^{22} Mg^{2+} ions
7. a. 16.1 g S
   b. 72.1 g H_2O
8. a. 1.00M
   b. 0.760M

9. a. 134 g
   b. 49.0 g
10. a. 20.0 dm^3
    b. 0.177 dm^3
11. 11.2% Na, 41.0% C
12. 66.7% C
13. 51.2% H_2O
14. a. $K_2Cr_2O_7$
    b. K_2CrO_4
15. MgO
16. $C_{54}O_6H_{102}$
17. $C_6O_7H_8$

CHAPTER 6

PROBLEMS

1. $2Mg(cr) + O_2(g) \rightarrow 2MgO(cr)$
2. $4Fe(cr) + 3O_2(g) \rightarrow 2Fe_2O_3(cr)$
3. $H_2O(l) + N_2O_3(g) \rightarrow 2HNO_2(aq)$
4. $Na_2O(cr) + H_2O(l) \rightarrow 2NaOH(aq)$
5. $3Fe(cr) + 4H_2O(l) \rightarrow Fe_3O_4(cr) + 4H_2(g)$
6. $MgBr_2(aq) + Cl_2(g) \rightarrow MgCl_2(aq) + Br_2(g)$
7. $Cl_2(g) + 2NaI(cr) \rightarrow 2NaCl(cr) + I_2(g)$
8. $2KNO_3(cr) \rightarrow 2KNO_2(cr) + O_2(g)$
9. $Zn(cr) + 2HCl(aq) \rightarrow ZnCl_2(aq) + H_2(g)$
10. $CaO(cr) + 2HCl(aq) \rightarrow CaCl_2(aq) + H_2O(l)$
11. $2Al(cr) + 3Pb(NO_3)_2(aq) \rightarrow 2Al(NO_3)_3(aq) + 3Pb(cr)$
12. $Cu(cr) + 2AgNO_3(aq) \rightarrow Cu(NO_3)_2(aq) + 2Ag(cr)$
13. $2K(cr) + 2H_2O(l) \rightarrow 2KOH(aq) + H_2(g)$
14. $Cl_2(g) + 2LiI(aq) \rightarrow 2LiCl(aq) + I_2(g)$
15. $2Al(cr) + 6HCl(aq) \rightarrow 2AlCl_3(aq) + 3H_2(g)$
16. $Fe(cr) + CuSO_4(aq) \rightarrow FeSO_4(aq) + Cu(cr)$
17. $Zn(cr) + H_2SO_4(aq) \rightarrow ZnSO_4(aq) + H_2(g)$
18. $Cl_2(g) + MgI_2(aq) \rightarrow MgCl_2(aq) + I_2(g)$
19. $2Na(cr) + 2H_2O(l) \rightarrow 2NaOH(aq) + H_2(g)$
20. $Mg(cr) + 2HCl(aq) \rightarrow MgCl_2(aq) + H_2(g)$
21. $Ca(OH)_2(aq) + 2HCl(aq) \rightarrow CaCl_2(aq) + 2H_2O(l)$
22. $3KOH(aq) + H_3PO_4(aq) \rightarrow K_3PO_4(aq) + 3H_2O(l)$
23. $2Al(NO_3)_3(aq) + 3H_2SO_4(aq) \rightarrow Al_2(SO_4)_3(aq) + 6HNO_3(aq)$
24. $Na_2SO_3(aq) + 2HCl(aq) \rightarrow 2NaCl(aq) + H_2O(l) + SO_2(g)$
25. $3NaOH(aq) + H_3PO_4(aq) \rightarrow Na_3PO_4(aq) + 3H_2O(l)$
26. $(NH_4)_2SO_4(aq) + Ca(OH)_2(aq) \rightarrow 2NH_4OH(aq) + CaSO_4(cr)$
27. $AgNO_3(aq) + KCl(aq) \rightarrow KNO_3(aq) + AgCl(cr)$

28. $3Mg(OH)_2(aq) + 2H_3PO_4(aq) \rightarrow Mg_3(PO_4)_2(cr) + 6H_2O(l)$
29. $FeS(cr) + 2HCl(aq) \rightarrow FeCl_2(aq) + H_2S(g)$
30. $(NH_4)_2S(aq) + Fe(NO_3)_2(aq) \rightarrow 2NH_4NO_3(aq) + FeS(cr)$
31. $2KNO_3(cr) \rightarrow 2KNO_2(cr) + O_2(g)$
32. $2PbO_2(cr) \rightarrow 2PbO(cr) + O_2(g)$
33. $2NaOH(cr) \rightarrow Na_2O(cr) + H_2O(l)$
34. $MgCO_3(cr) \rightarrow MgO(cr) + CO_2(g)$
35. $H_2SO_3(aq) \rightarrow H_2O(l) + SO_2(g)$
36. $CaCO_3(cr) \rightarrow CaO(cr) + CO_2(g)$
37. $2Fe(OH)_3(cr) \rightarrow Fe_2O_3(cr) + 3H_2O(l)$
38. $2NaClO_3(cr) \rightarrow 2NaCl(cr) + 3O_2(g)$
39. $2Ag_2O(cr) \rightarrow 4Ag(cr) + O_2(g)$
40. $2H_2O(l) \xrightarrow{\text{electricity}} 2H_2(g) + O_2(g)$
41. $2Na(cr) + Cl_2 \rightarrow 2NaCl(cr)$
42. $Br_2(g) + 2H_2O(l) + SO_2(g) \rightarrow 2HBr(aq) + H_2SO_4(aq)$
43. $CaO(cr) + H_2O(l) \rightarrow Ca(OH)_2(aq)$
44. $P_2O_5(cr) + 3BaO(cr) \rightarrow Ba_3(PO_4)_2(cr)$
45. $BaO(cr) + H_2O(l) \rightarrow Ba(OH)_2(aq)$
46. $SO_2(g) + MgO(cr) \rightarrow MgSO_3(cr)$
47. $CO_2(g) + H_2O(l) \rightarrow H_2CO_3(aq)$
48. $2Mg(cr) + O_2(g) \rightarrow 2MgO(cr)$
49. $N_2O_3(g) + H_2O(l) \rightarrow 2HNO_2(aq)$
50. $4Fe(cr) + 3O_2(g) \rightarrow 2Fe_2O_3(cr)$
51. 78.4 g $MgCl_2$
52. 6.07 g Cl_2
53. 1.95 g O_2
54. 0.747 g Cu
55. 9.18 g NH_3
56. 18.7 g HCl
57. 8.36 g Ag_3PO_4
58. 20.4 g NaOH

CHAPTER REVIEW PROBLEMS

1. $2HgO(cr) \rightarrow 2Hg(l) + O_2(g)$
2. $2H_2O(l) \rightarrow 2H_2(g) + O_2(g)$
3. $2Al(cr) + 3Pb(NO_3)_2(aq) \rightarrow 2Al(NO_3)_3(aq) + 3Pb(cr)$
4. $Cu(cr) + 2AgNO_3(aq) \rightarrow Cu(NO_3)_2(aq) + 2Ag(cr)$
5. $2K(cr) + 2H_2O(l) \rightarrow 2KOH(aq) + H_2(g)$
6. $MnO_2(cr) + 4HCl(aq) \rightarrow MnCl_2(aq) + Cl_2(g) + 2H_2O(l)$
7. $Cl_2(g) + 2LiI(aq) \rightarrow 2LiCl(aq) + I_2(g)$
8. $3F_2(g) + 3H_2O(l) \rightarrow 6HF(aq) + O_3(g)$
9. $2AgNO_3(aq) + K_2SO_4(aq) \rightarrow Ag_2SO_4(aq) + 2KNO_3(aq)$
10. $4NH_3(g) + 7O_2(g) \rightarrow 2N_2O_4(g) + 6H_2O(g)$
11. D.D. $Al(NO_3)_3(aq) + 3NaOH(aq) \rightarrow Al(OH)_3(cr) + 3NaNO_3(aq)$
12. D. $2SO_3(g) \rightarrow 2SO_2(g) + O_2(g)$

13. D.D. $2H_3PO_4(aq) + 3Mg(OH)_2(aq) \rightarrow Mg_3(PO_4)_2(cr) + 6H_2O(l)$
14. D. $NH_4NO_2(cr) \rightarrow N_2(g) + 2H_2O(l)$
15. D.D. $4NH_3(g) + 5O_2(g) \rightarrow 4NO(g) + 6H_2O(g)$
16. D.D. $BaCl_2(aq) + Na_2SO_4(aq) \rightarrow 2NaCl(aq) + BaSO_4(cr)$
17. D.D. $Fe_2O_3(cr) + 3CO(g) \rightarrow 2Fe(cr) + 3CO_2(g)$
18. D.D. $3Mg(OH)_2(aq) + 2(NH_4)_3PO_4(aq) \rightarrow Mg_3(PO_4)_2(cr) + 6NH_3(g) + 6H_2O(l)$
19. S.D. $2Al(cr) + 3CuCl_2(aq) \rightarrow 2AlCl_3(aq) + 3Cu$
20. S.D. $Fe(cr) + 2AgCH_3COO(aq) \rightarrow Fe(CH_3COO)_2(aq) + 2Ag(cr)$
21. $3Mg(OH)_2(aq) + 2H_3PO_4(aq) \rightarrow 6H_2O(l) + Mg_3(PO_4)_2(cr)$
22. $FeS(cr) + 2HCl(aq) \rightarrow FeCl_2(aq) + H_2S(g)$
23. $(NH_4)_2S(aq) + Fe(NO_3)_2 \rightarrow 2NH_4NO_3(aq) + FeS(cr)$
24. $H_2SO_4(aq) + 2KOH(aq) \rightarrow K_2SO_4(aq) + 2H_2O(l)$
25. $Al_2(SO_4)_3(aq) + Ca_3(PO_4)_2(cr) \rightarrow 3CaSO_4(cr) + 2AlPO_4(cr)$
26. $BaCO_3(cr) + 2HCl(aq) \rightarrow BaCl_2(aq) + H_2O(l) + CO_2(g)$
27. $2AgCH_3COO(aq) + K_2CrO_4(aq) \rightarrow 2KCH_3COO(aq) + Ag_2CrO_4(cr)$
28. $2(NH_4)_3PO_4(aq) + 3Ba(OH)_2(aq) \rightarrow Ba_3(PO_4)_2(cr) + 6NH_4OH(aq)$
29. $Cr_2(SO_3)_3(aq) + 3H_2SO_4(aq) \rightarrow Cr_2(SO_4)_3(cr) + 3H_2SO_3(aq)$
30. $Ca(OH)_2(aq) + 2HNO_3(aq) \rightarrow Ca(NO_3)_2(aq) + 2H_2O(l)$
31. a. $Cu(cr) + 4HNO_3(aq) \rightarrow Cu(NO_3)_2(aq) + 2NO_2(g) + 2H_2O(l)$
    b. $Cu(NO_3)_2(aq) + 2NaOH(aq) \rightarrow Cu(OH)_2(cr) + 2NaNO_3(aq)$
    c. $Cu(OH)_2(cr) \rightarrow CuO(cr) + H_2O(l)$
    d. $CuO(cr) + H_2SO_4(aq) \rightarrow CuSO_4(aq) + H_2O(l)$
    e. $CuSO_4(aq) + Zn(cr) \rightarrow ZnSO_4(aq) + Cu(cr)$
32. a. $Na_2CO_3(aq) + H_2SO_4(aq) \rightarrow Na_2SO_4(aq) + CO_2(g) + H_2O(l)$
    b. $2NaHCO_3(aq) + H_2SO_4(aq) \rightarrow Na_2SO_4(aq) + 2CO_2(g) + 2H_2O(l)$
       sodium hydrogen carbonate
33. $4FeS(cr) + 11O_2(g) \rightarrow 2Fe_2O_3(cr) + 8SO_2(g)$
34. $2NaHSO_3(aq) \rightarrow Na_2SO_3(aq) + SO_2(g) + H_2O(l)$
35. $Fe_2O_3(cr) + 3C(cr) \rightarrow 2Fe(l) + 3CO(g)$, 313 mol Fe
36. $2NH_3(g) + H_2SO_4(aq) \rightarrow (NH_4)_2SO_4(aq)$, 742.24 kg H_2SO_4
37. $2C(cr) + 2H_2O(l) \rightarrow CH_4(g) + CO_2(g)$, 667 kg CH_4
38. $2NO(g) + O_2(g) \rightarrow 2NO_2(g)$
    $2NO_2(g) + H_2O(l) \rightarrow HNO_2(aq) + HNO_3(aq)$
    5.00×10^2 kg HNO_3/year
39. $6CO_2(g) + 6H_2O(l) \rightarrow C_6H_{12}O_6(l) + 6O_2(g)$, 18.0 g H_2O

CHAPTER 7 _____

PROBLEMS

1. a. $^{50}_{24}Cr$ $24e^-$, $24p^+$, $26n$
   b. $^{37}_{17}Cl$ $17e^-$, $17p^+$, $20n$
   c. $^{26}_{12}Mg$ $12e^-$, $12p^+$, $14n$
   d. $^{193}_{77}Ir$ $77e^-$, $77p^+$, $116n$
   e. $^{29}_{14}Si$ $14e^-$, $14p^+$, $15n$
   f. $^{22}_{10}Ne$ $10e^-$, $10p^+$, $12n$

2. a. hydrogen
   b. beryllium
   c. oxygen
   d. magnesium
   e. calcium
   f. zinc

3. 24.31 u
4. 192.2 u

CHAPTER REVIEW PROBLEMS

1. T
2. F Atoms of the same element are identical in mass.
3. F Millikan is credited with the "oil drop" experiment.
4. F The mass of an electron is not equal to the mass of a proton.
5. T
6. F Thompson devised an experiment to determine the electron's mass.
7. F The atomic number is represented by the symbol Z.
8. T
9. F The isotopic mass difference is due to neutrons.
10. T
11. 51.996 u
12. a. 92   c. 2
    b. 34   d. 107
13. a. 24   c. 18
    b. 8   d. 36

14.

	Z	A	p	n	e
Ca	20	43	20	23	20
Pb	82	211	82	129	82
Pu	94	242	94	148	94
Cr	24	50	24	26	24

CHAPTER 8

PROBLEMS

1.

n	l	m	s	total capacity
4	3	3−, 2−, 1−, 0, 1+, 2+, 3+	±1/2	$4f^{14}$ 32 electrons
	2	2−, 1−, 0, 1+, 2+	±1/2	$4d^{10}$
	1	1−, 0, 1+	±1/2	$4p^6$
	0	0	±1/2	$4s^2$

2. 32 electrons

3.

	s	p	d	f
$l =$	0	1	2	3

4. three
5. two of opposite spin

6.

n	2	3	4	4	5
l	0	2	1	3	0
sublevel	$2s$	$3d$	$4p$	$4f$	$5s$

7. $l = 0, 1, 2, 3, 4$
8. $m = 2-, 1-, 0, 1+, 2+$
9. a, b, d are correct
10. a. fluorine
    b. magnesium
    c. gallium
    d. sulfur
11. a. Al $1s^22s^22p^63s^23p^1$
    b. Fe $1s^22s^22p^63s^23p^64s^23d^6$
    c. Cd $1s^22s^22p^63s^23p^64s^23d^{10}4p^65s^24d^{10}$
    d. C $1s^22s^22p^2$
    e. Ba $1s^22s^22p^63s^23p^64s^23d^{10}4p^65s^24d^{10}5p^66s^2$
    f. Hf $1s^22s^22p^63s^23p^64s^23d^{10}4p^65s^24d^{10}5p^66s^24f^{14}5d^2$
12. a. $1s^22s^1$ e. $1s^22s^22p^1$
    b. $1s^22s^22p^3$ f. $1s^22s^22p^5$
    c. $1s^22s^2$ g. $1s^22s^22p^2$
    d. $1s^22s^22p^4$ h. $1s^22s^22p^6$

13.

	$2s$	$2p$		
a.	↑			
b.	↑↓	↑	↑	↑
c.	↑↓			
d.	↑↓	↑↓	↑	↑
e.	↑↓	↑		
f.	↑↓	↑↓	↑↓	↑
g.	↑↓	↑	↑	
h.	↑↓	↑↓	↑↓	↑↓

14. a. Li·
    b. ·Ṅ·
    c. Be:
    d. ·Ö:
    e. Ḃ:
    f. :F̈:
    g. ·Ċ:
    h. :N̈e:

CHAPTER REVIEW PROBLEMS

1. position, speed
2. four
3. n
4. s, p, d, f
5. two of opposite spin
6. Pauli Exclusion Principle
7. outer energy level electrons
8. electron configuration of an atom
9. three
10. seven
11. ten
12. p
13. opposite spin
14. a. Li· $1s^2 2s^1$
    b. Ra: $1s^2 2s^2 2p^6 3s^2 3p^6 4s^2 3d^{10} 4p^6 5s^2 4d^{10} 5p^6 6s^2 4f^{14} 5d^{10} 6p^6 7s^2$
    c. Na· $1s^2 2s^2 2p^6 3s^1$
    d. Hg: $1s^2 2s^2 2p^6 3s^2 3p^6 4s^2 3d^{10} 4p^6 5s^2 4d^{10} 5p^6 6s^2 4f^{14} 5d^{10}$
    e. ·Ṡn: $1s^2 2s^2 2p^6 3s^2 3p^6 4s^2 3d^{10} 4p^6 5s^2 4d^{10} 5p^2$
    f. :K̈r: $1s^2 2s^2 2p^6 3s^2 3p^6 4s^2 3d^{10} 4p^6$

15. a. Ti: $4s^2 3d^3$ ⇅ | ☐ ☐ ☐

    b. Na· $3s^1$ ↑ | ☐ ☐

    c. Ȧl: $3s^2 3p^1$ ⇅ | ↑ ☐ ☐

    d. ·Ṗ: $3s^2 3p^3$ ⇅ | ↑ ↑ ↑

16. See Problems 14 and 15.

CHAPTER 9

PROBLEMS

1. a. IIIA, 13
    b. IIA, 2
    c. VIIA, 17
    d. VIA, 16
    e. VB, 5
    f. IIB, 12

2. a. boron
    b. beryllium
    c. chlorine
    d. sulfur
    e. vanadium
    f. zinc

3. a. $1s^22s^22p^63s^23p^64s^1$
    b. $1s^22s^22p^63s^23p^64s^23d^{10}4p^65s^24d^{10}5p^66s^24f^{14}5d^{10}$
    c. $1s^22s^1$
    d. $1s^22s^22p^63s^23p^3$
    e. $1s^22s^22p^63s^23p^64s^2$
    f. $1s^22s^22p^63s^23p^64s^23d^{10}4p^65s^24d^{10}5p^1$
4. period 5
5. chromium $(Z = 24)$,
    copper $(Z = 29)$
6. a. metal
    b. nonmetal
    c. metal
    d. metalloid
    e. metal
    f. metalloid
7. metals
8. C
9. D
10. A
11. B
12. F
13. G
14. H
15. E

CHAPTER REVIEW PROBLEMS

1. nonmetals
2. metal
3. Dmitri Mendeleev
4. alkali metals
5. noble gases
6. principal quantum number, n
7. $(n - 1)$ d sublevel
8. four pairs
9. $(n - 2)$ f sublevel
10. a. $1s^22s^22p^63s^23p^2$
    b. $1s^22s^22p^63s^23p^64s^23d^{10}4p^6$
    c. $1s^22s^22p^63s^23p^64s^13d^{10}$
    d. $1s^22s^22p^63s^23p^64s^23d^{10}4p^65s^24d^{10}5p^66s^1$
11. a. titanium $(Z = 22)$
    b. neon $(Z = 10)$
    c. chromium $(Z = 24)$
    d. plutonium $(Z = 94)$
    e. bromine $(Z = 35)$
    f. sodium $(Z = 11)$
12. a. $1s^22s^22p^63s^23p^64s^23d^{10}4p^65s^24d^{10}5p^5$
    b. $1s^22s^22p^4$
    c. $1s^22s^22p^63s^23p^64s^23d^8$
    d. $1s^22s^22p^63s^23p^64s^23d^{10}4p^65s^2$
13. a. nonmetal
    b. metal
    c. metal
    d. metalloid
    e. metal
    f. metal

CHAPTER 10 ⎯⎯⎯⎯⎯⎯⎯⎯⎯⎯⎯⎯⎯

PROBLEMS

1. a. Sr
   b. I
   c. Rb
   d. Mg
   e. P
   f. Ac
   g. Al
   h. Ba
2. a. Ca
   b. Cl^-
   c. As^{3-}
   d. Pb
   e. Mg^{2+}
   f. Te^{2-}
   g. C^{4-}
   h. Ag
3. a. 3+
   b. 3−
   c. 1−
   d. 2+
   e. 2+

f. 2−, 4+, 6+
g. 1+
h. 2+, 7+ (also 4+, 6+)

4. a. 4s
   b. 2p
   c. 2 − 4s, 1 − 4p
   d. 3p
   e. 2 − 5s, 2 − 5p
   f. 4p
   g. 4s
   h. 2 − 4s, 1 − 3d
5. a. O
   b. Sn
   c. F
   d. Ge
   e. I
   f. Ca
   g. Sb
   h. Al
   i. S

CHAPTER REVIEW PROBLEMS

1. increase
2. decrease
3. a. Na
   b. K
   c. Al
   d. Br
   e. N
   f. Ar
4. a. Fe^{3+}
   b. S
   c. U^{3+}
   d. Br^-
   e. Mo^{6+}
   f. As
5. a. 1+
   b. 2+
   c. 3+
   d. 4+ or 4−
   e. 3−, 3+, 5+
   f. 2−

g. 1−
h. 0
i. 1+

6. a. 1+
   b. 2+, 3+
   c. 3+, 4+, 6+
   d. 3+, 5+
   e. 2+, 3+, 4+, 5+
   f. 2+
7. decrease
8. increase
9. metals
10. a. more
    b. less
    c. more
    d. less
11. decrease
12. decrease
13. increase

266

CHAPTER 11

CHAPTER REVIEW PROBLEMS
1. false; . . . alkaline earth metals.
2. false; . . . allotropes of carbon.
3. false; . . electrons are in $4f$ sublevels.
4. true
5. true
6. false; When hydrogen loses one electron . . .
7. true
8. false; . . . is called the noble gases.
9. true
10. false; . . . are in Groups IA (1) and VIIA (17).

CHAPTER 12

PROBLEMS
1. a. ionic
    b. covalent
    c. covalent
    d. ionic
    e. covalent
    f. covalent
2. a. 55% covalent
    b. 85% covalent
    c. 60% ionic
    d. 97% covalent
    e. 90% ionic
    f. 93% covalent
3. a. bond length
    b. nonbonded distance
    c. ionic radius
    d. internuclear distance in the crystal
    e. internuclear distance in the crystal
    f. internuclear distance in the crystal
    g. ionic radius
4. covalent
5. ionic

CHAPTER REVIEW PROBLEMS
1. a. ionic
    b. covalent
    c. covalent
    d. ionic
2. a. increases
    b. decreases
    c. increases
3. a. ionic
    b. metallic
    c. covalent

CHAPTER 13

PROBLEMS

1. a. $\ddot{O}::C::\ddot{O}$ 16 electrons, linear

   b. $:\ddot{Cl}:\ B\ :\ddot{Cl}:$ 24 electrons, trigonal planar
      $:\ddot{Cl}:$

   c. $\left[\begin{array}{c} :\ddot{O}\quad \ddot{O}: \\ N \\ :\ddot{O}: \end{array}\right]^{1-} \leftrightarrow \left[\begin{array}{c} :\ddot{O}\quad \ddot{O}: \\ N \\ :\ddot{O}: \end{array}\right]^{1-} \leftrightarrow \left[\begin{array}{c} :\ddot{O}\quad \ddot{O}: \\ N \\ :\ddot{O}: \end{array}\right]$ 24 electrons trigonal planar

   d. $\begin{array}{c} :\ddot{O}: \\ H:\ddot{O}:P:\ddot{O}:H \\ :\ddot{O}: \\ H \end{array}$ 32 electrons, tetrahedral

2. a. $\begin{array}{c} H:\ddot{S}: \\ H \end{array}$ 8 electrons

   b. $\left[\begin{array}{c} H \\ H:N:H \\ H \end{array}\right]^{1+}$ 8 electrons

   c. $\left[\begin{array}{c} :\ddot{O}\quad \ddot{O}: \\ N \\ :\ddot{O}: \end{array}\right]^{1-} \leftrightarrow \left[\begin{array}{c} :\ddot{O}\quad \ddot{O}: \\ N \\ :\ddot{O}: \end{array}\right]^{1-} \leftrightarrow \left[\begin{array}{c} :\ddot{O}\quad \ddot{O}: \\ N \\ :\ddot{O}: \end{array}\right]^{1-}$ 24 electrons.

   d. $:C:::O:$ 10 electrons

   e. $\begin{array}{c} :\ddot{Cl}: \\ :\ddot{Cl}:C:\ddot{Cl}: \\ :\ddot{Cl}: \end{array}$ 32 electrons

   f. $\begin{array}{c} :\ddot{O}: \\ H:\ddot{C}:\ddot{O}:H \end{array}$ 18 electrons

3. NO_3^-

4. a. $(\sigma_{1s})^2\ (\sigma_{1s}^*)^2\ (\sigma_{2s})^2,$ B.O. $= 1$
   b. $(\sigma_{1s})^2\ (\sigma_{1s}^*)^2\ (\sigma_{2s})^2,\ (\sigma_{2s}^*)^2$ B.O. $= 0$
   c. $(\sigma_{2s})^2\ (\sigma_{1s}^*)^2\ (\sigma_{2s})^2\ (\sigma_{2s}^*)^2\ (\pi_{2py})^2\ (\pi_{2pz})^2,$ B.O. $= 2$

CHAPTER REVIEW PROBLEMS

1. a. 24 electrons
   b. 10 electrons
   c. 26 electrons
   d. 16 electrons
   e. 32 electrons
   f. 34 electrons

2. a. 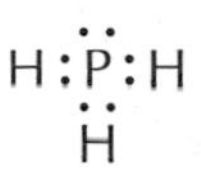 H:P̈:H   8 electrons
      H

   b. :S̈::C::S̈:   16 electrons

   c. $\left[:\ddot{O}:H\right]^{1-}$ 8 electrons

   d. $[:N:::O:]^{1+}$ 10 electrons

   e. 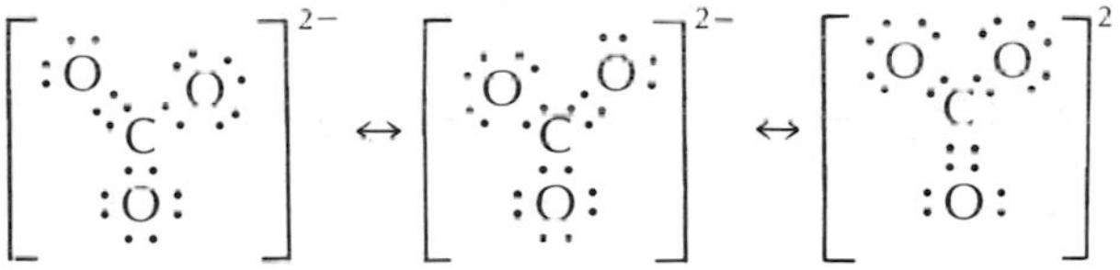 $\left[\begin{array}{c}:\ddot{O} \quad :\ddot{O}: \\ C \\ :\ddot{O}:\end{array}\right]^{2-} \leftrightarrow \left[\begin{array}{c}:\ddot{O} \quad \ddot{O}: \\ C \\ :\ddot{O}:\end{array}\right]^{2-} \leftrightarrow \left[\begin{array}{c}:\ddot{O} \quad :\ddot{O}: \\ C \\ :\ddot{O}:\end{array}\right]^{2}$

      24 electrons

   f. H·C:::N: 10 electrons

   g. 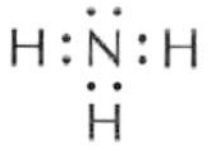 H:N̈:H   8 electrons
      H

   h. :C̈l:Ö:S̈:C̈l: 26 electrons

   i. trigonal bipyramid   40 electrons

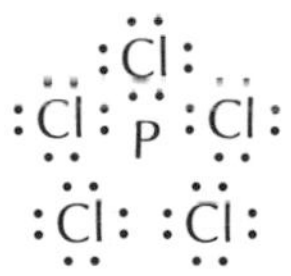

   :C̈l:
   :C̈l: P :C̈l:
   :C̈l: :C̈l:

3. CO_2 bonds are shorter than CO_3^{2-}
4. Bond angle, 107°, in NH_3 is less because of one unshared pair of electrons in nitrogen.
5. C $1s^2 2s^2 2p^2$. One $2s$ electron is promoted to occupy the empty p orbital. The half-filled s and three half-filled p orbitals hybridize to produce four sp^3 hybrid orbitals, each with 1 electron.
6. σ bond occurs when $s-s$, $s-p$, and end to end $p-p$ orbital overlap occurs.
   π bond occurs when the $p-p$ overlap is between p orbitals having parallel axes.

7. a. trigonal planar
   b. linear
   c. angular or bent
   d. tetrahedral
   e. tetrahedral
   f. octahedral
8. a. Construct a diagram similar to Figure 13-1 using the molecular orbital configuration.
   b. zero
   c. $(\sigma_{1s})^2$ $(\sigma_{1s}^*)^2$
   d. no
9. a. See 8a.
   b. two
   c. $(\sigma_{1s})^2$ $(\sigma_{1s}^*)^2$ $(\sigma_{2s})^2$ $(\sigma_{2s}^*)^2$ $(\pi_{2py})^2$ $(\pi_{2pz})^2$
   d. yes

CHAPTER 14

PROBLEMS

1. N—S is most polar
   a. I
   b. I
   c. Br
   d. N

2. a. $\overset{\cdot\cdot}{\underset{\cdot\cdot}{O}}$—$\overset{\cdot\cdot}{S}$=$\overset{\cdot\cdot}{\underset{\cdot\cdot}{O}}$: nonpolar-resonance structures, linear

   b. $\overset{\cdot\cdot}{\underset{\cdot\cdot}{Cl}}$—$\overset{\cdot\cdot}{As}$—$\overset{\cdot\cdot}{\underset{\cdot\cdot}{Cl}}$: polar-pyramidal structure
      |
      $\overset{\cdot\cdot}{\underset{\cdot\cdot}{Cl}}$:

   c. H—$\overset{\cdot\cdot}{\underset{}{Se}}$: polar-angular structure
      |
      H

   d. $\overset{}{:O:}$
      ‖
      S
           nonpolar-resonance structures, trigonal planar

3. Pyramidal NH_3 is polar and has stronger intermolecular forces than symmetrical CH_4.
4. F_2, Cl_2, Br_2, I_2
5. a. tetrachloroaurate(III) ion
   b. triamminechlorochromium(III) ion

    c. tetraamminecopper(II) ion

    d. tetraiodomercurate(II) ion

6. a. $Cr(H_2O)_6^{3+}$

    b. $Co(NH_3)_6^{3+}$

CHAPTER REVIEW PROBLEMS

1. $H—H$, $H \rightarrow S$, $H \leftarrow Ga$, $H \rightarrow Br$, $H \rightarrow Cl$, $H \rightarrow O$

2. a. polar $C \rightarrow O$

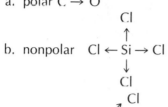

    b. nonpolar $Cl \leftarrow Si \rightarrow Cl$

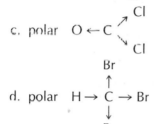

    c. polar $O \leftarrow C$

    d. polar $H \rightarrow C \rightarrow Br$

3. a. CH_3Cl

    b. N_2

    c. $AsCl_3$

    d. SO_3

    e. H_2Se

    f. CCl_4

4. polar molecule, negative ion

5. Shared pair of electrons is more strongly attracted by one atom in polar covalent bond.

6. complex ion

7. polar molecules

8. polar

9. a. tetrahydroxozincate(II) ion

    b. dithiosulfatoargentate(I) ion

    c. tetrachloroplumbate(II) ion

    d. hexaamminenickel(II) ion

10. a. $Fe(NH_3)_4^{2+}$, square planar or tetrahedral

    b. $Cu(H_2O)_6^{2+}$, octahedral

    c. $Ag(NH_3)_2^+$, linear

    d. $Sn(OH)_6^{2-}$, octahedral

11. hexacyanoferrate(II) ion

12. tetrachlorocuprate(II) ion

    tetraaquacopper(II) ion

CHAPTER 15 _____

PROBLEMS

1. 75 kPa
2. 111 kPa
3. 96.1 kPa
4. 15.46 kPa
5. a. 302 K
   b. 217 K
   c. 617 K
   d. 235 K

   e. 373 K
   f. 298 K
6. a. −105°C
   b. −18°C
   c. 273°C
   d. 27°C
   e. −220°C
   f. 0°C

CHAPTER REVIEW PROBLEMS

1. manometer
2. kinetic theory
3. barometer
4. absolute zero
5. 101.325 kPa
6. pressure
7. lighter molecule
8. 107 kPa
9. same

10. 84.8 kPa
11. 48.3 kPa
12. a. 243°C
    b. 428 K
    c. 299 K
    d. −259°C
    e. 694 K
    f. 100°C
13. SO_2

CHAPTER 16 _____

PROBLEMS

1. a. magnesium carbonate
   b. magnesium carbonate trihydrate
   c. magnesium carbonate pentahydrate
   d. neodymium(III) acetate monohydrate
   e. nickel(II) cyanide tetrahydrate
   f. praseodymium(III) carbonate octahydrate
2. a. $CaC_2O_4 \cdot H_2O$
   b. $Ce(BrO_3)_3 \cdot 9H_2O$
   c. $HBr \cdot 6H_2O$
   d. $FeC_2H_2O_4 \cdot 2H_2O$
   e. $Fe_2(C_2O_4)_3 \cdot 5H_2O$
   f. $LiI \cdot 3H_2O$

CHAPTER REVIEW PROBLEMS

1. Crystals are rigid bodies that have flat faces meeting at definite angles and having sharp melting points.
2. unit cell
3. space lattice
4. twelve

5. HCP, CCP(FCC), BCC
6. no
7. doped
8. polymorphous
9. hydrates
10. anhydrous
11. hygroscopic
12. deliquescent
13. efflorescent
14. There is no regular arrangement.
15. glass, paraffin
16. a. nickel(II) chloride hexahydrate
    b. magnesium perchlorate hexahydrate
    c. magnesium phosphate tetrahydrate
    d. calcium nitrate trihydrate
17. a. $CoCl_2 \cdot 6H_2O$
    b. $Ba(OH)_2 \cdot 8H_2O$
    c. $Ga_2O_3 \cdot H_2O$
    d. $MgHAsO_4 \cdot 7H_2O$

CHAPTER 17

PROBLEMS

1. Your answers need to have only 2 significant digits.
    a. $-118°C$
    b. 5080 kPa
    c. $-219°C$
    d. $-183°C$
2. a. solid
   b. gas
   c. liquid
   d. gas
3. a. solid changes to liquid
   b. gas condenses to liquid
   c. liquid changes to solid
   d. no change
4. a. 16.5 kJ
   b. 32.1 kJ
   c. 21.1 kJ
   d. 10.8 kJ
   e. 4.81 kJ
5. a. 4360 J
   b. 958 J
   c. 153 J
   d. 813 J
   e. 2550 J

CHAPTER REVIEW PROBLEMS

1. no
2. no
3. no
4. yes
5. weak
6. lower temperature, raise pressure
7. a. 10°C
   b. 20°C
   c. 35°C
   d. 285 kPa
   e. C.
   f. A.
8. 2090 J
9. 155 J
10. 546 kJ
11. 25.9g ice

CHAPTER 18

PROBLEMS

1. a. 106 cm³ O_2
    b. 48.2 cm³ H_2
    c. 472 cm³ SO_2
    d. 126.6 cm³ N_2
    e. 2.90 m³ N_2
    f. 0.982 dm³ Ne
2. 125 kPa
3. 266 cm³
4. a. 25.0 m³
    b. 16.7 m³
    c. 1.00×10^2 m³
5. 2.03 dm³
6. 211.1 kPa
7. 94.9 kPa
8. 53.6 kPa
9. 75.3 cm³
10. a. 47.4 cm³
    b. 69.9 cm³
    c. 128 cm³
    d. 2.20×10^2 cm³
11. a. 20.0 m³
    b. 5.00 m³

12. a. 294 cm³
    b. 67.3 cm³
    c. 91.0 cm³
    d. 324 cm³
    e. 2.64 dm³
    f. 11 cm³
13. 8.0°C
14. a. 550 cm³
    b. 210 cm³
    c. 111 cm³
    d. 180 cm³
15. a. 173 cm³
    b. 109 cm³
    c. 42.8 cm³
    d. 2.80×10^2 cm³
16. 548 cm³
17. 42 cm³
18. 221 kPa
19. 1.0×10^1 m³
20. 2.93 g/dm³
21. 2.96 g/dm³
22. 312 K or 39.3°C
23. 3.16/1
24. 0.0431 m/s

CHAPTER REVIEW PROBLEMS

1. a. 34.1 cm³
    b. 295 cm³
    c. 83.7 cm³
    d. 150 cm³
    e. 114 cm³
    f. 1.31 dm³
    g. 275 cm³
    h. 237 cm³
2. a. 1.67 g/dm³
    b. 1.64 g/dm³

3. 1.88 g/dm³
4. 2.74 g/dm³
5. 50 cm³
6. 45.0 kPa
7. a. 1.0×10^3 dm³
    b. 760 dm³
    c. pressure
8. 546 K or 273°C
9. 8.0×10^2 K or 527°C
10. 1.04/1

CHAPTER 19

PROBLEMS

1. a. 2.23 mol
    b. 0.0446 mol
    c. 0.29 mol

    d. 0,67 mol
    e. 0.11 mol
    f. 0.0893 mol

2. a. 14 300 g
   b. 4.7482 g
   c. 0.250 g
   d. 589 g
   e. 3800 g
   f. 5.3253 g
3. a. 9.0×10^1 dm^3 Br$_2$
   b. 131 dm^3 H$_2$S
   c. 8.91 dm^3 SO$_2$
   d. 189.6 dm^3 Cl$_2$
   e. 56.0 dm^3 NH$_3$
   f. 24.3 dm^3 NO$_2$
   g. 157 dm^3 O$_2$
   h. 6.14 dm^3 HCl
4. 63.8 g/mol SO$_2$
5. 128 g/mol HI
6. 16.0 g/mol CH$_4$
7. a. 0.0298 mol O$_2$
   b. 0.144 mol CO$_2$
8. a. 73.7 dm^3 H$_2$
   b. 46.5 dm^3 Cl$_2$
9. 87.3 g/mol PF$_3$

10. 1370 cm^3 H$_2$
11. 1880 cm^3 Br$_2$
12. 35.5 g CuO
13. 3110 cm^3 O$_2$
14. 8.04 g Al
15. 1.50×10^2 cm^3 H$_2$
16. 30.0 cm^3 O$_3$
17. 90.0 dm^3 H$_2$, 30.0 dm^3 N$_2$
18. 25.0 cm^3 Cl$_2$
19. a. 2.97 g KClO$_3$
    b. 1.16 g O$_2$
    c. 811 cm^3
20. NaOH, 0.25 mol Na$_2$SO$_4$
21. AgNO$_3$, 0.118 mol Ag
22. NaBr, 0.121 mol Br$_2$
23. 5.09 dm^3 NH$_3$
24. MgSO$_4$, 13.7 g Mg(CH$_3$COO)$_2$
25. 2.06 dm^3 O$_2$
26. 13.2 dm^3 Cl$_2$
27. 32.0 dm^3 N$_2$
28. 16.6 g Fe

CHAPTER REVIEW PROBLEMS

1. 22.40 dm^3/mol
2. 93.2 g/mol
3. a. 0.0893 mol NH$_3$, 1.52 g
   b. 0.205 mol SO$_2$, 19.7 g
4. a. 128 dm^3
   b. 267 dm^3
5. 46.6 g/mol
6. 365 cm^3 H$_2$

7. 0.542 g Mg
8. 30.0 dm^3 O$_2$
9. 84.75 dm^3 CO
10. 17.5 dm^3 C$_2$H$_2$
11. 200.0 cm^3 H$_2$O (g),
    50.0 cm^3 O$_2$ remain
12. 16.7 g NaHCO$_3$
13. 4.45 dm^3 H$_2$

CHAPTER 20 ———————————

PROBLEMS

1. a. $+1.20 \times 10^2$ kJ
   b. -6.91×10^2 kJ
   c. -124 kJ
2. a. $+181$ J/K
   b. -451 J/K
   c. $+167$ J/K
3. a. -1.67 kJ, spontaneous
   b. -74.3 kJ, spontaneous
   c. -69.5 kJ, spontaneous

4. a. -456 kJ, spontaneous
   b. -140 kJ, spontaneous
   c. -245 kJ, spontaneous
5. 188.8 J/mol·K
6. -749 kJ/mol
7. 137 kJ

CHAPTER REVIEW PROBLEMS

1. a. −422 kJ, spontaneous
   b. −358 kJ, spontaneous
2. a. −114 kJ
   b. −1317 kJ
3. a. −369 J/K
   b. +128 J/K

4. a. −42.9 kJ, spontaneous
   b. −192 kJ, spontaneous
5. +70. kJ
6. −1360 kJ
7. −634 kJ/mol
8. −125 kJ/mol

CHAPTER 21 —————————————————

PROBLEMS

1. a. 0.606M
   b. 0.244M
   c. 1.21M
2. a. 1.00 dm^3
   b. 4.00 dm^3
   c. 0.333 dm^3
3. a. 41.6 g $CaCl_2$
   b. 421 g KOH
   c. 71.0 g Na_2SO_4

4. a. 2.00m
   b. 2.40m
   c. 1.67m
5. a. 252 g KOH
   b. 22.5 g CH_3COOH
6. 684 g H_2O
7. 0.0807 CH_3CH_2OH, 0.919 H_2O
8. 0.183 $C_6H_5CH_3$, 0.817 C_6H_6

CHAPTER REVIEW PROBLEMS

1. a. 1.00M
   b. 0.800M
   c. 0.500M
2. a. 134 g $Na_2SO_4 \cdot 7H_2O$
   b. 49.0 g KH_2PO_4
   c. 6.30 × 10^2 g HNO_3
3. a. 20.0 dm^3
   b. 0.200 dm^3
   c. 12.8 dm^3
4. 7.85 g $Pb(CH_3COO)_2$, 0.0483M

5. a. 1.30m
   b. 0.111m
   c. 1.33m
6. a. 9.00 × 10^2 g $C_6H_{12}O_6$
   b. 18.3 g NaCl
7. 621 g $C_2H_4(OH)_2$
8. 0.500 CH_3OH
9. 5.79 g $Pb(NO_3)_2$
10. 58.4 g $FeSO_4 \cdot 7H_2O$

CHAPTER 22 —————————————————

PROBLEMS

1. −5.42°C, 2 ions
2. −1.85°C
3. a. 100.891°C, 3 ions
   b. 100.592°C, 2 ions
   5. 100.727°C, 2 ions
4. 42.9 g NaCl, 2 ions

5. 1991 g $C_2H_4(OH)_2$
6. 180 g/mol
7. 84.9 g/mol, 2 ions
8. 45.8 g/mol
9. 6940 kPa
10. 45.9 kPa

CHAPTER REVIEW PROBLEMS

1. $-2.47°C$, $84.1°C$
2. $-2.84°C$, $100.790°C$, 2 ions
3. 1.60×10^2 g
4. 2.63×10^2 g
5. 99.2 g/mol
6. 43.5 g/mol
7. 624 kPa
8. 142 kPa
9. 138 g/mol, $C_8H_{10}O_2$
10. 215 g/mol, $C_{10}H_6N_2O_4$

CHAPTER 23

PROBLEMS

1. $R = k[NO_2][O_2]$
2. 1.1 dm^3/mol·s
3. $R = 9.9 \times 10^{-4}$ mol/dm^3·s
4. a. right
   b. left
   c. left
   d. no change
   e. right
   f. left
   g. right
   h. left
   i. right
   j. left
   k. right
   l. no change
   m. left
   n. no change

5. 217
6. 0.0313M
7. a. $K_{eq} = \dfrac{[CH_3OH]}{[CO][H_2]^2}$

   b. $K_{eq} = \dfrac{[CH_4][H_2O]}{[CO][H_2]^3}$

   c. $K'_{eq} = \dfrac{[N_2]^2[H_2O]^6}{[NH_3]^4[O_2]^3}$

   d. $K_{eq} = \dfrac{[CO_2]^2}{[CO]^2[O_2]}$

8. 0.113
9. $4.52 \times 10^{-3}M$
10. $G = 26.4$ kJ
11. $K_{eq} = 0.461$

CHAPTER REVIEW PROBLEMS

1. a. $K_{eq} = \dfrac{[N_2O_4]}{[NO_2]^2}$

   b. $K_{eq} = \dfrac{[CH_3OH]}{[H_2]^2[CO]}$

   c. $K_{eq} = \dfrac{[O_2]^5[NH_3]^4}{[NO]^4[H_2O]^6}$

   d. $K_{eq} = \dfrac{[H_2]^4[CS_2]}{[H_2S]^2[CH_4]}$

2. $R = k[A]^2$
3. 4.5×10^{-4} mol/dm^3·s

4. a. $R = k[C_2H_4O]$
   b. 0.024 44 s^{-1}
5. a. right
   b. right
   c. left
   d. no change
6. 0.4999M
7. 35.9
8. 8.00×10^{24}
9. $+95.0$ kJ

277

CHAPTER 24

PROBLEMS

1. a. HCN, acid
       SO_4^{2-}, base
       HSO_4^-, conjugate acid
       CN^-, conjugate base
    b. CH_3COO^-, base
       H_2S, acid
       CH_3COOH, conjugate acid
       HS^-, conjugate base
2. a. Al^{3+} Lewis acid
       H_2O Lewis base
    b. NH_3 Lewis base
       Ag^+ Lewis acid
3. a. hydrochloric acid   g. nitrous acid
    b. nitric acid   h. hypochlorous acid
    c. sulfuric acid   i. sulfurous acid
    d. phosphoric acid   j. carbonic acid
    e. chloric acid   k. chlorous acid
    f. acetic acid   l. perchloric acid
4. a. sodium chlorate, chloric acid
    b. iron(II) perchlorate, perchloric acid
    c. ammonium bromate, bromic acid
    d. magnesium iodate, iodic acid
    e. manganese(II) iodide, hydroiodic acid
    f. barium nitrate, nitric acid
    g. lead(II) chloride, hydrochloric acid
    h. mercury(II) bromate, bromic acid
    i. zinc sulfate, sulfuric acid
    j. calcium hypochlorite, hypochlorous acid
5. a. $(NH_4)_2SO_4$, H_2SO_4 e. $Hg_2(BrO_3)_2$, $HBrO_3$
    b. $Ba(ClO)_2$, $HClO$ f. $Cr(NO_3)_3$, HNO_3
    c. $LiClO_3$, $HClO_3$ g. $MgCl_2$, HCl
    d. $CoSO_3$, H_2SO_3 h. $KClO_4$, $HClO_4$
6. a. $2Na + H_2O \rightarrow 2Na^+ + H_2 + 2OH^-$
    b. $6H^+ + 2PO_4^{3-} + 3Mg^{2+} + 6OH^- \rightarrow Mg_3(PO_4)_2 + 6H_2O$
    c. $Ba^{2+} + SO_4^{2-} \rightarrow BaSO_4$
    d. $3Mg^{2+} + 6OH^- + 6NH_4^+ + 2PO_4^{3-} \rightarrow Mg_3(PO_4)_2 + 3NH_3 + 6H_2O$
    e. $2Fe^{3+} + 3S^{2-} \rightarrow Fe_2S_3$
7. a. 1.85×10^{-5}
    b. 1.80×10^{-5}
    c. 6.16×10^{-10}

8. $[H_3O^+] = 4.18 \times 10^{-3}M$
   $[CH_3COO^-] = 4.18 \times 10^{-3}M$
   $[CH_3COOH] = 0.996M$
9. a. 7.90×10^{-4} c. 1.85×10^{-5}
   b. 1.80×10^{-4} d. 6.05×10^{-10}
10. 19.8% (using quadratic)
11. 0.001 35%
12. $4.58 \times 10^{-8}M$
13. $0.0350M$
14. a. $0.0319M$
    b. $0.0272M$

CHAPTER REVIEW PROBLEMS

1. a. produces H^+ (H_3O^+) ions in water solution
   b. proton donor
   c. electron-pair acceptor
2. a. hydrobromic acid   g. hydroiodic acid
   b. nitrous acid   h. acetic acid
   c. sulfuric acid   i. arsenic acid
   d. hydrosulfuric acid   j. iodic acid
   e. phosphorous acid   k. silicic acid
   f. chloric acid   l. carbonic acid
3. a. $Mg(OH)_2$, base   d. H_2SO_3, acid
   b. HCl, acid   e. NaClO, salt
   c. $Zn(NO_3)_2$, salt   f. KOH, base
4. a. HSO_4^-, acid   b. OH^-, base
       Cl^-, base CH_3COOH, acid
       SO_4^{2-}, conjugate base CH_3COO^-, conjugate base
       HCl, conjugate acid H_2O, conjugate acid
5. Ni^{2+} Lewis acid
   H_2O Lewis base
6. a. $H^+(aq) + OH^-(aq) \rightarrow H_2O(l)$
   b. $2K(cr) + 2H_2O(l) \rightarrow 2K^+(aq) + 2OH^-(aq) + H_2(g)$
   c. $Ag^+(aq) + Cl^-(aq) \rightarrow AgCl(cr)$
7. $3.17 \times 10^{-5}M = [H_3O^+]$
   $3.17 \times 10^{-5}M = [H_2BO_3^-]$
   $1.750M = [H_3BO_3]$
8. $1.02 \times 10^{-6}M$ (Simplified answer because the $[H_3O^+]$ from water is significant for such a weak acid.)
9. 1.77×10^{-5}
10. 4.32×10^{-7}
11. 3.03×10^{-5}
12. 0.00907%
13. $3.93 \times 10^{-5}M$
14. $0.0313M$

CHAPTER 25

PROBLEMS

1. $1.50 \ 10^{-16}$
2. 4.90×10^{-9}
3. 4.14×10^{-11}
4. 2.96×10^{-16}
5. 3.63×10^{-9}
6. 2.82×10^{-13}
7. $2.51 \times 10^{-18}M$
8. $3.97 \times 10^{-4}M$
9. $2.61 \times 10^{-9}M$
10. $1.21 \times 10^{-3}M$
11. 0.0699 g SrC_2O_4/dm^3, 0.558 g PbI_2/dm^3
12. no, $1.08 \times 10^{-30} < 4.07 \times 10^{-28}$
13. no, $2.50 \times 10^{-7} < 1.05 \times 10^{-6}$
14. yes, $2.3 \times 10^{-11} > 1.12 \times 10^{-12}$
15.   a. pH 4.0, pOH 10
        b. pH 12.3, pOH 1.74
        c. pH 9.21, pOH 4.79
        d. pH 1.39, pOH 12.6
16.   a. $1.91 \times 10^{-4}M$
        b. $2.24 \times 10^{-7}M$
        c. $1.00 \times 10^{-2}M$
        d. $6.3 \times 10^{-9}M$
17.   a. $1.00 \times 10^{-11}M$
        b. $1.78 \times 10^{-10}M$
        c. $3.2 \times 10^{-9}M$
        d. $7.9 \times 10^{-12}M$
18.   a. pH 11.4, pOH 2.6   d. pH 1.3, pOH 12.7
        b. pH 2.3, pOH 11.7   e. pH 12.5, pOH 1.5
        c. pH 0.82, pOH 13.2   f. pH 10.2, pOH 3.8
19. $4.0 \times 10^{-8}M$
20. $6.3 \times 10^{-5}M$
21. pH = 4.97
22. pH = 7.63
23.   a. $0.300M$ NaOH   c. $2.50M$ HNO$_3$
        b. 15.0 cm^3 acid   d. 17.5 cm^3 base
24. $4.80M$ NaOH
25. 21.4 cm^3 acid
26. $2.01M$ NH$_3$(aq)
27. $0.600N$ H$_3$PO$_4$, $0.200M$ H$_3$PO$_4$
28.   a. trial 1 $0.880N$, b. 52.8 g/dm^3
            trial 2 $0.930N$, 55.8 g/dm^3
            trial 3 $0.908N$, 54.5 g/dm^3

CHAPTER REVIEW PROBLEMS

1. a. 1.53×10^{-72}
   b. 1.00×10^{-25}
2. a. $2.51 \times 10^{-17}M$
   b. $1.41 \times 10^{-5}M$
3. 1.47 g $CaF_2/100.0$ dm^3
4. yes, $4.38 \times 10^{-4} > 1.12 \times 10^{-12}$
5. AgI precipitates first, $8.32 \times 10^{-14} < 1.78 \times 10^{-8}$

6.

	pOH	$[H_3O^+]$	$[OH^-]$
a.	11.1	$1.3 \times 10^{-3}M$	$7.9 \times 10^{-12}M$
b.	10.5	$3.2 \times 10^{-4}M$	$3.2 \times 10^{-11}M$
c.	7.8	$6.3 \times 10^{-7}M$	$1.6 \times 10^{-8}M$
d.	5.5	$3.2 \times 10^{-9}M$	$3.2 \times 10^{-6}M$
e.	11.0	$1.0 \times 10^{-3}M$	$1.0 \times 10^{-11}M$
f.	9.8	$6.3 \times 10^{-5}M$	$1.6 \times 10^{-10}M$
g.	6.2	$1.6 \times 10^{-8}M$	$6.3 \times 10^{-7}M$
h.	3.5	$3.2 \times 10^{-11}M$	$3.2 \times 10^{-4}M$

7.

	pOH	$[H_3O^+]$	$[OH^-]$
a.	13.0	$1.00 \times 10^{-1}M$	$1.00 \times 10^{-13}M$
b.	11.1	$1.26 \times 10^{-3}M$	$7.94 \times 10^{-12}M$
c.	2.90	$7.94 \times 10^{-12}M$	$1.26 \times 10^{-3}M$
d.	12.8	$0.0631M$	$1.58 \times 10^{-13}M$
e.	5.60	$3.98 \times 10^{-9}M$	$2.51 \times 10^{-6}M$
f.	1.00	$1.00 \times 10^{-13}M$	$1.00 \times 10^{-1}M$

8. 4.85
9. a. 6.00 cm^3
   b. 20.0 cm^3
   c. 8.80 cm^3
   d. 54.0 cm^3
10. $0.157M$
11. 5.69 cm^3
12. 6.00 cm^3
13. $0.667N$, $0.333M$
14. $0.980N$
15. 0.76 g/dm^3

CHAPTER 26 _____

PROBLEMS

1. a. 3+   e. 3+
   b. 2+   f. 6+
   c. 7+   g. 4+
   d. 5+   h. 5+
2. $2Cr(cr) + 3Sn^{4+}(aq) \rightarrow 2Cr^{3+}(aq) + 3Sn^{2+}(aq)$
3. $2Al(cr) + 6H^+(aq) \rightarrow 2Al^{3+}(aq) + 3H_2(g)$

4. $Zn(cr) + 2Ag^+(aq) \rightarrow Zn^{2+}(aq) + 2Ag(cr)$
5. $6NO_3^-(aq) + S(cr) + 6H^+(aq) \rightarrow 6NO_2(g) + H_2SO_4(aq) + 2H_2O(l)$
6. $Br_2(l) + SO_3^{2-}(aq) + 2OH^-(aq) \rightarrow 2Br^-(aq) + SO_4^{2-}(aq) + H_2O(l)$
7. $5Fe^{2+}(aq) + MnO_4^-(aq) + 8H^+(aq) \rightarrow Mn^{2+}(aq) + 5Fe^{3+}(aq) + 4H_2O(l)$
8. $Cu(cr) + SO_4^{2-}(aq) + 4H^+(aq) \rightarrow Cu^{2+}(aq) + SO_2(g) + 2H_2O(l)$
9. $3Cu(cr) + 2NO_3^-(aq) + 8H^+(aq) \rightarrow 3Cu^{2+}(aq) + 2NO(g) + 4H_2O(l)$
10. $2MnO_4^-(aq) + 5S^{2-}(aq) + 16H^+(aq) \rightarrow 2Mn^{2+}(aq) + 5S(cr) + 8H_2O(l)$
11. $CuS(cr) + 2NO_3^-(aq) + 4H^+(aq) \rightarrow Cu^{2+}(aq) + S(cr) + 2NO_2(g) + 2H_2O(l)$
12. $2NO_2(g) + ClO^-(aq) + 2OH^-(aq) \rightarrow 2NO_3^-(aq) + Cl^-(aq) + H_2O(l)$
13. $6Fe^{2+}(aq) + Cr_2O_7^{2-}(aq) + 14H^+(aq) \rightarrow 6Fe^{3+}(aq) + 2Cr^{3+}(aq) + 7H_2O(l)$
14. $2MnO_4(aq) + 10Cl^-(aq) + 16H^+(aq) \rightarrow 2Mn^{2+}(aq) + 5Cl_2(g) + 8H_2O(l)$
15. $6IO_3^-(aq) + 5H_2S(g) + 4OH^-(aq) \rightarrow 3I_2(g) + 5SO_3^{2-}(aq) + 7H_2O(l)$
16. $H_2SeO_3(aq) + 4Br^-(aq) + 4H^+(aq) \rightarrow Se(cr) + 2Br_2(g) + 3H_2O(l)$
17. $BrO_3^-(aq) + 2MnO_2(cr) + 2OH^-(aq) \rightarrow Br^-(aq) + 2MnO_4^-(aq) + H_2O(l)$
18. $3H_2S(g) + 2NO_3^-(aq) + 2H^+(aq) \rightarrow 3S(cr) + 2NO(g) + 4H_2O(l)$

CHAPTER REVIEW PROBLEMS

1. a. 4+
   b. 3+
   c. 1+
   d. 5+
   e. 5+
   f. 5+
2. $3AsH_3(g) + 4ClO_3^-(aq) \rightarrow 3H_3AsO_4(aq) + 4Cl^-(aq)$
3. $2HNO_2(aq) + 2I^-(aq) + 2H^+ \rightarrow 2NO(g) + I_2(g) + 2H_2O(l)$
4. $2MnO_4^-(aq) + 5H_2O_2(aq) + 6H^+(aq) \rightarrow 2Mn^{2+}(aq) + 5O_2(g) + 8H_2O(l)$
5. $2MnO_2(cr) + ClO_3^-(aq) + 2OH^-(aq) \rightarrow 2MnO_4^-(aq) + Cl^-(aq) + H_2O(l)$
6. $6Br_2(l) + 12OH^-(aq) \rightarrow 10Br^-(aq) + 2BrO_3^-(aq) + 6H_2O(l)$
7. $3N_2O_4(aq) + Br^-(aq) + 6OH^-(aq) \rightarrow 6NO_2^-(aq) + BrO_3^-(aq) + 3H_2O(l)$
8. $3H_2PO_2^-(aq) + 2SbO_2^-(aq) + OH^-(aq) \rightarrow 3HPO_3^{2-}(aq) + 2Sb(cr) + 2H_2O(l)$
9. $2CrO_2^-(aq) + 3ClO^-(aq) + 2OH^-(aq) \rightarrow 2CrO_4^{2-}(aq) + 3Cl^-(aq) + H_2O(l)$
10. $2Cu(OH)_2(cr) + HPO_3^{2-}(aq) \rightarrow Cu_2O(cr) + PO_4^{3-}(aq) + 2H_2O(l) + H^+(aq)$
11. $3HS^-(aq) + IO_3^-(aq) + 3H^+(aq) \rightarrow I^-(aq) + 3S(cr) + 3H_2O(l)$
12. $N_2O(g) + 2ClO^-(aq) + 2OH^-(aq) \rightarrow 2Cl^-(aq) + 2NO_2^-(aq) + H_2O(l)$
13. $H_2SO_3(aq) + MnO_2(cr) \rightarrow SO_4^{2-}(aq) + Mn^{2+}(aq) + H_2O(l)$
14. $IO_4^-(aq) + 7I^-(aq) + 8H^+(aq) \rightarrow 4I_2(g) + 4H_2O(l)$
15. $2CrO_4^{2-}(aq) + 6I^-(aq) + 16H^+(aq) \rightarrow 2Cr^{3+}(aq) + 3I_2(g) + 8H_2O(l)$

CHAPTER 27

PROBLEMS

1. a. +0.65 V
   b. +1.676 V
   c. +0.5297 V
   d. +0.74 V
   e. +1.204 V
   f. +0.115 V
2. a. Zn
   b. Pb
   c. Zn
   d. Pb
   e. $Pb^{2+}(aq)$
   f. $Zn(cr) \rightarrow Zn^{2+}(aq) + 2e^-$
   g. +0.6375 V

3. a. Au
   b. Al
   c. Al
   d. Au
   e. Al(cr)
   f. $Au^{3+}(aq) + 3e^- \rightarrow Au(cr)$
   g. +3.196 V
4. 849 s
5. 0.729 A
6. 6.70 A
7. 223 g

CHAPTER REVIEW PROBLEMS

1. a. +0.597 V, will occur
   b. −0.2931 V, will not as written
   c. −0.340 V, will not as written
   d. +0.90 V, will occur
   e. −0.6375 V, will not as written
2. +0.74 V
3. $Cr(cr) \rightarrow Cr^{2+}(aq) + 2e^-$
4. 0.373 mol e^-

5. 2.90×10^4 s
6. 3.29 g Cu
7. 164 g Zn
8. 1.40×10^2 g Cd
9. 216 g
10. 5.97 mol Na
11. 268 s
12. 0.723 A

CHAPTER 28

PROBLEMS

1. a. $^{208}_{82}Pb$
   b. $^{210}_{82}Pb$
   c. $^{235}_{92}U$
   d. $^{14}_{6}C$
   e. $^{5}_{2}He$
   f. $^{40}_{19}K$
   g. $^{8}_{3}Li$
   h. $^{238}_{92}U$
2. a. $^{7}_{3}Li + ^{2}_{1}H \rightarrow 2^{4}_{2}He$
   b. $^{3}_{1}H + ^{2}_{1}H \rightarrow ^{4}_{2}He + ^{1}_{0}n$
   c. $^{14}_{6}C \rightarrow ^{14}_{7}N + ^{0}_{-1}e$

   d. $^{9}_{4}Be + ^{4}_{2}He \rightarrow ^{12}_{6}C + ^{1}_{0}n$
   e. $^{14}_{7}N + ^{4}_{2}He \rightarrow ^{18}_{8}O + ^{0}_{+1}e$
   f. $^{26}_{12}Mg + ^{1}_{0}n \rightarrow ^{27}_{11}Na + ^{0}_{+1}e$
   g. $^{59}_{27}Co + ^{2}_{1}H \rightarrow ^{61}_{27}Co + ^{0}_{+1}e$
3. a. $^{214}_{82}Pb \rightarrow ^{214}_{83}Bi + ^{0}_{-1}e$
   $^{214}_{83}Bi \rightarrow ^{214}_{84}Po + ^{0}_{-1}e$
   $^{214}_{84}Po \rightarrow ^{210}_{82}Pb + ^{4}_{2}He$
4. 9.6 minutes
5. 7.3×10^{22} atoms
6. 80.7 days

CHAPTER REVIEW PROBLEMS

1. a. $^{22}_{11}Na \rightarrow ^{22}_{12}Mg + ^{0}_{-1}e$, beta
   b. $^{66}_{29}Cu \rightarrow ^{66}_{30}Zn + ^{0}_{-1}e$, beta
   c. $^{208}_{84}Po \rightarrow ^{204}_{82}Pb + ^{4}_{2}He$, alpha
   d. $^{27}_{14}Si \rightarrow ^{27}_{13}Al + ^{0}_{+1}e$, positron
2. a. $^{27}_{13}Al + ^{2}_{1}H \rightarrow ^{25}_{12}Mg + ^{4}_{2}He$
   b. $^{45}_{21}Sc + ^{1}_{0}n \rightarrow ^{42}_{19}K + ^{4}_{2}He$
   c. $^{63}_{29}Cu + ^{1}_{1}H \rightarrow ^{63}_{30}Zn + ^{1}_{0}n$
   d. $^{1}_{0}n + ^{235}_{92}U \rightarrow ^{136}_{53}I + ^{96}_{39}Y + 4^{1}_{0}n$

3. 244 years
4. 4860 years
5. 6.08×10^{22} atoms

CHAPTER 29 ─────────────

PROBLEMS

1. a. 3,4-dimethylhexane
   b. 2,2,3-trimethylpentane
   c. 2,2-dimethylbutane
   d. 3,3-diethylhexane
   e. 2,3,4-trimethylhexane
   f. 3,4,5-trimethylheptane
   g. 3,4,5-trimethylheptane
   h. 2,3,4-trimethylhexane
2. a. 2-methylpentane
   b. 2-methylbutane
   c. 2,3-dimethylpentane
   d. 3-ethylpentane
   e. 2,4-dimethylpentane
   f. 2,3-dimethylpentane
   g. 3-methylpentane
   h. 2,3-dimethylpentane
3. a. heptane
   b. 2,4-dimethylpentane
   c. 2,2,3-trimethylbutane
   d.
$$\underset{}{CH_3CH}\overset{\displaystyle CH_3 \quad\ CH_3}{\underset{\displaystyle |\qquad |}{}}-CHCH_2CH_3$$
   e.
$$CH_3CH_2\overset{\displaystyle CH_3}{\underset{\displaystyle |}{C}}CH_2CH_3$$
   $\underset{\displaystyle CH_3}{\underset{\displaystyle |}{}}$
   f. 3-methylhexane
   g. 2,2-dimethylpentane
   h.
$$\overset{\displaystyle CH_3}{\underset{\displaystyle |}{}}$$
$$CH_3CHCH_2CH_2CH_2CH_3$$

   i.
$$CH_3CH_2\overset{\displaystyle CH_2CH_3}{\underset{\displaystyle |}{C}}HCH_2CH_3$$

4. a. 2-pentene
   b. 1,2-dimethylbenzene
   c. cyclohexane
   d. phenylethyne
   e. cyclobutene
   f. 1-propyne
5. a. $CH_3CH_2C{\equiv}CCH_2CH_2CH_3$
   b.
$$\begin{array}{c} CH \\ /\!\!/ \ \backslash \\ CH \quad CH_2 \\ | \qquad | \\ CH_2 - CH_2 \end{array}$$
   c.
$$CH_3-\overset{\displaystyle CH_3}{\underset{\displaystyle |}{\underset{\displaystyle |}{\overset{\displaystyle |}{C}}}}-CHCH_2CH_2CH_3$$
   with CH_3 above and a benzene ring below the lower carbon
   d. $CH_2{=}CHCH{=}CH_2$
   e. benzene ring with $-CH_2CH_3$ and $-CH_3$ substituents
   f.
$$CH_3\overset{\displaystyle CH_3}{\underset{\displaystyle |}{C}}{=}CHCH\overset{\displaystyle }{\underset{\displaystyle |}{C}}H_3$$
   with CH_3 below

6. a. 1-chloropentane
   b. 1-chloro-3-methylbutane

   c.
   $$\underset{\overset{\displaystyle CH_3CHCH_2CH_2CH_3}{}}{\overset{\displaystyle Cl}{\overset{\displaystyle |}{}}}$$

   d.
   $$\underset{\overset{\displaystyle CH_3}{}}{\underset{\overset{\displaystyle CH_3CCH_2CH_3}{|}}{\overset{\displaystyle Cl}{\overset{\displaystyle |}{}}}}$$

   e. 3-chloropentane
   f. 2-chloro-3-methylbutane

   g.
   $$\underset{\displaystyle ClCH_2CHCH_2CH_3}{\overset{\displaystyle CH_3}{\overset{\displaystyle |}{}}}$$

   h.
   $$\underset{\overset{\displaystyle CH_3}{}}{\underset{\overset{\displaystyle ClCH_2CCH_3}{|}}{\overset{\displaystyle CH_3}{\overset{\displaystyle |}{}}}}$$

7. a. 1-bromo-3-ethyl-3-methylpentane
   b. 3-methyl-1, 4-pentadiene
   c. 3,3-dimethyl-1-butene
   d. chlorobenzene
   e. 2-pentene
   f. 2-methyl-2-butene
   g. 1-butene
   h. 4-methyl 2-pentene
   i. 2,3-dimethyl-2-pentene
   j. 2,4-dimethyl-1, 4-pentadiene
   k. 2,3,3-trimethyl-1, 4-hexadiene
   l. 1,4-dibromonaphthalene

8. a. $CH_3CH_2CH\!=\!CHCH_2CH_2CH_3$

   b.

c. $HCCl_3$

d.
$$\underset{\overset{\displaystyle CH_3CHCHCH_2CH_2CH_3}{}}{\overset{\displaystyle Cl}{\overset{\displaystyle |}{}}}$$

e.
$$\overset{\displaystyle CH}{\underset{\underset{\displaystyle CH\!=\!CH}{|\qquad\quad|}}{\overset{\displaystyle CH_2\qquad CH}{\diagup\quad\diagdown}}}$$

f.

g.

h.
$$\underset{\displaystyle Br\quad CH_3}{\underset{|\qquad\;|}{\overset{\displaystyle CH_3C\!=\!CCH_3}{}}}$$

CHAPTER REVIEW PROBLEMS

1. a.
   $$\underset{\displaystyle CH_3CH_2CHCH_3}{\overset{\displaystyle Cl}{\overset{\displaystyle |}{}}}$$

   b. $CH_3CH\!=\!CHCH_3$

   c.
   $$\underset{\displaystyle CH_3CH\!-\!CHCH_2OH}{\overset{\displaystyle CH_3\quad CH_2CH_3}{\overset{|\qquad\;|}{}}}$$

   d.
   $$\underset{\displaystyle CH_3}{\underset{|}{\overset{\displaystyle CH_3CCH_2C}{}}}\overset{\displaystyle O}{\underset{\displaystyle OH}{\diagup\!\!\diagdown}}$$

e. 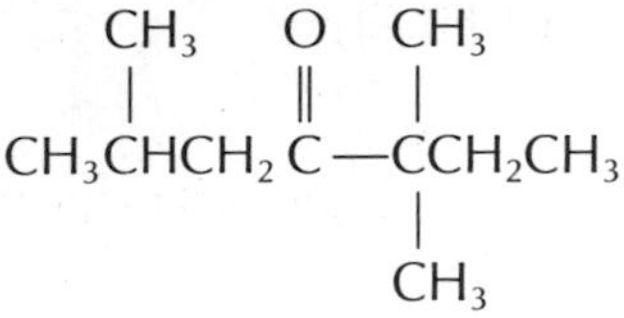
$$\underset{\underset{CH_3}{|}}{\underset{CH_3}{|}}CH_3CHCH_2\overset{\overset{O}{\|}}{C}-\overset{\overset{CH_3}{|}}{C}CH_2CH_3$$

m.
$$\underset{Cl}{\underset{|}{CH_3CH_2CHCH_2CH}}-\overset{CH_2CH_3 \quad CH_3}{\overset{|}{}}\underset{}{CH}\overset{\overset{O}{\diagup\!\!\!\!\diagdown}}{C}\underset{OH}{\diagdown}$$

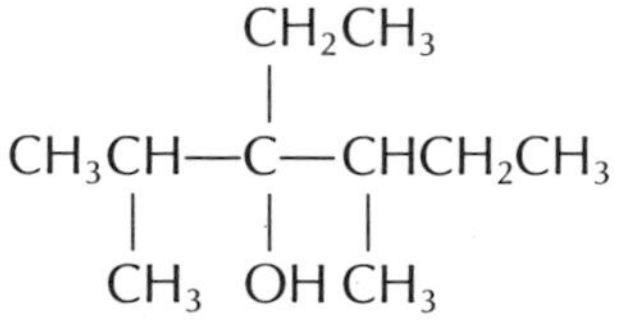

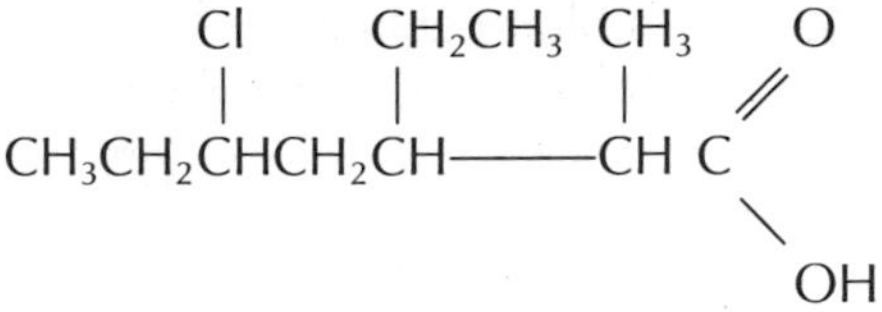

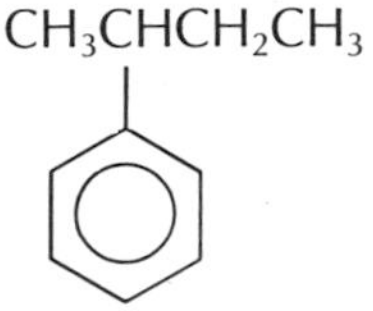

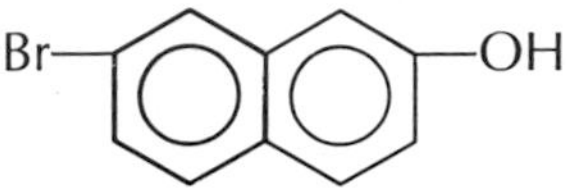

f. $CH\equiv C(CH_2)_5C\equiv CH$

n. $CH_3CHCH_2CH_3$ ⬡

g.

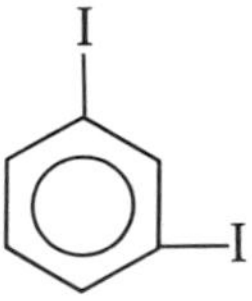

o. Br— ⬡⬡ —OH

h. 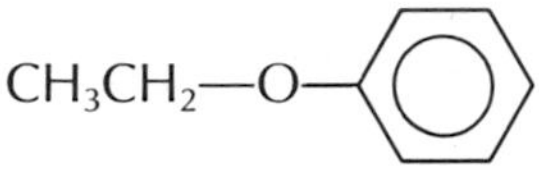 CH_3CH_2—O—⬡

p.
COOH
⬡
Br

i. $CH_3CH_2CH_2CH_2OH$

j. 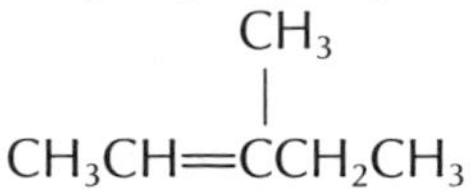
$$\underset{}{CH_3CH}{=}\overset{\overset{CH_3}{|}}{C}CH_2CH_3$$

k. 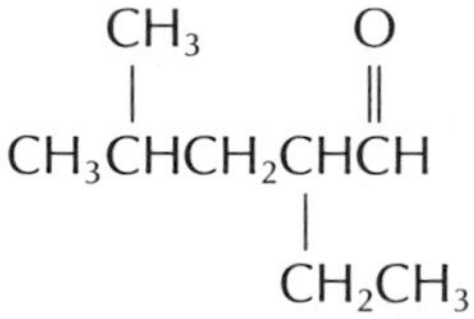
$$\overset{\overset{CH_3}{|}}{CH_3CHCH_2}\overset{\overset{O}{\|}}{CHCH}$$
$$\underset{CH_2CH_3}{|}$$

l.
$$\overset{\overset{CH_2CH_3}{|}}{CH_3CH}-\underset{\underset{CH_3 \quad OH \, CH_3}{|\quad\;\;|\quad\;\;|}}{C}-CHCH_2CH_3$$

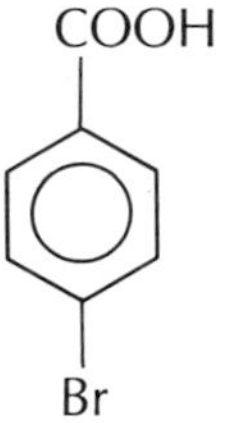

2. a. 2-methyl-3-pentanol
   b. 2-methyl-3-pentanone
   c. 3-methyl-1-butene
   d. butanal
   e. 4,4-dimethyl-1-pentanol
   f. 3-methyl-1, 4-hexadiene-3-ol
3. a. 1-chloro-2-methylbutane
   b. 2,3,3-trimethyl-1-bromobutane
   c. bromocyclopropane
   d. 3-chloropentane
   e. 2-methyl-2-butanol
   f. 3-bromo-2-pentene
   g. butanamine
   h. propanamide
4. a. CH_3CH_2OH, ethanol; alcohol
      CH_3OCH_3, methoxymethane; ether

b. CH_3CH_2CHO, propanal; aldehyde

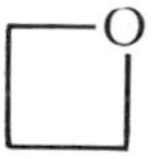

oxacyclobutane; ether

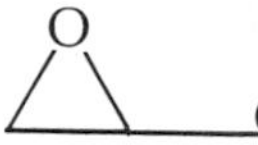

CH_3, methyloxacyclopropane, ether

$$CH_3\overset{\overset{\displaystyle O}{\|}}{C}CH_3,\ \text{propanone; ketone}$$

c. 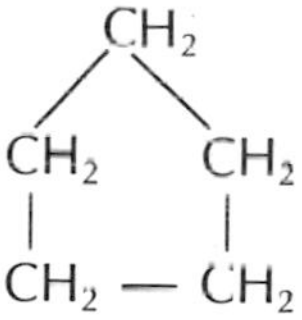
$$\begin{array}{c}
\overset{\displaystyle CH_2}{\diagup\ \ \diagdown}\\
CH_2\qquad CH_2\\
|\qquad\quad |\\
CH_2 \text{---} CH_2
\end{array}$$
cyclopentane; cycloalkane

$CH_3CH{=}CHCH_2CH_3$, 2-pentene; alkene (and other isomers)

5. a. 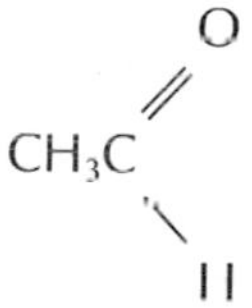 $CH_3\overset{\overset{\displaystyle O}{\diagup\!\diagup}}{C}\diagdown$

b. $CH_3\overset{\overset{\displaystyle O}{\|}}{C}CH_2CH_3$

c. $CH_3\overset{\overset{\displaystyle OH}{|}}{\underset{\underset{\displaystyle CH_3}{|}}{C}}CH_3$

d. 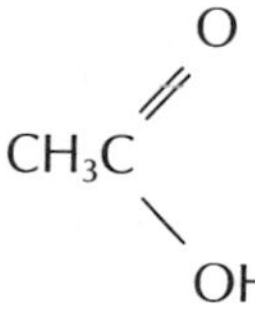 $CH_3\overset{\overset{\displaystyle O}{\diagup\!\diagup}}{C}\diagdown OH$

e. $CH_3\overset{\overset{\displaystyle Ch_3}{|}}{N}CH_3$

f. $CH_2{=}CHCH_3$

g. $CH_3C{\equiv}CCH_2CH_3$

h. 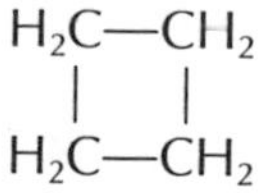
$$\begin{array}{c}
H_2C\text{---}CH_2\\
|\qquad\ |\\
H_2C\text{---}CH_2
\end{array}$$

i. 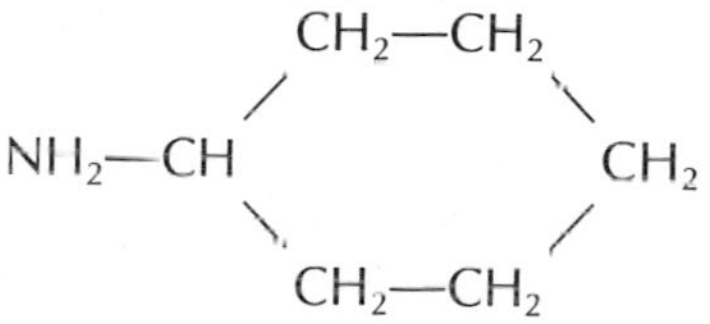
$$NH_2\text{---}CH
\begin{array}{c}
\diagup CH_2\text{---}CH_2 \diagdown\\
\qquad\qquad\qquad CH_2\\
\diagdown CH_2\text{---}CH_2 \diagup
\end{array}$$

j. $CH_3\overset{\overset{\displaystyle NH_4}{|}}{C}HCH_2CH_2CH_3$

k.

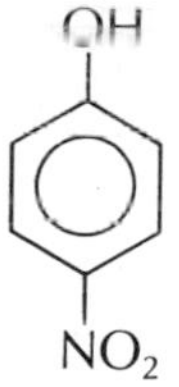

l.

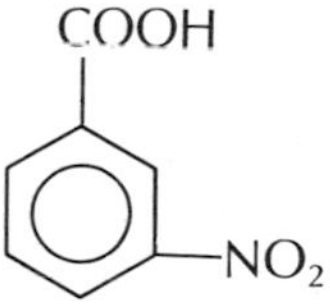

m. $CH_3C{\equiv}N$

n. 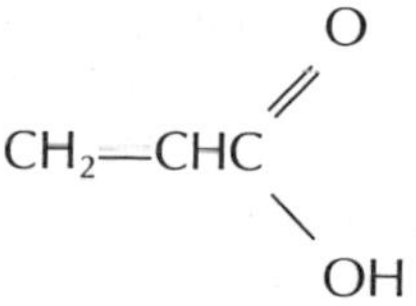 $CH_2\text{---}CH\overset{\overset{\displaystyle O}{\diagup\!\diagup}}{C}\diagdown OH$

287

CHAPTER 30 ───────────────

PROBLEMS

1. $C_3H_8 + 5O_2 \rightarrow 3CO_2 + 4H_2O$

2. $CH_2CH_2 + Br_2 \rightarrow CH_2-CH_2$
   $\quad\quad\quad\quad\quad\quad\;\; | \quad\; . \;|$
   $\quad\quad\quad\quad\quad\quad\; Br \quad Br$

3.

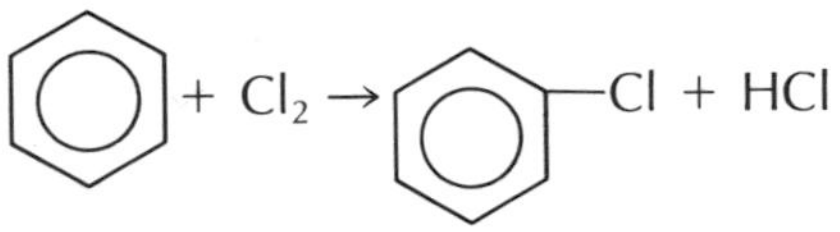

4.
$$\underset{CH_3CH_2CH_2\overset{\displaystyle |}{\underset{\displaystyle \;\;\;}{C}}HCH_3}{\overset{OH}{}} \rightarrow CH_3CH_2CH=CHCH_3 + H_2O$$

5.
$$CH_3CH_2\overset{O}{\overset{\|}{C}}-OH + CH_3CH_2-OH \rightarrow CH_3CH_2\overset{O}{\overset{\|}{C}}-O-CH_2CH_3 + H_2O$$

CHAPTER REVIEW PROBLEMS

1.
$$CH_3CH=CHCH_3 + HI \rightarrow CH_3CH_2\overset{I}{\overset{\|}{C}}HCH_3$$

2.
$$Br_2 + CH_2=CH_2 \rightarrow \underset{CH_2-CH_2}{\overset{Br \quad\;\; Br}{}}$$

3.
$$CH_3CH_2CH_2CH_2CH_2-OH + H\overset{O}{\overset{\|}{C}}-OH \rightarrow$$
$$CH_3CH_2CH_2CH_2CH_2-O-\overset{O}{\overset{\|}{C}}H + H_2O$$

4. $2CH_3CH_3 + 7O_2 \rightarrow 4CO_2 + 6H_2O$

5. $CH_3CH_2CH_2CH_2CH_2-OH \rightarrow H_2O + CH_3CH_2CH_2CH=CH_2$

6. DNA is used to transfer genetic information to the next generation.

7. A nucleotide contains a nitrogen base, a sugar, and a phosphate group.

8. saponification

9. amino acids

10. Carbohydrates provide energy and raw materials for cellular activity.

11. Saturated fats contain only single C—C bonds and are usually solids at room temperature. Unsaturated fats contain at least one multiple C—C bond.

12. unsaturated

INDEX

D

Dalton's law of partial pressure, 113–114
Decomposition reactions, 51
Deductive reasoning, 3
Deliquescence, 103
Delocalized electron, 81
Density, 16–17; of gas, 119–120
Derived units, 10
Diagonal rule, 63–64
Diffusion, 120–121
Dissociation, 168
DNA, 233
Double displacement reactions, 50

E

Efflorescence, 103
Electrochemistry, 199–205
Electrolytes, solutions of, 177–192
Electron, cloud, 61–62; configuration, 63, 67–68; delocalized, 81; dot structures, 65, 83–84; pair repulsion, 85–86
Electronegativity, 79
Elements, 19, 75–77
Elimination reaction, 230–231
Empirical formula, 30, 40–42; of hydrates, 43–44
Energy changes, measuring, 20–22
Enthalpy, 107, 135–136
Entropy, 135–136
Equations, see Chemical equations
Equilibrium, 155; constant, 158–159, 177; dynamic, 155; free energy and, 160–161
Ester, 224–225
Esterification reaction, 231
Ether, 225
Extensive property, 20

F

Factor label method, 11–13
Faraday's laws, 202–204
Fats, 232–233

First ionization energy, 73
Forbidden zone, 81–82
Formula(s), 23–32, 42–43
Formula mass, 34
Free energy, 135–136, 160–161
Freezing point, 107, 149, 150

G

Galvanic cell, 200–202
Gamma rays, 207–208
Gas, density, 119–120; diffusion, 120–121; ideal, 111, 124–126; laws, 111–121; volume, 126–129, 131–133
Gibbs free energy, 135–136, 160–161
Graham's law, 120–121
Graphs, 4–5

H

Half-life, 209–211
Halogen family, 68, 76, 220–222
Heisenberg Uncertainty Principle, 61
Hess's law, 140
Heterogeneous mixture, 19
Homogeneous mixture, 19
Hund's Rule, 64
Hybrid orbitals, 86–87
Hydrate, 39–40, 43, 103
Hydride ion, 75
Hydrocarbons, 213–220; aromatic, 218–220; halogen derivatives of, 221–222; naming, 214–217
Hydrogen ion, 75
Hydrolysis, 231
Hydroxyl group, 222
Hygroscopic substance, 103

I

Ideal gas, 111, 124–126
Inductive reasoning, 2
Inorganic compound, 76

Physical change, 20
Physical property, 20
Polymer, 230
Pressure, 97–98, 106, 111–114;
   osmotic, 152–153; standard, 117
Principal quantum number, 61
Protein, 232

Q

Quantum mechanics, 61
Quantum numbers, 61–63;
   principal, 61

R

Radiation, types of, 207–208
Radioactive decay, 207
Reactant, limiting, 129–131
Reaction, 47–56; decomposition,
   51; double displacement, 50;
   endothermic, 135; exothermic,
   135; organic, 229–232; rate, 156–
   157; redox, 194–197; reversible,
   155; single displacement, 49;
   spontaneous, 137–139
Reduction, 194
Resonance, 84–85
RNA, 233

S

Salts, 165
Saponification, 231–232
Scientific notation, 13–16
Shielding effect, 73
SI, 7
Significant digits, 7–9
Single displacement reactions, 49
Skeleton equations, 47

Solid, amorphous, 101;
   polymorphous, 102
Solubility product constant, 177–
   180
Solute, 19, 143; moles of, 149
Solution, 19, 143–154; of
   electrolytes, 177–192; normality
   of, 189; standard, 143, 186
Solvent, 19, 143
Specific heat, 21, 108
Specific rate constant, 156
State, changes of, 106–110
Stoichiometry, 52
STP, 117, 131
Substance, 19
Substitution reaction, 229

T

Temperature, 7, 107–108; Kelvin,
   114–115; standard, 117
Titration, 186–191
Transition element, 69, 76–77
Transmutation, 209

U

Unit cell, 101

V

Van der Waals forces, 92
Variables, 4
Voltaic cell, 200–202
Volume, 126–129, 131–133

W

Water of hydration, 39, 103
Weight, 7

International Atomic Masses

Element	Symbol	Atomic number	Atomic mass	Element	Symbol	Atomic number	Atomic mass
Actinium	Ac	89	227.027 8*	Neon	Ne	10	20.179 7
Aluminum	Al	13	26.981 539	Neptunium	Np	93	237.048 2
Americium	Am	95	243.061 4*	Nickel	Ni	28	58.69
Antimony	Sb	51	121.75	Niobium	Nb	41	92.906 38
Argon	Ar	18	39.948	Nitrogen	N	7	14.006 74
Arsenic	As	33	74.921 59	Nobelium	No	102	259.100 9*
Astatine	At	85	209.987 1*	Osmium	Os	76	190.2
Barium	Ba	56	137.327	Oxygen	O	8	15.999 4
Berkelium	Bk	97	247.070 3*	Palladium	Pd	46	106.42
Beryllium	Be	4	9.012 182	Phosphorus	P	15	30.973 762
Bismuth	Bi	83	208.980 37	Platinum	Pt	78	195.08
Boron	B	5	10.811	Plutonium	Pu	94	244.064 2*
Bromine	Br	35	79.904	Polonium	Po	84	208.982 4*
Cadmium	Cd	48	112.411	Potassium	K	19	39.098 3
Calcium	Ca	20	40.078	Praseodymium	Pr	59	140.907 65
Californium	Cf	98	251.079 6*	Promethium	Pm	61	144.912 8*
Carbon	C	6	12.011	Protactinium	Pa	91	231.035 88
Cerium	Ce	58	140.115	Radium	Ra	88	226.025 4
Cesium	Cs	55	132.905 43	Radon	Rn	86	222.017 6*
Chlorine	Cl	17	35.452 7	Rhenium	Re	75	186.207
Chromium	Cr	24	51.996 1	Rhodium	Rh	45	102.905 50
Cobalt	Co	27	58.933 20	Rubidium	Rb	37	85.467 8
Copper	Cu	29	63.546	Ruthenium	Ru	44	101.07
Curium	Cm	96	247.070 3*	Samarium	Sm	62	150.36
Dysprosium	Dy	66	162.50	Scandium	Sc	21	44.955 910
Einsteinium	Es	99	252.082 8*	Selenium	Se	34	78.96
Erbium	Er	68	167.26	Silicon	Si	14	28.085 5
Europium	Eu	63	151.965	Silver	Ag	47	107.868 2
Fermium	Fm	100	257.095 1*	Sodium	Na	11	22.989 768
Fluorine	F	9	18.998 403 2	Strontium	Sr	38	87.62
Francium	Fr	87	223.019 7*	Sulfur	S	16	32.066
Gadolinium	Gd	64	157.25	Tantalum	Ta	73	180.947 9
Gallium	Ga	31	69.723	Technetium	Tc	43	97.907 2*
Germanium	Ge	32	72.61	Tellurium	Te	52	127.60
Gold	Au	79	196.966 54	Terbium	Tb	65	158.925 34
Hafnium	Hf	72	178.49	Thallium	Tl	81	204.383 3
Helium	He	2	4.002 602	Thorium	Th	90	232.038 1
Holmium	Ho	67	164.930 32	Thulium	Tm	69	168.934 21
Hydrogen	H	1	1.007 94	Tin	Sn	50	118.710
Indium	In	49	114.82	Titanium	Ti	22	47.88
Iodine	I	53	126.904 47	Tungsten	W	74	183.85
Iridium	Ir	77	192.22	Unnilennium†	Une	109	266*
Iron	Fe	26	55.847	Unnilhexium†	Unh	106	263*
Krypton	Kr	36	83.80	Unniloctium†	Uno	108	265*
Lanthanum	La	57	138.905 5	Unnilpentium†	Unp	105	262*
Lawrencium	Lr	103	260.105 4*	Unnilquadium†	Unq	104	261*
Lead	Pb	82	207.2	Unnilseptium†	Uns	107	262*
Lithium	Li	3	6.941	Uranium	U	92	238.028 9
Lutetium	Lu	71	174.967	Vanadium	V	23	50.941 5
Magnesium	Mg	12	24.305 0	Xenon	Xe	54	131.29
Manganese	Mn	25	54.938 05	Ytterbium	Yb	70	173.04
Mendelevium	Md	101	258.098 6*	Yttrium	Y	39	88.905 85
Mercury	Hg	80	200.59	Zinc	Zn	30	65.39
Molybdenum	Mo	42	95.94	Zirconium	Zr	40	91.224
Neodymium	Nd	60	144.24				

*The mass of the isotope with the longest known half-life.
†Names for elements 104-109 have been approved for temporary use by the IUPAC. The USSR has proposed Kurchatovium (Ku) for element 104, and Bohrium (Bh) for element 105. The United States has proposed Rutherfordium (Rf) for element 104, and Hahnium (Ha) for element 105.